LIGHTNINGS
TO SPITFIRES

MEMOIRS OF AN RAF FIGHTER PILOT AND FORMER
OFFICER COMMANDING THE BATTLE OF BRITAIN
MEMORIAL FLIGHT

This book is dedicated to my friends and colleagues in the Royal Air Force who lost their lives flying in the service of their country, who faced the risks willingly and died doing what they loved, especially:

Dave Hampton	7 April 1975	Lightning F.6
Chris Jones	23 November 1978	F-4 Phantom FG.1
Ian Dixon	28 October 1983	Tornado GR.1
Dave ('Frosty') Frost	13 July 1984	Lightning F.6
Martin ('Tetley') Ramsay	6 March 1985	Lightning F.6
Neil ('Clachy') Maclachlan	25 January 1988	Red Arrows Hawk T.1
Pete ('Stoney') Stone	20 June 1989	Harrier T.4
Steve ('Alf') Moir	21 July 1989	Tornado F.3
Bill Vivian and Des Lacey	15 June 1998	Tornado F.3

And to those they loved and who loved them, whom they left behind.

Also, to my wife, Elaine, who lived with those risks daily and who put up with so much to support me through my long career as an RAF pilot.

LIGHTNINGS
TO SPITFIRES

MEMOIRS OF AN RAF FIGHTER PILOT AND FORMER
OFFICER COMMANDING THE BATTLE OF BRITAIN
MEMORIAL FLIGHT

CLIVE ROWLEY

AIR WORLD

AIR WORLD

LIGHTNINGS TO SPITFIRES
MEMOIRS OF AN RAF FIGHTER PILOT AND FORMER OFFICER
COMMANDING THE BATTLE OF BRITAIN MEMORIAL FLIGHT

First published in Great Britain in 2021 by
Air World
An imprint of
Pen & Sword Books Ltd
Yorkshire – Philadelphia

ISBN 978 1 39901 562 2

Typeset by SJmagic DESIGN SERVICES, India.

Printed and bound in the UK by CPI Group (UK) Ltd, Croydon, CR0 4YY.

Pen & Sword Books Limited incorporates the imprints of Atlas, Archaeology, Aviation, Discovery, Family History, Fiction, History, Maritime, Military, Military Classics, Politics, Select, Transport, True Crime, Air World, Frontline Publishing, Leo Cooper, Remember When, Seaforth Publishing, The Praetorian Press, Wharncliffe Local History, Wharncliffe Transport, Wharncliffe True Crime and White Owl.

For a complete list of Pen & Sword titles please contact

PEN & SWORD BOOKS LIMITED
47 Church Street, Barnsley, South Yorkshire, S70 2AS, England
E-mail: enquiries@pen-and-sword.co.uk
Website: www.pen-and-sword.co.uk

Or
PEN AND SWORD BOOKS
1950 Lawrence Rd, Havertown, PA 19083, USA
E-mail: Uspen-and-sword@casematepublishers.com
Website: www.penandswordbooks.com

Contents

Glossary

A&AEE	Aeroplane and Armament Experimental Establishment
AAA	Anti-Aircraft Artillery
AAR	Air-to-air-refuelling (also known as 'tanking')
AC	Alternating current
ACE	Allied Command Europe
ACL	Air Combat Leader
ACM	Air Combat Manoeuvring
ACMI	Air Combat Manoeuvring Instrumentation (Range)
ACT	Air Combat Training
AD	Air Defence
ADV	Air Defence Variant (of Tornado)
AEF	Air Experience Flight
AFTS	Advanced Flying Training School
AI	Air Intercept (designation for fighter radars)
AIM	Air Intercept Missile (e.g. AIM-9L)
AMLCD	Active Matrix Liquid Crystal Display
AMRAAM	Advanced Medium-Range Air-to-Air Missile (also known as AIM-120)
AOA	Angle of Attack
AOC	Air Officer Commanding (an RAF Group)
APC	Armament Practice Camp
ASAP	As Soon As Possible
ASRAAM	Advanced Short-Range Air-to-Air Missile
ATC	Air Traffic Control
AWACS	Airborne Warning and Control System
AWC	Air Warfare Centre
BBMF	Battle of Britain Memorial Flight
BFT(S)	Basic Flying Training (School)
BVR	Beyond Visual Range

GLOSSARY

CAP	Combat Air Patrol
CBFFI	Commander British Forces Falkland Islands
CBLS	Carrier Bomb Light Stores
CCF	Combined Cadet Force
CFB	Canadian Forces Base
CFI	Chief Flying Instructor
CFIT	Controlled Flight into Terrain
CFS	Central Flying School
C-in-C	Commander-in-Chief (actually AOC-in-C – Air Officer Commanding in Chief)
CSP	Capability Sustainment Programme
CTTO	Central Trials and Tactics Organisation (forerunner of the Air Warfare Centre)
DACT	Dissimilar (types) Air Combat Training
DH	Direct Hit
DRA	Defence Research Agency
ECCM	Electronic Counter-Counter Measures
ECM	Electronic Counter Measures
EFT(S)	Elementary Flying Training (School)
EWO	Electronic Warfare Officer
FEZ	Fighter Engagement Zone
FIPZ	Falkland Islands Protection Zone
FOX 1	Launch of a semi-active radar missile
FOX 2	Launch of an infra-red homing missile
FRA	First Run Attack
FTRS	Full-Time Reserve Service
FTS	Flying Training School
GCA	Ground Controlled Approach (to a runway)
GCI	Ground Controlled Intercept
GPS	Global Positioning System
GPWS	Ground Proximity Warning System
HAF	Hellenic (Greek) Air Force
HAS	Hardened Aircraft Shelter
HIMAT	High Mass Altitude and Temperature
HOTAS	Hands on Throttle and Stick
HQ	Headquarters
HUD	Head-Up Display
IADS	Integrated Air Defence System
IDS	Interdictor Strike (variant of Tornado)

IFF	Identification Friend or Foe
IRCCM	Infra-Red Counter-Counter Measures
IRCM	Infra-Red Counter Measures
IRE	Instrument Rating Examiner
IRT	Instrument Rating Test
ISS	Individual Staff Studies
IWI	Intercept Weapons Instructor (Lightnings)
JP	Junior pilot
JP 3	Jet Provost T.3
JP 5	Jet Provost T.5
JTIDS	Joint Tactical Information Distribution System ('Link 16' Datalink)
LLA	Lincolnshire's Lancaster Association (charity)
LLSP	Low Level Search Pattern
LTF	Lightning Training Flight
LUAS	Liverpool University Air Squadron
M	Mach (number) – speed relative to the speed of sound (M1.0)
MASUAS	Manchester and Salford University Air Squadron
MBE	Member (of the Order of the) British Empire
MEZ	(Surface -to-air) Missile Engagement Zone
MFF	Mixed Fighter Force
MoD	Ministry of Defence
MPA	Mount Pleasant Airfield (Falklands)
MPC	Missile Practice Camp
NATO	North Atlantic Treaty Organization
Navex	Navigation exercise
NBC	Nuclear Biological and Chemical
NCO	Non-Commissioned Officer (e.g. Sergeant)
NVGs	Night Vision Goggles
OASC	Officer and Aircrew Selection Centre
OC	Officer Commanding
OC Eng. Wing	Officer Commanding Engineering Wing
OCU	Operational Conversion Unit
OEU	Operational Evaluation Unit
Ops	Operations
PAN Call	International standard radio call notifying an urgent situation that does not pose an immediate danger to life or the aircraft.

GLOSSARY

PBF	Pilot Briefing Facility
PI	Practice intercept
PLB	Personal Locator Beacon
PPL	Private Pilot's Licence
PSI	Pounds per Square Inch (pressure)
QFI	Qualified Flying Instructor
QRA	Quick Reaction Alert
QTI	Qualified Tactics Instructor
QWI	Qualified Weapons Instructor
QWIL	Qualified Weapons Instructor Leader
RAAF	Royal Australian Air Force
RAF	Royal Air Force
RHWR	Radar Homing and Warning Receiver
RMAF	Royal Malaysian Air Force
RNEFTS	Royal Navy Elementary Flying Training School
RNLAF	Royal Netherlands Air Force
RNoAF	Royal Norwegian Air Force
RPM	Revolutions per minute
RSAF	Royal Saudi Air Force
SA	Situational Awareness
SAM	Surface-to-Air Missile
SAR	Search and Rescue
SASO	Senior Air Staff Officer
SEP	Specific Excess Power
SEPECAT	*Société Européenne de Production de l'avion Ecole de Combat et d'Appui Tactique*
SHAR	Sea Harrier
SIFF	Successor Identification Friend or Foe
SNEB	*Societe Nouvelle des Etablissements Edgar Brandt* (rockets)
STANEVAL	Standards Evaluation (Unit)
STCAAME	Strike Command Air-to-Air Missile Establishment
TACEVAL	Tactical Evaluation (usually for NATO)
TD circle	Target Detection circle
TFM	Tactical Fighter Meet
TI	Tactics Instructor
TLP	Tactical Leadership Programme
TMO	Trials Management Officer
TRD	Towed Radar Decoy

TWU	Tactical Weapons Unit
UAS	University Air Squadron
UN	United Nations
USAF	United States Air Force
USAFE	United States Air Forces in Europe
VHF	Very High Frequency
VIFF	Vectoring in forward flight (by Harriers)
VIP	Very Important Person
VVIP	Very-Very Important Person (usually Royalty)
Visident	Visual Identification
VR	Volunteer Reserve
WRAF	Women's Royal Air Force (merged with the RAF in 1994)

List of Plates

Every effort has been made to trace copyright owners and obtain permission for the photographs in the book; however, the provenance of some is uncertain. If there have been any errors or omissions we apologise and will be pleased to make appropriate acknowledgements in any future editions. A number of the photographs are UK MoD Crown Copyright and have been released under the Open Government Licence (OGL). Their publication in this book does not imply any endorsement or official sanction of the book. Photographs not credited are from the author's own collection.

Plate Section 1 (mono)

1. Bournemouth School Combined Cadet Force RAF Section at RAF Colerne in 1968.
2. Pilot Officer Rowley with a Jet Provost T.5 at RAF Leeming in August 1972.
3. Award of RAF pilot's 'wings' on 4 August 1972.
4. The author with a Hunter F.6 of 4 FTS RAF Valley in 1973.
5. Lightning F.2A XN790 tail letter L of 19 Squadron, based at RAF Gutersloh, Germany.
6. The author with the refuelling hose from a Victor tanker in August 1974. *(Tony Paxton)*
7. Battle Flight scramble at Gutersloh.
8. A McDonnell Douglas F-4 Phantom in the gunsight of Clive Rowley's Lightning F.2A.
9. B Flight pilots of 19 Squadron, June 1975. *(UK MoD Crown Copyright 1975, OGL)*
10. A pair of Lightning F.2As of 19 Sqn taking off in close formation at Gutersloh in 1976.

11. Reheat fire damage to Lightning F.2A XN789 F which occurred during a sortie with the author as the pilot on 11 May 1976.
12. Lightning F.2A XN786 M in which the author had a second reheat fire. *(Pete Hodgson)*
13. The jet pipe failure which caused a reheat fire warning and control restriction when the author was flying Lightning F.2A XN786 M on 4 August 1976.
14. Flying Officer Clive Rowley, aged 25, towards the end of a three-year front-line tour on Lightnings in Germany in October 1976.
15. Award of the Queen's Commendation for Valuable Service in the Air in October 1976. *(UK MoD Crown Copyright 1976, OGL)*

Plate Section 2 (colour)

1. Scottish Aviation Bulldog T.1s, Central Flying School course, 1977.
2. Clive & Elaine Rowley's wedding in 1978.
3. Hawk T.1 of 63 Squadron, No. 2 Tactical Weapons Unit (TWU), Chivenor, in 1982.
4. 63 Squadron TWU staff instructors at Chivenor in 1983.
5. Lightning F.3, XR749, DA of the OC Lightning Training Flight (LTF), in 1986.
6. OC LTF with the Flight's engineers outside the LTF hangar at Binbrook in 1987.
7. OC LTF in the cockpit of Lightning F.3 XR718 DA in 1987. *(Chris Allan)*
8. The author in a fully-armed 5 Squadron Tornado F.3 shadowing one of the two Russian Tupolev Tu-95 Bear Deltas intercepted north of Scotland on 8 September 1988.
9. The author and his 5 Squadron navigator, Flt Lt Rich Sanderson, during an armament practice camp in Cyprus in 1989.
10. A Tornado F.3 of 5 Squadron starts up for a combat air patrol sortie in one of the sun shelters at Dhahran, Saudi Arabia, during Operation GRANBY (DESERT SHIELD) in August 1990.
11. The author welcomed home from operations by daughter Suzanne and wife Elaine after a flight of 7 hours and 45 minutes from Saudi Arabia on 17 September 1990.
12. The author in a Tornado F.3 of the Operational Evaluation Unit (OEU), leading two *Luftwaffe* MiG-29s – former foes – back to Decimomannu, Sardinia, in 1991.

LIST OF PLATES

13. Tornado F.3 of the F.3 OEU dropping infra-red decoy flares over the China Lake ranges in the Californian high desert in February 1992 during a trial.
14. Walking away from an OEU Tornado F.3 in Cyprus with navigator John Prescott.
15. Squadron Leader Gordon 'Scotty' Scott and the author with the then highly-classified Tornado F.3 Towed Radar Decoy (TRD) pod during trials at Eglin AFB Florida in 1995.
16. Tornado F.3s of 1435 Flight in the Falkland Islands. The author flew with the Flight over the Islands on a number of detachments to Mount Pleasant Airfield. *(Cpl Darren Smith MoD Crown Copyright 2013, OGL)*
17. With wife Elaine and daughter Suzanne after an investiture at Buckingham Palace to receive the MBE from HM The Queen in 2002.
18. The author in the rear cockpit of a Tornado F.3 of 56(R) Sqn with the Chief of the Air Staff, Air Chief Marshal Sir Peter Squire in the front cockpit in April 2002.
19. The Tornado F.3 Operational Conversion Unit – 56(R) Sqn – aircraft, ground crew, staff instructors and students in March 2003. *(UK MoD Crown Copyright 2003, OGL)*
20. The author flying BBMF Hurricane IIC PZ865 in 1996 during his first display season with the Flight.
21. The author in BBMF Spitfire Vb AB910 before his first public Spitfire display.
22. The author flying BBMF Spitfire Vb AB910 in May 1997, photographed from the BBMF Lancaster rear turret. *(UK MoD Crown Copyright 1997, OGL)*
23. The BBMF fighter pilots for the 2000 display season.
24. The author airborne in the cockpit of BBMF Spitfire Vb AB910 in 2002. *(UK MoD Crown Copyright 2002, OGL)*
25. Officer Commanding the RAF Battle of Britain Memorial Flight (BBMF) in 2004. *(Sgt Jack Pritchard UK MoD Crown Copyright 2004, OGL).*
26. BBMF Lancaster, Hurricane and Spitfire over Buckingham Palace in July 2005. *(SAC Scott Robertson UK MoD Crown Copyright 2005, OGL)*
27. The author in a Spitfire leading two Eurofighter Typhoons for a flypast over the AOC's salute at Coningsby's Annual Formal Inspection in September 2005. *(UK MoD Crown Copyright 2005, OGL)*

28. The author's last Spitfire display at the end of the 2006 display season and after eleven years with the BBMF.
29. Clive Rowley with an appropriately marked Spitfire PR XIX in September 2006 at the end of his eleven years flying with the BBMF.
30. Recalled for a special appearance at the BBMF's 50th anniversary air show at Duxford on 5 May 2007. The author flew Spitfire AB910 on the left of this picture. *(Mike Cook – free use)*
31. The author as a volunteer reservist flight lieutenant, relieved at having performed a successful forced landing in a farmer's field, off the airfield at Cranwell in August 2012 in a Grob Tutor after one propeller blade disintegrated at only 500 feet. *(Paul Smith)*

Prologue

4 August 1976. I am taxiing out towards the runway in Lightning F.2A XN786 (tail letter 'M'). I've been flying Lightnings with No. 19(F) Squadron at RAF Gutersloh, in Germany, for over two and a half years; I have 575 hours of flying on type and 850 hours total flying. Although I'm only 25 years old, and still considered a junior pilot on my squadron, I'm confident and assured in what I'm doing, but hopefully not overconfident. I've had my mettle tested with a couple of serious airborne emergencies in recent months and, having dealt with them successfully, my confidence is perhaps justified. Unbeknown to me though, my skills and my confidence, my ability to remain calm under pressure, indeed my courage, are about to be tested to the limit.

As I taxi out, I complete the pre-take-off checks from memory. These are now second nature. Finally, I check that the ejection-seat safety pins are all stowed and the seat is live and ready to fire when the handle is pulled.

I call on the radio for permission for our formation of two Lightnings to take off. Having received clearance, I move onto the runway, line up pointing down the centre of the left-hand half and bring the aircraft to a halt, the nose dipping slightly as the nose-wheel oleo leg compresses when I apply the brakes. My number two is the Boss, Wing Commander Bob Barcilon. He lines his aircraft up alongside me on the right-hand half of the runway. He looks across at me and gives me a 'thumbs up'. I give him the 'wind up' signal, rotating my gloved index finger. I parallel the two throttles and then advance them both smoothly forward to wind the two mighty Rolls Royce Avon jet engines behind me up to 92 per cent rpm. Any more power than this will make the wheels slide even with the brakes fully on. An increased roar behind me accompanies the engine indications on the gauges. A quick check around the cockpit shows that all is well and I look across at the Boss. He gives me another 'thumbs up'; he's ready to go. I tap the front of my flying helmet on the 'forehead' twice and then give a pronounced nod of my head to indicate brakes release.

We both release the brakes simultaneously; the acceleration is instant as we start to roll down the runway and we move the throttles forward to maximum 'cold' (non-reheated) power, checking the engine indications are normal. I nod again and we both push the throttles through the 'gate' to select reheat. A double 'thump' from behind me and a kick in the back tell me both reheats have lit and I check the jet-pipe nozzle positions and jet-pipe temperature indications to confirm all is well. I then bring the power back a bit from full reheat to give my Number Two something to play with. On my right, the Boss is doing all that I'm doing and working to stay in formation with me. Others will be watching and reputations are at stake. All this has taken mere seconds, but we are already accelerating through 150 knots. I start to raise the nose wheel and, as we accelerate through 180 knots, I continue to pull back on the control column to lift off only about half a mile down the runway. (Nought to 200 miles per hour in half a mile – not bad.)

As soon as I'm safely airborne, it's brakes on to stop the wheels rotating (there's a lot of energy in wheels doing 200 mph) and select undercarriage up, even though we're only feet above the ground. The aircraft is accelerating rapidly and the nose-wheel will not retract fully if the speed reaches 250 knots before it is stowed and locked up because it retracts forwards into the airflow. Rapid and apparently quite 'punchy' undercarriage retractions immediately after lift off are therefore the normal and necessary procedure for Lightning pilots. With the speed building through 300 knots, I nod my head again and we both cancel the reheats. The aircraft continues to accelerate rapidly in 'cold' power to the climbing speed of 450 knots. I roll gently into a right turn onto the northerly climb-out heading and as I roll out of the turn, I wave the Boss away. He breaks out in a 'punchy' manner to position his aircraft in tactical, 'battle' formation, about a mile to my right and level with me. The speed is now at 450 knots and we're climbing rapidly through 2,000 feet.

Suddenly all hell lets loose! There is a terrific thump, accompanied by a violent deceleration, the like of which I have never experienced before, which throws me forward in my straps. The thought flashes through my head that I've hit something I haven't seen, but it's not that. A few seconds of violent vibration confuses my senses further and, as the vibration ceases, an audio warning alarm sounds loud in my earphones. I look to the standard warning panel and see that the red 'Reheat Fire 1' warning has illuminated. This is not good. Many Lightnings have been lost over the years to reheat fires.

PROLOGUE

Faster than it takes to say it or read this, I carry out the drill for a reheat fire, a drill honed by many practices in the simulator, and now almost instinctive. I throttle the number one engine back to idle, operate the catch on the throttle and bring the throttle fully rearwards, closing the high-pressure fuel cock for that engine and shutting it down. I also turn off the switches for the low-pressure fuel cock and the fuel pumps, and select the air-to-air refuel switch to the 'refuel' setting to de-pressurise the fuel tanks to prevent fuel transferring through what may be damaged pipes in an effort to stop the spread of any fire. In the Lightning there is no fire extinguisher for the reheat zones so that's all that can be done for now.

I start to pull up into a steeper climb to bring the speed back toward 250 knots, the recommended speed for ejection, and I press the transmit switch on the throttle to tell the Gutersloh air traffic controller and my Number Two of my predicament (hopefully sounding reasonably calm, even if I don't feel it): 'Mayday, Mayday, Mayday. Hotel One Two. Reheat Fire One. Standby.' As I pull back on the control column whilst making this call, I realise that the controls are stiffening and jamming. The control rods to the tail plane run close to the number one engine jet pipe, this might well indicate a serious fire and I might be about to lose control, so I add, 'Standby for ejection.' A surge of fear, almost panic, runs through me, seeming to start in the pit of my stomach and surging up to my brain. I find myself suppressing it immediately and I am pleased to discover that I am then feeling completely calm. The adrenalin is still there, my mind is reacting quickly to every stimulus, but I am strangely detached and composed.

*****

More than four decades later, I sometimes still shake when retelling the story of that incident, which I can remember as if it was yesterday. Now retired from full-time and reserve service with the RAF and indeed from flying altogether, I have decided that perhaps I should commit to paper some of the stories of my forty-four years of flying with the Royal Air Force.

Part of me wonders if it is presumptuous of me to imagine that anyone will be interested and, as a result, I have hesitated and 'stalled' over this project, but many friends and colleagues who have patiently listened to my stories over the years have encouraged me to 'write a book'. I hope that my words may give the reader some idea of what it was like to be a fighter pilot in the RAF in the last three decades of the twentieth century and into the twenty-first. Of course, every pilot's experiences will be different and these are only mine, but for those who have not been fortunate enough to share these experiences first-hand, the hair-raising and the entertaining, I hope this book will provide a good read.

My story is perhaps somewhat unusual because I flew continuously in full-time service with the RAF from 1971 to 2006, flying fast-jets until I was 52 years old. With nine years of flying as a volunteer reservist after that, I accumulated over 8,500 hours, all in aircraft which I could turn upside down. I achieved this somewhat unusual feat because I accepted 'Specialist Aircrew' terms of service at the age of 40, giving up any further chance of promotion above my rank of squadron leader in return for being allowed to remain in flying appointments. Even as Spec Aircrew, this wasn't guaranteed, but I managed to 'wangle' flying job after flying job. For most of my career in the RAF, apart from time spent as a flying instructor, I was a specialist fighter pilot, spending most of my working life attempting to perfect the 'art' of intercepting, engaging and destroying enemy aircraft in the air.

During this long career as a fighter pilot I witnessed, first-hand, quantum jumps in the development of aircraft, equipment and weapon systems and the subsequent and parallel evolution of fighter tactics.

The Hawker Hunter, on which I received my initial tactical training, was armed only with cannon and the air combat tactics which we were taught were little changed from the Second World War or the Korean War: first you had to get behind your opponent, inside 500 yards, before you could shoot.

The Lightning and its potential adversaries had heat-seeking air-to-air missiles, the lethal range of which was much greater than cannon, but which still had to be fired in the target's stern sector. Air combat tactics with such weapons still required the attacker to get behind the target before shooting, albeit at greater range and with air combat taking up more sky.

The Tornado F.3 and its opposite numbers were equipped with all-aspect 'heat-seeking' and semi-active radar-guided missiles. The arena in which we 'fought' had now become much more lethal and required entirely different tactics in both beyond visual range (BVR) combats and close-in visual fighting. These tactics were refined further when the aircraft were subsequently equipped with active radar-guided missiles (the AMRAAM) and the latest generation of all-aspect long-range 'heat-seekers' (the ASRAAM).

I was, therefore, intimately involved in the evolution of weapons systems and tactics over three 'generations' of fighter aircraft and weapons development. Perversely, I was to finish my full-time flying career in the extremely privileged position of being one of the few pilots to fly the Battle of Britain Memorial Flight's Second World War-era Spitfires and Hurricanes, literally going back several generations.

I am very aware that many RAF pilots who served through the same period as me will have equally good or better stories to tell, but many do not perhaps possess the desire to 'put pen to paper'. I am also aware that, in my own case, I have no real combat experience, where others do. Aside from a brief involvement in the DESERT SHIELD operations of the First Gulf War in 1990, I saw no actual combat. However, fast-jet flying in the RAF, especially in the earlier stages of my career, was not without its risks which I and my friends and colleagues willingly accepted for the chance to fly high-performance aircraft. Some of my friends paid the ultimate price for their love of flying, losing their lives in peacetime flying accidents. It is to them that I have dedicated this book. They lost their lives serving their country just as surely as those who have died on operations and they are commemorated on the walls of the Armed Forces Memorial at the National Memorial Arboretum at Alrewas, Staffordshire. I will never forget them and I remember them as they were when I knew them, especially during the silences at Remembrance Day ceremonies when other veterans are thinking of their friends and colleagues who paid the ultimate price. As the poem goes, 'They shall grow not old, as we that are left grow old.'

I consider myself extremely lucky to have survived my forty-four years of military flying – in all honesty as a young pilot I really didn't expect to, although I hoped I might – and to have been allowed to experience the thrills of being an RAF fighter pilot. It really wasn't easy to succeed in this most challenging and demanding of professions that is open to all but which is occupied by only a very small percentage of the population. In fact it was a constant and massive struggle for me during the early years. Being blessed with certain natural talents was only a small part of the story; the rest was sheer hard work and determination.

*****

If you want to know what happened after I radioed 'Standby for ejection' during the Lightning reheat fire in 1976, you will have to read on; you see, that was just a taster.

Chapter 1

Beginnings

Apparently I was 7 years old when I announced to my mother that I was going to be a fighter pilot when I grew up. I don't remember this 'Eureka' moment but I do know that by the age of 11 it had become very much my clear ambition. Indeed, I entered my 'eleven-plus' examination with the mind-set that this was the first hurdle that must be successfully jumped if I was to achieve my aim. There is no doubt that I was single-minded about becoming a fighter pilot from a very young age.

I was born in 1951 in Brentwood, Essex, the first-born son of Phyllis and Clifford Rowley. I was later joined by two younger brothers, and so grew up as the eldest of three siblings. From a very early age I showed good co-ordination and a desire for action.

My upbringing was humble, as part of a loving and happy, but not very well-off Christian family. My father was a gentlemen's hairdresser – a barber – with a shop in Barkingside, near Ilford, on the north-eastern outskirts of London. The wider family was very much a London family. My grandparents on my father's side died before I was born, so I never met them. Grandfather Rowley had been a London bus driver and had met my father's mother when she was a conductor on the London buses in the 1920s. My surviving granddad on my mother's side was also a London bus driver for thirty-two years.

As a boy I enjoyed sport, but I had no real prowess as a sportsman. I was a fairly quick sprinter over short distances, and walking or cycling was the family's normal mode of transport as we did not own a car, so this ensured that I grew up physically fit. Equally, I wasn't particularly academic and, whilst I was conscientious at junior school, I found learning hard work. A school report from February 1960 (when I was 9 years old) written by Mr Lawrence, a teacher I liked, said 'Clive is a grand little trier … he has a long way to go, but his perseverance should help him to succeed'. With the benefit of hindsight Mr Lawrence was very astute, as that could sum up my life.

If I had any natural talents at a young age they were mainly in practical skills. As my mother would say, 'Clive is good with his hands.' Like many boys of my age at that time, I built things with toys like Meccano and learned all sorts of mechanical lessons and skills as a result. I continued to impress with my hand/eye co-ordination and I also developed some musical talent, becoming quite a decent pianist and later teaching myself to play the guitar (musical talents that I'm afraid have faded with lack of practice over the years).

I'm fairly sure that Captain W.E. Johns and his 'Biggles' books had something to do with my thoughts turning more seriously to becoming a fighter pilot. I started reading 'Biggles' books when I was about 7 and, eventually, I had read them all. By the age of 11 I had started a notebook and, whenever one of the books contained some details on how a pilot actually controlled an aircraft, I noted it down; my own 'how to fly an aeroplane' notes.

It seems strange to say so now, but I was also influenced by my boyhood opinion that there was bound to be another war and I would have to be in it. This viewpoint is perhaps less surprising when you remember that my grandfather and his generation had fought in the First World War (my grandad had been a Royal Navy rating on a destroyer in the Battle of Jutland) and my father and his generation had fought in the Second World War. Meanwhile, conscription under National Service did not end until 1960, which was also when the Malayan Conflict ended, by which time I was 9 years old. It seemed to me as a boy, that it was inevitable that the next war would involve my generation and I decided that, if I could, I would choose the capacity in which I had to fight. I wanted to be a fighter pilot, not because it was a safe option – indeed it seemed heroically dangerous – but because I believed that a fighter pilot had more control over his own destiny than most fighting men. These were my views with all the wisdom and experience of a 10- or 11-year-old boy. In retrospect it is strange that one so young should view war as inevitable and have the capacity to be so analytical about it.

*****

When I was 11 years old my family moved to Bournemouth where my father had bought a barber's shop with the family accommodation over it. This move, as it turned out, was a remarkably fortunate twist of fate in my plans to become an RAF pilot. I had taken and passed the eleven-plus examination in Essex and, as Bournemouth was an education authority that still had a selective system with grammar schools, I was offered a place at Bournemouth School, the boys' grammar school in the town. Not only was Bournemouth School a good school with a somewhat old-fashioned and traditional style, but it also had a Combined Cadet Force (CCF) with a strong RAF Section which I would be able to join when I reached the required minimum age.

Unfortunately, I found the academic side of my secondary schooling dull and uninteresting and I was not motivated to apply myself to the work. I really could not see the point of learning some of the more esoteric subjects (what possible use was Latin to a pilot?) and my results were not good, with a general consensus from the teachers in their reports that I was capable of doing much better if only I would apply myself more. As an indication of my lack of academic ability and interest, I was allowed to drop Chemistry as a subject and take up woodwork and technical drawing instead, which I loved.

I was now singularly focused on becoming an RAF pilot and would not be deflected from this ambition, despite my mother being sure that the RAF would not take someone from as lowly a background as mine to be an officer (how wrong she was about that) and that I should 'have other strings to my bow'. I took every opportunity to learn more about flying and the RAF, and this was my principal interest. I had a poster of a BAC Lightning jet fighter on my bedroom wall, little realising that I would one day be piloting an identical machine. I made Airfix kits of aircraft, which dangled from the ceiling of my bedroom, and I learned much about the intricacies of aircraft from them. I quite deliberately took every opportunity to improve my co-ordination and reactions with games and tricks, reasoning that these would be required skills at the pilot aptitude tests. In competition with my friends, it was apparent that I did indeed have quicker reactions and better co-ordination than most.

During this phase of my life my closest friends outside of school, which was three and a half miles from my home, were two lads who lived locally, Nigel and Angus. We were almost identical in age (our birthdays being only two weeks apart), we possessed a similar, somewhat irresponsible, outlook on life and shared a mischievous sense of humour. Nigel and Angus attended the local secondary modern school, not my grammar school, but this did not matter. We became inseparable outside school hours – three musketeers – and did everything together, often getting up to no good. Interestingly, all three of us eventually joined the RAF in different capacities; Nigel first,

3

as an apprentice logistician (he left the service as a flight sergeant), me next as an officer and pilot, and then Angus who, after completing an apprenticeship in industry, joined the RAF as a flight engineer, initially in the rank of sergeant, and served for a full career, being commissioned in the process. At one stage in the 1970s we were all three in the RAF, all in entirely different ranks and occupying different messes, none of us allowed into the others', not that the rules necessarily stopped us, but that's another story. Most importantly, we remained firm friends regardless of the rank differences and the fact that, theoretically, the other two were supposed to call me 'Sir'. As if!

*****

In 1965 I finally reached the minimum age for joining the CCF and in the Cadet Force environment I thrived; I attended every possible cadet camp and took every opportunity for air experience flying. My first ever flight, in a de Havilland Chipmunk T.10 training aircraft from the grass airfield at Hamble, at the age of fourteen, convinced me more than ever, if indeed I needed to be convinced, that flying was for me. When the bouncing and rumbling from the wheels across the grass ceased as we lifted off and I was airborne for the first time, I knew this was what I wanted to be doing. Although the smell of petrol in the Chipmunk, along with turbulence and the disorientating effects of aerobatics, sometimes made me feel slightly queasy, I was never airsick, and loved it all. I was somewhat overawed by the RAF pilots who took me flying and must have seemed quite shy and uncommunicative in the back cockpit. I'm not sure that I impressed any of them, but my mind was made up; this was for me, if the RAF would have me.

On Friday afternoons at school, lessons ceased for the senior years and Cadet Force activities took over. I enjoyed all of it; parading and marching, shooting (for which I had quite an eye, gaining my marksman badges on both 0.22 and 0.303 rifles) and even the academic study needed to pass the various stages of the proficiency exams, in which the subjects were directly aviation related.

At the age of 16 I volunteered and was selected for a two-week gliding course at Old Sarum airfield near Salisbury during the school Easter holidays. The initial flights were made in Slingsby T.21 Sedburgh wood-and-fabric gliders with side-by-side seating for the instructor and pupil. Most of the course, though, was flown in Slingsby T.31 Tandem Tutor gliders, also made of wood and fabric, and with the instructor seated behind the pupil. I successfully completed the course and flew solo three times in a totally unpowered winch-launched glider. This being my first ever solo, at the age of only 16, I can still recall the occasion and the emotions vividly. The very fact that anyone was prepared to trust me with my own life and with the glider amazed me and gave my confidence a great boost. Those long-forgotten cadet gliding instructors who taught me and trusted me to fly solo as a 16-year-old cadet deserve my gratitude.

I found myself being promoted up the cadet ranks within the CCF, being given positions of increasing responsibility and being required to instruct other cadets in the various activities. At the age of 16, with the rank of Cadet Corporal, I took charge of a flight of junior cadets, teaching them various subjects needed for the Proficiency Certificate, such as meteorology, principles of flight, navigation, flying, engines and airframes. Then, as a Cadet Sergeant and later Flight Sergeant, I took charge of the NCO Cadre, training cadets to become junior leaders themselves. Ultimately, in my final year at school, I achieved the lofty rank of Cadet Warrant Officer in charge of the RAF Senior Section.

Unfortunately, however, my success within the CCF was not replicated in my academic studies at school. Poor results in the GCE O Levels at age 16 meant that I barely qualified to enter the sixth form, which was critical to my plans. Fortunately, I was allowed to continue at school and, therefore, with the CCF. The minimum academic qualifications to enter the RAF as an officer and pilot at that time were five O Levels, including Maths, English and a science. As I started my sixth-form A-Level studies, I still had not passed the Physics O Level I needed to satisfy the science requirement. I re-sat the exam four times, without any formal teaching in the subject after the first attempt, knowing that it was essential to gain a pass to continue on my chosen path. Eventually, on the fourth attempt, I gained a pass. I am convinced this was only because one question required me to draw and label a human eye. This was something that I had been made to do on numerous occasions as a punishment for misbehaviour during Physics classes in the Third Form, and could therefore do brilliantly. Having eventually passed the Physics O Level and, therefore, with the minimum academic qualifications 'under my belt', my interest in my sixth-form studies waned further, as A Levels were not strictly required to be accepted by the RAF as a pilot.

*****

During my first year in the sixth form, I applied for an RAF cadet flying scholarship, a very formal application process requiring much form filling and a recommendation from my CCF. I was then invited to the Officers and Aircrew Selection Centre (OASC) at RAF Biggin Hill for a selection process, which included an interview, a medical and the standard RAF pilot aptitude tests. This was daunting, but obviously essential to my ambitions. I passed the medical without any difficulty and did well at the pilot aptitude tests (I was never asked to undergo them again). I must have impressed at the interview and was duly awarded one of the RAF's valuable cadet flying scholarships. This was no small thing and I was delighted when told of my success by a wing commander before leaving the OASC. The RAF would now pay for thirty hours of flying instruction at a selected flying club, taking me almost to private pilot's licence (PPL) standard (only an additional five hours' flying were needed in those days). It also meant that my score in the aptitude tests and my medical fitness were up to the standards required for entry to RAF pilot training.

I completed the Flying Scholarship during the school summer holidays of 1968 with Bournemouth Flying Club at Hurn, my local airfield. Each day of the holiday I drove to the airport on my Lambretta scooter, which I had purchased earlier that year (this was, after all, the era of the 'mods'). The flying was conducted on Cessna 150s, high-wing, light aircraft, with civilian instructors. I went solo after ten hours of dual flying, completing thirty minutes of circuits and landings from Sandown airport on the Isle of Wight where we 'deployed' for summer evening flying because Hurn Airport closed at 17:00 in those days. I flew five sorties that day, including two solos, with the last being the return flight to Hurn, landing at 19:15 as dusk approached. Quite a day. I was ecstatic, and exhausted.

There were seven other cadets on the flying scholarship course with me and, as we approached the end of the thirty hours flying paid for by the RAF, the Chief Flying Instructor (CFI) called us each into his office to discuss whether we were going to continue with the additional five hours required for a PPL, which would have to be paid for individually. The CFI and owner of the Flying Club was 'Noddy' Bernard, an ex-RAF wartime pilot with a somewhat coarse turn of phrase and a mischievous sense of humour, both no doubt honed by his time in the service and on bomber operations. He was also an excellent and extremely sympathetic instructor. When my turn came for the interview I explained that, much as I would love to continue with the additional five hours flying to qualify for a PPL, neither I nor my parents could possibly afford it. I had already discussed this with my mother and father and I had accepted that it was quite beyond our means. Much to my eternal amazement, Noddy told me that I had done very well on the course, my flying impressed him and he thought I could make it as an RAF pilot; it would be a shame to have to stop now without gaining a PPL. Therefore, he would give me the extra five hours flying free of charge, but I was not to tell anyone else. This was an incredibly generous gesture and I was, in fact I still am, quite moved by it and remain very grateful. I wonder what potential he saw in that young 17-year-old. That gesture, as much as anything in my life so far, set me on my way to becoming a professional pilot.

The summer holidays were over before I had finished the course and flown the hours needed for a PPL but that did not matter. The last few hours were completed at weekends through the autumn and into the winter. Finally, I flew the final test, the general flying test with Noddy, who was also a CAA examiner, and I was awarded a PPL, still aged only 17 and before I even had a driving licence for a car. Surely, I was on my way now to fulfilling my dream of becoming a fighter pilot? Well it was a first step anyway. I just had to convince the RAF to take me on.

*****

During my final year at school I made a formal application to join the RAF. At this time there were three methods of entry as an officer: Direct Entry, which required five GCE O Levels, the Cranwell Cadetship scheme, which required two A Levels as the minimum academic entry standard, and graduate entry via university and a degree. The university route was not for me and, in any case, with my academic record, it was out of my reach. I thought that it was worth trying for a Cranwell Cadetship.

I left school in June 1969, having taken my A Level exams and awaited the results. I was also waiting to be called to the Officer and Aircrew Selection Centre (OASC) in connection with my application for a Cranwell Cadetship. In the interim, I took a temporary job as a bus conductor on the Bournemouth Corporation yellow buses. Bournemouth being a holiday town there were always additional holiday-season jobs on the buses and it paid well. As both of my grandfathers had been busmen, I was following a family tradition.

During that summer I was called to the OASC at Biggin Hill and went through the full officer and aircrew selection process for a Cranwell Cadetship without repeating the pilot aptitude tests that I had already passed. I actually enjoyed the experience. The famous 'hangar games' in teams, designed to test individuals' aptitude for leadership and their ability to work in a team, were fun, as were the team and individual problem-solving tests. The written papers were less amusing, but no great problem. I let myself down in the interview though. For some reason I took an instant dislike to both the officers behind the desk and allowed them to rile me such that I did not make a good impression. I think they thought me immature, which was probably fair at the time.

The outcome was my first major disappointment on my path to becoming an RAF pilot as I was not offered a place, but was told I could re-apply in twelve months' time (presumably having done some growing up). This was quite a blow. Perhaps my dream was beyond reach after all. To compound matters further, when the A Level results came through, I had failed to achieve any A Level passes. My lack of effort on my academic studies had caught up with me. My next application to the RAF would be as a direct entrant with a grand total of seven GCE O Levels (three of which were English – language, literature and general studies – and one woodwork) – not a sparkling set of academic qualifications to set before a selection board but just more than the required minima.

Meanwhile, I had to see out the next twelve months and so continued to work as a bus conductor. The Bournemouth buses were still generally crewed by a driver and a conductor at that time and the company was happy to keep me on. The work was actually good fun and working early or late shifts didn't bother me. Meanwhile, most of my surplus cash was ploughed back into flying at the Bournemouth Flying Club. I needed to have that 'second string to my bow' that my mother had long been recommending. It was my intention, if the RAF would not take me, to build up sufficient flying hours to become a civilian flying instructor, then eventually to gain a commercial pilot licence and break into commercial flying. My dream of becoming a fighter pilot now seemed less achievable but I was not going to give up on being a professional pilot, whatever it took.

There were two unexpected benefits to me from my year spent working as a bus conductor. Firstly, I was dealing with people of all types, all day long and this was very good for my general confidence and maturity. Secondly, I was crewed each week with a different driver, spending every hour of that working week with him. The shifts were much more enjoyable if you could get on and work together. This introduction to working as part of a two-man team and getting along with all sorts of different individuals of all ages, with many different personal interests, was really good for me. I grew up considerably from the boy who had left school a year before.

BEGINNINGS

It was a more mature 19-year-old who re-applied to the RAF in 1970, knowing that this was probably going to be the last chance. The OASC was familiar to me now, this being my third selection process. All the tests were completed without difficulty and I felt that I made a favourable impression. The interview with the selection board went much better than the previous attempt; even though there was so much depending on the outcome, I felt relaxed and confident and made a real effort to appear more mature. When it was all over, I knew I had done my best and I went home to await the letter which would inform me of the results, one way or the other.

The official letter from the RAF arrived soon after, on 19 November 1970. It said:

> I am directed to inform you that you have been selected for training as a pilot leading to appointment to a commission in the General Duties Branch (Officer Cadet Entry) of the Royal Air Force. Your subsequent appointment to a commission will depend upon satisfactory completion of a course at the Officer Cadet Training Unit. Provisional arrangements have been made for you to enter the Officer Cadet Training Unit, Royal Air Force Henlow, on 6th December 1970. If you wish to accept this offer, please inform this Centre as soon as possible, using the prepaid envelope. You should confirm that the date proposed for you to enter training is acceptable.

Having made me wait for a year from my previous application they now wanted me to start in just over two weeks' time. I accepted the offer by return post. It seemed to have been a long road to get to this point. I knew that this was just the beginning, but I was in.

Chapter 2

Officer Training

On 7 December 1970 I was formally enrolled and sworn in to the Royal Air Force as an officer cadet, on a par with and paid the same as a leading aircraftsman. I was now earning about a quarter of what I did as a bus conductor and was subjected to the full force of service discipline. It was an environment that any military novice from time immemorial would recognise, where the individual's motto has to be *illegitimi non carborundum* – 'Don't let the b******* grind you down'. I was ready for this and it didn't trouble me.

Physical fitness was a significant element of the officer training course, especially in the early stages. Gym work was based on circuit-training exercises and a policy that whatever standards you set at the start of the course had to be improved upon significantly by the end. The physical training instructors were merciless. There were cross-country runs around the old airfield at Henlow and swimming proficiency tests. Team sports were also plentiful. Wednesday afternoons were sports afternoons and, to make up the shortfall of the 'lost' half day of work, we normally worked Saturday mornings. 'Long weekends' of two full days were only occasionally granted. I was a member of my training squadron's soccer team and played regularly in eleven-a-side and five-a-side matches.

Our fitness was really put to the test during the so-called 'camps' away from Henlow, at locations such as the Stanford Training Area in Norfolk when we force-marched many miles every day at a brisk pace, carrying heavy backpacks and sometimes other loads as well. I think I surprised myself, having never been particularly 'sporty', at how I threw myself into the physical conditioning and sporting side of life and how relatively well I performed. It would be true to say that by the end of seven months of officer training I had never been fitter, and sad to say that I never would be again. It is a source of regret amongst many RAF officers that their first best uniforms, their 'Number Ones', were tailored for them at this stage of their careers when their waist lines were at their absolute slimmest. Most of those first uniforms did not see out a full career, at least not without some letting out.

As with any military basic training, there were aspects of the course designed to teach not only specific skills and routines, but also to inculcate the concept of discipline, self-discipline and teamwork. If one person messed up the whole team suffered. Kit and room or block inspections formed part of this. After a full evening spent preparing, or 'bulling', the accommodation block for inspection, it could be very disheartening on return from a hard day's work, to find personal belongings and clothing scattered everywhere, because some minor aspect was not up to scratch. Such an environment makes everyone pull together and work as a team, with those who are stronger in certain areas helping the weaker members. People got to know each other really well under the duress of these circumstances and strong friendships were formed.

Drill (marching) was another element of the training which took considerable time and effort and helped to develop those military concepts, whilst also teaching the specific moves and procedures. My background as an air cadet helped me here – I'd been performing RAF drill since I was 14 years old – but I had never before done rifle drill with fixed bayonets or sword drill. I enjoyed these disciplines although some of the drill instructors were truly fearsome. It is interesting, in these more politically correct and enlightened days, to note that there was never, in our interpretation, any sign of bullying. It was tough but fair. The drill instructors were all RAF Regiment NCOs, they called us 'Sir' (pronounced 'Suh') or 'Gentlemen' collectively, but had a way of delivering the 'Suh' which was somehow denigrating. The fearsome Training Wing Warrant Officer, Mr Jordan, told us, 'Gentlemen, I will call you "Suh". You will call me "Suh". The difference is you will mean it.'

Not surprisingly, leadership training was a major part of the Officer Training Course with lectures on the theory of leadership and practical exercises to put the theory and our individual leadership skills to the test. During these practical exercises we were each under scrutiny, not only to see how we performed as leaders, but also how we behaved as team members. The conditioning of the team, to make individuals less co-operative by making them cold, tired, hungry and wet, was very much part of the system. Otherwise, leading would have been too easy, as everyone in the team would want to help their colleague and friend whose turn it was to take charge. On many occasions on these exercises I felt that I was being pushed beyond my limits and then found that these were not actually real limits. I discovered reserves of energy, of character and of determination that I had not previously been required to tap into and hadn't known I possessed. This was an interesting discovery and I developed a new assured confidence as a result of knowing myself and my personal capabilities better.

There were also classroom lessons on academic subjects – so-called Professional Studies – that future officers needed to absorb. We were taught and then allowed to practise the procedures to be used for hearing charges (orderly room procedures) and also for conducting interviews of various types, including welfare problems, during practical sessions. The standard of knowledge and understanding in these subjects, and our ability to find our way around the various manuals for the appropriate regulations, were tested with professional studies exams. The future pilots and navigators had several more years of flying training ahead of them before they would command men and women in the normal course of their duties. For most, it would not be until they reached much higher rank that they would be frantically trying to recall what they were taught about these specifics during officer training. In my case, it was 1986, fifteen years later, in the rank of squadron leader before I was required to hear a charge.

So focused was I on entering flying training and becoming an RAF pilot, that officer training seemed an inconvenience, a hoop that had to be jumped through, before I could get my hands on one of Her Majesty's aircraft and get on with the real business. This was a mistake. In the RAF that I was joining, you could not become a pilot without first becoming an officer. The combination of my not taking the business of becoming a commissioned officer seriously enough and, perhaps as a consequence, not performing well enough in some areas, resulted in my failing to graduate and being 're-coursed' at the end of the four-month course to repeat the last three months again. At least I wasn't suspended from training completely like many others, but I was being given a second chance. I wasn't alone in this; several of my friends and colleagues were re-coursed with me, but it was still a serious setback.

I realised at this point that if I was going to get the chance to become an RAF pilot, I had to pass the officer training course first and I needed to apply myself more to that end. I also began to feel, almost without consciously realising it, that they don't just give away the Queen's Commission and anything that took so much effort must be worth having. It was with a completely different attitude that I undertook the second course, very determined and viewing the chance to become a commissioned officer as something I now really aspired to. Perhaps I'd been brainwashed, or maybe it was just a continuation of growing up, a process that the training was doubtless accelerating.

When I was eventually told that I had passed the course and would be graduating and becoming a commissioned officer, it was a great relief. In my final debrief, my flight commander, whom I liked and whose opinion I respected, praised my overall performance and told me I had good potential. He also said, 'If you have a fault, Rowley, it is that you do not abide fools lightly.' That was the first time that I had heard that expression, but it was not to be the last. I knew that he was right and, to be honest, I couldn't really see why that characteristic was a fault. If I could do it, couldn't anybody?

It was a much more mature, well-trained and very proud 20-year-old who was commissioned as an acting pilot officer in the RAF on 24 June 1971. I had grown up enormously in the six and a half months that I had been in the RAF and I had changed more in that short time than most people of that age would in years. In some respects, I could almost be called responsible.

When our flight drill sergeant, who had helped to develop us from boys to men and officers, finished his final inspection of us before sending us onto the graduation parade, he saluted us all for the first time, as from now on he would always have to do. Although we were marching on to the parade wearing the white officer cadet tabs on our lapels and the white band around our caps, we also wore the stripes of commissioned officers on our sleeves. The white tabs and bands would be removed after we marched off. Our sergeant's show of respect for our new commissions, which we had now earned, meant more to us than anything. It was really a very moving and a very proud moment.

The first hurdle had been successfully jumped. Flying training was next.

Chapter 3

Flying Training

RAF Church Fenton

Before starting flying training, and after some brief leave, I was sent to RAF Church Fenton, near York, to complete the Academic Studies Course, which didn't sound like something I was going to enjoy. All direct-entry student pilots entering flying training had to complete this short course to brush up on their mathematics and science knowledge. I don't remember the detailed content of the course but I do remember it being as bad as I had expected. I had, of course, obtained only marginal passes in GCE O Level maths and physics at school and the squadron leader in charge of the course commented on my report that 'These obvious weaknesses in maths/science were reflected in a poor performance throughout the course'. My academic failings were costing me again. I was re-coursed once more for further training during which my performance apparently 'improved considerably and reached an acceptable standard'.

Also based at Church Fenton was an Aviation Medical Training Centre where we future pilots were given instruction in the physiological effects of flying by RAF doctors, who were aviation medicine experts. Part of this training included being taken to 25,000 feet in the decompression chamber and then being given experience of what it was like to become hypoxic by having the oxygen supply turned off. For me, as the hypoxia took effect, a feeling of euphoria crept over me, which could clearly be dangerous if it was not recognised. The simple tasks of subtracting numbers and drawing something, which I had been given, first became difficult as I struggled with the lack of oxygen, then suddenly became no cause for concern, no problem at all, as the euphoria set in. When back on oxygen and recovered, the scribbling on my pad, which had seemed fine at the time, was almost indecipherable and the mathematics was definitely not accurate. This was a useful and interesting experience, one that my long flying career subsequently demanded I repeated on another nine occasions by which time the value had begun to diminish. Doesn't starving the brain of oxygen kill off brain cells? That could explain a lot.

At Church Fenton we were also subjected to an ejection-seat experience on a rig, a procedure that was later stopped due to some students receiving injuries to their necks and spines. The rig was mounted on a truck, with a gantry which was about thirty-feet high when swung up to the vertical; a Martin Baker Mk 4 ejection seat was mounted on the gantry. When my turn came, I strapped myself very tightly into the seat at the bottom of the rig, feeling somewhat apprehensive. We were made to use the ejection-seat face-blind firing handle for this demonstration. I pulled the handle to its full extent over my flying helmet and face, and was now unable to see what was happening. The one-second pause, which simulated the time taken for the cockpit canopy to separate from the aircraft, seemed like an eternity. Then there was a loud bang and a massive acceleration up the rig, accompanied by a not-insignificant amount of back pain. The pain and sensation of acceleration ceased and I moved the blind away to find myself swaying gently, thirty feet up, near the top of the gantry. I was then slowly winched back down to the ground. Quite a fairground ride. The pain of the 'ride' and the subsequent stiff back and neck I experienced for the rest of the day and night convinced me that ejection definitely needed to be considered only as a last-ditch option and wasn't a decision to be taken lightly, especially as this practice ejection had been done with only the primary cartridge in the gun, rather than all three cartridges that would be present in the real seat. I'm not sure that this was really what the training was trying to get across, when the flight safety message of the day was 'Eject in time'. However, that said, I don't think I was ever really influenced by the experience, except to be sure that I always strapped into an ejection seat with great care, with the lap straps as tight as I could get them, to minimise the risk of spinal damage if I did have to eject. It would be true to say that every time I strapped into an ejection seat over the next thirty-two years, I did so as if this was going to be the time that I had to use it.

*****

Because I had previously completed an air cadet flying scholarship which, of course, was training provided under the auspices of the RAF and paid for from the public purse, I was to be 'through jet trained'. Those students who had not completed a flying scholarship were required to undergo a short

15

elementary flying training (EFT) Course at RAF Church Fenton on the de Havilland Chipmunk. This was an introduction to flying and something of a weeding-out course. One of the good friends I had made during officer training was chopped from flying training during his Chipmunk EFT without even going solo. That was a shock to me as well as for him. The first of my friends and colleagues had fallen by the wayside in what was to become a familiar manner. Quite clearly, the expectations the flying training system had of us were unforgiving in the extreme and, whilst you might be given a second chance, you were not going to get many more

Of the twelve young student pilots on my academic studies course at Church Fenton, three were suspended from flying training at various stages. Only two of us eventually became fast-jet fighter pilots and the others ended up flying multi-engine aircraft. These were by no means exceptional numbers. Of course, at the time, I had no way of knowing what the outcome would be.

Basic Flying Training – RAF Leeming

I was posted to No. 3 Flying Training School at RAF Leeming, in North Yorkshire, on 6 September 1971 where I embarked on the Basic Flying Training course with relish. The aircraft we flew for the first seven months of the course (about sixty hours flying time) was the Hunting/BAC Jet Provost T.3. The 'JP 3' was a low-wing single-jet two-seat basic trainer with a slightly bulbous and blunt, tadpole-like, nose to accommodate the side-by-side ejection seats for the instructor and student in an unpressurised cockpit. The straight wings had wingtip fuel tanks fitted. The 'JP 3' was powered by a Rolls Royce Viper 102 pure jet engine that produced a relatively puny 1,750 lbs of thrust. By the time that I started flying the 'JP 3' it had been in service for eleven years. I didn't think it was a pretty aircraft but that didn't matter; it was a jet and was definitely a step beyond anything I'd flown before. The theoretical maximum ('Never Exceed') speed was 350 knots, although you didn't often see that; it could cruise at 240 knots at low level and it was stressed for 6G, which, considering that the pilots were not equipped with anti-g suits, was quite enough.

During the first half of the course, the days were occupied with a mix of ground school and flying. This still permitted two flights per day on many days and on 8 October, eight flying days into the course, with just over ten hours of dual instruction under my belt, I was sent on my first solo, for one circuit of the airfield in the 'JP', at the nearby satellite airfield of RAF Topcliffe. Every trainee pilot has probably wondered whether his instructor really knows what he's doing in letting him go off on his own for the first time. I felt the same moment of doubt as we stopped in front of the air traffic control tower for my instructor, Flight Lieutenant Al Gaunt, to climb out and go up to the 'glasshouse' to monitor my solo. That said, I felt ready, and my first solo in the RAF, and in a jet, went without a hitch and was a good confidence boost.

The course continued through the circuit consolidation phase, general handling away from the airfield, which included stalling, spinning and aerobatics, simulated airborne emergencies and practice forced landings. Medium-level navigation, low flying and low-level navigation, and instrument flying were also introduced. The flying was exciting and great fun – I loved it all – although of course it was also very hard work, requiring intense concentration to achieve the standards expected and to learn and advance at the rapid rate required. I often flew twice a day on my allocated flying days and would frequently feel absolutely shattered at the end of the day; but it was that satisfied sort of tiredness of both body and mind which allows easy sleep.

During this stage of the course I was allocated a newly-trained instructor, straight out of the Central Flying School course and previously a Canberra photo-reconnaissance pilot who had spent much of his time flying at low level. Flight Lieutenant Paul Draper proved to be an excellent instructor, despite his relative lack of experience as a QFI. I liked him and we had an easy, friendly, working relationship. He invited his three allocated students to his house; we met his lovely wife and admired his Triumph sports car, at least until he bent it on the notorious Gatenby Lane that connected RAF Leeming to the A1 trunk road. One of his best traits as a flying instructor was his ability to identify the cause of the errors I made, possibly because he had made similar mistakes himself in training, remembered the reasons and knew the cure. A special relationship develops with anyone that you fly with regularly, based on shared risks and because the intensity of the environment opens up personalities. There is no hiding behind a personal veneer or façade in a cockpit.

Paul and I shared one risk too far one day. As we taxied in from the end of the runway at the end of another training sortie, I reached to get the ejection-seat-pan-handle safety pin from the block on the cockpit coaming to make the seat safe before unstrapping. I was horrified to find that it was not in the pin block but was still in the ejection seat. I had flown the entire sortie with the ejection-seat-pan handle made safe. If I had needed to eject in a hurry and had attempted to pull the seat handle it would not have moved. There were no secrets between us and I immediately owned up to Paul, my instructor, shamefaced and horror-struck, at what had happened. His reaction wasn't what I had expected. He had, he confided with great honesty, noticed my error during my pre-take-off checks and had not corrected me immediately, meaning to draw it to my attention before we took off to make a point of it; then he forgot. Clearly, he felt very responsible for this serious error, too. The honesty between us was refreshing and an indication of the trust that had developed between us. I learned the lesson. Never again did I ever make that mistake with ejection-seat pins, a mistake that has cost others their lives.

The ground school lectures and study, which made up half of our working time during this stage of the course, were hard work, but different from any learning and studying that I had done before. Here it was directly related to the job and to flying and so I was much more motivated than I'd been at school. Subjects like aerodynamics, 'tech', meteorology, navigation, Morse-code and airmanship were clearly all things that we needed to understand and that we would be using daily. That wasn't to say that I found it easy to study, learn and store the information I was being taught but now I could accept that this was worth some effort as I needed to know this stuff.

Apart from the mainstream subjects, we occasionally received further lectures on the physiology of flight, under the heading of aviation medicine. I remember one particular lecture from one of the station's RAF doctors, which unfortunately for him was the last lecture of the day, the graveyard shift. When he announced that we were going to learn about the balance organs, the semi-circular canals in the inner ear, a subject which we had covered prior to starting the course, we suggested that our time would be better spent by finishing early. The young doctor was obviously fully prepared for this and said that we could wrap up straight away if one of the class could come up to the front and explain the workings of the inner ear using the cut-away model he had brought with him. One of our number, John Tonks, was 'volunteered' and he proceeded to move up to the front and give what we thought was an excellent explanation of the workings of the semi-circular canals using the model. An early finish looked on the cards. The doctor told him to sit down and said that he was also impressed with what he had just seen and heard, especially as this was a model of the uterus. We realised that we didn't know as much about the human body as we thought we did. He had our attention; it was one of the best pieces of instructional motivational technique I have ever witnessed.

FLYING TRAINING

In order to assimilate the ground school knowledge that was being pumped into us, I worked late into the evenings in my room in the officers' mess. Never before had I worked so hard or applied myself so much to academic subjects. It paid off. I had to re-sit one exam but, overall, I did well in the ground school subjects. In fact, amazingly for someone who had been such a dullard at school, only one other student of the twelve on my course achieved an overall mark in the ground school exams higher than mine.

*****

Poor weather meant that I flew only once in January 1972 but I was able to get a long weekend to jointly celebrate my twenty-first birthday with my two boyhood friends from Bournemouth, Nigel and Angus, whose twenty-first birthdays fell within the fortnight after mine. Nigel was now a senior aircraftsman in the RAF and Angus a sergeant but we didn't tell anyone in the service about our all-ranks weekend in Paris, not least because we got up to no good at all.

*****

In April 1972 I passed the Basic Handling Test with my flight commander, and it was time to convert to the Jet Provost T.5 for the advanced phases of the course. The 'JP 5' was a step up from the 'JP 3'. It was powered by a Viper 200 series jet engine with 2,500 lbs thrust, over 40 per cent more than the JP 3. The JP 5s we flew at Leeming did not carry tip tanks and weighed less than 7,000 lbs. The aircraft also had a pressurised cockpit with an electrically-operated sliding canopy, which gave it, to my mind, a more attractive look than the JP 3. The theoretical maximum speed of the JP 5 was 380 knots; it could cruise quite comfortably at 300 knots at low level and, at this speed, fuel management became quite a factor. It could climb at 4,000 feet per minute to a service ceiling of over 36,000 feet. This was true jet performance and I was excited about starting to fly it.

I quickly got to grips with the extra performance of the JP 5 and began to enjoy the new advanced exercises of the course, such as high-level flying (climbing to altitudes that I'd never been to before), maximum-rate turning (sustaining 6G in a spiral descent), night flying and close formation. In addition to these new exercises, we continued to develop our skills in general handling and aerobatics, medium- and low-level navigation and instrument

19

flying. Of the new skills, close formation and tail-chasing were perhaps the most exciting and, in pure flying terms, perhaps the most demanding. Once I began to overcome my initial fears of causing a mid-air collision and began to realise that I actually could maintain station mere feet away from the lead aircraft with both of us travelling at great speed, and learnt to relax on the controls, it all became great fun.

Over the last three months of the Basic Flying Training course, on the days when the weather was good, I routinely flew twice a day and often three times in a day. This provided excellent continuity in the training and assisted rapid progress; it was very rewarding and satisfying but sometimes very tiring too. The intense concentration needed to achieve the required standards and the inevitable effect of the more demanding flying on my nerves meant that sometimes when I returned to my room in the mess at the end of the day, I lay down on my bed for a short nap, promptly fell asleep and only awoke later in the evening having missed dinner. This did not bother me as I knew that sleep was the best way for me to recharge my personal 'batteries' and that I would then be sharp and ready for the next flying day.

During this stage of my course, RAF Leeming was visited by a Spitfire flown by the famous display pilot Ray Hanna. A Jet Provost display team duo, the 'Gemini Pair', which was famous for 'mirror-image' formation flying, was based at RAF Leeming and their team manager was Squadron Leader Henry Prince. He had been a Red Arrow when Ray Hanna led the team and he had persuaded Ray to bring the Spitfire to Leeming to fly in formation with the Gemini Pair for air-to-air publicity photographs. The following day, Ray Hanna took off in the Spitfire and flew an amazing 'beat up' of the airfield before departing. I stood alone by the corner of one of the hangars and watched in awe as he appeared round the hangar with 90 degrees of bank applied and with his wingtip mere feet from the ground, continuing to give the airfield a right royal and entirely illegal beat up for several minutes. This was the first time that I had seen the beauty, power and charisma of a Spitfire in flight; it set a long-held ambition in place in my mind. What if one day I could fly one? This was an ambition that I never expected to fulfil but which, beyond my wildest dreams at that time, I would in fact achieve twenty-five years later.

*****

The course seemed to rush towards its conclusion with various flying tests: 6 June, Night Handling Test; 14 July, Instrument Rating Test; 26 July, Final

Navigation Test; 27 July, Final Handling Test. I prepared as well as I possibly could for each test. I was always slightly nervous but only in a way that heightened my focus rather than dulling my brain. I didn't really suffer from so-called 'testitus' as some other students did. I felt that I performed as well as I could in each test and drew favourable comments and good grades from the examiners.

On Friday 4 August 1972, the twelve RAF student pilots (and one Jordanian Air Force student) of Number 51 Course paraded, as the graduating flight, on the main aircraft servicing pan in front of the air traffic control tower at RAF Leeming for the presentation of their pilot's 'wings'. When my turn came to march forward for the reviewing officer, Air Vice Marshal Gill DSO, to place the RAF pilot's flying badge onto the left breast of my uniform tunic, it was, and still is, one of the proudest moments of my life. I remain intensely proud that I earned the right to wear RAF pilot's wings. When the various prizes for the course were announced, I found myself marching forward again, first to collect the Glen Trophy awarded to the student who 'shows the greatest proficiency in general flying' and then again to collect the Sword of Merit awarded to the best all-round student of the graduating course. For someone who had never won any prizes for anything, this was just amazing, especially as this was all that had ever mattered to me. I felt humbled, astonished and very proud. I was glad that my parents were there to share these moments of success with me.

Of the twelve RAF students on my course, two were posted to train on helicopters, four were sent for multi-engine aircraft training and the remaining six, including me, were posted for 'fast jet' Advanced Flying Training at RAF Valley, the next step on the road to becoming a fighter pilot. As it turned out, only two of us would succeed in getting into those coveted fighter cockpits at the first attempt which indicates the difficulty involved. For now, I was briefly replete. I had achieved all and more than I could have hoped for at this stage.

Advanced Flying Training – RAF Valley

RAF Valley, on Anglesey, is a slightly strange RAF station not quite like anywhere else and, it seemed to me, a long way from anywhere else. Sitting on the exposed north-west coast of the island, it often suffered from gales, low cloud or fog, especially in the winter months, which was when my course was scheduled to take place. Perversely, when the rest of the UK was suffering from bad weather, Valley could be bathed in sunshine and it was a very useful and frequently-utilised weather diversion airfield.

The Advanced Flying Training Course at No. 4 Flying Training School was principally flown on the Folland Gnat jet trainer, although a squadron of Hawker Hunters on the far side of the airfield took some students through the course. The Gnat was a small aircraft, diminutive even, which tall people had trouble fitting into. I knew that I had a long back and a tall sitting height, even though I am just six-feet tall, and that this might be a problem. Before any student pilots were sent to RAF Valley they had to be measured and assessed as anthropologically suitable and within the sitting height required for the Gnat. When I was measured, I had scrunched myself down on the measuring rig and managed to produce an acceptable sitting height measurement. However, this subterfuge did not last long at Valley.

On 9 October 1972 the first event on the first day of the course was the station Commander's welcome address. When the group captain had finished speaking to us, he singled several of us out, including me, to be assessed for size in a Gnat cockpit that day, obviously based on previous experiences with taller students. My cockpit check in the Gnat was a disaster; I was so tall, sitting in the front cockpit wearing my bone dome flying helmet, that it was impossible to close the canopy; it was clearly a non-starter. So, it was off to the other side of the airfield to No. 3 Squadron to be assessed in a single-seat Hawker Hunter F.6. This nearly went horribly wrong, too. With the ejection seat fully lowered and wearing my bone dome, I could close the canopy but the flight lieutenant flying instructor standing outside was not happy about my ability to reach the top handle of the ejection seat over my head. In truth it was a squeeze to get my hands between the top of my bone dome and the canopy but there was always the bottom handle, wasn't there? Eventually, he agreed that I fitted and the crisis was over. I was to train on the Hawker Hunter. The Hunter was a fighter, not just a trainer. Indeed, it was only recently that the Hunter had been withdrawn from operational service with the RAF in the Middle East. I would be flying the single-seat F.6 versions in due course, as well as the two-seat T.7s. I couldn't have been happier.

The Hunter ground school took almost two months to complete and covered the systems and cockpit controls and indications, as well as how to deal with emergencies that might occur. Much of this was learned and practised in the Hunter simulator, which was really an emergencies trainer with no visual flying cues. We also learned more on general subjects associated with the sort of flying we were about to embark upon, such as high speed and supersonic aerodynamics.

*****

The single-seat versions of the Hawker Hunter are amongst the most graceful looking aircraft ever to take to the skies, with their slim fuselages, shapely 35-degree-swept mid-mounted wings, swept tail and fin and their neat triangular engine air intakes in the wing roots.

The aircraft used at 4 FTS at Valley had been modified as pure trainers with no armament; the four Aden cannon had been removed, along with the blisters under the nose, which were fitted to operational aircraft to collect spent ammunition links. Some wag in the past had nicknamed these lumps 'Sabrinas' after an actress of the day. This modification made the Valley Hunters particularly slick and meant that they actually performed better than the operational variants. The Valley Hunters were painted in a raspberry-ripple red-white-and-grey Training Command shiny gloss paint scheme. We almost always flew with the 100-imperial-gallon-capacity fuel drop tanks fitted under the wings.

The single-seat Hunter F.6 weighed in at around 17,000 lbs. Its single Rolls Royce Avon 207 jet engine produced 10,145 lbs of thrust, so its performance was respectable and, coming straight from the Jet Provost, pretty startling to me at first. It could climb at over 17,000 feet per minute to a service ceiling of 50,000 feet although, in practice, this was limited to 45,000 feet by the oxygen regulator capability. It was capable of flying at 620 knots at low level and at Mach 0.92 (M0.92) level at 45,000 feet. In a shallow dive from high altitude it could go supersonic. The Hunter cockpit was rather old-fashioned, even in 1972. It was fitted with a Martin Baker Mk 3 ejection seat and the instrumentation and cockpit displays were not ergonomically arranged; in fact, they were scattered around the cockpit in a most haphazard fashion with individual warning lights and 'dolls-eye' indicators. To complicate things further, the cockpit layouts were not all the same The Hunter had conventional hydraulically-powered controls, with a manual reversionary mode in the event of hydraulic or engine failure, which could also be selected for training purposes. In manual, the controls were very heavy indeed.

The Hunter T.7 that I was to fly first for dual instruction was, to my mind, slightly less beautiful to look at than the single-seat F.6, principally because of the rather bulbous nose needed to accommodate the side-by-side seating for two pilots in the cockpit. The T.7 also had a less powerful engine, being fitted with a 100-series Avon engine with a rated thrust of 7,500 lbs. As the T.7 with its two-man cockpit was heavier than the F.6, this meant that the performance was less sprightly. I also found the T.7's flying controls to be heavier than the F.6's.

On 4 December I flew a Hunter T.7 for the first time with my nominated instructor, Flight Lieutenant Pete Hitchcock. Pete was a real gentleman and a genuinely nice man; he had previously been a Lightning pilot flying F.2As in Germany with the famous 92 Squadron, where he had earned a Martin Baker tie after ejecting from a Lightning which failed to recover from a spin. Our paths subsequently crossed many times over the years as he rose up the ranks and he was in a position to influence my career to my benefit on at least two further occasions, not least as the squadron leader pilot desk officer 'poster' in 1986. Incidentally, my flight commander on the Hunter squadron at Valley was the then Flight Lieutenant Peter Squire, who subsequently became the Chief of Air Staff. He retired as Air Chief Marshal Sir Peter Squire GCB DFC AFC ADC FRAeS (his DFC was earned leading the Harriers of 1 Squadron in the Falklands War in 1982). He never forgot me and, whenever we met in subsequent years, he always shook my hand and addressed me as Clive. Having flown with him on the course in a Hunter in 1973 when he was a flight lieutenant, I next flew with him as his instructor in a Tornado F.3 twenty-nine years later, in 2002, when he was the Chief of the Air Staff.

On that first sortie in a Hunter T.7 I realised what a jump I was making from the sedate pace of the Jet Provosts, which I had so far been flying, up to the true fast-jet performance of these beasts. One of the aims of that first forty-minute familiarisation flight was to show the student what the aircraft could do and to impress upon him the rate at which things happened, and the need to anticipate events and think ahead, which, as all student pilots know, is easier said than done. I also had to get used to the idea of flying in a heavy and cumbersome immersion suit, with life jacket and anti-g trousers. We were now routinely flying over the sea, in this case the Irish Sea, and during the winter months the sea temperature was such that survival time in the water would be very short without the protection of a waterproof immersion suit and sufficient warm clothing underneath. The anti-g trousers fitted tightly around the legs and stomach and inflated when G was pulled, a necessary aid to the pilot being able to retain full vision and remain conscious whilst sustaining 6G as the Hunter could do (the aircraft was actually stressed to 7G).

FLYING TRAINING

On take off the initial acceleration down the runway was impressive; the nose-wheel was lifted off at 120 knots and the aircraft unstuck from the runway at 145-150 knots. The undercarriage had to be raised before the speed reached 250 knots. The aircraft was initially held in a shallow climb to build the speed quickly towards the climbing speed of 370 knots. It was necessary to anticipate this by about 15 knots and to pitch up into the climbing attitude to hold 370 knots. At about 23,000 feet the best climbing speed became M0.85. I was now travelling faster than I had ever done before, in the climb. We flew a few aerobatics with much higher entry speeds than I had been used to, for example we used 425 knots for a loop, and it took a lot of sky to complete each manoeuvre. When turning, small amounts of bank achieved very poor rates of turn at normal cruising speeds and it was necessary to use bank angles that would be considered steep turns in slower aircraft. Another difference from my earlier flying was how much it was necessary to scan the instruments when flying visually, as it was not easy to select visual attitudes. Back in the visual circuit the downwind leg was flown at 220 knots, tipping into the finals' turn at 180 knots. The final approach was flown at 150 knots. The swept-wing characteristics of the aircraft meant that there was a higher nose attitude than I was used to on the approach to land. All in all, it was an exciting revelation and rather daunting.

*****

As the course progressed, I realised that I was now playing with the big boys, in the first eleven as it were, and that this was going to be far harder than anything I had done so far. There were eight student pilots on my course, of whom four were university graduates who had completed their Basic Flying Training at Cranwell. These individuals were older and considerably more mature than me; they also seemed to have bigger brains. They were impressive in their performances on the course and took easily to the academic challenges. All of these university graduates subsequently did very well in their respective careers in the RAF and they all rose to Air rank.* I was one of the youngest, if not the youngest, of the students on the course. The other three direct entrants did not find it easy either. Unfortunately, two of them were 'chopped' from the course, one being sent to multi-engine aircraft training and the other, a friend of mine, found that

---

* Air rank refers to RAF senior officers from air commodore to marshal of the Royal Air Force who are equivalent to Royal Navy Flag officers, i.e. those in the admiral ranks, or Army general officers.'

his flying days were over just as he was about to get married. In truth, the distractions of his long-range romance had been instrumental in his failing the course.

After just over twenty hours of flying in the T.7, including thirty minutes solo, and having gained an instrument rating on the Hunter, I was let loose in a single-seat F.6 on 8 January 1973. Most pilots will have particular memories of their very first solo or maybe of their first solo on another type. For me, this was one of the most memorable, as it was my first-ever flight in a single-seat jet fighter. I remember pausing after I had strapped in, and before I started the engine, to take in the fact that there was no empty seat beside me; I was able to lean my elbows on both sides of the cockpit and look out over the centre of the nose through the armoured windscreen. It was a tight fit but it felt right. I was about to fly a single-seater.

Flying the Hunter F.6 for the first time was everything that I had been led to expect it would be. The controls were lighter and more responsive than the T.7, to the extent that it took some care to avoid over-controlling and inducing a pilot-induced oscillation (PIO) in roll immediately after take off. The acceleration after take off was markedly quicker too. Overall, the single-seat Hunter was just a delight to fly and I revelled in taking it to 620 knots over the sea. Shortly after this flight I flew supersonic for the first time (something that later became completely routine to me and, as such, a non-event).

I found formation flying in the Hunter much more demanding than I had done in the lighter Jet Provost. The greater inertia of this heavier aircraft was more difficult to control and required a greater sense of urgency than I initially showed. Speed control was not easy either, as there was so much power on hand and slowing down such a slick aircraft wasn't straightforward and required good anticipation. I knew that I was struggling with this phase and woke up in a sweat one night having had a terrible nightmare in which I had caused a mid-air collision in formation over the airfield, the ensuing crash writing off most of the aircraft on the ground. I did not normally dream, or at least didn't remember my dreams, and had never had nightmares, but clearly the stress was beginning to affect me and I was suffering from a loss of faith in my ability. Fortunately, I achieved an acceptable standard in formation flying and my confidence and ability in this important skill improved further as I progressed in my subsequent flying career.

I also struggled with low-level navigation at the increased speeds we were flying at (six or seven miles per minute). I tended to use ground features too close to my own aircraft and did not employ 'big-feature' navigation techniques, using obvious features, well ahead, as I later learned to do. The difficulties I experienced with low-level navigation at this stage of my career later made me very sympathetic to students who suffered similar problems when I subsequently became a Tactical Weapons Unit instructor on the Hawk at RAF Chivenor. Indeed, I was made the Low-level Navigation Phase Officer with special responsibility for helping those students who were struggling with the techniques. It is perhaps a truism that being able to recognise and understand the common mistakes from personal experience, and knowing the solutions, makes one a better instructor.

Despite my struggles with some elements of the course, my confidence overall must have been holding up and I think I never really doubted that I had what it took. I just needed to prove it to my instructors. One instructor in particular who I flew with frequently, Flight Lieutenant Mike Phillips, another ex-Lightning pilot, gave me a particularly hard time and must have believed that my confidence would not be badly affected by his instructional style. He would send me out to the aircraft to do the external checks whilst he was signing the F700 maintenance log. I was conscientious with my checks and took too long over them as far as he was concerned. He would appear striding across the pan shouting, 'Come on Rowley, get a move on, you'll never make a fighter pilot!' Strapping into the ejection seat alongside him in a Hunter T.7, there would be a blur of arms from his side and he would be strapped in and shouting, 'You'll never make a fighter pilot, Rowley' at me again as I completed the process at my own pace. I just grinned at him and got on with it but he wasn't entirely wrong to press me because not long into the future, if I was successful, I could be 'scrambling' at double-quick speed as he had done on a fighter squadron. I crossed paths with Mike on several occasions during my subsequent career when we were both flying at the same airfields and he will feature again in this tale.

In mid-March 1973, with just over seventy hours on Hunters, I completed the course. Although I had not done particularly well and the report on my performance was not the best, I had passed. I was graded average except for aerobatics and night flying which were graded high average, and I was placed sixth out of the eight students on the course. Considering that the last two had been 'chopped' from the course, this meant that, effectively, I was bottom of the class. Having been top on my basic flying training course, I was now bottom at advanced flying training, which just went to show how the difficulty level had been 'ramped up'.

I had made up my mind that I wanted to fly single-seat fighters if I could and my choices for future postings reflected that. The student who came top of our course, Bill Rimmer (who later retired as an Air Vice Marshal) was 'creamed off' to become a qualified flying instructor (QFI). The order of merit in postings after that was generally Harrier for the better students; Lightning for those considered able to cope with the high workload of the aircraft's single-seat cockpit; and then the two-seat aircraft, the F-4 Phantom and Buccaneer, where a new pilot could be helped by an experienced navigator. I was role-disposed to the Lightning and felt pleased with that outcome. Clearly, I had done sufficiently well to be considered suitable for single-seat fighters, or maybe the instructors thought that navigators would not put up with me.

There was another stage of training to complete before I would fly the Lightning. The next step was the Tactical Weapons Unit course at RAF Chivenor. I was leaving Training Command and moving to Strike Command.

Tactical Weapons Unit – RAF Chivenor

I was fortunate to have only a couple of weeks between the AFTS course at Valley and the Tactical Weapons Unit (TWU) course at No. 229 Operational Conversion Unit, RAF Chivenor. Many student pilots at that time were suffering long gaps between their various courses. I was originally given a course start date some distance into the future but someone scheduled to be on the course starting in April 1973 broke his leg and I was moved forward to replace him with just two weeks' leave in between courses.

The TWU course was another stage on the long road to becoming an RAF fighter pilot and, as with each step so far, another big jump. Up until now the focus of the training had been entirely on the business of flying the aircraft – pure flying. Now there was an assumption that we knew how to fly and we were about to learn how to operate and 'fight' the aircraft. There was an expectation that flying the aircraft could no longer take up most of your brain power but rather that this would be a more instinctive process, as spare capacity would now need to be focused on the tactical aspects.

The squadron I was posted to at Chivenor, 234 Squadron, was a proper fighter squadron, with a proud fighting history and plenty of squadron memorabilia to go with it. We were treated much more like grown-ups than students in many respects and shared the squadron crew room with the instructors, rather than being segregated in separate crew rooms as was the practice in Training Command.

The living arrangements in the officers' mess at Chivenor were somewhat primitive at that time and the accommodation could at best be described as 'historic'. The wooden buildings were all of Second World War-vintage and had changed little since. Whilst the public rooms had character, the individual officers' rooms were in lines of wooden huts that resembled a wartime prisoner-of war camp. Each officer was allocated his own small room with no facilities whatsoever. The toilets and ablutions were in a separate wooden block between the lines of huts which was often a cold or wet trek from one's room.

I stuck these arrangements for only a week or so and then, having discovered that we could get permission to live out if we requested it, and having been offered a share of a rented cottage, I moved out. With two other student pilots, Rod Berrington and Tim Aaron, we rented a cottage in the small hamlet of Lake just outside Barnstaple. Off-duty life in North Devon throughout the summer of 1973 was pretty idyllic, the more so when we had to move from the cottage because of planned refurbishments and our landlady, Lady Wrey, found us other rented accommodation in the old servants' wing of a large mansion at Braunton, in its own grounds on a hill overlooking Chivenor airfield and the Taw estuary. We worked hard and we played hard and the fact that the flying was so much fun just added to that summer being one that I remember as amongst the best of my life. (Rod Berrington, with whom I shared a house whilst at Chivenor was quite a character with a string of girlfriends. He subsequently became a Lightning pilot and later, having left the service, moved to South Africa and married. He was murdered in 2009 in Johannesburg when he was shot by a burglar.)

I had one advantage when I started the TWU course as flying was conducted on the Hunter: the T.7, the F.6, the F.6A (fitted with a brake parachute) and the FGA.9. Having flown the Hunter at Valley, I did not have to convert to a new type like those students who had flown the Gnat during their advanced flying training. For me, the conversion phase of the course was, therefore, straightforward with some trips missed out from the syllabus as I didn't need them.

As soon as the conversion and close-formation phases were complete, we were taught tactical and 'battle' formation from 250 feet up to 40,000 feet. Battle formation meant flying line abreast about a mile apart as a pair. Turns were executed by crossing over with an appropriate delay and what seemed like some advanced choreography to us at the time. We practised on bicycles on the aircraft servicing pan, trying to learn the geometry and work out who avoided whom.

Next came the so-called 'cine-weave' phase in which we were taught to use the gunsight to accurately track a hard-manoeuvring target (the target flew a 4G break turn initiated on the attacker's 'Commence' call, turning through

90 degrees and then reversing into a barrel roll in the opposite direction). At first this seemed virtually impossible to follow, let alone to track with the gun-sight 'pipper' whilst simultaneously ranging with the twist grip on the throttle to keep the diamonds in the sight matched to the target's wingspan. With practice, however, I rapidly became quite proficient at this skill.

Although we were using nothing more dangerous than cine film at this stage, it was made very clear to us that this was not a game. I remember being slightly shocked at first when we were told that the aiming point was the target aircraft's cockpit – the pilot being the most vulnerable part of the target aircraft – rather than the centre of the aircraft. In other words, we were being taught to aim to kill the pilot. This was perhaps the first time that I had been made to realise what my job as a fighter pilot would be, if called upon to do it 'for real'. To a degree this was actually a psychological exercise conducted by the staff at the TWU because, later on, I was trained to aim at the centre of the target aircraft for the best chance of scoring multiple and therefore lethal hits with the cannon.

There were some aircraft accidents during this time, which focused my mind on the dangers associated with flying fast jets. On 27 April 1973, only eleven days after I arrived at Chivenor, a student pilot on the senior course flew his Hunter into the stays of the huge TV mast on Caradon Hill, near Liskeard, Cornwall, in poor weather. The impact took a large chunk off the wingtip of his aircraft, which then rolled violently out of control. With no alternative but to eject he put his head back and pulled the ejection-seat-pan handle. As he did so, he saw the ground not far above him as the aircraft rolled inverted and, believing that he was going to be ejected into the terrain, he thought he was about to die. Fortunately for him the aircraft was rolling so rapidly, that by the time the cockpit canopy had separated from the aircraft and his ejection seat fired, the aircraft was passing the right way up and his ejection was successful. I remember that, when the pilot later re-appeared in the 234 Squadron crew-room, his attitude was that whatever disciplinary action the service intended to throw at him paled into insignificance against how close he had come to dying. His attitude, at this life-defining moment, put things into perspective for me no end, as until then I think I may have been guilty of being more worried about being in trouble than being dead. (The student pilot involved in this accident went on to fly Buccaneers and had a full and successful RAF career.)

On 5 June a staff pilot flying a Hunter FGA.9 of 79 Squadron, our sister squadron at Chivenor, was forced to eject after his engine failed at low level, the aircraft crashing near Bideford in Devon. Then on 27 July another pilot was forced to eject from a 234 Squadron Hunter F.6 following a fire warning which, it eventually transpired, was spurious; the aircraft crashed near Chawleigh, North Devon. Clearly, this business was not without its risks and it was obviously luck of the draw to whom it happened. An engine failure in any single-engine aircraft will immediately result in the aircraft becoming a glider and not necessarily a very good one at that.

In looking after our Rolls Royce Avon engines, we always timed the engine wind-down when the engine was shut down back on the parking pan at the conclusion of each flight. After one sortie, I closed the engine down and started the stop-watch to time the engine run down as we always did. As I did so the engine produced a strange squealing noise and the RPM fell instantly to zero. The ground crew, too, had heard the noise and, when I told them the run-down time, they checked the engine and confirmed that it had, in fact, seized. I couldn't think of a better moment for it to have occurred and, although I was not particularly concerned about it, I felt that I'd been lucky that day.

It seems amazing to note in these days of impressive safety records that during 1973 the RAF lost twenty-eight aircraft, tragically with the deaths of nineteen aircrew, whilst a further twenty-one were forced to eject, many suffering injuries as a result. My reaction to all these accidents, some of which resulted in the ejections or deaths of people I knew, was very pragmatic. There was a part of me that felt that it was probably only a question of time before it would be necessary for me to resort to a 'Martin Baker let-down' but that really didn't bother me. I think that I felt that those who had been killed were almost always the victim of some sort of mistake or error (pilot error as it was called in those days) and I naively believed that I was very careful and would not make those fatal mistakes. In some ways this was simply a naive defence mechanism that was subsequently to be challenged and I became much more realistic later on. I was not blind to the risks but accepted them entirely as part of the life and career that I had chosen. I was only too willing to accept them in return for the excitement that fast-jet flying offered.

After proving that we could use the gunsight to produce cine film of the required standards, we were allowed to fire real 30mm ball ammunition from the Aden cannon whilst conducting air-to-ground and later air-to-air gunnery practice. It was the most fantastic fun, especially the sound of the guns firing in the nose of the Hunter just a few feet in front of you but it was not without its risks. In a 10-degree dive strafe attack at Hunter speeds, the time interval between ceasing fire at the minimum permitted range and impacting the ground was only just over two seconds. I was not a natural 'weaponeer' and my assessment of ranges at these sorts of speeds was inconsistent, as were my scores.

As a student on the air defence course I was not exposed to other ground-attack weapons events, such as bombing and SNEB rockets, as my compatriots on the ground-attack course were but I did get to try air-to-air gunnery when they did not. Air-to-air gunnery was conducted against a 'flag', a long rectangular banner target made of a sort of netting, towed by an ancient Meteor jet. We fired shells dipped in coloured paints so that we could see how many had hit the target, after it was dropped back at the airfield, by counting the holes; not many in my case.

Other elements of the Tactical Weapons Unit course saw us completing more low-flying navigation exercises, now as part of a tactical formation. I still struggled with low-level navigation at seven miles per minute, as I had at Valley but I was learning. By the time I reached the so-called 'Strike' phase, in which we flew simulated attack profiles against ground targets, I had improved and produced acceptable results.

Another phase of the course, which was more extensive for the air defenders, was called 'Tactics', later known as air combat training (ACT). The tactics we were taught were really quite old-fashioned, little different from those used by the earlier generation of fighter pilots in the Second World War, but just taking up more sky, and not necessarily suited to the air-to-air missile environment that was now upon us in the 'real' world. The instruction of air combat was rather lacking compared with the way that such teaching evolved in later years. The instructor who was your opponent seemed to have only one thought in mind – to win at all costs – and the instruction passed on in the air and in the debriefs was limited. I spent most of my time in the dogfights, pulling as hard as I could towards my opponent, in heavy buffet with my helmet banging on the cockpit canopy, spiralling downwards towards a stalemate at base height. I didn't often get 'shot down' but neither did I ever look like getting many 'kills' myself. Fortunately, I was to have some great teachers of this 'dark art' later on in my career.

My TWU course ended officially on 3 August 1973, my last sortie of the course – a 2v2 'Tactics' air-combat-training sortie – having been flown only the day before. My course reports from both the station commander and the Wing Commander Flying indicated that they were more impressed by my attitude than by my results; they saw potential in me as a fighter pilot and were prepared to give me the chance to prove it. I remain grateful to them for the chance and, if I may be permitted to say so myself, perhaps they were right.

Chapter 4

Fledgling Lightning Pilot

Explosive Decompression

Before starting the Lightning Operational Conversion Unit (OCU) course, I had to attend another Aviation Medicine Course at RAF North Luffenham, this time specifically aimed at future Lightning pilots. The Av Med specialist doctors delivered lectures covering the physiological effects of flight, with greater emphasis on high-altitude considerations. In addition, we were issued with all the various flying kit needed for the Lightning, including anti-G suits and pressure jerkins.

At that time, the Lightning was officially limited to a ceiling of 56,000 feet. This was the maximum altitude at which the combination of personal equipment and the oxygen regulator in the aircraft could keep the pilot alive in the event of a cockpit de-pressurisation whilst a rapid descent was made to lower levels. The Lightning cockpit was, of course, pressurised and the cabin altitude would not normally exceed 25,000 feet, regardless of how high the aircraft was taken above that. However, in the event of a loss of pressurisation, perhaps caused by the failure of the canopy seal, the pilot would suddenly and instantly be exposed to the very low pressure of the altitude that he was at. To remain conscious at these very high altitudes it is not sufficient to breathe 100 per cent oxygen; the oxygen needs to be delivered under pressure. Without the correct pressure for the altitude, the pilot's useful consciousness time can be measured in mere seconds. The maximum oxygen pressure I had experienced on the ground training rigs and in the de-compression chamber up to this point was 45 millimetres of mercury pressure. At 56,000 feet it was necessary to breathe oxygen at 70 millimetres of mercury pressure to remain conscious for long enough to descend to lower levels. In order to cope with oxygen being pumped into the lungs at this extreme pressure, some external assistance was needed. This was provided by a pressure jerkin which inflated around the chest. Without this external bracing there would be a risk of the lungs rupturing although not, as we joked at the time, of the pilot being blown up like a balloon.

We had to learn to breathe normally with this extreme level of pressure breathing, with the assistance of a pressure jerkin and the G-suit and, of course, wearing the flying helmet and oxygen mask. The training was initially conducted at a bench. When the pressure came on you rolled down the chain toggle on the oxygen mask to clamp it tight to your face against the pressure. The breathing process then became a reverse of normal breathing. Normally we breathe in deliberately and relax to breathe out. With pressure breathing the oxygen is pumped into you, so that the moment you relax, your lungs fill very quickly and you then have to make a considerable effort with your diaphragm to breathe out against the constant flow of oxygen under pressure. This inevitably leads to an unusual concentration on breathing, something that normally happens without conscious effort, and this can lead to breathing at the wrong rate, usually too fast, which can in turn lead to hyperventilation with initial symptoms, such as light-headedness, similar to hypoxia. All very complicated and rather daunting.

The oxygen pressures that we were subjected to and the length of time that we were exposed were gradually increased. With practice we learned to monitor and control our own breathing rates up to the full 70 millimetres pressure. The effects of breathing at the highest pressures were quite marked, I suppose it inevitably increased your blood pressure, your hands appeared swollen, as did the neck, and the oxygen tended to blow up through the tear ducts into the eyes, making your eyes water. It was all very strange.

Eventually, we were ready to be explosively decompressed in the chamber, from 25,000 feet to 56,000 feet in three seconds. We had to breathe 100 per cent oxygen for some time beforehand to ensure all the nitrogen naturally present in our blood had been expelled. Otherwise we would run the risk of any nitrogen bubbles in the blood causing 'the bends', which could be extremely painful and even fatal. For this extreme set of circumstances, the decompression was carried out individually, strapped into a seat so that the G-suit and pressure jerkin could work against the harness. Sitting in the decompression chamber waiting for my explosive decompression felt rather like being a condemned man in a gas chamber. The countdown commenced from five to zero and then there was an almighty clang as the valves operated, the air in the chamber turned to cloud and the temperature dropped markedly. Having breathed out all the air in my lungs during the countdown I found them instantly full again as I rolled down the toggle on the mask. I seemed to be expelling gas of one sort or another from every available orifice in my body. You could see why it was recommended that you kept off the Ruddles ale and avoided baked beans and broccoli. Then it was into the fight to control the breathing against the pressure whilst the altitude was rapidly reduced as if in a maximum-rate descent. Somewhere on the way down we were asked to switch on the microphone in the oxygen mask and simulate a Mayday call. Mine was entirely unintelligible as the top of my mouth, affected by the pressure, wasn't where my tongue normally found it and I could hardly form the words. With the additional problem of having to force out against the pressure of the oxygen, my ability to speak was seriously compromised.

It was a great relief to get back down to more normal altitudes and eventually back to 'ground level'. It was all quite exciting and very interesting. This episode indicates the lengths that the RAF went to with our training to ensure that we were as prepared as possible for the extreme environments in which we were going to operate as pilots in high-performance jet fighters. Although I never again had to go through an explosive decompression to 56,000 feet, refresher and re-currency training during my long military flying career meant that I was decompressed in a chamber to 45,000 feet a total of six times.

Lightning Operational Conversion Unit – RAF Coltishall

On Monday 3 September 1973 I joined Number 77 (Long) Lightning Conversion Course at RAF Coltishall, a few miles north-east of Norwich. 'Colt', as the base was known to those who served there, was a famous RAF airfield with a proud wartime history. It had been home to the Lightning Operational Conversion Unit (OCU) since the aircraft had first come into service in 1960 and it was a very happy station.

The conversion unit consisted of two separate squadrons, each commanded by a wing commander. No. 65 Squadron, to which I was posted, operated Lightning F.1A and T.4 aircraft and trained pilots for the RAF Germany squadrons, whose Lightning F.2As shared the same weapons systems, radar and missiles. No. 65 Squadron and its instructor pilots also held a war role and it was declared to NATO as an operational squadron, hence it having a proper squadron identity. I had, by pure chance, got myself in the right place to be posted to RAF Germany and those low-level, olive-green Lightnings, if I performed well enough. It was a good start. The other squadron on the station was labelled as 2(T) Squadron; it flew the Lightning F.3 and T.5, training pilots for the UK and Cyprus squadrons.

LIGHTNINGS TO SPITFIRES

The English Electric (later BAC) Lightning was a remarkable piece of British ingenuity and engineering; the first British aircraft able to sustain supersonic speeds in level flight and the first to achieve twice the speed of sound, Mach 2. Its Rolls Royce Avon reheated engines were stacked one above the other in an unusual arrangement in the relatively thin but tall fuselage. The wings were swept back 60 degrees, the radar was contained in a bullet fairing in the centre of the nose intake, and the two air-to-air missiles were mounted on the sides of the fuselage under the cockpit. The cockpit and the pilot seemed to be almost an afterthought, squeezed onto the top and front of this 'rocket ship'. On the ground, sitting on its tall, spindly undercarriage and thin high-pressure tyres, the Lightning seemed an ungainly beast but, in the air with the undercarriage retracted, its highly-swept-wing planform gave it a sleek and purposeful shape which made it look fast even when it was flying relatively slowly. In 1973 the OCU Lightnings still wore their shiny silver polished-metal finishes; they were yet to be covered with camouflage paint and they looked wonderful.

In the afternoon of that very first day on the course, I flew Lightning T.4 XM996 with Flight Lieutenant Paul Holmes, a QFI, on 'Convex 1', the familiarisation sortie. This sortie was intended to introduce the students to the Lightning, to give them the opportunity to experience the full performance of the aircraft and to impress and motivate them for the ground school and flight-simulator training that would follow before any further flying. The sortie began with a reheat take off and climb, which gave a brakes off to 36,000 feet time-to-height of about two and a half minutes whilst covering a ground distance of only sixteen nautical miles. This was a truly awesome experience, even for someone used to the fast-jet performance of the Hawker Hunter. On this first sortie my instructor flew the take off and climb but, not long after this first familiarisation, I was executing this same reheat take off and climb myself, on my own in a single-seat Lightning F.1A, a fantastic experience.

For take off the maximum power that could be applied against the brakes was 92 per cent of maximum 'dry' (non-reheated) power, otherwise the aircraft would slide forward. When the brakes were released, full dry power (100 per cent) was set as the aircraft started to move and then, if doing a reheat take off, full reheat was engaged. There was an initially alarming double thump as the reheats lit and an almighty kick of acceleration. The aircraft reached lift-off speed (170 knots) about 600 yards down the runway.

It was very easy during this excitement to over-rotate the Lightning as you pulled it off the ground which could result in the tail bumper contacting the runway. (Even when the take off was correctly executed, the tail bumper was only inches off the ground). This was definitely to be avoided, as the brake parachute cable ran around the tail bumper and could easily be cut by such contact with the runway, meaning that stopping after landing without the parachute was going to be fraught – all the 7,500 feet of runway would be needed to stop with wheel brakes only – and the brakes would be burned out in the process. (In well over 1,000 take offs in Lightnings over subsequent years, I only hit the tail bumper and chopped the brake parachute cable on one occasion, which was still one too many.) As soon as the aircraft was safely airborne it was necessary to raise the undercarriage immediately, or the limiting speed of 250 knots would quickly be exceeded before the undercarriage had retracted and the nose wheel would not then retract forwards against the airflow.

Once airborne and 'cleaned up' in a reheat climb, the speed rapidly increased to the optimum climbing speed of 450 knots and it was necessary to raise the nose to the climbing attitude of 30 degrees as the aircraft accelerated through 420 knots. The aircraft was then climbed at 450 knots until passing about 16,000 feet, and then M0.9 above that. A moment's inattention or a distraction could easily lead to the aircraft going supersonic in the climb if the nose attitude was allowed to drop, which wouldn't make you popular with anyone below who suffered from the supersonic 'bang'. The level off took at least 1,500 feet of anticipation and, with such a steep climb angle, the easiest method, even at night or in cloud, was to roll inverted, pull to achieve level flight and then roll upright, meanwhile manipulating the throttles back into the dry power range in order to maintain M0.9 and avoid accelerating transonic. On my first exposure to this amazing performance I was wondering if I would ever be able to keep up, as we seemed to be levelling off at 36,000 feet when most aircraft would just be settling into the climb after take off.

Having seen the extraordinary aircraft performance I was going to have to learn to deal with, it was then into the ground school and the simulator for two and a half weeks. I learned how the systems in the Lightning worked and I was taught the necessary cockpit checks, procedures and drills to cope with the emergencies that might develop when systems failed, as they frequently did. A particular problem with the Lightning was that pipes containing inflammable hydraulic fluid and jet fuel, under pressure, were crammed into tight spaces within the aircraft's fuselage, often close to heat sources such as the engines and jet pipes. If a leak of fuel or hydraulic fluid occurred, it was likely to lead to a major and, possibly, catastrophic fire. In addition, the Lightning's flying controls were purely hydraulically powered with no manual back up. There were only two hydraulic systems supporting the flying controls, each driven from one of the engines and if both systems failed for any reason, for example if one engine failed and then the other hydraulic system failed, the controls would freeze solid and the pilot would be forced to eject. Failures of this type occurred quite frequently. During the twenty-eight years that the aircraft was in service, an amazing seventy-six Lightnings crashed or were totally written off from 280 built for the RAF. The chances of being involved in a serious incident or accident were therefore quite high, and Lightning pilots took the ground and simulator emergency training very seriously.

During the simulator training and the subsequent conversion flying, it became apparent that, whilst the Lightning was not a particularly difficult aircraft to fly, it did have some vices, particularly at slow speeds, and also things tended to happen quickly and could go wrong equally fast. The aircraft was always short of fuel, virtually from take off, and the fuel contents and the distance from home or the nearest suitable airfield needed to be monitored constantly and carefully. Use of reheat would eat into the available fuel very quickly indeed. There, surely, has never been a Lightning pilot who hasn't, at some point, been below his minimum landing fuel some distance from the airfield. The aircraft demanded respect and the cockpit workload could be very high indeed; pilots needed to stay well ahead of the aircraft to keep up with the pace of events and had to possess high levels of what is known as 'airmanship'.

Good airmanship is something that separates a superior pilot from an average one. With the scientific development of the psychology of flying and flying training, one method of structuring airmanship, later taught by the RAF, was a 'decision loop': recognise, assess, prioritise, decide and act. Airmanship was not taught as scientifically as that back in 1973 but that is the essence of what was required. In order to cope with the pace of events, a Lightning pilot needed to be very 'on the ball'; he needed to be able to think quickly and clearly and use good judgement. Good pilots cope with high workloads by prioritising correctly and continuously, with long periods of intense concentration, so that the instantaneous workload never exceeds their capacity. This was something that I was just beginning to learn to do but the airmanship skills I developed whilst flying the Lightning stood me in good stead for the rest of my flying career.

The conversion or 'convex' phase of the course included general handling and aerobatics, circuits and landings, instrument flying – leading up to the award of an instrument rating on the Lightning – close and tactical formation flying, and high-altitude and supersonic handling. One peculiarity of the Lightning was that, during circuit and landing training, the pilot only allowed the aircraft's wheels to touch the runway on the final landing. On touchdown the Lightning's wheels and tyres were spun up from stationary to 170 miles per hour the instant the tyres touched the runway. The aircraft's thin wheels and their high-pressure tyres would not survive very much of that treatment. At best the tyres could be expected to last no more than about fifteen landings and on days when the crosswind was strong it was not uncommon for the ground crew to have to change the wheels and tyres after only three landings. All Lightning approaches, which were not for the final landing, therefore culminated in a very low overshoot – with practice at about a foot above the runway; there were no practice touch-and-go or 'roller' landings. This was easier to do than might be thought. Approaches were always flown with the airbrakes out; selecting them 'in' arrested any further descent and caused the Lightning to 'float' along the runway; any increase in power then had it heading skywards again.

After only six flights, totalling three hours and fifty minutes flying time, I was sent solo in the two-seat T.4 and then for the next two sorties in single-seat Lightning F.1As. Strangely, my first solos in the Lightning are not experiences that I particularly remember. Perhaps it was just the next step, a natural progression, and everything was just falling into place.

The supersonic handling flights were interesting, as we explored speeds and capabilities well beyond anything I had experienced so far. The supersonic 'convex' sortie was flown dual first, with an instructor in a Lightning T.4, and was then repeated solo in a single-seat F.1A. At an altitude of 36,000 feet the aircraft was accelerated to around M1.5 in full reheat. This meant that I exceeded the speed required to join the '1,000 miles per hour' or 'Ten Ton' Club, with my instructor as the necessary witness on the dual sortie. I still have the framed certificate that my membership warranted. The whole thing was quite tongue in cheek and became much less meaningful when every Concorde passenger was flying considerably in excess of 1,000 mph a few years later but, at this time, membership of the 'Ten Ton' club was still fairly exclusive. Accelerating transonic through about M0.97 there was a second or two of very light buffet, the so-called 'cobblestone' effect, which could easily be mistaken for some clear air turbulence. When the Mach meter wound up through M1.0 this was the only indication that the aircraft was now supersonic: there was no noise, no vibration, no fuss; this was what the Lightning was designed to do. At M1.04, the altimeter height suddenly jumped up by 1,800 feet, and indications on the other pressure instruments also jumped as the pressure errors disappeared when the supersonic shock wave moved back past the static vents. (Strangely, the Lightning altimeters only ever read accurately when the aircraft was supersonic; when the aircraft was subsonic there were always errors, which increased with speed and which had to be compensated for when trying to fly an accurate height.) At six miles high there were no visual indications that you were accelerating towards 1,000 mph and beyond.

Having achieved M1.5 the aircraft was then set into a 5G turn, which caused the speed to reduce. The high-G turn was held until the aircraft decelerated through the transonic regime to subsonic speed. As the Lightning decelerated back through the transonic band it was likely to experience a strong pitch up, which could cause a loss of control, and it was necessary to reduce the pull on the control column, and therefore the G, to counter this pitch-up effect. This sortie had become known amongst the OCU students as the 'Wing Commander Spinning Exercise'. In June 1973, four months before I flew the exercise, an experienced wing commander on a refresher course had flown the same manoeuvre solo in a Lightning T.4. When he hit the transonic cobblestones in the decelerating turn, the pitch up was so violent that the aircraft entered a spin, from which he was unable to recover. He ejected safely at 10,000 feet and was rescued from the North Sea. The aircraft crashed twenty-three miles north east of Great Yarmouth and was destroyed. With the knowledge that even this experienced wing commander had been caught out by the Lightning's transonic handling, I was extremely careful when I flew the exercise solo.

The conversion phase culminated with a Final Handling Test which I flew on 25 October 1973 with the OC Operations Wing, Wing Commander Dave Seward, who had previously been the leader of the famous 56 Squadron 'Firebirds' Lightning aerobatic display team. I passed the test and the next week flew a dual night check in a T.4 followed by a forty-minute solo night flight in an F.1A, which my logbook records as night general handling and practice diversion to Honington. I was now qualified to fly the Lightning both by day and by night.

*****

Having been taught how to fly the Lightning, it was time to learn how to operate the radar and weapons system and to do the job that it was intended to do, all-weather air defence. The air intercept (AI) 21 pulse radar in these early marks of Lightning was basic and limited in both its capability and its detection range. Control of the radar was extremely 'manual'; there was virtually no automation, or at least none that we used. Tactical thinking had moved away from locking the radar to a target as soon as possible, which gave steering cues in the scope, as this was also likely to alert a target's radar warning receiver. The radar hand controller mounted on the left side of the Lightning's cockpit behind the throttles was a masterpiece of ergonomic design. It incorporated seventeen different controls and switches which could be manipulated entirely by feel as each was different in shape, feel and operation. The fact that there were so many switches and controls is indicative of the radar needing considerable pilot input. To start with, just pointing the radar in the right place with the gain set correctly to be able to see radar contacts on the screen was a feat in itself. To conduct practice intercepts (PIs) on the targets took a considerable amount of mental capacity and mental arithmetic to calculate the target's heading and height and to achieve the necessary lateral displacement, so that a 60-degree banked 2G turn would provide a roll-out one to one-and-a-half miles behind the target, in range to fire a Firestreak missile.

Meanwhile, of course, the business of flying the aircraft and managing the cockpit and fuel still needed constant attention. I recall one occasion when, flying solo in a Lightning F.1A, I was conducting practice intercepts against a Canberra target at about 36,000 feet, on a day when there was extensive high-level milky cirrus cloud that meant there was no visual horizon and flying needed to be done on instruments. Rather than scanning the radar as another instrument, I spent too long looking into the radar 'boot' and forgot about instrument flying for a second or two. A strange sensation alerted me to check the instruments, which were revolving wildly as my lack of concentration on the main and vital business of flying the aircraft had allowed the aircraft to get into what is euphemistically known as an 'unusual position', from which I had to recover before getting back to locating the target on the radar and completing the intercept. This was not too much of a problem at 36,000 feet but was clearly to be avoided at lower levels.

*****

During this phase of the course, in November 1973, news reached me that a Hunter T.7 from No. 4 FTS at RAF Valley had crashed whilst on the approach to RAF Shawbury in Shropshire. Both crew members had been killed. The instructor was Squadron Leader Chip Kirkham, a hugely experienced Hunter pilot and instructor, and a thoroughly nice man, with whom I had flown in January of that year. I was saddened but accepted that, quite clearly, this type of flying could be very unforgiving.

Life at 'Colt' was fun even though the course was such hard work. The officers' mess was lively, the bar was packed every evening at the end of the working day and there were all sorts of high jinks and practical jokes played on people. Weekends were usually our own and the station's proximity to the Norfolk Broads and numerous excellent Norfolk pubs and, of course, to Norwich City meant that we were not short of entertainment. Sundays tended to be rather quieter as everyone recovered from their Friday and Saturday night excesses. One of the flight commanders on 65 Squadron, Squadron Leader Dave Hampton, known as 'Quingle' as that was how his signature looked, sometimes invited the two young bachelors on the course, Tim Neville and me, round to his married quarter for Sunday lunches. We got to know his wife and his young children and enjoyed the family atmosphere that, being so far from our own homes, we missed. This was a great kindness of the Hamptons and it was with deep sadness that I learned some time after I left the OCU, in April 1975, that Quingle had been killed when his Lightning F.6 crashed into the sea in a spin, off Cyprus, and he had ejected too late.

*****

On 16 January 1974 I flew the final check ride of the Lightning OCU course. The sortie was flown in a two-seat Lightning T.4 and started from being held at 'cockpit alert', strapped in and waiting scramble instructions. Meanwhile, another Lightning, flown by an OCU instructor, was sent out over the North Sea as a target. The scramble message came through on the 'telebrief' – a secure landline plugged into the aircraft – with vectors (headings) and angels (height) to fly, and the details of the fighter control agency to call on the radio. Sitting in the right-hand seat of my aircraft to monitor and assess my performance was one of the flight commanders, Squadron Leader 'Dickie' Duckett, who was an experienced Lightning pilot and an ex-Red Arrow, who subsequently became the leader of the 'Reds'. My instructions were to intercept and identify a target which, of course, turned out to be the other Lightning. Having executed a reheat take off and climb to height and conducted a successful radar intercept on the evading target, I identified the type to the controller and he ordered me to 'shadow'.

The target then started to evade violently; its behaviour became increasingly aggressive and, eventually, the controller cleared me to engage the 'bandit'. By now though, I was not in a position of advantage and a full-blown 'dogfight' ensued with much use of reheat as I attempted to complete my task. In the excitement, I forgot to monitor my fuel for a few minutes, until Dickie Duckett reached across and pointed at the fuel gauges. I realised with some horror that I was well below the required fuel to get back to Coltishall, the nearest airfield, with anything like the stipulated minimum fuel on the ground. I cancelled the reheats, called a 'knock it off' on the radio and set course for home, feeling embarrassed and shamefaced. My examiner asked me my intentions and I explained my plan to fly the most economical recovery for a straight-in visual approach, keeping air traffic informed of my fuel emergency.

As I flew this recovery to Coltishall, the target Lightning flew alongside us. Its pilot, Flight Lieutenant Jack Brown, didn't say very much on the radio until we were about twenty miles out from the airfield. Jack then asked what our fuel state was. Dickie Duckett told him, quite accurately and honestly, even though we were below the minimum required by the rule book. Jack Brown simply said, 'Roger, do you mind if I go in first.' I realised, for the first time, that he was even shorter of fuel than me. Obviously, this was not a good outcome for my final check ride but my shortcomings were mitigated to a degree by the fact that the staff pilot in the target aircraft landed with even less fuel. They couldn't really castigate me over it, could they? That said, it was a very valuable lesson for a new Lightning pilot, one hard learned and never forgotten.

It was decided that I should fly the sortie again, the next day, this time with the Officer Commanding Operations Wing, Wing Commander Dave Seward. On this second attempt everything went well and I was deemed to have passed the course. For whatever reason, I think that Wing Commander Seward had decided that I had what it took. Once again, someone had spotted potential in me, given me a second chance and my keen and hard-working attitude had won the day. I had just over sixty hours on the Lightning and I was now going to join a front-line squadron – the famous 19 Squadron based in Germany – as a fighter pilot. It had taken just over three years since I joined the RAF to reach this point and I couldn't have been happier. I was not yet, officially, the fighter pilot that I had yearned to be since I was a boy. I had yet to become operational but I was getting ever closer.

Chapter 5

Lightning Squadron RAF Germany

I arrived as a brand-new, junior Lightning pilot on No. 19(F) Squadron at RAF Gutersloh, Germany, in January 1974, when the Cold War was still very much at its height and the Soviet Union's relations with the West remained strained if not exactly hostile. The RAF base at Gutersloh was an ex-Luftwaffe Second World War airfield, situated in a low-lying and flat area of Westphalia, some twelve miles south-west of the town of Bielefeld and just south of a range of forested hills called the Teutoburger Wald. The airfield was only sixty-eight miles from the nearest point of the border with Soviet-occupied East Germany. This was significant, as the possibility of an attack by the Soviet Bloc against Western Germany and, therefore, NATO was still present in everyone's minds, unthinkable as the outcome might have been.

I had just turned 23 years old; it was three years since I had joined the RAF as an officer cadet and only two years and three months since I had started my flying training, and here I was on the front line. I had been lucky to get through the training system and on to a squadron so quickly. Many trainee RAF pilots at this time found their progress blocked by delays between courses and they took much longer to get to this stage of their careers. Arriving with me on the same day was 21-year-old fellow Flying Officer, Tim Neville. We drove out to Gutersloh together in my car and for the next three years we became good friends as we shared the experiences of learning to be fighter pilots, life on the squadron and the rather wild bachelor lifestyle enjoyed by single RAF officers living in an officers' mess in Germany.

No. 19 Squadron was a famous fighter squadron, with a proud history going back to the First World War. In August 1938 the squadron had been the first RAF front-line unit to be equipped with the Spitfire. Thirty years before I joined, it had been one of the first RAF squadrons to re-equip with the North American Mustang III, which it flew on long-range bomber-escort and interdiction missions for the remainder of the Second World War. Most

RAF pilots will have good memories of their first operational squadron, the first unit they were able to develop a fierce loyalty towards and feel proud of its operational worth. I am no exception and I have very fond memories of the three years that I spent flying Lightnings with 19 Squadron at Gutersloh.

The Lightning F.2A

From 1965 up to early 1977 there were two RAF Lightning squadrons based in Germany, Numbers 19 and 92 Squadrons. From 1968 these squadrons operated the Lightning F.2A. Only thirty-one examples of this mark of Lightning were produced. By 1974, when I arrived at Gutersloh, the F.2As had been painted with plain dark-green upper surfaces, covering their previous silver metal finish, in recognition of the primarily low-level role they were expected to undertake in the event of war.

The Lightning F.2As were modified F.2s, with the addition of the large ventral fuel tank and the cranked and cambered wings of the Lightning F.6, modifications which significantly increased the aircraft's operational effectiveness. Many Lightning pilots who, like me, have flown most marks of the aircraft believe that the F.2A was the best to fly operationally, as it was the ideal compromise. It carried the most internal fuel (10,300 lbs) and the two Rolls Royce Avon 211R engines produced a total of almost 29,000 pounds of thrust in full reheat, endowing the aircraft with more than sufficient power, whilst being more economical than the slightly more powerful engines of the Lightning F.3 and F.6. The F.2A had the larger square-topped fin and the arrester hook fitted to the F.6 but retained the nose-mounted 30mm Aden cannon of the earlier marks. Equipped with the AI 21 air intercept pulse radar, the F.2A did not have the capability to carry Redtop missiles; instead it carried two of the slightly less-capable, but arguably more reliable, Firestreak infra-red-homing air-to-air missiles. (The Firestreak was essentially a pursuit weapon that had to be fired from within a 30-degree sector either side of the target's tail.) This weapon suite was no particular disadvantage in the low-level overland environment of Germany. In fact, the F.2A's older system offered some positive benefits, especially the gunsight (the 'pilot attack sight'), which was almost a small head-up-display, providing weapon-aiming information and, when the radar was locked on to a target, a target indicator, radar range and closure rate.

During the period when the Lightning F.2A was operational in Germany, it generally outperformed all comers in the quick reaction low-to-high-level visual interception role that was so crucial to NATO's forward air defence against possible attack from the East. The Lightning's outstanding performance and its simple weapon system made it a match for any other aircraft that it was likely to tangle with, either in training or for real. Most of the fighter and fighter-bomber types on both sides at that time were either cannon-armed only or, if fitted with air-to-air missiles, had a capability no better than the Lightning and its Firestreak heat-seeking missiles. The only exception to this in the 1970s was the McDonnell Douglas F-4 Phantom in service with the RAF, which was equipped with a pulse-doppler radar and semi-active radar missiles. This advanced weapon system provided the RAF F-4s with a beyond-visual-range (BVR) capability that could provide the Lightning pilot with some difficulties in surviving to the visual merge. In a visual fight with an F-4, however, the Lightning pilot would fancy his chances, as he did with all the other potential opponents, as long as he fought to his aircraft's strengths.

For an aircraft designed as an interceptor, the Lightning proved to have excellent air-combat-manoeuvring (ACM) dog-fighting capabilities with a good turn rate and an excess of power, especially below 15,000 feet. As an indication of the power available it was possible to set the aircraft into a 5G turn at 450 knots at low level and then, with full reheat selected, fly a climbing 5G spiral maintaining speed and G up to 15,000 feet, quite impressive for that era.

Being something of an elite force, the Lightning pilots felt confident about their ability to do the job asked of them; they were proud of their aircraft and their prowess, and were able to hold their heads high in the NATO fighter community. There was quite a spirit – an esprit de corps – amongst the Lightning pilots at Gutersloh, which was evident on the ground and in the air.

Training to be Operational

My own work-up to achieve operational, or 'Op', status was going to take several months and started immediately. In my first month on the squadron I flew twenty-nine hours, often flying twice or three times a day. There was much to learn and I was expected to learn quickly.

It all started with a couple of trips in one of the squadron's two Lightning T.4, two-seat trainers, 'T-birds' or 'Tubs', with the squadron QFI and then with one of the instrument-rating examiners (IREs), to familiarise me with the local area and procedures. Then I flew the requisite squadron commander's arrival check with the Boss, Wing Commander Peter Vangucci. He wanted to see that the Operational Conversion Unit had not sold him a pup.

After one more T-bird sortie with one of the squadron weapon instructors (known as IWIs, intercept weapons instructors, in the Lightning Force), I was ready for my first flight in an F.2A Lightning, and my first in a Lightning with the big ventral tank. The RAF never operated a two-seat version of this mark of the Lightning. With its extra fuel and increased weight, the F.2A always required full reheat for the take off (usually cancelling it at 300 knots unless conducting a reheat climb) whereas with the small ventral tank versions I had flown so far reheat was optional and 'dry power' take offs were often carried out. The F.2A was delightful to fly; having the additional fuel was a real bonus, it went supersonic easily and it felt like a real fighter. I loved it. I also thought that its cranked wing made it nicer to land. You could almost flare it on to the runway – really more of a check of the rate of descent than an actual flare – although you were still touching down at the not inconsiderable speed of 155 knots (almost 180 mph).

Unless and until war broke out, the Gutersloh Lightnings were tasked with defending the integrity of the airspace of the northern half of the Federal Republic of Germany and of policing the Buffer Zone. This was a thirty-mile-wide sterile strip between east and west Europe into which Allied aircraft were not allowed to fly without special permission, partly for their own safety and also so that any airborne presence in the zone was immediately detected. The Gutersloh Lightning squadrons provided a Quick Reaction Alert (QRA) force, called 'Battle Flight' in the Second Allied Tactical Air Force (2 ATAF), with two aircraft always available on a high alert state, to police the Buffer Zone and to defend the airspace.

Much, although not all, of my early operational work-up training was geared towards qualifying me to conduct these missions and to hold alert on Battle Flight. I flew many radar intercepts in all weathers, by day and by night, with varying levels of assistance from ground intercept controllers, to intercept and identify, shadow, shepherd or engage a target, usually another Lightning. The training also included the techniques for dealing with any Soviet aircraft that might want to defect.

One of the best aspects of flying Lightnings in Germany was the variety of the tasking and the flying. Along with training for Battle Flight, I started to experience some of these other missions.

'Tanking'

Only three weeks into my tour I had my first taste of air-to-air refuelling from a Victor 'tanker'. The Lightning T.4s – the two-seat trainers – were not capable of air-to-air refuelling and had no refuelling probe, so there could be no dual instruction in 'tanking' and the first attempt at this tricky art had to be done solo in a F.2A. You received a brief and were shown a photograph of a Lightning 'plugged in' to the refuelling drogue trailing behind a Victor's wing but, in effect, you were going to have to learn how to do it yourself. My first impression when I arrived alongside the Victor was how enormous it was. I had, up to then, never flown in formation with such a large aircraft and it took me a while to get in close. The Lightning's refuelling probe was a long fixed pipe sticking out forward from the port wing. You actually had to duck under it when you climbed the ladder into the cockpit. The teaching for air-to-air refuelling was not to look at your probe tip as you approached the refuelling basket as this would cause you to over-control the aircraft. Rather, you flew in formation with reference to the tanker's wing and the hose-drum unit under it, straight in front of you, and ran a particular instrument on the cockpit coaming up the hose, until the refuelling basket latched neatly onto your probe tip. That was the theory. The problem was that as you got closer to the basket the air pressure 'bubble' around your own aircraft affected the shuttlecock-like drogue, the basket, pushing it out to the left. If you moved your aircraft at all sharply it caused the basket to jiggle about. It really wasn't easy to start with. After all, you were trying to fly formation to within an accuracy of about two feet in three dimensions. One coarse fighter pilot's description of tanking was that it was 'like trying to take a running f*** at a rolling doughnut'. I think it took me about twelve 'stabs' at the basket on my first attempt at tanking but I finally made contact and took on the fuel. This was a skill that was not only very important to all Lightning pilots, who never seemed to have enough fuel, but also one at which we all eventually excelled.

Firing the Guns

I had my first experience of firing the guns in the Lightning when I flew one of the occasional sorties, usually flown as a 'four-ship', to fire the Aden cannon, simply to exercise them, not at any target, but just 'air-into-air'. This gun firing was carried out over a sea range off the coast of Holland

and was usually done in a weave with some G applied, to ensure that there were no problems with the cannon jamming under G. The Aden cannon in the F.2A variant of the Lightning were mounted in the upper part of the nose above the air intake and the breeches of the cannon ran back almost to the pilot's shoulders as he sat in the cockpit. When the guns were fired there was a tremendous racket and considerable vibration in the cockpit, which made it quite exciting. On this particular sortie, the event was even more exciting than usual for the leader of our four-ship, Flight Lieutenant Steve Giles.

When we arrived over the range, Steve got permission to fire from the controller, peeled off from our echelon starboard formation and called 'firing now'. I saw smoke from his guns and he went into an apparently very 'punchy' overbanked descent into cloud. I called 'firing now' and got on with my weaving and firing, loving the cacophony of noise and amazed at the vibration. I then heard Steve's voice on the radio, sounding rather distressed, transmitting, 'Mayday, Mayday, Mayday, control restriction, standby for ejection', or words to that effect. In his aircraft the link chute, which carried the spent links from the cannon ammunition belt into a canvas bag, had become disconnected with the vibration from the guns. The spent links had therefore been pushed onto a fibreglass shroud covering the control rods, forcing it onto the rods like a calliper brake. The rudder was jammed with some left rudder applied and the aileron movement was severely restricted. Fortunately, with both hands on the control column and sheer brute strength, Steve managed to centralise the ailerons and get the aircraft levelled off. We all joined up and the No. 3 (Squadron Leader John May, one of the flight commanders) carried out a visual inspection of Steve's aircraft, reporting no external damage. Having made our way back to Gutersloh, the three serviceable Lightings landed, making sure we got down before Steve made a mess of the runway. He managed to land his aircraft from a long straight-in approach, although the hook skipped over the approach end cable on the runway and he was forced to deploy the brake parachute to stop. Being unable to move the rudder pedals to steer or apply differential braking, he was fortunate to remain on the runway and stop safely. Steve was awarded a Green Endorsement in his logbook for getting the aircraft back safely.

An interesting aside to this story concerns Steve's wife, Anita. Although she knew roughly when her husband was due to fly each day, she had never taken any closer interest. At the time that Steve put out his Mayday call that day (0930) she was posting letters in the RAF Gutersloh post office. In her own words, she said that she had a sudden compelling urge to see Steve land. She rushed out of the station in the car, down the public highway for about a mile, dumped the car on a verge and then ran, with their eighteen-month-old son in her arms, along a canal bank for a quarter of a mile to the runway threshold. She said that she had about 100 yards to go when three Lightnings broke into the circuit and landed. About two minutes after she had reached the threshold, she saw a 'drunken, wallowing Lightning coming in low'. It hit the ground in a shower of sparks (because the hook was trailing on the ground) and careered up the runway with fire engines in hot pursuit. This strange tale of premonition highlights the point that it is easy to forget the impact that an RAF pilot's rather dangerous and risky job had on their loved ones, who carried with them an almost constant and usually unspoken concern.

War Role and the Low-Level Search Patterns

Almost every month there was some sort of NATO exercise that the Gutersloh Lightning squadrons took part in. Only operational pilots could fly on these exercises and until I became 'Op' I usually flew in one of the T-birds with another squadron pilot to experience what went on. Gradually, I was exposed to the wartime roles of the Lightning in Germany and flew training missions in F.2As to prepare me for the time when I, too, would be operational and able to take part in the exercises. One aspect, which quickly became apparent, was that as an air defence pilot you were very likely to be scrambled into a sortie for which you had no time to plan or brief, for any of the variety of tasks that you could be expected to undertake, with no prior notice. Training for this relied on the use of standard operating procedures and required a degree of flexibility. It became an aspect of the role that I loved.

In common with Lightning squadrons in other theatres, there was a requirement in 2 ATAF to be able to conduct all-weather intercepts and engagements under close limited loose or broadcast control from a fighter controller on the ground, including against high-flying and/or supersonic targets. These events were routinely practised, with intercepts against targets at speeds up to M1.6 and high-flying targets up to 56,000 feet conducted in a special corridor, which was cleared for supersonic flying overland above 36,000 feet. We also practised engagements against radar 'jamming' targets, often at night, with the Canberra T.17s of 360 Squadron providing the jamming. All this was common to Lightning operators in other theatres;

but in Germany the nature of the potential threat and the integrated nature of the NATO defences resulted in some significant differences in the concept of operations.

The wartime airborne threat in Germany was principally made up of Soviet Bloc fighter or fighter-bomber aircraft rather than the heavy bomber threat that faced UK Lightning squadrons. It was, therefore, essential that Germany-based Lightning pilots were trained to a high standard in fighter-versus-fighter air combat manoeuvring. Most engagements were expected to occur at low level, as enemy aircraft would probably attempt to use terrain masking to avoid radar detection and engagement by the numerous NATO surface-to-air missile (SAM) sites. Manned fighter aircraft were only a part of the overall NATO integrated air defence system. In a shooting war NATO air defence fighters would have had to operate in fighter engagement zones (FEZs) from the surface up to a specified altitude. The FEZs were surrounded to the East, West and above by missile engagement zones (MEZs), in which the SAM batteries would have freedom to engage, and pursuit of targets by fighters would normally have to be broken off. Therefore, Germany-based Lightning pilots had to become expert at engaging targets at low level overland.

The Lightning's pulse-only radar was effectively useless against low-level targets overland due to the ground clutter swamping the target returns and, because assistance from ground-based radars was also limited, detection of targets had to be principally achieved by visual means, the Mark One Eyeball. This requirement led to the setting up of a system of low-level search patterns (LLSPs) within the FEZ. The LLSPs were racetrack-shaped visual combat air patrols (CAPs) flown at 90 degrees to the expected threat direction (since this was from the East, the racetracks were orientated North-South). Each racetrack pattern was eight miles long to permit a straight leg of one minute flown at 360 knots in each direction with a 2G/60-degree-banked turn at each end. Each search pattern was identified by a number and each adjoined another, forming an unbroken chain running north-south through the FEZ. There were actually two parallel lines of LLSPs, one line some distance west of the other.

In order to provide cross cover as well as to concentrate firepower, we normally operated with a pair of fighters manning a LLSP and with other pairs on adjoining CAPs. A pair of Lightnings on a LLSP would fly in standard battle formation, line abreast at approximately one and a half miles spacing, and would fly 'inwards turnabouts' at the ends of the patterns, turning towards each other to provide the maximum cross cover. To optimise the visual detection of targets it was necessary to fly as low as was permitted by the rules, which was 250 feet, in order to skyline other aircraft. As the Lightning had no radar altimeter the height above the ground was judged by eyeball and it is likely that we were often flying lower. When manning LLSPs for training we were permitted to engage any military aircraft that we detected. As these engagements were effectively unplanned and un-briefed there was supposed to be no evasive manoeuvring involved. As far as we were concerned that was up to the targets, not us, and some interesting low-level, hard-turning and running fights sometimes developed. The Gutersloh Lightning pilots became extremely proficient and confident at manoeuvring their aircraft aggressively at low levels. They thought nothing of being inverted at perhaps 1,500 feet, as they flew lag pursuit barrel rolls to re-position their aircraft to maintain the tactical advantage.

The emphasis on low-level engagements is perhaps epitomised by the technique that was taught for taking gun shots against very low-level targets. The cannon were, of course, considered as primary weapons at that time. Due to the fact that the Lightning had been designed exclusively as an air defence fighter rather than for the ground-attack role, the two cannon in the nose of the F.2A were mounted with a slight upwards inclination. This was a useful feature in a turning combat situation as, when trying to guns-track a target, there was already some degree of lead established into the turn by the physical mounting of the guns. However, against a straight and level target, this gun mounting angle meant that the shooter would be below the target when tracking it. This was not a problem against a target at a reasonable height, but against one flying at ultra-low level it would not be possible to track it safely from below and so a special low-level gun-attack procedure was taught to the Germany Lightning pilots. This involved an attack from close behind the low-level target and from some 1,000 feet above. The pilot of the attacking Lightning rolled his aircraft inverted and pulled the nose down into a steep dive to put the target in the gunsight before rolling back the right way up and taking a quick guns' shot. The break-out needed to be prompt and aggressively flown to avoid descending below the target or flying into the ground and the attacker could then re-position for a further attack if necessary. For our training sorties the target was flown at 500 feet to build in a safety buffer. I was first taught this technique by my flight commander, Squadron Leader John 'Spon' Spencer – a highly respected weapons instructor – in one of the T-birds, three months into my work-up to becoming operational. I thought he was very brave to sit there beside me whilst I hurled us at the ground in an inverted dive. There was little margin for error or time for him to intervene if I overcooked it. Later the same day, I was sent off to do the exercise again on my own in a single-seat F.2A. He must have had confidence in me and it certainly built my own confidence in manoeuvring the aircraft aggressively at low level. In truth, the inverted low-level guns attack technique had limited merit in most real circumstances; it was usually better to goad the target into turning or wait for it to crest over a ridge.

All navigation for Lightning pilots at low level over Germany was by map and stopwatch with no modern navigation aids; familiarity with the LLSP operating area assisted greatly with this. Even so, it could be tricky to find one's way back to a particular LLSP after a prolonged running fight against determined, evading opposition, which was the sort of fight you might perhaps find yourself involved in, for example, against formations of RAF Buccaneers.

Sometimes, when other Lightnings were in adjacent patterns, the first pilots to detect and engage targets would call these other fighters into the melee as reinforcements. If there were multiple targets, for example a six-ship of fighter-bombers such as Harriers, these engagements could get quite large and complicated. The Lightning pilots, therefore, needed to be able to maintain high situational awareness in multiple-aircraft fights, perhaps whilst engaging a specific target of their own and whilst co-ordinating other fighters using the radio. This essential skill was practised and honed not only in the LLSPs but also in multi-aircraft air combat training (ACT) at medium levels. During my three years with 19 Squadron the unit flew over a thousand 4v2 ACT sorties to hone these skills, as well as conducting ACT in smaller numbers down to 1v1, dissimilar ACT against other types of fighters and, of course, frequent 'low-level affiliation' sorties as the low-level training engagements became known. I was personally involved in many of them.

Operational at Last

On Monday 17 June 1974, some six months after I had arrived on the squadron, I finally reached the standards required to be declared 'Operational' (this later became known as Combat Ready). This was the moment that I had worked towards for many years. My final 'Op Check' was flown in a T.4 Lightning with my flight commander, Squadron Leader John Spencer. I don't particularly remember the sortie, and my log book gives no clues, but it would have involved a 'scramble' from cockpit readiness and would have tested me in the procedures, techniques and skills required both to hold alert on Battle Flight and to operate in a wartime scenario, with another Lightning as my prey. As the sortie lasted only thirty minutes it suggests considerable use of reheat and must have been fairly intense. I passed the test and my logbook simply records 'Operational at Last'. My total flying in the RAF was just over 400 hours and I had 170 hours on the Lightning, with thirty-six of them at night, but I could finally call myself a fighter pilot. I had achieved the ambition I set myself when I was 7 years old and had pursued ever since. Of course, I still had plenty to learn and many more qualifications to pursue. I was under no illusions about that; but I still felt very proud.

The very next day, I flew on my own in a Lightning F.2A on an Exercise COLDFIRE sortie, manning one of the low-level search patterns and prepared to take on any targets I could find. That is a sortie I have not forgotten, as my flawed belief that I was the 'fighter' and everyone else was a 'target' was immediately shown up for its naivete. On my own in a low-level search pattern, I checked behind me as I turned at one end of the pattern and was appalled to see a Lockheed F-104 Starfighter, of the Royal Netherlands Air Force as it turned out, arcing in behind me, fortunately still out of range but clearly intent on getting some guns film of a Lightning. I lit the reheats and broke hard into him, forcing him to overshoot (the F-104 was not a great turner with its tiny wings). Throttling back and popping the airbrakes, I reversed the turn, attempting to fly the Starfighter out in front of me and to get behind him, selecting guns on the master armament selector as I did so. Much to my surprise the Dutch F-104 pilot (I could clearly see the national markings now) was up for the fight and before I knew it we were getting into a slow-speed 'scissors' at very low level as we weaved across each other, each trying to fly slower that the other to get behind and into position for a guns shot. I was gradually winning but had never expected to be flying this slowly and aggressively in a Lightning, this close to the ground. I began to realise why the work up to combat-ready, to allow me to partake in these exercises, had been so long, careful and extensive. These were big boys' games. The Dutch pilot obviously realised that he wasn't going to win this slow speed fight and, as we reversed towards each other one more time, he engaged his afterburner and bugged out over a ridge. It was the first time I witnessed the phenomenal acceleration of the F-104, which outpaced my Lightning as I followed him. However, he had simply opened the range from guns range into missile range. As I prepared to take the missile shot, he suddenly pulled up into cloud, foiling that intent, as the infra-red missiles could not see the target in cloud. I hesitated for only a moment and then followed him up into cloud, switching on my radar transmitter. As it happened, we popped out of cloud fairly quickly and now he was a sitting duck for a simulated missile shot, with camera film to prove it when I got back home. Then I just had the problem of how to get back down through the cloud. I was very impressed with that Dutch pilot's aggression and never forgot the lesson he taught me – that I, too, could become a target if I wasn't careful.

Battle Flight

The RAF Germany Interceptor Quick Reaction Force, known as Battle Flight, was permanently manned at Gutersloh twenty-four hours a day, every day of the year, with two pilots and six ground crew always able to launch one, or if necessary, both fully-armed Lightnings rapidly. Due to the proximity of the border, Battle Flight aircraft were maintained on a five-minute readiness state rather than the ten-minute alert state held by UK QRA fighters. This was not an easy obligation to meet, particularly if a scramble was ordered when the pilots were sleeping overnight or at other inopportune moments during a twenty-four-hour shift of duty in the 'Shed', the nature of which can be left to the reader's imagination. Overnight, pilots had to attempt to sleep in full flying kit, including anti-G suit and boots, but without their life-jackets which would be left hanging up at a convenient location on the run to the aircraft, perhaps on the Lightning's pitot tube or on one of the aircraft's missiles. The pilots' helmets would already be plugged into the aircraft and balanced on the top of the windscreens. As far as I know, the five-minute reaction time was never exceeded and this was a source of pride amongst the Gutersloh Lightning pilots; no-one wanted to be the first to spoil the record.

In order to meet the five-minute state, reaction to the scramble bell had to be instant and rapid. Woe betide anyone who got in the way of the stampeding pilots and ground crew on their run to the aircraft located in the Battle Flight hangars attached directly to the domestic accommodation. For some years after I finished my Germany Lightning tour the sound of a bell the same as the Battle Flight scramble bell would have me leaping about instinctively, adrenalin rushing, before I realised that I was not in fact required to react.

After running to their aircraft and climbing the ladders to the cockpits, the pilots would pull on their helmets and strap in rapidly, assisted by a member of the ground crew. This was normally accomplished within about one minute and thirty seconds of the bell first sounding. Most pilots found that, to save time, they had to leave their ejection-seat leg restraints undone until airborne, not connecting them until at the top of the climb; usually their flying gloves would be left on the cockpit coaming to be donned when time permitted. After checking in with the Wing Operations Centre using the secure Telebrief landline, the scramble message would be broadcast by the ops controller and acknowledged by the pilot. This gave details of climb-out direction and height ('angels'), who to call on the radio and on what frequency, for example, 'Vector zero seven zero, climb Angels two five, call "Bandbox" on stud fifteen, Scramble, Scramble, Scramble'. Normally only one fighter would be scrambled but, very occasionally, both would be launched together. A double scramble tended to cause anxiety amongst any observers, as this was the reaction that could be expected to a genuine infringement of West German airspace by Soviet Bloc aircraft, either with hostile intent or perhaps one wishing to defect.

The Lightning was extremely well designed for fast scramble starts – in fact this was one of its fortes – and it could be ready to taxi within seconds of initiating the start sequence. One slight 'gotcha' at this stage was that the Lightning had to be left on state with the parking brake selected off to prevent the wheel brakes from sticking on. It was, therefore, essential that the pilot remembered to put the parking brake on before starting the engines because, otherwise, as the aircraft was not chocked, it would roll forward as the engines developed thrust during the start up.

As he taxied out of the shed the pilot had to knock out the piece of red-painted wood which had been holding the canopy up whilst the aircraft was on state. It always seemed incongruous to me that such jet-age machinery required such a basic piece of apparatus to function effectively. The fact of the matter was, though, that the canopy of the Lightning would sag down and eventually close if left for a significant period of time without the engines (and hydraulic pumps) running as the canopy accumulator pressure would gradually exhaust. The wooden strut was therefore essential to hold the canopy open to allow immediate access to the cockpit, the only alternative being time-consuming pumping by the ground crew with the hand pump. At Gutersloh, the Battle Flight Shed was located a short distance from the runway and it took about ninety seconds to taxi at high speed to the runway for take off. Most pilots found that they were unable to complete the full pre-take-off checks in this condensed time and simply used the informal check list, 'Hood, Pumps, Pins' (canopy closed and locked, fuel pumps on and ejection-seat pins removed and stowed).

Battle Flight scrambles obviously took priority over any other aircraft and the take off would usually begin from a rolling start. A reheat climb to altitude was the norm even if, subsequently, a descent to low level was required for the intercept. With the Lightning's fantastic time-to-height performance, a pilot could easily find himself levelling off at altitude just over six minutes after the initiation of the scramble, when he had been sitting comfortably in the crew room, perhaps halfway through his dinner or, even worse, asleep in bed. It was a strange feeling on a no-notice scramble to catch up with events at 30,000-odd feet, realising that up until then one had been running on some sort of personal 'autopilot'.

Having been declared 'Operational' I could now hold Battle Flight duties and did my first twenty-four-hour stint in the Shed two days later on 19 June 1974. Every newly-operational Battle Flight pilot knew that, at some unknown point during their first day, they would be required to scramble, as a practice, to demonstrate that they could be airborne within five minutes. With that in mind, I spent the day sitting around in full kit, including my life-jacket, and in a high state of agitation unable to concentrate on much else. When the scramble bell rang, I did my very best to be as fast as I could, taking off on the practice scramble and flying for one hour and fifteen minutes. When I returned, I checked my scramble time. It had been four minutes and fifty seconds. I had only ten seconds spare on the five-minute limit and that from being fully prepared and awake. Clearly, I was going to have to cut that time down by strapping in more quickly.

Life at RAF Gutersloh

Life for the bachelor officers at RAF Gutersloh was pretty idyllic. Not only were we enjoying a fulfilling and exciting working life as Lightning pilots, but we also had plenty of fun off duty. We were living the dream. All the Lightning pilots were extremely professional at work and in the air, but off duty they seemed to go out of their way to appear to be the exact opposite and it was very difficult to get them to be serious about anything.

We bachelors lived in the old Luftwaffe officers' mess at Gutersloh, with our rooms in separate blocks arranged around a large grass square. Each block had a German batman, or 'bat lady', to clean our rooms and our shoes, make our beds and wake us with a cup of tea in the mornings, a service which has understandably long since faded into history. My bat lady was Emmy who was old enough to have been doing the same duties during the war for German officers and who scolded me for late rising at a weekend like a mother. The main building of the mess may well once have been a German farmhouse. With its tower, German-style roof and ivy-covered walls, it looked nothing like the traditional officers' mess in the UK.

At the top of the tower was 'Göring's Room', as it was known, a small room with a trick beam in the ceiling that was rumoured to have been visited by the former head of the wartime Luftwaffe and was named after him. The 19 Squadron pilots often used this room for squadron beer calls, especially if someone was being declared operational on the squadron and had to drink their yard of ice-cold lager before being awarded their squadron badge to wear on their flying suits to show their operational status. When I drank my 'op' yard of beer, which you had to do without removing the vessel from your lips once started, the onlookers reckoned they drank more beer watching me than I did drinking the two and half pints in the yard. Apparently, it was some sort of record for the slowest yard ever, but at least I wasn't sick out of one of the windows as many of the rapid drinkers were. In the basement of the mess building was a *keller* bar with old murals of German fairy tales painted on the walls. Initially not much used during my time at Gutersloh, I was instrumental in getting it refurbished and up and running, with relaxed dress rules from the rest of the mess public rooms, and it became a very popular haunt.

All service personnel based overseas were paid an additional local overseas allowance, supposedly to make up the difference in the price of buying things that might cost more overseas than back home. Quite how this was calculated was something of a mystery, but the fact was that it increased our salaries significantly. Meanwhile, almost everything that a bachelor would want to buy in Germany, including alcohol, hi-fis, new cars and petrol, was tax-free and so considerably cheaper than back home.

Weekends at Gutersloh for the bachelors invariably involved parties either in our own mess or at one of the other British bases in Germany, of which there were many within easy driving range. There was never any shortage of girls for the parties, mainly British Army nurses or British teachers at the military schools.

The married pilots on the squadron lived either in the nearby married quarters or in apartments in nearby German towns. They and their wives were very much part of the social scene off duty; they socialised in the mess frequently and the bachelor officers were often invited to their homes. We all knew each other really well; it was an enlarged family, which replaced the ones we were separated from back home, and we formed some life-long friendships.

The Boss

Just a few months into my tour the Officer Commanding 19 Squadron, Wing Commander Peter Vangucci, reached the end of his time in command and we got a new Boss. Peter Vangucci's last flight in a Lightning was also the very last flight for the squadron's only remaining Mark 2 (small ventral tank) Lightning before it was retired. His flight ended with an impressive beat up of the airfield.

The new Boss was Wing Commander (later Air Commodore) Robert 'Bob' Barcilon, who was one of the best bosses I ever worked for; we kept in touch up to his death in 2016. His pedigree and skills as a pilot were unquestionable, he had been part of the famous 111 Squadron Black Arrows Hawker Hunter aerobatic formation team in the late 1950s and had flown in the renowned twenty-two-ship loop. He was much respected by us all and led his pilots with a gentle but firm hand and considerable sympathy, whilst also demanding high standards. Most importantly, he stood up for his squadron fiercely against those above him, which endeared him to us further. We, in turn, were fiercely loyal to him.

Bob Barcilon was relatively small in stature with a slightly hawkish sort of face and he walked quickly. Within weeks of his arrival the squadron ground crew had taken to calling him the 'Pink Panther' as they thought that he bore a resemblance to the cartoon character. We junior pilots were aware of this. He wasn't. One day the ground crew asked some of us junior pilots if we thought it was a good idea to paint a pink panther on the side of the Boss's personal Lightning (XN781, tail letter B). This aircraft already bore the 'Top Cat' emblem stencilled on the left side of nose. This was a silhouette of a cat's backside with its tail up and the words 'Top Cat. Often licked. Never beaten!' underneath it. We thought the pink panther idea was splendid.

In due course, overnight one night, a large pink panther was painted under the cockpit of the Boss's aircraft above the roundel, beautifully done, in colour, the animal facing backwards and holding the wing commander's pennant – which was already present – on a stick. As luck would have it, the following morning a 'generation' exercise was called. This involved an early morning call-out and then the rapid generation of as many fully-armed and serviceable aircraft as possible. As the aircraft became ready, the pilots allocated to them were brought to cockpit readiness to check in on the radio with Wing Operations.

At this time the squadron's dispersal area on the far side of the airfield was undergoing reconstruction, with NATO hardened aircraft shelters being built, and so was unusable. Unusually, therefore, the aircraft were lined up on the pan in front of the squadron's hangar. I went out to my aircraft, checked in on the radio and was told to maintain cockpit readiness. Next to me, on my right, was the Wing Commander's Lightning with its new pink panther resplendent on its port side.

Soon afterwards, the Boss appeared striding out towards his aircraft to put it on state. He conducted his external 'walk-round' checks without noticing anything unusual, with his two ground crew doing pink panther walks behind him whenever he wasn't looking. He then climbed up the ladder past the pink panther, did a double take, went back down a couple of rungs to peer at this new piece of nose art and obviously asked the ground crew what it was. I couldn't hear with my bone dome on but the ground crews' gestures clearly indicated total ignorance and innocence. The Boss then got on with his job. He took it amazingly well and embraced his new nickname. Pink Panthers began to appear everywhere, including on the back of his flying helmet and on his flying suit. I particularly liked the rubber Pink Panther head in the squadron line hut that could be twisted into different shapes according to the ground crew's perception of the Boss's mood.

I learned much from the leadership of Bob Barcilon, things that I did not forget and tried to replicate when my turn for command came later in my career. I had cause to be grateful for his sympathetic handling of me on several occasions. I also learned from him about how to be a better fighter pilot. Once I had grasped the basics, he taught me to be, in his words, 'more underhand and sneakier', to try to kill victims without them even knowing I was there. At the time it seemed to me to be far less fun than rushing into a fight in reheat and forcing a dogfight, but it was undeniably very effective and he was, of course, absolutely right.

Tanking Calamity

As Germany-based Lightning squadrons we did not get as much air-to-air refuelling (tanking) practice as our UK compatriots. Spookily enough, the Victor tankers only seemed to be available over Germany on Fridays, meaning the crews had to land at Gutersloh and stay for the weekend. They were always royally hosted by us, in keeping with our policy of making sure our reputation as good overseas hosts was maintained.

In August 1974 on my fifth-ever tanking trip, with gaps of several weeks between each of them, I think I was probably getting slightly overconfident about this tricky skill. My leader, Flight Lieutenant Ian Wilde, had already plugged into the starboard hose of the Victor when I tried to do the same on the port hose. As my probe tip was about to reach the basket I took a sneaky peek at it to see whether it was going in, something that was not recommended. Seeing that I was going to miss the basket slightly to its right, I put on a large boot full of left rudder to slide my probe into it. Unfortunately, the probe tip contacted the rim of the basket, didn't engage it and pushed it sideways. In retrospect, I probably had too much overtake and, as I throttled back and popped the airbrakes out to back off, I was surprised and horrified to see a very large lateral 'whip' developing in the hose, which quickly snaked back to the pod (the hose drum unit or HDU) under the tanker's port wing, and grew more as it whipped back toward me. The next thing I knew there was a loud bang as this hose with a mind of its own whacked my Lightning somewhere under the nose and my aircraft was tipped with 90 degrees of bank toward the Victor's fuselage on my right. It was rather frightening for a second until I got the aircraft wings level again. My leader had spotted this violent manoeuvre out of the corner of his eye and quickly disconnected from the basket on the other side. Having averted a collision, my sense of relief immediately evaporated when I realised that the tanker's hose – all fifty-five feet of it – was missing and had fallen off, over Germany! I transmitted on the radio, '[Tanker call-sign], your hose has fallen off.' This didn't go down well and a right royal flap ensued.

I had to get a visual inspection from my leader, who reported a possible dent in the intake, and I conducted a low-speed handling check before landing back at Gutersloh to face the music.

Unfortunately, the stainless steel, double skin of the Lightning's engine intake had been dented and the skins were squashed together by the impact of the hose or basket. The engineers were suggesting that the aircraft would need to be stripped back to frame six and might take several months to repair. I was not popular.

I had more immediate concerns and spent the weekend worrying about what had happened to the tanker's hose which I had knocked off. Had it, for example, caused a multiple pile up on a German autobahn? How many deaths or injuries might I be responsible for? No news was good news but the damage to the aircraft was still threatening my thus-far good relationship with the Boss.

Fortunately, an expert metal panel beater, named Ted, was sent out from BAe Warton to see if he could beat out the dent. His skills saved the day and my bacon. The Boss suggested, in a way that was clearly an order, that I might buy Ted lots of beer and present him with a framed picture of the aircraft. It seemed a small price to pay.

The fifty-five feet of tanker hose was found a couple of weeks later in a German farmer's field and returned to RAF Gutersloh. The Boss made me have my photograph taken for the squadron diary, looking a little sheepish with the hose wrapped around me like a huge python.

Air-to-air Gunnery

In August 1974 No. 19 Squadron deployed en masse to Decimomannu air base, near Cagliari in Sardinia – 'Deci' to the RAF – for the annual armament practice camp or APC. This was an opportunity to use the range over the sea off Sardinia for air-to-air gunnery training.

We had been practising for a couple of weeks at Gutersloh prior to deploying, cine-only, filming the attacks against a 'banner' or flag target towed by a Canberra aircraft without firing any actual shells from the two Aden 30mm cannon in the F.2A Lightning's nose. Now we had the opportunity to fire 'ball' (non-explosive) ammunition at the banner with the aim of achieving 'ACE' status for as many pilots on the squadron as possible. In this case ACE was actually Air Command Europe, although ace status sounded great to us. This was actually a qualification that counted towards the annual TACEVAL score when NATO evaluators assessed the Gutersloh Lightning Wing's operational effectiveness.

To achieve ACE status at air-to-air gunnery, pilots across NATO had to achieve at least 15 per cent hits from the number of rounds fired at the target on two shoots within six. This may sound a low score and requirement but was actually quite difficult to achieve and should be considered in the light of the knowledge that even a couple of hits with explosive 30mm cannon shells against the types of aircraft targets we were likely to encounter would probably prove lethal.

The Canberra towed the 'banner' target at only 180 knots and the Lightning's attack speed was 360 knots, quite slow for such a swept-wing aircraft, but giving an overtake on the target of 180 knots. Firing range was between 500 and 300 yards at which point you were three seconds from flying into it. In most circumstances this amount of overtake would be considered excessive against an actual airborne target and it certainly made the time available very limited to correct the tracking in the gunsight and to assess the range to fire. Air-to-air gunnery was a skill that I would improve on with experience and more gunsight time, but at this stage I found it very difficult, although it was great fun and I did manage to ACE qualify, as did many of the pilots on the squadron.

Supersonic and Stratospheric

One day in December 1974 I was scheduled to be flying a training sortie involving a supersonic intercept against a supersonic target at high level. The normal profile for this routine training exercise was to have a Lightning target flying at 40,000 feet at M1.3, whilst the fighter aircraft would begin the intercept at 36,000 feet accelerating up to M1.6. The Lightning was easily capable of these heights and speeds, although the extensive use of reheat would shorten the sortie length, usually to around forty-five to fifty minutes in the Mark F.2A Lightning.

On this particular day, the Lightning due to be my target went unserviceable just before we walked out to fly. There was no spare aircraft and my chances of flying were looking doubtful. Then it was suggested that, as the Boss was flying an air test in another Lightning, which would involve a supersonic run at M1.6, if I asked him nicely, perhaps he would agree to my intercepting him. I duly made my request to the Boss, who was not particularly enamoured by my proposal as the air-test profile was extremely fuel critical; he would not be able to make any adjustments for me but I was free to intercept him if I could. This was something of a red rag to a bull for this young flying officer fighter pilot: a gauntlet had been thrown down and I was determined to show him what I could do.

I telephoned the German fighter controller who would be controlling my intercept and explained the vital need to get this one right.

The intercept went perfectly with some expert help from the fighter controller. I gained radar contact at decent range and, with help from the controller, manoeuvred so that I had the ideal lateral separation for a 2G turn in behind the target to allow me to continue accelerating. By the time that I rolled out in missile range behind the Boss he was at 40,000 feet and beginning to decelerate down through about M1.4. I was doing M1.6 and my aircraft was still accelerating nicely. I took a simulated Firestreak missile shot and continued to close on the Boss, intending to fly past him close, to give him the benefit of my supersonic shock wave and to let him know that the intercept had been successful. When I sat as the target on these types of sorties, I never ceased to be amazed at the speed that the fighter closed and shot past. It was fun to feel the 'thump' of the shockwave as it passed. My Lightning was now accelerating through M1.7, which was the release to service maximum speed limit for the F.2A, although we all knew that each and every F.2A had been tested to M2.0. With that in mind, I let the speed build up to M1.8, which is what I was doing as I shot past the Boss's Lightning a couple of hundred yards off his starboard wing. Having passed him I now needed to slow down and, without giving it too much thought, I pulled the aircraft up into a 15-degree climb from 40,000 feet. As I did so, I throttled both engines gently back to idle/fast idle (minimum power). Even without the benefit of full power, the aircraft climbed rapidly to 65,000 feet, which was my second 'rule bust' of the day, as the maximum altitude at which our equipment would keep us alive in the event of a pressurisation failure or canopy loss was 56,000 feet. Not that I was wearing the pressure jerkin anyway.

Approaching 65,000 feet it was noticeable how dark the sky had become; the horizon had a definite curve to it and the light was being reflected from below rather than coming from above. There was also a strange relationship between the indicated air speed and Mach number; as I topped out at M1.1 the airspeed was only about 180 knots, just above the normal approach speed. I had gently rolled inverted a couple of thousand feet below this but, not surprisingly, given the thin air, the controls were somewhat lacking authority and it took a few seconds to get the nose to adopt a descending attitude, during which time the thought briefly crossed my mind that I was going into orbit.

There are many Lightning pilots who have reached much higher altitudes than this but it was a most interesting experience, albeit not one that I chose to repeat. After my return from my fifty-minute sortie, the Boss did not comment on any of my 'tomfoolery', obviously unaware of the limits I had bust that day.

Air Combat Training

As my tour progressed, I flew more and more air combat training sorties with many being 1v1 against other pilots on my squadron, and some being 'dissimilar air combat training' (DACT) against other RAF types. I also flew in many of the squadron's 4v2 sorties, often leading four-ship formations despite my junior position on the squadron.

I particularly remember one of the 1v1 ACT sorties I flew in April 1975 against the other flight commander on the squadron, Squadron Leader John May, who was a highly-respected fighter pilot with considerable experience on the Lightning. This was part of an intense combat work up for me to achieve an air combat leader (ACL) qualification. Against such strong opposition a junior pilot couldn't really expect to win a 1v1 combat, but at least one could hope not to lose. I had decided upon a game plan that might just give me a chance.

The 1v1 'fights' typically started at 15,000 to 20,000 feet with the two Lightnings in line-abreast battle formation about a mile apart. At the call, 'Outwards turn for combat, GO', both aircraft turned outwards 60 degrees and maintained speed at M0.9, with the pilots looking back over their shoulders to retain visual contact with their opponent. When about six miles apart the leader called 'Inwards turn for combat. GO' and from this point the fight was on (later it became a requirement to call 'tally' before the fight was on). From here the pilots could use whatever power they wished and manoeuvre however they wanted to.

Later, and for very good reasons, the rules of combat incorporated a minimum 'bubble' around each aircraft, initially 500 feet and later 1,000 feet, to avoid mid-air collisions, but that rule had yet to be introduced. We would 'dust each other off' on the first pass, as close to each other as we dared, with a closing speed of eighteen miles per minute or 600 yards per second. If you gave your opponent too much space, he would use that as turning room against you.

I crossed very close aboard with the other Lightning, with him on my left, both of us at M0.9. Just before I passed him, I banked hard left towards him, feinting a climbing turn to the left. As we crossed, he broke hard right into what we later termed a 'single circle' (contra-rotating), fight. When I had passed him and he was unsighted on me I reversed my turn hard to the right and with the reheats now fully lit I slashed down hard into a right-hand turn pulling 6G, losing height to maintain my speed at M0.9 and straining hard against the sustained G force. Twisting in my straps to keep my eyes on my opponent, as I came round the corner I saw he was in a climbing turn to the right and I was much lower than him; potentially I had wasted some energy here but I seemed to have gained an advantage. Then I began to realise that he probably couldn't see me. He wasn't flying with any great purpose against my position relative to him and he wasn't keeping his 'lift vector' on me. You were supposed to call on the radio the moment you lost sight of your opponent for safety reasons, but of course any pilot would delay that call for as long as possible in order not to give the game away. It seemed that my little game plan might just be working and I was now getting into an advantageous position in his rear quarter, although not yet within the 30-degree cone off his tail for a Firestreak missile shot. When his 'lost tally' call came, I revelled in my reply, 'Roger. Continue'. He couldn't see me but I could certainly see him. From such an advantageous position and despite his best efforts, in a few minutes I was able to take a simulated missile shot that I was sure would be declared valid, as indeed it was, when the film was assessed later.

At this point my game management head came into play. I had an unexpected 'victory' over a senior pilot but if I called the 'kill' immediately we would have sufficient fuel for a further split and he would probably even up the score. I therefore hung on behind him for as long as possible into a very slow speed fight at base height, before calling 'Fox Two' (missile kill), 'Knock it off. Knock it off.' From his radio response I clearly had one very irritated squadron leader in the other aircraft (apparently no-one had 'shot him down' since 1968) and he demanded a reset. I pointed out that my fuel was really insufficient for a further fight but he was insistent. We set up for another combat split and, as I was the leader, I ensured that as we crossed on the first pass I was pointing towards base. I simply went straight through and 'bugged out' leaving him miles behind. Overall score: One: Nil.

After we had landed and I had signed my aircraft in, I arrived in the squadron operations room some minutes after Squadron Leader May who had obviously relayed the outcome of the sortie to my flight commander, Squadron Leader John Spon Spencer, a fearsome fighter pilot, who was running the 'ops' desk. As I walked in, no doubt grinning, I was brought rapidly back to earth as Spon glowered at me and spat out the words: 'Rowley, you're fighting me at 09:00 tomorrow morning.' There were no congratulatory comments and I feared my success in this particular 'combat' was going to be short lived.

It was actually several days later when the 1v1 against Spon took place and he put me right back in my place and ensured that I was not going to become overconfident. On this sortie he unsighted me and I was shot down by him, twice. Spon was a qualified weapons instructor and one of the finest exponents of air combat manoeuvring and tactics that I have ever met. He ran a wonderfully instructive debrief after the sortie in which he completely reconstructed our fights in detail, in several colours on a whiteboard, picking out the mistakes I had made and explaining how he had won the fights, with each lesson numbered. I learned so much and I was definitely put back in my box.

I flew two more 1v1 ACT sorties that same day, another against him in which I fared better and held him off, and a third in the T.4 trainer with the Boss, Wing Commander Barcilon, which I briefed, led and debriefed and after which I was awarded a coveted Air Combat Leader (ACL) qualification and a clearance to fly ACT down to a minimum height of 5,000 feet, only fifteen months into my first tour. Soon afterwards I also became a qualified four-ship leader. An ACL on the squadron was expected to be able to brief, lead and fully debrief any ACT sortie, including the like-type 4v2 sorties we flew frequently. Recalling and reconstructing the events of these sorties in detail and drawing the lessons in a comprehensive debrief was particularly demanding.

At the end of my second year on the squadron, my assessment hand-written into my log book by the Boss was: 'High Average as an all-weather fighter pilot. Above Average in Air Combat.' That meant a lot.

Missile Firing

In May 1975 I got my first chance to fire a Firestreak air-to-air missile. These opportunities tended to be once per tour for most fighter pilots. During routine training we carried 'acquisition rounds' on our Lightnings, which looked like the real missile and were fitted with the infra-red seeker head but had no rocket motor and no explosive warhead. We could simulate missile firings right up to and including trigger press with all the correct in-cockpit indications, just no missile being fired. There was no need to fire real missiles more frequently than we did.

The actual missile firings were either with ready-use war rounds – missiles with the full explosive warhead that could equally well have been used in a shooting war – or sometimes with missiles that had telemetry fitted in place of a warhead for trials purposes. The missile firings exposed the pilots to the experience and also tested the reliability and capability of the weapons. The firings were carried out in Aberporth range, over the sea in Cardigan Bay, Wales. The targets were remotely-piloted Jindivik drones, which looked rather like a Jet Provost without a pilot or cockpit. The drones were flown from Llanbedr airfield on the coast of Cardigan Bay and they towed an infra-red flare on a long 'string'. With luck, the missiles would home onto the flare and leave the Jindivik unscathed, although sometimes the drones were hit. The missile-firing sorties were mounted from RAF Valley, which was very close to the range, and where Strike Command's Air-to-Air Missile Establishment was based.

We deployed four Lightnings, under the leadership of our flight commander, Squadron Leader John 'Spon' Spencer, to RAF Valley the day before the first missile firings. It was two years since I had left Valley as a student pilot graduating from the Advanced Flying Training course; it was good to be back as an operational front-line fighter pilot in a mighty Lightning.

I fired my first air-to-air missile, a Firestreak ready-use war round, on a low-level firing at 500 feet over the sea, against a flare towed by a Jindivik. For the first time, I experienced the superb close control provided by the radar controllers on the ground at Aberporth as they set up the geometry between the firing aircraft and the target so as to ensure the missile was flying into a clear area and also to ensure that the firing occurred during the thirty-second burn time of the flare (otherwise their precious Jindivik drone would be shot down). At any point up to trigger press the controller could call a 'Stop. Stop. Stop.'

The effect of pulling the trigger was quite startling. There was an enormous 'BANG' and a 'whoosh' from just outside the cockpit, where the missile was mounted right alongside it. It was as if an express train had just rushed past, inches away. The missile shot off its launch rail, breaking the shear bolt as it did so, accelerating to about M1.5 above launch speed with a plume of white rocket smoke behind it. (The remaining broken half of the shear bolts which were removed from the missile shoes by the armourers were nice little souvenirs of Lightning missile firings. I have three in my collection.)

I was obliged to break away after firing to allow the photo-chase Lightning, which had been flying in close formation with me, to film the missile as it sped toward the target and exploded. I quickly reversed my breakaway turn, just in time to see the missile warhead – basically a very large grenade – explode in an ugly orange-and-black fireball. All very exciting.

We spent the weekend at Valley, during which we put on a party for the officers' mess with duty-free booze from Germany, literally gallons of our favourite squadron tipple, Harvey Wallbanger cocktail, which consists of vodka, orange juice and Galliano liqueur, and which we were experts at mixing. We had persuaded the friendly Welsh customs officer on arrival that the duty-free alcohol we were bringing into the country was entirely for consumption in the officers' mess, so he waived any duty charges.

On the Monday we set off back home to Germany with our four-ship of Lightnings. Our flight commander and leader, John 'Spon' Spencer, had a word with the Valley station commander to get permission from him for us to complete a flypast as we departed the airfield. Apparently, all such flypasts had been stopped after some fighter pilot hooliganism; one flypast by Lightnings from a UK squadron had actually broken windows in the mess with a sonic boom. The station commander agreed to a flypast by our four-ship, as he knew John Spencer, and stipulated a minimum height of 500 feet. In our briefing Spon told us this and said that meant 'Not below me'. I thought it was going to be a waste of time. I was wrong.

We took off individually in a noisy five-second stream, blasting off in full reheat, and joined up for a four-ship close formation echelon flypast over the airfield. From this formation we broke away individually, following the leader at five-second intervals into a 270-degree turn, out over the sea, to run back in over the top of the Strike Command Air-to-Air Missile Establishment (STCAAME) which had been hosting us. Spon had briefed us that were to be in 1,000-yard trail at 450 knots in dry power, then full reheat to accelerate to 550 knots over the top of STCAAME, before pulling 6G to the vertical for a 'vertical departure'. I was the number two in the formation, behind Spon, and as I followed him round over the sea, descending to get level with him, with 'Not below me' ringing in my ears, I found that I simply couldn't fly that low. I seemed to have rocks on the coast flashing past my ears, I was perhaps lower than 100 feet, but I simply couldn't fly as low as Spon. Reheats in, 550 knots over the roof of the STCAAME building, 6G pull up and then rocketing vertically upwards, topping out at 28,000 feet. Wow! That was fun.

We never received any feedback from Valley, good or bad. This was to be the first of many such airfield 'beat ups' of this sort that I got away with, something that in today's RAF would get you court martialled but which in those days was accepted as fighter pilot spirit.

North of the Arctic Circle

In September 1975 I was included in the Away Team for a NATO squadron exchange with a Royal Norwegian Air Force (RNoAF) F-104 Starfighter squadron based a Bodø (pronounced Buda), about fifty miles north of the

Arctic Circle. NATO squadron exchanges were a regular feature in RAF squadrons' annual calendars. Sometimes they were a one-way event and sometimes a team from each unit swapped bases to work with the Home Team left behind. The Norwegian squadron that hosted us at Bodø, 332 Squadron, operated its polished-metal, silver F-104s in the Air Defence role, whilst its sister squadron at the base, 334 Squadron, flew green-painted F-104s in the low-level fighter bomber and maritime-attack roles.

We took more pilots than the five Lightnings we deployed, and I flew to Norway in an RAF C-130 Hercules support aircraft with our ground crew and equipment. The Lightnings were supported on the 'trail' to Bodø by an RAF Victor tanker as it was too far from Gutersloh in one hop without air-to-air refuelling. The detachment commander was our OC A Flight, Squadron Leader John May.

We were royally hosted by the Norwegians with whom we had a natural affinity. We flew some interesting sorties, including low-level radar intercepts over the sea, standard fare for UK Lightning squadrons, but a skill which we could not practise overland at Gutersloh. I flew in a low-level affiliation sortie, over the sea, against four of the 334 Squadron F-104s, whose pilots were clearly in their element at ultra-low level and high speed over the sea. We also flew a four-ship fighter sweep northwards, almost to the North Cape, on a day when the weather allowed an excellent view of the Norwegian mountains and coastline from 36,000 feet. This flight took us closer to Russian airspace than any of us had ever been before. On the return leg southwards, back towards Bodø, we were bounced unexpectedly by a single silver 332 Squadron F-104. Fortunately, our very many hours of practising for just this eventuality meant that he was spotted before he got into a firing position and he was then chased through the mountains and valleys at low level by our leader, whilst the other three of us followed along covering his tail from height. In truth, I think we were reluctant to descend to low level as our fuel was tight. Not as tight as the leader's, apparently, after he'd got his 'kill' and climbed back up.

We departed Bodø on the morning after a final party with the Norwegians, when we had hosted them with plentiful supplies of Harvey Wallbangers and duty-free whiskey, which they drank in copious quantities. The detachment rules from our leader were that none of us were to go to bed before the Norwegians, so we were perhaps feeling a little 'shabby' the following morning, but nothing that wouldn't be fixed by some 100 per cent oxygen once in the cockpit.

We were briefed by Squadron Leader John May for a flypast and beat up over Bodø similar to the one that I had been involved in at Valley a few months earlier. The final flypast would culminate in a vertical climb to join the Victor tanker at 30,000 feet for the trail back to Gutersloh. Once again, I was the number two. After take off we joined up in close formation in a neat five-ship echelon for the first flypast. Then we peeled off to fly along the long straight taxiway parallel to the main runway at Bodø, which would take us over the aircraft parking pan at the end of it, where the 332 Squadron pilots would be standing to wave us off. The brief was 450 knots, reheats in, 550 knots pull to the vertical over the pan. As I followed my leader along the taxiway at 450 knots I decided to fly as low as I could. A subsequent photograph, sent to us in an album of photos of the exchange by 332 Squadron and which we received at Gutersloh a couple of weeks later, showed that I was really quite low, perhaps fifty feet. Reheats lit, 550 knots over the pan and a 6G pull into a vertical climb, topping out at 30,000 feet. Great fun.

When we had landed back at Gutersloh after a transit flight of two hours and forty minutes with air-to-air refuelling from the Victor tanker en route, we were welcomed home by the rest of the squadron pilots and the married pilots' wives, with bottles of beer. Unusually, for such a simple flight home, Squadron Leader May called us into a briefing room, beer bottles in hand, for a debrief. It transpired that the senior pilot who was behind me on the 'beat up' at Bodø had snitched on me about how low I was. Apparently, according to him, when he arrived over the pan at the end of the taxiway immediately after me, the Norwegian pilots were no longer standing. Why, the flight commander wanted to know, had I been below him? I needed to think fast if I was to avoid serious trouble.

'I can't understand it, Sir,' I said, 'I had you on the horizon.'

'Did you?' he replied, looking puzzled, and then, 'Hang on, there was a mountain in front of me.'

'Oh yes, Sir,' I said, 'That would explain it.'

He obviously knew I was making excuses, but it seemed my 'cheek' had won the day; he may even have been secretly pleased to see such spirit. At any rate, nothing more was heard of it until the photo album arrived when he rushed into the crew room to show me the photo of one very low Lightning.

'Probably not me, Sir,' I said, 'Could have been any of us.'

Night Frights

The RAF Germany Lightning pilots did not do as much night flying as their UK-based compatriots, who tended to operate a strict regime of alternate weeks of day and night shifts. We did only about 15 per cent of our flying in the dark, whilst still remaining current in all disciplines at night, especially for Battle Flight duties and with so-called 'visidents'. A visident involved using the radar to close to minimum radar range (300 yards) in the dark on a target that could be lights out, to get visual and then creep into close formation to identify it.

My logbook shows that I also regularly flew night supersonic intercepts, practice intercepts at all levels above 5,000 feet overland with various types of loose and broadcast control from the ground, occasional night air-to-air refuelling and also frequent sorties against the 360 Squadron Canberra T.17s, which jammed our radars. The jamming meant that the Lightning radar did not show a range to the target and instead of seeing a blip you saw a 'spoke' which showed up on the scope in azimuth only. However, using the techniques that had been developed it was still possible to conduct an intercept, even against a jamming target that was weaving, to roll out behind it and assess the range for a missile shot to 'kill' it. After several such practice intercepts, we liked to complete the sortie by flashing past on one side of the Canberra, with the reheats blazing in the dark, just because we could.

*****

One night I was planned to be flying one of two Lightnings which would conduct 'bat and ball' alternate intercepts against a 360 Squadron radar-jamming Canberra T.17, with the other Lightning flown by the 19 Squadron QFI, Flight Lieutenant Phil Owen. It was winter but the weather forecast was good and the station Met man had assured us that the ground temperature was going to remain above freezing all night and runway icing was not going to be a problem. We duly launched into a cloudless night sky.

I was trailing my leader up the climb using my radar to follow him when it failed and would not reset. There was nothing more I could do and no point in continuing with the planned sortie profile, as there was nothing I could usefully contribute. I arranged to return to base from the top of climb to spend the rest of the sortie pounding the instrument pattern. Most unusually, therefore, I was recovering to base with a Lightning almost full of fuel.

Soon after I had made initial contact with the Gutersloh air traffic control (ATC) approach controller, he radioed, 'From OC Ops Wing.

The runway is icing up. You are to burn off fuel and land ASAP.' Now a Lightning pilot needs some persuading to waste fuel unnecessarily and, as things were obviously not going according to plan on the ground, I asked for confirmation that I was definitely to burn off my precious fuel to land ASAP. The controller confirmed that those were the instructions.

The Lightning did not have a fuel dump facility, presumably because it seemed totally superfluous in the original aircraft which had so little fuel to start with and which could burn what it did have so quickly. The recommended technique for burning off fuel was to slow down to below the undercarriage limiting speed (250 knots), configure 'dirty' with undercarriage and flaps down and airbrakes out, select full reheat and fly round and round in small circles keeping the speed below 250 knots by pulling G and buffet.

I decided not to burn down to absolute minimums, but only to a fuel state commensurate with landing and stopping on what was apparently going to be a slippery runway, taking into account that the Lightning was never an easy aircraft to stop from its landing speed of 155 knots (almost 180 mph). If the brake parachute failed, which was a relatively frequent occurrence, Gutersloh's runway was marginal in length at the best of times.

As I was about to complete my last orbit before commencing my approach, the undercarriage indications in the cockpit suddenly changed from three green lights (all three undercarriage legs locked down) to three greens and a nose-wheel red (red meaning unlocked). I cancelled the burners, rolled out of the turn pointing towards base with that homing-pigeon instinct that Lightning pilots developed and confirmed the strange contradictory undercarriage indications. I decided that although the snag was almost certainly only an indication problem, I had better tell someone. I announced to the ATC controller that I was ready to commence the feed-in to a ground-controlled approach (GCA), but that I had three undercarriage greens and a nose-wheel red. He didn't believe me and we went through a bit of a question-and-answer session to convince him. The duty pilot came up on the radio frequency and we went through the question-and-answer session again. We agreed that we should treat the problem under the heading of 'Undercarriage – Unusual Positions', which required the undercarriage to be recycled up, then down. The recycle duly produced three greens with no reds. The next line in the drill said: 'If three greens obtained, leave down.' Fine, there should be no need to raise it now, so problem solved.

As I approached the top of descent for the GCA at six miles from the airfield the talkdown controller asked me what my fuel state was. This immediately rang alarm bells in my head, which seconds later were proven warranted as, having given him my fuel state, he said, 'From OC Ops Wing. The runway requires de-icing before aircraft can land. You are to hold off and endure.'

'But I've just burnt off to land on his instructions,' I radioed.

'Hold off and endure,' replied the controller with, apparently, very little sympathy for my predicament.

These new instructions were easier to issue than to comply with. Having completed the drills for the undercarriage problem I was supposed to be leaving the gear down, but, with the Dunlops dangling, my endurance could be measured in very few minutes and I could not make it to the crash diversion airfield if a diversion was necessary. There was nothing else for it: the wheels would have to come up.

'Tell OC Ops that I'm having to raise the undercarriage and I'm closing down one engine,' I transmitted. I still didn't detect any sympathy in the controller's response but I definitely had his attention now. Closing down one engine in the Lightning could save significant amounts of fuel and there was still plenty of power. I had never done this before, outside of the simulator, but this was undoubtedly a time for it. It's a funny thing, but when you fly an aircraft designed with only one engine it never seems a great cause for concern but, when you lose the built-in redundancy of your two-engine mount, it is a most uncomfortable feeling.

I flew to overhead the airfield and orbited at circuit height and at endurance speed, watching the fuel-gauge indications decreasing all too rapidly. Around me things were not going smoothly. One of the Konsin Spreader de-icing machines broke down on the runway. To add to everyone's problems the Canberra I had been planned to work with that night returned to the airfield with an air-speed-indicator failure. Phil Owen was in formation with it in his Lightning, in the dark, calling the Canberra's airspeed to its pilot on the radio. Each radio call asking for an estimate of how much longer before the runway would be clear was met with an estimate which was rapidly proven over-optimistic and replaced with a longer one.

Finally, I reached the fuel state at which I would either have to land or divert. Diverting on minimum fuel in a Lightning meant landing at the diversion airfield virtually on fumes. Miraculously, my announcement of this intention produced a clearance to land from my next circuit. I turned downwind, re-lit the No. 2 engine for a bit of insurance on the approach, and carried out the pre-landing checks including lowering the undercarriage. To my horror the undercarriage indicator showed two main wheel greens and a nose-wheel red. Bugger. The nose wheel might not be locked down. I shut down the No. 2 engine again, announced my problem and went around from finals, now below minimum landing and diversion fuel. I recycled the undercarriage up then down and was much relieved to get three greens, indicating all wheels locked down. I re-lit the No. 2 engine for the second time that night and landed from the next approach. Everyone else got down safely behind me.

With everyone back on the ground the flight commander who was running the 19 Squadron programme that night, Squadron Leader John May, had no hesitation in deciding that this was clearly a night when any further attempt at flying would be tempting fate and we were 'stacking' to the bar. I joined the rest of them after I had written a full and rather critical flight safety report, reflecting what this particular Flying Officer thought of some of the proceedings that night.

*****

On a February night in 1975 I took off from RAF Gutersloh in Germany, as the number two in a pair of Lightning F.2As. The leader was one of the squadron's weapon instructors, Flight Lieutenant Graham Clark, an experienced, expert and fine fighter pilot. I followed Graham up the climb in 'AI trail', 'tied on' to him with my radar. Climbing at 450 knots, we went into cloud at 4,000 feet and popped out shortly afterwards at 20,000 feet into a starry night sky. As we did so Graham's voice came up on the radio with, 'Err, Two, I've got a bit of a problem.' He then went on to explain that he had some sort of AC electrical failure, he had lost his main attitude indicator and, in addition, his standby artificial horizon was also unserviceable. This meant that he was now above 16,000 feet of solid cloud, in the dark, with no attitude references at all in his cockpit.

There was little alternative but for me to lead Graham down through the cloud in close formation. Night close formation in cloud was something that I'd never done up to that point. I closed up on him using my radar and night visident procedures and then moved carefully into loose formation on his starboard side. Graham handed the lead to me and slid into close formation on my left wing. I made the necessary arrangements with air traffic control and started the descent. It was extremely dark in the cloud. Now and then I took my eyes off my instruments for a second and sneaked a glance out to my left to see how Graham was doing. If our Lightings' flashing anti-collision lights were on when I looked, I could see some of his aircraft just off my wingtip; if the lights were off it was simply black. It started to get turbulent and I flew with both hands on the control column, my eyes glued to the instruments, trying to smooth out the bumps. I thought Graham must have been having a really hard time hanging on to me, but then his calm voice came up on the R/T with a cheery, 'Bumpy in 'ere i'n'it?' The skill and coolness he demonstrated that night in holding close formation with me in the dark through 16,000 feet of thick, bumpy cloud, were to me, as a junior pilot at the time, simply exceptional.

As we broke cloud at 4,000 feet, I was in a gentle left-hand turn. I decided to keep the turn going until we were pointing at base so that I could tell Graham that the airfield was on his nose and let him recover visually on his own. Halfway round the remainder of this turn, I stole another glance outside to see how he was doing. I was shocked to see the silver underside of his Lightning, illuminated by the anti-collision lights, breaking away from me, seemingly from inside my wingtip. Heart racing, I rolled away, realising I had almost collided with him. It transpired that after emerging from the cloud and becoming visual with the surface, Graham, quite reasonably, broke out of close formation from me and then flew straight and level. I was unaware of this and continued to turn left towards him. Fortunately, he had looked out towards me fractionally before my continued left turn had caused a collision and he broke away, averting disaster. Back on the ground later, he was kind enough to share the responsibility with me, which allowed me to feel slightly better about it.

*****

One night, returning to Gutersloh after a sortie, for a visual night circuit to land, there was an unexpected cloudburst over the airfield. Fortunately, the cloud base was high enough to permit a visual circuit, but it was absolutely bucketing down with rain and was very dark. As I turned finals it was actually quite difficult to see the runway clearly through the Lightning's windscreen. I decided that, even if my brake parachute failed, I didn't want to be airborne any longer in that weather and I would, therefore, do a precautionary landing.

On a normal landing in the Lightning, touching down at about 155 knots (almost 180 mph), the throttles were retarded to idle/fast idle, the brake 'chute handle was pulled and, if the tug of the brake parachute was felt, then light braking could be commenced. If the brake 'chute failed, the landing was aborted, full dry power was applied and the aircraft was flown off for another circuit to land 'precautionary' without the 'chute. If there was insufficient fuel for a further circuit, the precautionary landing technique was used anyway, as you were going to stay down and stop regardless of whether the brake 'chute functioned correctly or not. On a precautionary landing as soon as the wheels touched the runway, the throttles were both brought to idle, hard braking was commenced and then the brake 'chute handle was pulled. If it worked, the brakes could be released; if not you were already braking hard to stop in the remaining runway without it. It generally took the remainder of a 7,500 feet runway to stop without a 'chute and the brakes were then normally too hot to taxi in.

I touched down gently on the runway, throttled both engines back to idle, hit the brakes and pulled the brake 'chute handle. The 'chute deployed but, as I didn't seem to be slowing as much as expected, I continued to brake hard. Then there was a 'bang' and the aircraft lurched to the left, immediately followed by another bang from the right. The aircraft began slewing from side to side, still doing about 130 knots and it became very difficult to keep straight. Indeed I momentarily thought I would leave the runway onto the grass, which would probably have been catastrophic. For the first time, but unfortunately not the last, I experienced how frightening it is not to be fully in control of an aircraft at high speed on the ground, especially in the dark. I announced to the ATC local controller on the radio that I had a double tyre burst, as that seemed the most likely explanation, and I fought the aircraft to a halt halfway down the runway, the starboard wheel was not far from the right-hand edge and the aircraft was pointing well to the left. My No. 2, who was on finals to land behind me, had to overshoot and divert to the crash diversion on minimum fuel as I had now blocked the runway.

Having stopped, I quickly made the cockpit safe and climbed out which was never easy to do from a Lightning without a ladder. It involved lowering oneself over the side onto the dummy Firestreak missile mounted beneath the cockpit and jumping to the ground. Once standing on the runway I realised just how much water there was; it was raining hard and the standing water was over the toes of my flying boots. It was at least a couple of inches deep. The wheels of my Lightning were glowing red in the dark and they had both been worn distinctly flat. The fire trucks took longer to get to me than I had hoped. Apparently, the RAF firemen had just tucked them up inside the fire section garage to prevent them from getting wet. My return to the squadron was in one of the fire trucks, whilst the squadron ground crew sorted out a rapid wheel change for the Lightning on the runway, before it could be towed back, ever aware that the runway could not be blocked in case of a Battle Flight scramble.

I had been the victim of the phenomenon of dynamic aquaplaning, where wheels will slide on top of a wedge of water under the tyre and can actually be braked to a halt on top of the water without any actual retardation and with a loss of directional control. When my aircraft had been slowed below the minimum aquaplaning speed by the brake parachute, the wheels broke through the water to the surface beneath, at which point, with the brakes applied, the effect was the same as landing with the brakes on. Hence both tyres bursting. The very thin main wheel tyres on the Lighting were inflated to over 300 psi, so when they burst it could be quite dramatic. I learned about aquaplaning from that.

*****

In January 1976 the squadron suffered a mid-air collision at night, with fortunately relatively minor damage and both Lightnings landing safely. The sortie profile was a 2v1 night intercept with the lead fighter conducting a passing, offensive visident on the target, which was another Lightning. The aim was to use the radar to get visual with the target and then pass close enough to identify the aircraft type, call 'hostile, clear engage' on the radio and break away so that the second fighter, trailing the first one, a mile behind on radar, could take a simulated missile 'shot'.

The pilot of the lead fighter, a very experienced weapon instructor, did not get the correct indications in the pilot attack sight – the mini head-up display and weapons aiming sight – when he switched the range scale from miles to yards by selecting the master armament selector knob from missiles to guns. This selector was poorly positioned low down in the cockpit on the right side. The pilot looked into the cockpit to confirm his selection and when he looked up again, he was about to collide with the target. He bunted under the target Lightning's port wing and the aerial on top of the fin impacted the port aileron of the other aircraft. Neither pilot was aware that the aircraft had touched, although they realised that they had come close. The damage became apparent on the ground, as did the significance of how close this had been to an accident. A board of inquiry ensued.

The Inquiry queried why offensive passing visidents were being flown at all, despite this having been a standard procedure for many years. The end result was that the visident rules were amended in the regulations. In addition, the Inquiry had realised that it was routine to fly in close formation on completion of a night visident if the target could be seen from minimum radar range. It, therefore, became a requirement for all RAF Germany Lightning pilots to be trained and checked in night close formation.

So it was that, in April 1976, I found myself one dark and cloudy night, first, leading a night pairs close-formation sortie and, then, being checked out as wingman in a Lightning T.4. The sortie profile was a night close-formation pairs take off, climb to height through cloud, some close-formation manoeuvring, a descent back down through cloud in close formation and a pairs' GCA for a pairs landing, all in the dark. This was before the days of night-vision goggles and the external lighting on the Lightning was nothing much to write home about. All it had was the standard dim navigation lights, one on each wingtip (green on the starboard and red on the port) and two small white lights either side of the lower jet pipe at the rear. The anti-collision lights were not strobe lights, just flashing white lights. For close formation at night, the wingman could ask for the anti-collision light to be on or off as he wished. The options, therefore, were either to formate on one wingtip navigation light with not much more of the leader's aircraft visible, or to have the leader's aircraft illuminated by the anti-collision light, when it flashed on. When it was off you couldn't see anything, having lost night vision.

On my dual check in the T.4, with the very brave Squadron Leader John Spencer once again risking his neck to my limited skills, I found it to be just about the most demanding and dangerous thing I've ever been asked to do in an aircraft. When the leader's anti-collision light was on I could see enough to formate but if, for example, I was slightly wide I would start to move in only for the light to go off. When it flashed on again, I would be too close, and so it continued. I didn't hit the leader or lose him and fall out of formation, and we landed safely. In the debrief Spon said to me, 'I've never known you be so quiet for so long. All I heard from you throughout the entire sortie was heavy breathing and when we went into cloud you simply said "F****** Hell!" I think that probably summed the experience up perfectly. It was awful.

Near Mid-air Collision

The risk of mid-air collision always exists in the fighter game when you are often flying in confined airspace close to other aircraft. Over the years there have been some tragic mid-air collisions, some between members of the same formation or sortie and some between random aircraft that just happened to be in the same place at the same time. The so-called 'big sky' theory that suggests that the odds of two aircraft being in exactly the same place at the same time in a three-dimensional environment are remote and it is therefore very unlikely to happen may be believed by some, but not by those who have had the misfortune to disprove it.

My first such experience came in June 1976. We had some Armée de l'Air Mirage F1s and their pilots visiting the squadron and working with us for a week. One day I was tasked to lead one of the French pilots in his Mirage into the low-level search patterns, hoping to find some freelance 'trade' and show him how we operated. The visibility that day was typical for that part of Germany, very hazy and probably on the minimum we could accept for low flying, which was five kilometres (three miles). We were very used to operating in such conditions.

Flying in battle formation with the Mirage one mile off my left wing I was paying special attention to him, not wanting to lose him and also, as ever, checking his six o'clock in case we were unexpectedly bounced. I may have been looking across at him and behind him for perhaps about eight seconds. As I turned my head to the front to look forwards, a SEPECAT Jaguar aircraft flashed across the top of my cockpit canopy, absolutely head-on, no more than ten feet above me, with a 'whoosh'. I was left with a sort of photographic impression of a Jaguar on my retina. It had happened so quickly, in a split second, that there had been no time to be scared or to react; we had not hit and now it was over. I simply called a 'turnabout' to the French pilot, wrenched my Lightning round through 180 degrees in reheat, and chased after the Jaguar at high speed to take a simulated missile 'shot'. I doubt if its pilot ever saw us.

Back on the ground I mulled over what had happened and why I had come so close to dying in a fireball from a head-on collision. I was flying at an estimated 250 feet, the minimum altitude allowed by the rules, judged by eyeball and experience. The Jaguar was also flying at 250 feet, probably very accurately using his radar altimeter, something the Lightning did not have until later in its life. I had obviously been ten feet low in my estimate. I had been flying at 360 knots; the Jaguar was probably cruising at 420 knots, giving a closing speed of 13 nautical miles per minute, or just over 430 yards every second. From the maximum visual range that we had that day, three nautical miles – which was legal for low flying – I had precisely 13.8 seconds to spot a head-on Jaguar with that closing speed, a very small camouflaged shape to pick out against the background. As I hadn't spotted him in the first five seconds of that thirteen and then I had spent the rest of that time looking across at my wingman, it was no wonder I hadn't seen it until it was far too late. I took the lesson away but reasoned that there wasn't very much you could do about that; you just needed to be lucky.

During my subsequent long military aviation career there were to be several more occasions when I got close to similar mid-air collisions. Several of them were near collisions with military fast jets that were heading towards me on a 90-degree angle. The problem with those was that they approached, as all collisions do, on a steady azimuth, in this case about 45 degrees off the nose, with no relative movement, no 'sightline spin' as fighter pilots call it, and so are not only very difficult to spot but are often hidden behind the windscreen arch. On two occasions, once in a Hawk jet and once in a Tornado F.3, I was saved by navigators in the rear cockpits, who called the contacts to me and eventually called 'PULL UP', which fortunately I reacted to immediately. One other near collision between me in a Hawk and a Tornado GR.1, when we missed by about fifty feet, happened in cloud and was the fault of the Air Traffic Control radar controller on the ground. In order to survive a career in military aviation you definitely need some luck.

Emergencies

I was extremely fortunate to get into the last year of my three-year tour in Germany before I experienced any of the nasty emergencies that the Lightning could throw at you. When they did happen, the outcomes were also extremely fortunate.

On 5 May 1976, shortly after take off in Lightning F.2A XN776, my aircraft suffered an AC electrical system failure, which meant that, along with various other things, the AC electric fuel pumps that provided fuel to the engines failed. The Lightning F.2A emergency drill for this type of failure imposed a maximum limit of 85 per cent rpm on both engines, as any higher throttle setting could cause the engines to flame out. With a heavy aeroplane, as I had on this occasion, full of fuel just after take off and with no way of dumping it, this was barely enough power to stagger around and land the aircraft. There was a taught technique, which I had often practised in the simulator, for a heavyweight, AC-failed pattern. Fundamentally, this involved flying at more than 300 knots to minimise drag until lined up with the runway and committed to the approach. The pattern was also flown at a height from which you could afford to lose 500 feet for every 90-degree turn and still have sufficient height for the approach. There was no chance of an overshoot from the approach or of a second attempt. Once slowed down to approach speed, down was the only way the aircraft was going. The training paid off and I flew the pattern, approach, and landing successfully and without difficulty, although I found the whole thing somewhat disconcerting.

*****

Only six days later, on 11 May 1976, I was flying Lightning F.2A XN789 – the personal aircraft of Squadron Leader John Spencer, OC B Flight – on a supersonic intercept against another Lightning, flown by Flight Lieutenant Phil Owen, the squadron QFI.

Accelerating through M1.25 at 38,000 feet with both engines in full reheat, I felt a slight pulsing in the power and, looking in at the engine instruments, I saw that the top temperature control on the No. 2 (top) engine was intermittently trimming back the rpm. I throttled back to an intermediate reheat setting and, as I did so, the No. 2 reheat self-cancelled. I re-selected reheat on that engine by rocking the throttle outboard and pushing it fully forward, and it lit normally. I was accelerating again; perhaps it was just a 'glitch'; my attention returned to the radar and the intercept. Thirty seconds later, the warning system audio alarm sounded and a Reheat Fire 2 warning illuminated on the standard warning panel. A reheat fire warning might be spurious but, if it was real, the outcome could involve earning a Martin Baker tie and landing by parachute rather than as planned. Many Lightnings were lost to reheat fires over the years.

I immediately and rapidly carried out the reheat fire drill, instinctive actions drummed into me during the regular simulator training I'd received. I cancelled reheat on both engines and throttled the No. 2 engine back to idle, operated the catch on the throttle and brought the throttle fully rearwards, closing the high-pressure fuel cock for that engine and shutting it down. I also turned off the low-pressure fuel cock and the fuel pumps, and selected the air-to-air refuel switch to refuel to stop pressure transferring fuel through pipes that might be damaged. There were no fire extinguishers for the reheat zones of the Lightning, so that was all that could be done for now.

I declared a 'Mayday' on the radio, adding that I had a Reheat Fire 2, and hoping I sounded a lot calmer than I felt. About ten seconds later the fire warning light went out. I hoped it might have been a false alarm, but wondered if the fire was so bad it had burned through the fire wire. I really didn't fancy the prospect of ejecting at supersonic speed and at such high altitude, so I now started working hard to slow down and descend, in case ejection became necessary. The ideal ejection parameters we were told were 10,000 feet and 250 knots, although, personally, I always felt that 10,000 feet was a long way to come down in a parachute, the harness of which might be pinching certain sensitive parts of one's anatomy. I was now heading towards the pre-meditated ejection area, the Dummersee lake and its surrounding marshland, about thirty miles north of Gutersloh. If I had to eject, the aircraft would hopefully cause no harm to anything or anyone on the ground in this unpopulated area.

Meanwhile, Phil Owen in the target aircraft had been vectored towards me very slickly by the fighter controller and he joined into close formation to give my aircraft a visual inspection. From the port side he could see nothing amiss; perhaps it was just a spurious warning. He then moved to the starboard side and found something: 'Oh yes,' he said on the radio, 'You've definitely had a fire.' He sounded really quite enthusiastic about his discovery. I was glad he was pleased. He described what he could see, a large jagged hole about a foot in diameter on the top of the rear fuselage beneath the base of the fin. Even more worryingly, he also reported what he said looked like smoke or fluid venting from the hole, and he asked me to check that I had completed the drill and turned off the fuel to the No. 2 engine. I double checked and confirmed that I had.

The Lightning reheat fire drill required the pilot to hold off for a minimum of five minutes before commencing recovery. This requirement was as a result of experience gained with reheat fires earlier in the Lightning's life, and was intended to give confidence in the integrity of the tail plane control rods at the rear of the aircraft, which could easily be damaged by a fire and which might then fail, leading to loss of pitch control, as had happened. By the time that I had waited my five minutes from the initial fire warning, my useable fuel (that in the left wing) was getting quite low. I did not want to transfer fuel from the other tanks as I didn't know whether the fuel transfer pipes had been damaged. So I requested permission to commence my recovery with the Gutersloh air traffic controller we were now talking to. His immediate response was, 'From your squadron commander, you are to remain in the ejection area for another two minutes.' I pointed out that my fuel was now low, I had already completed the five-minute hold-off and that I would really like to recover now. After a brief pause, during which my future was presumably being discussed on the ground, I was allowed to commence recovery. I completed a slow-speed handling check on the way back to Gutersloh, slowing down to approach speed in the landing configuration with undercarriage down, flaps down and airbrakes out, to ascertain that I still had control.

I landed from a straight-in visual approach, my 'Mayday' status ensuring I had priority over other traffic. Phil stayed with me all the way home, flying a loose formation position, keeping out of my way, but keeping an eye on me, which was comforting. He overshot on my right as I was about to land. The landing was quite normal, albeit on one engine, which was no big deal in the Lightning as there was plenty of power from just one engine even without reheat. The brake 'chute worked normally and stopping was no drama. As I pulled off the runway at the far end and shut down, I had 600 lbs of useable fuel remaining, not a lot. I was immediately surrounded by fire trucks, tractors and assorted senior officers.

Thinking that the panic was now over, I carefully confirmed that everything was switched off and made safe in the cockpit before vacating. Whilst doing this, I suddenly noticed the Boss, Wing Commander Bob Barcilon, frantically signalling from the ground beside the cockpit for me to get out. The firemen had positioned one of their ladders against the cockpit so, without further delay, I scrambled down it to see what all the fuss was about. Moving to the rear of the aircraft, the cause of everyone's concern became apparent. Highly inflammable hydraulic fluid was pouring from the vicinity of the hole in the fuselage and running down over the very hot jet pipe inside it. The firemen were poised with hoses ready lest it all caught fire and quite bizarrely, not to say bravely, Wing Commander Peter Swindlehurst, the Officer Commanding Engineering Wing (OC Eng. Wing) was standing on the top of an A-frame ladder in his shirt sleeves with his hand in the hole, attempting to stem the flow of hydraulic fluid with a large rag. I suddenly realised that, now that my part in the drama was over, my hands were beginning to shake.

At the end of what had been a rather exciting day, and once I had completed all the various paperwork that an incident of this nature generates, I went to the officers' mess bar and was enjoying a well-deserved beer or two. The squadron junior engineering officer came looking for me to explain what had been found. For some reason the No. 2 (top) engine had lost about 25 per cent of each of the four exhaust-cone support fairing shrouds at the rear of the engine and two pieces of fairing, one quite large, had lodged in the reheat burner ring. It seemed that these lodged pieces of metal had sufficiently disturbed the reheat flame distribution to cause excessive heating and failure of the jet pipe skin. Once that had happened, burning through the aluminium alloy structure and fuselage skin was inevitable. Effectively, the No. 2 reheat had burned out through the side of the aircraft.

Considerable damage had been caused to the rear fuselage on the starboard side and the rudder powered flying control unit by the hole had been damaged by the heat. It was leaking fluid from the No. 1 control system. In the Lightning the flying controls were entirely hydraulically powered with no manual back-up. If both hydraulic systems failed, the controls went solid and ejection was the only alternative. With the No. 2 engine shut down and with it the No. 2 hydraulic system, the flying controls were being supported only by the No. 1 system. This was losing fluid at such a rate that, had I stayed airborne for much longer, I would have had a complete flying controls failure and been forced to eject, possibly at a late stage on the approach. The engineers actually calculated that I probably had only two minutes remaining before the controls would have failed completely. I had been very lucky indeed.

When I went back to my room later that evening there was a piece of Lightning propped against my door, a panel with a jagged hole in the middle, obviously beyond repair and looking like it had been damaged by flak. Stuck to it was a note from OC Eng. Wing that simply said, 'A Souvenir?' I have kept that panel ever since and it is now mounted properly on a wooden panel on my lounge wall, looking rather like a piece of modern sculpture of dubious artistic merit, with a 19 Squadron badge on it and a brass plaque which simply says: 'THE HOLE, Reheat Fire damage to Lightning F.2A XN789 on 11th May 1976'. This strange wall decoration has a special place in my heart and my home, as it reminds me of a day when I was very lucky to keep up my record of having the same number of landings as take offs and that all pilots need luck as well as skill.

*****

Three months later, on 4 August 1976, I was flying Lightning F.2A XN786, tail letter M, the personal aircraft of the other flight commander, Squadron Leader John May, when I experienced another nasty reheat fire warning and a pitch control restriction.

The beginning of this incident, up to the point of my radio call 'Standby for ejection', was described in the prologue to this book. Shortly after the incident I wrote to my parents describing what had happened. This was a letter that my mother kept. I was obviously trying to explain to my parents the details of the event, whilst trying to avoid worrying them too much. The words are, perhaps, not how I would write today but this is how I described it immediately after the event, aged 25; it does have a certain immediacy. This is what I wrote:

Dear Mum and Dad,

I'm afraid I've been up to my tricks again. I had another reheat fire in the air on Wednesday, only even more serious this time. I'd only just taken óff, with the Boss as my number two, and was climbing through about 2,000 feet when there was a terrific explosion down the back end and I got a Reheat Fire 1 warning. I closed down the No. 1 engine, switched off the fuel to it, and the warning light went out. I then put out a 'Mayday' call saying that I'd had a reheat fire. When I tried to pull up and slow down, I noticed the pitch controls were going stiff, which is normally a sure sign of a big fire, as the control runs for the tail plane are down by the No. 1 reheat pipe. I said so on the radio and warned, 'Standby for ejection'. I was expecting the controls to go solid at any moment and really thought I was going to have to eject. I couldn't get any higher than 3,500 feet because of cloud, but I slowed down to 250 knots, which is the best speed to eject and I had all my straps as tight as they would go, my visor down and everything ready to go. In fact, I would have been justified in ejecting there and then. At this point it started to rain and the thought went through my head that I was going to get wet.

I experimented with the controls and discovered that the ailerons and rudder were okay; it was just the tail plane that was very stiff and jamming. By using brute force, with two hands on the control column, I found I could keep control, albeit a little jerkily. Having ascertained that I could maintain control I started a gentle turn to the south, to turn away from the town of Osnabruck and into an area where there was less cloud, which then allowed me to climb gently to 9,000 feet to have a bit more height to play with.

The Boss came in close and had a look all around the back of my aircraft to see if he could see any signs of fire or damage. Initially, he saw nothing, but after a couple of minutes the fin started to swell 'before his very eyes' and he reported some sort of explosion in the fin.

We decided to do a slow speed handling check to see if I could maintain control. I slowed down to 200 knots with the undercarriage and flaps down and found I could keep control, but full (dry) power on my one good engine wasn't enough to stay level, so I brought the undercarriage and flaps up again and accelerated in a descent to 300 knots which was a comfortable speed to stay level.

With approval from the duty pilot on the ground we decided that I would have a go at landing it, keeping lots of height in hand and only putting the gear down at a late stage when I was happy. I routed well clear of Gutersloh town in case anything went wrong and set up for a long straight-in approach. As I was so heavy with fuel the approach speed was 195 knots (almost 225 mph). At a late stage of the approach I lowered the undercarriage and flaps, and put the airbrakes out, although the airbrakes didn't work due to damage. About one mile out I pushed the nose down to get onto the correct approach angle. I then found myself pointing at the approach lights at about 300 feet unable to get the nose to come up, with the control column jammed in pitch no matter how hard I pulled. With both hands on the control column pulling hard and no hand for the throttle, the speed built up to 220 knots. Then the control column moved more than I meant it to, the nose came up more than I had intended and I was pushing to get it down. Without much actual control from me, the speed bled back to 195 knots and the aircraft thumped onto the end of the runway, more by luck than judgement. The Station Commander who was watching from the ATC tower apparently said it looked like a nice landing. He wasn't sitting where I was. The brake parachute worked, which was a stroke of luck, as you can't rely on it with the No. 1 engine shut down. Once I was over the first, 'approach end' cable, which I was going too fast to engage, I lowered the hook, but I stopped before engaging the overrun cable. I was immediately surrounded by fire engines. Needless to say, I was out like a shot.

After all that effort to get the thing down, the aircraft is so badly damaged that they have decided it's not economical to repair and it will be written off. At least I'm alright. It appears that there had been a failure of the No. 1 jet pipe, which broke into two pieces and disintegrated. Some of it fell out the back and the rest of it was jammed up against the back of the engine in a great twisted pile of junk. Looking down the jet pipe the damage is incredible. It looks as though someone has thrown a hand grenade in there.

One engineering officer, who is very experienced on Lightnings, says he's never seen such a badly damaged aircraft get back safely. Apart from the damage caused by the hot gas leak, all the junk was blocking the airflow back from the engine, like a cork, and it had nowhere to go. So the air pressure was going into the back end of the fuselage and sort of blowing it up like a balloon. The whole back end is distorted and that's why the fin is swollen. The floor between the two engines was blown up and there is a fire wire for the No. 2 engine right by the hole. I was very lucky not to have had a Fire 2 warning in addition to the Reheat 1 fire warning. I probably would have ejected if that had happened. Also, there is a recuperator full of highly-inflammable hydraulic fluid that is squashed flat, but fortunately didn't split. The engineers keep shaking their heads and telling me I don't know how lucky I was. I do though and I'm very happy to be safe.

I was flying again the next day but, in truth, it actually took me a little while to get over the trauma of the whole experience. I was helped in that by being able to talk it through with my friends and colleagues but, alone in my room, I did face some demons and fear that I couldn't continue to survive many more of these incidents unscathed. I had experienced three nasty emergencies within three months and I almost felt that fate was 'targeting' me personally. I've always found that sleep helps to calm and reset my mind but, unusually, I did suffer some nightmares for a brief while – the falling into a black hole sort – from which I woke up in a cold sweat. On the other hand, I reasoned that things come in threes, don't they? I'd had three incidents in a row, so surely that was it. That wasn't the view that the Boss took. He had seen me wreck one of the flight commanders' personal aircraft and have a really good go at the other. I was banned from flying the Boss's aircraft ever again, as he was convinced his would be next.

One thing the last emergency had done was to teach me something about myself which had previously remained untested. I had discovered that, when faced with clear and present danger, I could control my fear, push any emotions into the background and think calmly, clearly and quickly. Surely a very good attribute for a fighter pilot and something that was to stand me in good stead on several future occasions. This was an interesting discovery for me and was very good for my confidence and self-belief.

When the official Aircraft Accident Report was published in March 1977 it stated:

> Many Lightnings have been lost in circumstances similar to these; it was only thanks to the skill and determination of the pilot that this aircraft was recovered safely, thus enabling a full engineering investigation to be carried out.

*****

Two months after the incident, in October 1976, I was on leave in the UK and was having breakfast one morning with BBC Radio One playing in the background. The news came on and the newsreader announced, 'An RAF Lighting pilot based at RAF Gutersloh in Germany … .' My ears pricked up. 'Flying Officer Clive Rowley, has been awarded the Queen's Commendation for Valuable Service in the Air … .' Crazy as it seemed, I was on the news. This was absolutely the first I had heard about this. I had no idea that I had been recommended for an award and hadn't expected it. As far as I was concerned, I was just doing my job. The station commander at Gutersloh, Group Captain (later Air Vice Marshal) Peter Collins, had received a letter some days before which he later gave to me. It was stamped 'Honours in Confidence' and was titled 'Award for Gallantry, Fg Off C.M. Rowley – 19 Sqn.' It went on to say that The Queen had approved the award of the Queen's Commendation for Valuable Service in the Air to me, that it would be published in the supplement to the *London Gazette* on 19 October 1976 and remained 'in confidence' until then. It asked the station commander to inform the recipient, me, the day prior to the official announcement. As I was away on leave, he had been unable to contact me, so the first I knew of it was when my name was on the BBC News.

Once it was all confirmed, I was delighted to have been recognised and I was very proud to be allowed to wear the oak leaf signifying the Queen's Commendation on my uniform under my pilot's wings, especially as I was still only 25 years old and still just a flying officer. It was unusual for someone of such lowly rank and junior years to sport the oak leaf. It was to be very lonely on my chest for the next fifteen years.

The citation for the award in the supplement to the *London Gazette* stated:

> Queen's Commendation for Valuable Service in the Air. Flying Officer C.M. Rowley.
>
> For his outstanding courage, presence of mind and airmanship when, on 4 August 1976, he brought his badly damaged Lightning back to base. Had he abandoned it, the aircraft could well have inflicted considerable damage, death or injury on heavily populated areas.

Official congratulations followed. There was a signal, personal for me, from the Commander-in-Chief (C.-in-C.) RAF Germany, a letter from the Parliamentary Under-Secretary of State for Defence for the Royal Air Force, and even a letter from the Headmaster of my old school. There was also considerable publicity with the news being carried in several newspapers and aviation magazines. The memento I liked best was presented to me by the 19 Squadron ground crew immediately after the incident. It was a cartoon of Biggles walking away from a crashed and smoking Spitfire with a speech bubble that said, 'Not to worry, Chaps. I'm O.K.' and their own sarcastic comment 'With the sincere gratitude of the ground crew No. 19 (F) Squadron August 1976', no doubt referring to the amount of work that I had created for them.

The certificate that went with a Queen's Commendation for Valuable Service in the Air was presented to me in person by the C.-in-C. RAF Germany, Air Marshal Sir Michael Beetham GCB CBE DFC AFC, who went on to become Chief of the Air Staff and to retire as a Marshal of the Royal Air Force. He had been a Lancaster pilot during the Second World War, completing thirty operations; he had also been the reviewing officer at my commissioning parade at Henlow in June 1971. At that stage of my career I was still in trepidation of such senior officers and it seemed the scariest part of the whole thing.

End of Tour

With the end of my three-year tour in Germany getting closer, I became more realistic about where I might be posted next. No. 19 (Lightning) Squadron was disbanding 'en masse' in January 1977, with a new 19 Squadron being formed at RAF Wildenrath equipped with the F-4 Phantom FGR.2. The other Lightning squadron at Gutersloh, 92 Squadron, would follow the same path three months later. This meant that there would be a glut of about thirty ex-Lightning pilots on the market, all looking for good postings. Some went to the F-4 and some, not surprisingly, to the Lightning squadrons at Binbrook in the UK; some even got ground tours, but there was little else on offer.

Flying Lightnings in the UK wasn't the next step that I wanted. One day in the future I wanted to be able to call myself a good pilot in an all-round sense, not just a good Lightning pilot. Also, at this stage of my life and career I wasn't ready to give up my coveted single-seat cockpit, with all the challenges and satisfaction that comes with being entirely responsible for the aircraft and for the success or failure of a sortie, without having to share it with a navigator. So, I didn't want to be posted to the F-4 either.

My three-year tour in the front line in Germany had been intense and all-consuming. It had been hard work and had taken something of a toll on me. It is interesting to note that between 1974 and 1976, five RAF Lightnings had crashed, with two pilots killed and three having ejected (none of them from the Germany squadrons). In the last year alone, the RAF had lost twenty-five fast-jet aircraft with fourteen aircrew killed. Accident rates were so much higher than we are used to today. I was feeling tired and I was beginning to think that I was in need of a 'rest tour'.

I also decided that a formal qualification could be a useful addition to my flying career, so I volunteered for the Central Flying School (CFS) to become a Qualified Flying Instructor (QFI). I more than met the minimum standards and my application was accompanied by strong recommendations from my squadron commander and the station commander, who both thought I would make a good instructor. Unusually for a fast-jet fighter pilot, I also placed a request to become an instructor at the elementary level, flying the Scottish Aviation Bulldog trainer, as I thought it would be interesting to teach students to fly from scratch, rather than to teach them to fly at a later stage of their training. In addition, I wondered if some piston-engine propeller experience might one day help me to get closer to flying a Spitfire. My application for CFS was accepted, as was my request for Bulldogs, and I was posted initially to RAF Cranwell for the ground school phase of the CFS course, starting in February 1977. Once that was completed, the Bulldog flying part of the QFI course would take place at RAF Leeming in North Yorkshire where I had completed my Basic Flying Training in 1971-72.

On Christmas Eve 1976 I was promoted to flight lieutenant, having done my time as an acting pilot officer, pilot officer and flying officer. As my

Germany Lightning tour ended, I was just short of 26 years old and it seemed that I was finally going to have to start growing up.

The reports written about me during my tour had a recurring theme of determination and hard work overcoming deficiencies in natural skill as a pilot, but at the end of the tour I was delighted to be rated above average as a fighter pilot and well above average as a combat pilot and leader. The station commander wrote in my final report that 'Rowley is particularly impressive in his handling of emergencies in the air, of which he has had more than his share.'

I had just over 650 flying hours on the Lightning and just short of 1,000 hours total flying. As someone who had just wanted to be a fighter pilot, I really couldn't have asked for more than an 'Above Average' rating in my logbook, but now it was off to new pastures and new challenges.

Chapter 6

Bulldog Instructor

Central Flying School Course

The ground school phase of the Central Flying School (CFS) course took place at RAF Cranwell, where the CFS Headquarters was located, and lasted almost two months. There was much to learn, to a higher standard than we had needed as student pilots. The subjects included Aerodynamics, Meteorology and 'Tech' (the technical details of the aircraft you were going to fly and be instructing on). In addition, there was some excellent tuition on instructional techniques to be employed on the ground and in the air, including the psychology of students and how to present a lesson in a classroom environment.

We were tested not only to ensure that we had the requisite level of knowledge in the subjects themselves, but also in our ability to teach them to a group of students, simulated by our course-mates. I found it very interesting and enjoyable. Amazingly, for someone who had been such a dullard at school, the final results saw me in second place out of twenty students on the ground school course. A perfect result as far as I was concerned, as coming top could see you recommended for an appointment as a ground instructor, a fate worse than death.

*****

In April 1976 I arrived back at RAF Leeming, where I had undergone my Basic Flying Training, to complete the flying part of the CFS course on the Bulldog. To my amusement, the building we worked in was the same one I had occupied as a student on the Basic Flying Training course some years earlier. It was good to see that the coffee bar we had built as students from local stone was still standing in the crew room, as it did for many years afterwards. It was not something that could be easily removed.

The Scottish Aviation Bulldog T.1 was a two-seat side-by-side dual-control low-wing training aircraft, which had been developed as a more powerful, increased-wingspan version of the civilian Beagle Pup. It was powered by a 200 hp Lycoming four-cylinder air-cooled engine, driving a two-bladed variable-pitch propeller, and featured a comfortable cockpit, with a fully-transparent sliding canopy. The Bulldog was fully aerobatic, with limits of just over 5G to minus 2G and a limiting airspeed, in a dive, of 185 knots. The pilots wore backpack parachutes and standard RAF flying helmets, with a boom microphone rather than a mask, as the aircraft service ceiling meant that oxygen was neither required nor available.

I found the Bulldog very enjoyable to fly, although I quickly had to learn to use my feet on the rudder pedals more than I was used to in the air to keep the aircraft in balance and pointing the same way it was going. With propeller-driven aircraft a number of factors mean that any change in speed or power setting will upset the directional balance, which will be indicated by the slip ball in the turn-and-slip indicator moving away from the middle. Keeping the ball in the middle became an important element of accurate flying. There was also an additional lever – the RPM lever – for controlling the constant-speed propeller which was something I had not had to deal with before.

The speed at which the aircraft covered the ground was also very different from my recent experience. On my first conversion sortie with a CFS instructor we took off on a beautiful clear day and climbed to height toward the Yorkshire Dales to the west of Leeming, eventually levelling off some ten minutes later at 8,000 feet. The training of RAF pilots relies heavily on the use of various mnemonics to remember checks. The relevant one in use by Training Command for this point of the sortie was 'FEEL': Fuel, Engine, Electrics and Location. When it came to 'Location', as far as I was concerned I could now be anywhere. In a Lightning I would be about ninety miles from base in that time. I took out my map and started matching ground features to the map. The CFS instructor took control, turned back through 90 degrees, dropped a wing and said, 'Look. Leeming.' Heading into the wind we hadn't travelled very far at all and the airfield was still clearly visible. It was embarrassing but also amusing. Clearly, I was going to have to adapt to this slower rate of progress.

CFS taught you to become a master of your craft and to make the aircraft do exactly what you were asking it to do. The ability to fly accurately was vital to effective demonstrations and teaching in the air, and it was also an expected skill. Up to this point in my flying career I had tended to believe that as long as I achieved the 'end game' with an aircraft, the exact details of how we got there were unimportant. Now we were being told that it did matter. I bought into this mindset and it was to change my personal attitude to flying (and other aspects of life) forever. From here on I strove for accuracy and perfection in everything, rarely of course achieving either for very long, but constantly trying to be that master of my craft. In some ways it perhaps takes some of the carefree fun out of flying, if you are forever dissatisfied unless your aircraft is exactly on the parameters you have set for it, but it undoubtedly makes you a better pilot.

The conversion to the Bulldog was short and quick. I went solo after two dual flights and the phase was completed in just three weeks. Then it was on to the 'patter' exercises in which we learned, practised and 'gave back' the various airborne training sequences of the elementary flying training syllabus. Being able to talk about what you are doing whilst flying the aircraft accurately and precisely is a fundamental skill of a flying instructor. The patter is best presented in a non-conversational style with short phrases at exactly the correct moment. Most exercises were broken down into building-block components. Turning, for example, would be broken down into entry, maintain and exit, which would not necessarily be taught in that order: maintain, exit, entry would probably be the slickest and easiest. At the elementary training stage it was generally considered to be a bad idea to talk to the students whilst they were flying the aircraft, due to their limited capacity at that stage of training and the likelihood of distraction.

*****

My course-mates on the Bulldog CFS course were all more experienced than me, with all but one of them coming from a multi-engine large aircraft background, mainly Vulcans and Nimrods. The exception was Brian Skillicorn who had been a helicopter test pilot. He was a brilliant pilot and flew vintage aircraft with the Shuttleworth Collection at weekends.

During the brief night-flying phase of the course I reached what for me was a considerable milestone, my first 1,000 hours total flying. I think I had been making a bit of a fuss leading up to it although the rest of the course had many more hours than this and 1,000 did not mean much to them at all. As it seemed to matter to me, they were kind enough to meet me from the night sortie in which I clocked up the 1,000 hours, with beer, to congratulate me.

As the end of the CFS course approached there was an aerobatic competition for the students. Those who got through the elimination stage, which included me, were worked down to 1,000 feet over the airfield for the competition. It was won by Brian Skillicorn and I came second. He had some very unusual and advanced aerobatic manoeuvres in his display sequence, including a so-called *Cap Lomcovak* (Czech for headache) where, at the top of a stall turn in knife-edge flight, the aircraft is made to pivot around its wing line before the stall turn is completed. He wouldn't reveal to me his secrets of how this was done and it later took me hours of individual experimenting, to the point of making myself feel ill, to perfect the manoeuvre myself.

*****

When it came to postings, I had asked to go to a university air squadron. I was posted to RAF Woodvale as a QFI with Manchester and Salford University Air Squadron. I didn't know Woodvale but it sounded fine. Then it was discovered that I was a bachelor and the hutted accommodation for the officers' mess at RAF Woodvale was not considered suitable for a permanent living-in officer. My posting was changed to send me to Queen's University Air Squadron in Belfast, Northern Ireland. However, the pilot originally posted there actually wanted to go and didn't want to swap with me. After some negotiation we were both allowed to keep our original postings. It is on small things like that, completely beyond your control, that your fate hangs and your life could be changed in an instant, forever. If I hadn't been posted to Woodvale, I would never have met my wife.

Chipmunk

Having finished the CFS course, I discovered that the UAS to which I was posted was on block leave for a month, having just returned from the month-long intensive annual flying camp. This was the normal annual routine for the UASs. There seemed little point in turning up there to do nothing for a month. Meanwhile, a signal had been sent around the RAF asking for volunteer pilots to help out with flying at various Air Cadet camps at RAF bases. This meant flying the DH Chipmunk T.10 tail-wheel trainer, which was still used by the air experience flights to provide such experience to cadets. I had never flown a tail-wheel aircraft and thought that my education as a pilot was somewhat lacking in this respect, especially as

I still harboured that hidden and far-fetched desire to maybe one day fly a Spitfire, so I volunteered.

For two weeks in August 1977 I returned to RAF Coltishall, where I had trained on Lightnings in 1973, but which was now home to several SEPECAT Jaguar squadrons and which was hosting air cadet camps during the school summer holidays. The flight commander and the Chipmunk aircraft of No. 2 Air Experience Flight (AEF) had been deployed to Coltishall from Hamble for the summer.

The AEF flight commander, Flight Lieutenant Pete Houghton, was not best pleased when he discovered that I was not Chipmunk-qualified, although I had volunteered sincerely, not thinking that to be a requirement. I was left to my own devices for a couple of days during which I devoured the Chipmunk *Pilot's Notes*, learned the checks from the flight reference cards and asked him many questions, which at least showed a professional interest. Pete Houghton was a wartime pilot who had also flown Meteors and he turned out to be an absolutely brilliant instructor. In fact, he held the highest category of instructional qualification, A1. He answered all my questions superbly, often with diagrams. My obvious interest led to him taking me flying and it appeared that he was impressed with what he saw. For my part I never forgot some of the things he taught me, especially about the techniques for landing tail-wheel aircraft. Years later I was saying the same things to pilots on the Battle of Britain Memorial Flight.

After three hours and thirty minutes of dual instruction with him, I had passed the Chipmunk Flying Ability Test. Then, having completed the requisite five hours Chipmunk flying with some solo sorties, I flew thirty-one cadets over the next week and built some useful tail-wheel experience. Over the next couple of years, I was able to fly Chipmunks with the AEF at Woodvale from time to time and built my tail-wheel hours and experience further.

University Air Squadron Instructor

RAF Woodvale is not quite like anywhere else in the RAF. On the west coast of England, just south of the holiday town of Southport with its nightlife, the small airfield is nestled behind the sand dunes and between the towns of Ainsdale, immediately to the north, and Formby, to the south. The resident units were two University Air Squadrons – Manchester and Salford University Air Squadron (MASUAS) and Liverpool University Air

Squadron (LUAS) – operating the Bulldog, plus an air experience flight, which flew Chipmunks. The airfield was run under contract, with the air traffic controllers and all of the engineers being civilians. The ten RAF officers on the station, who were also the flying instructors, were the only full-time RAF personnel on the base. None of the normal support facilities of an RAF station were present at Woodvale, which was parented by RAF Sealand, a maintenance unit, where we had to go for things like annual medicals and stores. The squadron leader in command of one of the UASs at Woodvale was the Station Commander and the other was OC Operations. Woodvale was definitely out of the mainstream of the RAF and was the more charming for it.

UASs vary in size, but MASUAS had about fifty students divided between five instructors, although the instructors did not fly exclusively with their own allocated students. As undergraduates, the students' main focus had to be successful completion of their degrees. UAS activities, including flying, came second, although some seemed to have that the other way round and were to be found at the airfield at every opportunity. A handful of students were on bursaries and committed to a career in the RAF, already holding the rank of acting pilot officer, whilst all the others were cadet pilots, who in many cases would never be accepted by the RAF. These students had been recruited by the UAS itself via a formal selection process but with no aptitude testing. This provided an interesting spread of ability and natural aptitude, or in some cases lack of it, for the instructors to work with.

The normal working week for the UASs was Wednesday to Sunday, with flying on Wednesday, a 'town headquarters' night for ground training on Thursday evening with a late finish, and flying at the airfield from Friday afternoon through to Sunday. Our days off were usually Mondays and Tuesdays.

When I arrived at Woodvale, as a brand-new B2 category QFI, I was still only 26 years old, only a few years older than the students themselves, I was still a bachelor and looked younger than my years. There was an amusing incident on my first night in the officers' mess when I met some of the senior students in the TV room and they mistook me for a new student. Some of the third-year student pilots actually had more hours on the Bulldog than I did when I arrived.

Initially, for some months, I lived in the officers' mess, where the civilian staff did their very best to look after their only living-in officer. I was allocated two rooms in one of the accommodation huts, so that I could have a lounge as well as a bedroom. There was a particular problem on Mondays and Tuesdays – the UAS 'weekend' – when I was off duty and literally the only person living in the mess. I would be asked at breakfast what I fancied for dinner as it would be cooked specially for me. On a Monday or Tuesday in order to get a drink from the bar, which was locked up and unmanned on those days, I had to become the bar officer, so that I could have a key, help myself and note the purchase in my bar book to go on my mess bill. Eventually, I got fed up with this off-duty lifestyle and, after a prolonged campaign, aided by my squadron commander, I was granted permission to live out with a rent allowance paid by the RAF. I moved into an apartment in the Birkdale area of Southport and looked after myself.

That squadron commander, Squadron Leader Mike Schofield, OC MASUAS, was absolutely brilliant with me, appreciating what I 'brought to the party' as a young and punchy ex-Lightning pilot. He liked the relationship that I had with the students and the example I set to them. He encouraged me no end and let me have my head. Mike was a good pilot and instructor and finished his RAF career as Captain of the Queen's Flight.

Many of the students that I flew with and instructed at Woodvale went on to become pilots in the RAF, several of them fast-jet pilots. One of those I flew with frequently, early in my time with MASUAS, was Chris Moran, who went on to fly Harriers. I was to meet him again when he was an Air Vice Marshal and the Air Officer Commanding (AOC) 1 Group, whilst I was the Officer Commanding the Battle of Britain Memorial Flight (BBMF). We flew together again in a BBMF Chipmunk in April 2004. Subsequently, he was promoted to Air Chief Marshal, knighted and became Commander-in-Chief of Air Command. Chris Moran was a keep-fit fanatic and triathlete; sadly, he collapsed and died after a triathlon in May 2010, aged just 54.

Another student pilot I flew with on MASUAS was Brian Weatherly who also became a Harrier pilot. Sadly, he lost his life in June 1986 whilst he was the RAF Germany Harrier display pilot. His Harrier got into difficulties in the hover and pitched vertically nose down, Brian ejected parallel to the ground and did not survive.

Three other Woodvale UAS students became Lightning pilots at Binbrook and we met again when I was posted there in 1984. It is always a good idea to be nice to those below you in rank or position, as you never know when the roles may be reversed. One of my students with whom I flew most at Woodvale was Alan Page. When I arrived on 11 Squadron at Binbrook to fly Lightnings again, in 1984, he was made my mentor for my work up to Combat Ready and gave me quite a hard time. Two years later he was working for me when I was given command of the Lightning Training Flight and he was one of my instructors.

*****

In November 1977, at a party in the officers' mess at Woodvale, I met the Southport girl, Elaine, who was to become my wife. She had come along with a girlfriend and we were drawn together – eyes across a crowded room and all that – spending the whole evening talking and dancing together. We quickly became boyfriend and girlfriend and, indeed, best friends, which we have been ever since. I proposed to her on St Valentine's Day in February 1978 in the Valentine's card I handed to her personally at lunchtime that day, nervously awaiting her response whilst she read it. Elaine has always maintained that it was the only romantic thing that I ever did. In truth I thought writing the proposal down in the card meant that I couldn't chicken out at the last moment. She said 'Yes'.

We were married in her local church in the Churchtown area of Southport in September 1978. The vicar was an ex-wartime RAF Lancaster rear gunner whose experiences had turned him to the cloth after the war. He was pleased to be conducting the marriage ceremony for someone wearing his service's uniform and sporting RAF wings too. As we exited the church there were the traditional two lines of uniformed RAF officers forming an archway with their swords for the bride and groom to walk through. Some of the sword bearers were RAF friends from my previous tour at Gutersloh, and some were instructor colleagues at Woodvale. Soon afterwards, Elaine and I moved from my flat in Southport into our first married quarter in Formby. Elaine worked in a bank in Southport Monday to Friday; I worked Wednesday to Sunday, so we hardly ever had a day off together.

*****

In November 1978, only two months after Elaine and I were married, I was deeply saddened to learn of the death of one of my friends and sword-bearers from our wedding, in an accident in an F-4 Phantom FG.1. Flight Lieutenant Chris Jones had been on 19 Squadron at Gutersloh with me for virtually all of my three-year tour. We had been fellow bachelors living in the officers' mess and we were good friends. I was with him at the party at the NATO headquarters at Brunssum, in the Netherlands, when he met the lovely WRAF officer, Dot, who became his wife, and I was at their wedding at Gutersloh a few months later. Chris was an extremely capable and aggressive fighter pilot. He was clever, too. Chris had been posted from the Lightning to F-4 Phantoms and had recently completed the qualified weapon instructor (QWI) course, no mean achievement; he was on track for greater things. On the night of 23 November 1978 he was flying a 111 Squadron Phantom FG.1 from RAF Leuchars in Fife, Scotland, when the aircraft crashed into the sea, ten miles from Bell Rock, during the approach to Leuchars. Chris and his navigator, Mike Stephenson, were both killed. The FG.1 variant of the Phantom did not have a battery as part of the electrical system and I believe that Chris's aircraft suffered a double generator failure with a loss of everything electrical, including lighting, in the dark. Why they didn't eject immediately I don't know; perhaps he thought he'd got it under control.

Chris's death came as a great shock to me and also to Elaine who had only met him at our wedding a few weeks before and was no doubt now wondering what she had married into. For me it caused a complete shift in my attitude towards the chances of being killed in an aircraft. Up to that point I'd had a rather head-in-the-sand 'it won't happen to me' attitude, based on being able to believe that whatever had caused the various accidents I heard and read about, I wouldn't make that sort of mistake: I was more careful than that. Now, I thought that if it could happen to Chris, whose abilities I knew were as good as or even better than mine, then it could also happen to me. No longer could I take the 'it won't happen to me' viewpoint. Fortunately, I was able to rationalise it all and, from then on, my attitude was that I would do everything in my power to minimise the risks over which I had any control; everything beyond that, which was not under my control, there was just no point worrying about. That attitude worked for me and saw me through the rest of my flying career without stress ever becoming an issue and my enthusiasm for flying remaining undiminished. Neither did it stop me taking calculated risks but they were carefully calculated; I think that I became quite good at risk assessment and hazard awareness.

*****

That same month I was told to pack up my desk at MASUAS and move across to the Liverpool UAS (LUAS) building where I was to be the Chief Flying Instructor (CFI). This came as a surprise, as I hadn't sought additional responsibility and was already making clear my determination to remain in flying posts throughout a full career rather than follow the path of promotion, which would inevitably lead to ground staff tours. This attitude tended to frustrate those in command who wrote my reports as they saw their remit to be pointing everyone in the career promotion direction. Nevertheless, there I was on LUAS as the CFI, with two other instructors of the same rank, but much greater seniority, age and experience, theoretically working for me. Why one of them hadn't got the job ahead of me is still a mystery to me. I was now responsible for the day-to-day running of the flying programme and the supervision that went with that, liaising with the engineers over aircraft availability and planning and organising things such as the deployment for the month-long summer camp, in this case to RAF St Mawgan in Cornwall. I actually enjoyed the organising and the admin that went with it, although I pretended to hate paperwork.

In April 1979 I passed my re-categorisation test to become an A2 category instructor, which was defined as Above Average. It had taken me three attempts and I had studied hard for the mammoth ground-school examination which took four hours, as well as for the flying test.

The annual camp saw us deploying our four aircraft to St Mawgan from early July to early August 1979. The transit flight across the Bristol Channel from South Wales to Cornwall was one of those occasions when my attitude to risk was shown to be quite different from the other instructors on the UAS, who all had multi-engine backgrounds. As we crossed the water of the Bristol Channel in a four-ship of aircraft, three of them were flying at only a couple of thousand feet with no chance of making the coastline if their single engine failed. I was at 10,000 feet within gliding range the whole time. They had the 'it won't happen to me' mentality; I didn't. After landing, they all wanted to know what I had been doing up there. In the four weeks at St Mawgan I flew over sixty-five hours, often flying four or five instructional sorties each day. It was intense, tiring, rewarding and successful.

At the end of October 1979 my tour at Woodvale came to a sudden and abrupt end with a short-notice posting to RAF Leeming to join the CFS Standardisation Squadron. It appeared that I had been head hunted by the unit which had prepared me for my A2 re-categorisation; they had been impressed with what they had seen of me and they wanted me to teach other UAS instructors preparing for an 'A2 re-cat'. Nothing I said would alter anyone's minds, I had to go.

Central Flying School Standards Instructor

We moved ourselves, with a rented truck, from our married quarter in Formby to a nice married quarter in The Square at Leeming. When we were 'marched in' by the Warrant Officer Families Officer he asked if we'd be needing a cot. We said we didn't. He said we would. He was right. Our daughter, Suzanne, was born ten months later in Catterick Military Hospital.

It wasn't easy for Elaine, who couldn't yet drive, being stuck on the married patch at Leeming, miles from anywhere, with a baby and an energetic young Labrador dog to deal with, whilst I was at work Monday to Friday. There were only very occasional buses to the local town of Northallerton. We very much valued our weekends when we could get out and do things as a family, including the shopping, with visits to Ripon and York as well as trips out into the beautiful countryside of the North York Moors and the Yorkshire Dales.

I worked in a very small team of standardisation instructors, separated from the main CFS Standards Squadron in a building opposite. Without any great oversight or supervision, we were pretty much left to get on with the job ourselves. I worked closely with the other Bulldog standards instructor, Flight Lieutenant Dave Walby, who it transpired had been largely instrumental in head hunting me for the job. He was a brilliant pilot and instructor, with a background on Vulcans but an attitude that could easily have made him a fighter pilot. I learned much from him, especially about instructing. We took QFIs from the UASs all over the country and from the Royal Navy Elementary Flying School (RNEFTS) – which also flew the Bulldog – and put them through a two-week course to work them up for their re-categorisation to A2 standard. This involved a half day of ground school on most days, making sure that they had the knowledge, understood the details and could teach the subjects to a student with full use of the whiteboard and four coloured pens. The other half of each day we flew, practising the likely test profiles and sequences and ensuring the instructors had the latest 'best practice' for the sequences and the patter. We had a high success rate when we put instructors forward for their A2 re-cats and the nature of the job undoubtedly improved my knowledge and instructional skills too. Sometimes, when we didn't have any instructor students on a course, I would fly with elementary student pilots of the RNEFTS or the co-located Northumberland UAS.

In November 1979 I was flying a general handling sortie with one of the RNEFTS instructors, Flight Lieutenant Harvey Spirit, who had been a fellow Lightning pilot with me on 19 Squadron in Germany. Harvey had subsequently ejected from a Hawker Hunter with an engine failure and damaged his back such that he could no longer fly on ejection seats. He was now a Bulldog QFI with RNEFTS. We were flying visual circuits at RAF Topcliffe with full cloud cover above us when I was surprised to see two parachutes emerge from the cloud on the downwind leg of the circuit. I immediately pointed these out to Harvey and then reported them to air traffic control on the radio. The local controller informed us that the parachutes were the crew of a Bulldog that had just been abandoned in the overhead. It transpired that the student pilot had lost control in turbulent cloud and the instructor had been unable to recover the situation, so they abandoned the aircraft and took to their parachutes. We located them in a field just outside the airfield, both apparently unharmed and waving at us, and we indicated to air traffic control where they were by orbiting above the field. With crash crews and an ambulance on the way to them we were then sent off to find the Bulldog crash site, which we located in another field near Skipton-on-Swale where, fortunately, it had crashed without harming anyone or anything. This had turned out to be a more exciting sortie than we had been expecting. I was subsequently required to assist the board of inquiry as an expert witness.

In the spring of 1980 I was put forward for the CFS in-house aerobatic competition, the Brabyn Trophy. Over a period of weeks I was selected as the Bulldog aerobatic pilot and worked down to fly my aerobatic sequence over the airfields with a minimum height of 500 feet. My aerobatic sequence was quite advanced for the Bulldog, starting with a dive towards the display line at 90 degrees to it, reaching maximum speed to pull up from 500 feet into a vertical 360-degree roll with a stall turn at the top. It also included some fancy manoeuvres, such as a so-called 'salmon leap' (pulling up to the vertical, yawing off 45 degrees, rolling through 360 degrees and completing the stall turn to be pointing vertically downwards), an eight-point hesitation roll from inverted to inverted, which took some time and was only really viable with the slow speed of the Bulldog, ideally into a strong headwind, and the *Cap Lomcovak*, which I had copied from Brian Skillicorn after much practice. On the day of the competition, which was held at Leeming, with a strong wind blowing down the line, I was up against two Jet Provosts and a Hawk jet trainer. Much to my surprise I won. I could call myself the champion aerobatic pilot of the Central Flying School and I was able to keep the beautiful Brabyn Trophy, a silver Meteor, on my mantelpiece until I was posted.

*****

With the end of my tour looming I became more realistic about likely postings and had to drop some of my more fanciful ideas. It became obvious that I was going to be sent back into the fast-jet world and my desk officer wanted to post me back to Lightnings at Binbrook. I learned that the recently reformed No. 2 Tactical Weapons Unit (TWU) flying the Hawk at RAF Chivenor was potentially in need of QFIs on the staff. I hadn't flown the Hawk and it seemed like a super little jet. Also, I knew how pleasant it was to be based at Chivenor, having been a student there on the Hunter in 1973. I spoke with my desk officer and asked if I could volunteer as a TWU instructor. The job of the posting desk officers is to fit pegs into holes and here he had a perfectly-shaped peg for one of his holes. He bit my arm off and posting notices duly arrived. Before actually joining the staff on the TWU at Chivenor I would have to complete the TWU Long Course and a staff work-up on the Hawk at Brawdy, starting in February 1981.

My instructional tour, which as it transpired was a mere interlude in a career of fast-jet flying, came to an end in November 1980, just after I had reached 1,000 hours flying on the Bulldog. I had achieved that total in only slightly over three and a half years, averaging 285 hours flying per year during that tour. Most sorties were of an hour or less, so that number of flying hours represents a similar number of sorties

Before I left Leeming, I managed to scrounge some Jet Provost flying in an attempt to speed up and re-build my G-tolerance ready for the fast-jet world. The RAF system, in its wisdom, saw no need for me to have any sort of official refresher flying course after more than three years flying at 150 knots or less. During December 1980 I flew fifteen hours on Jet Provost T.5As with the Refresher Flying School (RFS) at Leeming, including a couple of solos, mostly involving low-level navigation sorties, close formation and tail chases. It was extremely useful flying and very good of the RFS to provide it as it was completely unofficial.

Just before Christmas 1980 we packed up our married quarter at Leeming and 'marched out'. We moved to RAF Brawdy, near Haverfordwest in Pembrokeshire, Wales, where we 'marched in' to another rather grotty looking married quarter, with olive-green rendering and mould on the walls, and windows with metal frames that were not double glazed and streamed with condensation. This was to be our home for the next six months. At least the married quarter patch was situated on the edge of Haverfordwest town and not at the airfield, so Elaine could walk into town.

Chapter 7

Tactical Weapons Unit
Hawk Instructor

The Hawk

Before commencing the Tactical Weapons Unit (TWU) Long Course at Brawdy I managed to scrounge an unofficial introduction to the Hawk at RAF Valley by pulling some strings with ex-Lightning friends who were Hawk instructors there. In January 1981 I sat through a short ground school for the Hawk at Valley, including some simulator time. I then attended the required course at the Aviation Medical Training Centre at North Luffenham, where I was once again rendered hypoxic at 25,000 feet in the decompression chamber and explosively decompressed from 25,000 feet to 45,000 feet. Back at Valley I scrounged eleven hours flying in Hawks. I even flew solo which, considering that this was not an officially recognised course, was very good of the particular instructor who let me do it. This was to be a most valuable introduction to the aircraft because, at Brawdy, with the other ab-initio students on the Long Course all being Hawk-qualified, there were no plans to treat me any differently and there would be no special conversion to type for me; I was just expected to get on with it.

The Hawker Siddeley Hawk T.1, well known as the mount of the Red Arrows, was a brilliant little jet to fly. Designed from the outset as an advanced jet trainer with a combat capability, the prototype had first flown in 1974 and the T.1 variant entered service with the RAF in 1976, replacing the Folland Gnat as the advanced trainer at Valley and, over the next few years, taking over from the Hawker Hunter at the TWUs. The Hawk had a neat and comfortable two-seat tandem cockpit fitted with gunsights and Martin Baker Mk 10B zero-height, zero-speed, rocket-assisted ejection seats. The design of the fuselage gave the instructor in the rear seat excellent visibility forwards over the top of the front-cockpit ejection seat and the all-round view from the cockpit was superb. The Rolls Royce Turbomeca Adour two-shaft low bypass turbofan engine produced 5,200 pounds of thrust and was both reliable and economical with fuel. The flight controls were hydraulically powered and a ram-air turbine continued to provide hydraulic power in the event of an engine failure. (The Hawk could glide well for a fast jet and if a runway was within gliding range an engine failure did not necessarily mean that ejection was the only option.)

At the TWUs the Hawk almost always carried a gun-pod – with a single 30mm Aden cannon – under the fuselage on the centreline station, and frequently carried weapons on the wing pylons, usually either Carrier Bomb Light Stores (CBLS) containers for practice bombs (four practice bombs in each, eight total) or SNEB rocket pods. Unlike the red-and-white painted Training Command Hawks, the TWU Hawks were camouflaged with the same schemes as front-line RAF fighter aircraft, initially grey and green and later air defence grey.

The Hawk was delightful to fly, being sensitive and responsive on the controls. I warmed to the feel of the aircraft immediately and found that its handling inspired confidence. It flew more like a straight-wing aircraft than a swept-wing one and on the approach to land you pointed it at the runway threshold (rather than pointing your feet at it with the nose up in the air as in a Lightning). The Hawk had an excellent rate of roll; in fact, it was very easy for the pilot who wasn't flying the aircraft to have his head smacked against the canopy as it got 'left behind' if the flying pilot unexpectedly rolled it rapidly. The impressive turn rate and radius endowed the Hawk with excellent manoeuvrability. It was a great little dog-fighter which could hold its own in a turning fight against the likes of F-15s and F-16s and which would out-turn most of the RAF's front-line aircraft of the time. The airframe was very strong with high G limits; 7.2G to minus 3.5G in the configurations we used at the TWUs. Occasional over-stresses up to 9G rarely did any damage to the aircraft beyond a few popped rivets, although they could be more damaging to the pilot's neck, as I was to discover later when another pilot did it to me. The Hawk's maximum airspeed was limited to 550 knots (500 knots with underwing stores fitted) at lower levels and M0.88 at height, although it could be pushed supersonic in a dive up to M1.2 when not carrying underwing stores.

If the Hawk had a fault as a fast-jet training aircraft it was perhaps that it was actually a little too easy to fly and it was difficult to instil the importance of fuel management into student pilots, as simply pulling up and slowing down almost always brought you back onto the 'fuel line'.

My first experiences of the Hawk at Valley were spoiled only by having to wear, once again, the heavy and cumbersome winter flying kit with G-suit, external immersion suit, life preserver, bone dome and oxygen mask. My first couple of trips wearing all the kit, strapped tightly into the ejection seat and pulling considerably more G than I had been used to for the last four years, felt very uncomfortable and constricted. I soon got used to it again though, which was just as well, as this was to be my working environment for the next twenty-two years.

Tactical Weapons Unit Course Brawdy

When I started flying at Brawdy on the TWU Long Course in February 1981, my suspicions about how little sympathy I would get for my limited experience on the Hawk were confirmed. After three dual flights to familiarise me with the local area, the procedures and the diversion airfields, I flew a solo sortie. The very next trip was an instrument-rating test, which, somehow, I passed. Then it was straight into the tactical flying elements of the course with tactical battle-formation flying and cine-weave gunsight-tracking exercises.

The next month, with only fifteen hours flying on the course behind me, I was regularly visiting Pembrey Range, just north of the Gower Peninsula on the south Wales coast near Kidwelly, to strafe, bomb and rocket ground targets. It was all enormous fun as I had never before dropped bombs, even practice ones, having been on the Air Defence TWU course as a student, and I had never fired the SNEB rockets. Whilst I enjoyed the weapons work tremendously, I found myself more concerned about flying the aircraft back home from the range to land, as I still had so few hours on type.

In April and May, with most of the weapons work on the course completed, I was exposed to the TWU teaching for air combat manoeuvring on 1v1 and 2v1 combat sorties, with the aircraft simulating being gun-armed only. My air combat skills honed on Lightnings in Germany had apparently not faded too much as a result of my tour as a Bulldog QFI and I was graded above average in this phase of the course. I also flew on low-level navigation exercises, flying around Wales at 250 feet and 420 knots, and then using those techniques in simulated attack profile sorties, initially with a pair of Hawks and then as a four-ship. These sorties involved low-level navigation, in battle formations, to attack simulated ground targets, later with a bounce aircraft, another Hawk, added into the mix, trying to shoot us down and

Above: Bournemouth School Combined Cadet Force RAF Section during an Easter Camp at RAF Colerne in 1968. Cadet Rowley is in the middle row third from left, sporting a gliding badge.

Below: Pilot Officer Rowley with a Jet Provost T.5 on completion of the Basic Flying Training Course at 3 FTS RAF Leeming in August 1972.

Left: A very proud day. Award of RAF pilot's 'wings' on 4 August 1972.

Below: The author with a Hunter F.6 of 4 FTS RAF Valley, during Advanced Flying Training in 1973.

Above: Lightning F.2A XN790 tail letter L of 19 Squadron, based at RAF Gutersloh, Germany. XN790 carried the author's name under the cockpit as 'FLG OFF C M ROWLEY'. Photo taken by the author from another single-seat Lightning.

Right: The author with the refuelling hose from a Victor tanker, knocked off over land whilst attempting to connect in August 1974. See 'Tanking Calamity'. (*Tony Paxton*)

Above: Battle Flight scramble at Gutersloh. The requirement was to be airborne within five minutes of the bell sounding.

Below: A McDonnell F-4 'Phantom' in the gunsight of Clive Rowley's Lightning F.2A. In the mid-1970s the Lightning was at least a match for any other aircraft that it was likely to meet, either in training or for real.

Above: B Flight pilots of 19 Sqn, June 1975, with top buttons undone and fighter pilot poses. Left to right: Sqn Ldr John 'Spon' Spencer, Fg Off Tim Neville, Flt Lt Al Martin, Fg Off Clive Rowley, Flt Lt Paul Cooper, Flt Lt John Brady, Flt Lt John Dobson and Flt Lt Phil Owen. (*UK MOD*)

Below: A pair of Lightning F.2As of 19 Sqn taking off in close formation at Gutersloh in 1976.

Above: Reheat fire damage to Lightning F.2A XN789 F, which occurred during a sortie with the author as the pilot, on 11 May 1976.

Below: Lightning F.2A XN786 M in which the author had a second reheat fire. (*Pete Hodgson*)

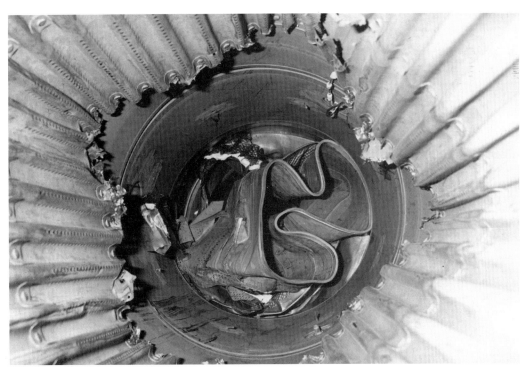

Above: The jet pipe failure which caused a reheat fire warning and control restriction when the author was flying Lightning F.2A XN786 M on 4 August 1976.

Right: Flying Officer Clive Rowley, aged 25, towards the end of a three-year front-line tour on Lightnings in Germany in October 1976.

Award of the Queen's Commendation for Valuable Service in the Air in October 1976. The certificate was presented by Air Marshal Sir Michael Beetham (C.-in-C. RAF Germany). Left to right: Sqn Ldr John 'Spon' Spencer, Air Marshal Beetham, author, Wg Cdr Bob Barcilon (OC 19 Sqn), Gr Capt Peter Collins (RAF Gutersloh Station Commander) and Sqn Ldr John May. (*UK MOD*)

needing to be countered. It was most pleasing to discover that the problems I had suffered with low-level navigation in advanced training at Valley in 1972-3 had now been overcome and I was assessed as high to above average in the low-level environment. In May we also completed some air-to-air gunnery, firing coloured ball rounds at a sleeve banner target towed by Brawdy's venerable Gloster Meteor F.8, named 'Winston', flown by the inimitable handlebar-moustachioed Flight Lieutenant 'Puddy' Cat.

On completion of the TWU Long Course I remained at Brawdy for another month to undergo the TWU staff work-up and standardisation course. At the end of that period I had been awarded a QFI 'ticket' on the Hawk, upgraded my instrument rating and had learned and been cleared to instruct the various elements of the TWU course to student pilots. Apart from transferring my instructional skills to a fast jet and to teaching tactics – how to operate and fight the aircraft – rather than just how to fly it, an interesting aspect was the need to sometimes monitor and instruct a solo student from another 'chase' aircraft instead of being in the same cockpit.

In June 1981 I moved my family to Devon, where we had purchased a house on the western outskirts of Barnstaple, a ten-minute drive from RAF Chivenor where I would be based with No. 2 TWU for the next two and half years. This was our fifth home in three years; but this one was ours.

TWU Instructor Chivenor

RAF Chivenor airfield is on the Taw Estuary, near Braunton, in north Devon, and was where I had completed the TWU course as a student pilot on the Hawker Hunter in 1973. The base was closed in 1974 and put on 'care and maintenance'. When I arrived there for the second time in mid-1981, to be part of the TWU staff, it had been re-opened as the home of No. 2 TWU for only a few months. There had been a considerable amount of new building work and I was pleased to see that the old wooden huts that formed the officers' mess in my student days had been replaced with a very modern brand-new brick building with excellent facilities. The airfield had two squadrons operating the Hawk in the TWU role, Nos. 63 and 151 Squadrons. I was posted to the former whose Hawks proudly wore the unit's yellow-and-black chequerboard 'fighter bars' on the aircraft's rear fuselage.

After the obligatory CO's arrival dual check I was straight into tactical instructional sorties with the current course, flying numerous air combat training (ACT) sorties and simulated attack profiles. In my first month with 63 Squadron I flew almost thirty hours.

It was not at all uncommon for the TWU instructors to fly two or sometimes three ACT sorties in one day, as I did frequently. These combat sorties subjected the Hawk aircrew to considerable amounts of sustained G, up to 7G, with the need to twist your head around to keep tally on the other aircraft and with the additional weight of the flying helmet multiplied by the G. I found that at the end of a day when I had flown two or three combat sorties, the muscles from my shoulders to my neck would be really sore and tight. During my tour on Hawks I had to start buying shirts with collars the next size up, due to the extra neck muscle I gained. It was quite interesting to see the effects of these air combat training sorties on the student pilots and even on experienced Hawk instructors from Valley when they came to the TWU. Despite being familiar with flying aerobatics in the Hawk, it wasn't the same as air combat manoeuvring when you have to move your head around more. The effect was to create dizziness and, when they climbed out of the aircraft after the sortie, they weaved their way off like drunks until they became more used to it.

Bombing

When I arrived at Chivenor the TWUs, and indeed the RAF, was in the process of converting to a new type of practice bomb with different ballistics from the old one, so I flew a 10-degree dive-bombing sortie on Pembrey Range with a QWI, Flight Lieutenant Stu Robinson, to learn the differences. He demonstrated the first bomb and received a 'DH' (Direct Hit) on the radio from the range controller who was observing where the practice bomb landed from the flash and smoke it produced. It couldn't have been a better demonstration. I copied what Stu had just shown me and got the same result, much to his surprise. We shared the eight bombs, four each, and every single one was a DH.

I was also taught and practised level bombing from 200 feet on the Pembrey Range as this method of delivery had been introduced into the course syllabus. The QWI for my dual level-bombing check-out sortie was John Marden. John was a really nice chap who went on to fly Jaguars. He subsequently became very ill and ultimately received a heart-and-lung transplant. Remarkably and inspirationally, he regained his fitness, returned to duty and was allowed to fly fast jets once again, albeit not solo. In August

1991, as the Wing Commander OC Operations Wing at RAF Coltishall, John was flying a two-seat Jaguar T.2 with Wing Commander Bill Pixton at low level over Wales. The aircraft was involved in a mid-air collision with a civilian light aircraft, a Cessna 152, which was found to have been operating at low level, photographing houses, without the necessary permission or notification. Both aircraft were destroyed in the crash, the Cessna pilot was killed and, although both Jaguar pilots ejected, only Bill Pixton survived. It seemed doubly sad that John died in such a way, aged only 40, after all that he had been through. This was planned to be John's last flight in a Jaguar before being posted. His family were waiting at RAF Coltishall for his return. He never did.

Board of Inquiry

On 21 October 1981 a two-seat Hawker Hunter T.7 from RAF Brawdy crashed into the sea fifty miles south-west of Brawdy. The two pilots, the instructor, Flight Lieutenant Dave Oakley, and his student, Squadron Leader Aubrey-Rees, ejected and were rescued by a search-and-rescue helicopter. A board of inquiry was convened and my name was pulled from the hat to be the type expert on the board, although I wasn't one. The president of the board was the Squadron Leader Operations at RAF Chivenor, Squadron Leader Becker.

We had to hot foot it to Brawdy, with me flying us both there in a Hawk the very next day. We started by interviewing the two pilots, who were recovering from their ordeal in hospital. Whilst it was an unwanted and enforced break from flying for me, the whole thing turned out to be a very interesting and educational experience, which shaped my thinking forever afterwards. From then on, I always thought about 'the subsequent board of inquiry' and whether I would be able to justify my actions if I ever found myself in front of one.

This accident had occurred as the TWU Hunter instructor was teaching visual recoveries from the vertical to the student. He put the aircraft into a steep climb, probably the true vertical, with rapidly reducing airspeed (at the time there was nothing to say you shouldn't do this) and gave control to the student. He did what he had been taught and centralised the controls, waiting for the aircraft to fall out and adopt a nose-down attitude with increasing airspeed, before flying it out. Much to their surprise the Hunter went into an inverted spin, something which no one outside the Boscombe Down test-pilot community had any experience of at that time. The instructor carried out the correct recovery actions for an inverted spin but, when the aircraft had not recovered by 10,000 feet, they both ejected.

It was decided that, as there was no suggestion of any technical failure, no attempt would be made to recover the aircraft wreckage from the deep water where it had crashed which in any case might not have been possible. The briefing we received from HQ 11 Group suggested that, as the accident had been caused by a loss of control, it must surely be the result of aircrew error; the hierarchy clearly expected the instructor pilot to be hung out to dry. The more we investigated the more we came to believe that the pilots had, in fact, done nothing wrong. Our views were backed up by test pilots' evidence which indicated that a Hunter could enter an inverted spin from those circumstances and that normal pilots could not be expected to recover from an inverted spin, which even test-pilot students fully prepared and briefed had difficulty doing. We concluded that it was an 'Operating Hazard' with no blame attached to the pilots. It took a while for the Group HQ to agree but, in the end, our findings were accepted.

Two years later, in 1983, the pilot of the Hunter, Dave Oakley, was involved in a mid-air collision between two Harriers conducting air combat training at 10,000 feet over Cambridgeshire and he was forced to eject for a second time. Sadly, the two pilots in the other Harrier, a T.4, were killed. The instructor was Flight Lieutenant John Leeming, an ex-Lightning pilot whom I knew, who had flown Sea Harriers with the Royal Navy during the Falklands War.

Instrument Rating Examiner

In late November 1981, despite the fact that my recent flying had been limited by my time spent on the ground with the board of inquiry, I was sent on a pre-planned Instrument Rating Examiner course at Brawdy. It was only seven sorties with some ground school and in early December I was awarded a Master Green instrument rating on the Hawk – the highest standard of instrument rating that exists in the RAF – and I became an Instrument Rating Examiner, qualified to conduct instrument rating tests on other pilots. I was now a qualified flying instructor, tactics instructor and instrument rating examiner on the Hawk and, as such, I was quite useful to my TWU squadron.

Hawk to Woodvale

In February 1982 I took a Hawk to RAF Woodvale, where I had been a University Air Squadron instructor just a few years previously, in order to show off the jet to the students and to attend a town headquarters night to give them a presentation on the TWU course. The idea was to motivate and to inspire the prospective fighter pilots amongst the Liverpool UAS students. I took Flying Officer Pete Lloyd with me in the back seat of the Hawk. He had been a student on Liverpool UAS during my time as an instructor and he was now a search and rescue Wessex helicopter pilot with 22 Squadron at Chivenor. He would talk to the UAS students about his role.

There was considerable interest in the camouflaged Hawk, with its centreline gun-pod and underwing CBLS practice bomb-carriers, after we had landed at Woodvale. The town headquarters evening went well, too. The next day the weather wasn't that great with an overcast at about 1,000 feet and visibility that was close to the minimum for low flying. I began to forget all ideas of any sort of beat up as I departed Woodvale. However, the UAS instructors had different ideas and tried their best to persuade me to put on a show. I resisted for a while but was eventually goaded into it. The only thing I can say in my defence was that I had a clear plan as to what I was going to do before I took off and I stuck to it. The history of aviation accidents indicates that making it up as you go along usually ends badly.

As Woodvale has built-up areas to the north and south of it, I turned onto east and headed inland immediately after take off to remain clear of the towns. I headed east for one minute and then turned back hard left onto west to run back towards the airfield at low level at about 420 knots. The visibility meant that, initially, I couldn't see the airfield but then I picked up an aerial mast that I knew was on its edge. Passing the mast, I banked hard left and ran past the hangar across the pan where the UAS Bulldogs were parked, probably at about 100 feet. Then I reversed hard right into a 6G turn around the air traffic control tower. As I passed it, I flew through a flock of whirling sea gulls, fortunately without hitting any. Continuing the turn I remained inside the airfield boundary and after 360 degrees I passed once again over the pan, this time in a 6G turn. Expecting that the gulls would by now have dispersed, I was surprised to find myself flying through them a second time as I completed the turn, again fortunately without hitting any. Then I rolled wings level, pointing out to sea, pitched up about 15 degrees and 'twinkle rolled' as I disappeared into the cloud.

Even in 1982 there were very few places in the RAF where you could get away with that sort of behaviour and there were never any repercussions. Today, such a thing would probably appear as a smart-phone video online within minutes and you would be court martialled.

Falklands War – Harrier Air Combat Training

In April 1982 Argentina invaded and occupied the British sovereign territory of the Falkland Islands in the South Atlantic. In response, the British sent a large task force, totalling some 120 ships, to the area, including two aircraft carriers, HMS *Hermes* and HMS *Invincible*, with Royal Navy Fleet Air Arm Sea Harriers and later, from mid-May, RAF Harrier GR.3s onboard. After several weeks at sea, British amphibious forces landed at San Carlos on the north-western side of the East Falkland Island on 21 May and the land battle began, with the Argentine air force attacking the British forces from the air. As is well known, the British eventually re-took the islands and hostilities ceased on 14 June. A total of 255 British servicemen and 907 Argentinian were killed during the seventy-four days of conflict; many more were injured.

Meanwhile, back home in the UK, everyone watched the daily updates and reports on TV. For those of us flying with the RAF there was considerable frustration that, for most of us, there was no part we could play in the war. As the Ministry of Defence was uncertain how long the fighting would continue, RAF Harrier reinforcements were being prepared for possible deployment with intensive operational training, including the employment of the Sidewinder AIM-9L 'Lima' all-aspect infra-red missiles, newly fitted to the Harrier GR.3 for the war. (AIM is the US designation used for air-to-air missiles and stands for 'Air Intercept Missile'.) Two of my fellow TWU instructors on 63 Squadron at Chivenor were whisked back into the Harrier force, which they had not long left, in order to bolster the number of available pilots. Flight Lieutenant Ross Boyens found himself flying Harrier combat missions over the Falklands with 1 Squadron, whilst Flight Lieutenant Pete Collins was part of the potential reinforcements.

In early June the Harrier Force in Germany submitted a request for TWU Hawks to be deployed to RAF Gutersloh to act as simulated Argentinian A-4 Skyhawks and 'aggressors', to assist with the dissimilar air combat training for the reinforcement Harrier pilots employing their new AIM-9L Sidewinder missiles. From 63 Squadron two ex-Lightning air defence pilots were selected to go, Flight Lieutenant Dave Beveridge and myself. Dave had been on my original Lightning conversion course at Coltishall in 1973; he had flown Lightnings in the UK and was now a QWI with 63 Squadron at Chivenor. He was one of the finest exponents of 1v1 air combat manoeuvring that I have ever met. He was an extremely aggressive fighter pilot and not only had natural ability in combat, but also had a deep understanding of the science involved. He was extremely generous in sharing his secrets with me and had already taught me much about air combat manoeuvring in the Hawk. Dave was a natural choice for this particular job with the Harriers at Gutersloh, and I felt honoured to be considered in the same company and be chosen to go too.

We flew out to Gutersloh in two Hawks on 3 June, with RAF ground crew occupying our back seats to service the aircraft whilst we were deployed. During that week we each flew six dissimilar air combat training sorties against the Harriers, some 1v1, but mostly 2v2. The idea was to train the Harrier pilots in the tactics they would need to use against the manoeuvrable Argentinian A-4 Skyhawks and not for us to win every fight, as that wouldn't be good for the Harrier pilots' confidence or morale. After all, they were potentially about to deploy into a shooting war. We were restricted to being gun-armed only which theoretically put us at a significant disadvantage against the Harriers with their new all-aspect infra-red air-to-air missiles. Dave and I found that we could work extremely effectively together as a fighting pair, with a great unspoken understanding, and we seemed to fare much better against the Harriers in air combat than anyone had expected. We also found that the Harriers' use of their vectored thrust nozzles for VIFFing (vectoring in forward flight) at slower speeds, whilst it created a sudden unexpected pitch rate and a braking effect, could be easily countered by pulling up into a so-called 'high yo-yo' and re-committing aggressively onto what was now a sitting duck with limited energy. Dave seemed to appreciate my ability to keep overall situational awareness in a fight and to co-ordinate with use of the radio even when we were split and couldn't see each other. I certainly respected his ability in close combat and his unerring ability to gain the advantage and take a 'kill'. As a result of our success we found our hands tied more and more to balance the odds.

On one 2v2 sortie we were briefed by a US Marine exchange Harrier pilot that we were to fly as a pair up and down a 'towline' at a fixed altitude with no control from the ground and we were not allowed to react until the Harriers committed onto us from our high six o'clock. We would have to rely solely on our eyes to spot them and, as usual, we would be gun-armed only. Meanwhile, the two Harriers would be vectored by a fighter controller into our Hawks' six o'clock, with a height advantage, ready to dive down on us; they would be 'armed' with simulated Sidewinder AIM-9Ls – they carried acquisition rounds with the IR seeker head fitted – as well as their cannon. Each time this was set up in the air, we spotted the Harriers high in our six o'clock, countered their initial attack by breaking into them at high G and then won the individual 1v1 combats which developed, achieving gun kills against them. When it came to the debrief, after landing from the sortie, the US Marine Harrier pilot who led it said to us, 'Before we took off, I was wondering how to couch this debrief in terms so as not to embarrass you guys. After the second fight I realised that wasn't going to be a problem.'

The Falklands War ended before the Gutersloh Harriers needed to deploy, but our week in Germany made us feel that we had played a small supporting role, and it had been great fun.

Mixed Fighter Force

In 1982 the RAF decided to augment the UK air defence forces by employing the TWU Hawks and instructors in a war role as day-only fighters. The Mixed Fighter Force (MFF) concept was simple and intended to increase the number of fighters available on combat air patrols (CAPs) at any one time. Without an air-intercept radar (and with no radar warning receiver or defensive aids either) the Hawks operating alone could only provide point defence or visual CAPs; even if close fighter control was available, locating enemy aircraft would be like trying to find the proverbial needle in a haystack. By flying the Hawks in company with radar-equipped F-4 Phantoms (occasionally with Lightnings and later with Tornado F.3s), usually two Hawks to one fighter, the radar-equipped aircraft could detect the targets, take semi-active radar missile (Fox 1) shots before the merge and lead the Hawks into a visual engagement where their superb turning ability gave them a good chance of achieving 'kills'. That was the theory. In practice it was less successful and not very popular with the 'real' fighter crews. The concept was employed only up to the late 1980s and then slipped into history.

My first experience of the MFF concept was in March 1982, not long after I had qualified as a four-ship leader at the TWU. I was given the task of planning, organising and leading a detachment of four Hawks from

Chivenor to Leuchars, in Fife, Scotland, to participate in a large UK air defence exercise named MALLET BLOW. We flew several sorties of MFF during the week – in my case I flew six sorties – with our Hawks being 'towed around' by F-4 Phantoms and we engaged various targets provided by RAF and NATO fighter aircraft. The concept and the exercise were declared successful; my part in it and my air defence expertise drew praise in my next annual report.

In July that year we were similarly involved in another UK air defence exercise, Exercise PRIORY, intended to put the UK air defence system fully to the test. This time we deployed to Coningsby, in Lincolnshire, which was to be our base in time of war. We worked with the F-4 Phantom crews of 64(R) Squadron, the Phantom Operational Conversion Unit. The F-4 crews were told to 'tow' their Hawks into a fight at no more than 500 knots. In fact, they really wanted to hit the merge much faster than that; they didn't really want to be at less than 550 knots. The result was that as soon as the F-4 crews gained radar contact they raced off, leaving the Hawks behind. This didn't really matter as it was relatively easy to keep visual on the large and smoky F-4s and the 'enemy' aircraft would tend to see them and start mixing it with them, at which point the small Hawks arrived into the fight often unseen. On one particular sortie from this exercise we had six Hawks behind two F-4s, and we engaged six further F-4s acting as enemy aircraft. It was a memorable fourteen-aircraft dog fight.

Further deployments to Coningsby to participate in UK air defence exercises and on MFF operations with the 64(R) Squadron F-4s occurred in April and July 1983. These were notable on a number of counts, not least because in 1983 the RAF modified some of its Hawks to T.1A standard, giving them the ability to carry two Sidewinder AIM-9L all-aspect infra-red air-to-air missiles on the wing pylons. Although the missiles were integrated onto the Hawk in a relatively basic manner, with boresight capability only, and firing ranges had to be judged visually, it significantly increased the capability of the aircraft over its previous armament of a single Aden 30mm cannon.

In April, operating from Coningsby on an Exercise PRIORY, I flew several sorties, two of which were leading a pair of Hawks on MFF operations with F-4s, with the RAF Chivenor station commander, Group Captain (later Air Commodore) Jerry Saye, an ex-Harrier pilot, as my wingman, to expose him to the air defence procedures and MFF operations. The Air Officer Commanding 11 Group had decreed that on this exercise as many RAF fighter controllers as possible were to be flown in the back seats of Hawks to give them a view of proceedings from the cockpit. One of the 151 Squadron Hawks from Chivenor, which was also deployed to Coningsby along with us, came back from an exercise sortie with no rear canopy and a 'pole' sticking up out of it, and without the fighter controller passenger who had been in the back seat on take-off. He had apparently decided that he'd had enough of low-level air combat and ejected over the North Sea, much to the surprise of the pilot. Fortunately, the passenger was picked up unhurt by a search-and-rescue helicopter having apparently carried out a decent dinghy drill for which he had received only a verbal briefing. The pilot suffered plenty of jibes from his colleagues over the 'careless loss of a passenger'. The AOC's idea of flying as many fighter controllers as possible on exercises wasn't repeated.

During another Exercise PRIORY in July that year, once again operating from Coningsby, I was involved in one MFF sortie that I have never forgotten. Our MFF formation consisted of two F-4s with our four Hawks. We intercepted and engaged three Dutch RNLAF F-16As over the North Sea. The F-16A was a fabulous little dogfighter with a simple track-while-scan radar and armed with AIM-9L infra-red missiles and a gun. The Dutch pilots loved nothing more than getting gun 'kills' in a fight. As soon as the F-4 crews gained radar contact on the F-16s they were off like robbers' dogs at high speed towards their targets, leaving the Hawks trailing behind as usual. The F-4 crews called 'Fox One' missile shots on the way to the merge and then a dogfight fur ball ensued, into which our four Hawks plunged headlong, without apparently having been seen by the Dutch pilots up to that point. I latched onto an F-16 turning hard left at high G, with impressive vortices streaming off his wing-root extensions, a sight that is locked in my memory banks. I was in guns' range, but couldn't quite get the pipper of the gunsight onto the target, although I was holding my own in the turn, maintaining the G and the airspeed on the light buffet. Perhaps the F-16s were not using reheat due to the need to have enough fuel to return to the Netherlands. Behind me was another F-16 trying to get a guns' kill on me, but he was also stuck in lag, and behind him was another of our Hawks, queuing up for a shot. I managed to get the pipper on to 'my' F-16, took the gun 'kill' with film to prove it and then snap-rolled to wings level and pulled up into a loop, planning to roll off the top, leaving the F-16 behind me to his fate with the other Hawk. As I reached the top of the loop still inverted, an F-4 pursued by another F-16 shot up in front of me in a vertical climb. The risk of a mid-air collision in this tight nine-aircraft fur ball was very high indeed and I decided not to poke my nose back into it until I had sussed where everyone was. Then someone called 'Knock it off' and, as quickly as it had begun, it was all over. The sortie warranted an exclamation mark in my logbook, my code for an extra special sortie or fight.

Night Bird Strike

On 20 October 1982 a 151 Squadron Hawk aircraft suffered a multiple bird strike at 350 feet on a night approach to Chivenor's runway. The student pilot, Flight Lieutenant Rawles, was flying his first solo night familiarisation sortie. At least one bird was ingested into the engine which flamed out and lost power. An eyewitness saw the aircraft trailing a fifteen-to-twenty-feet flame from its jet pipe. The pilot ejected at 185 feet, suffering slight face and back injuries. Five seconds later the aircraft crashed into the undershoot of the runway, lost its undercarriage, suffered considerable damage to wings, flaps and lower fuselage, slid through rough ground and came to a halt on the airfield. The pilot landed safely in the Taw Estuary, inflated his survival dinghy, climbed into it and was rapidly being taken out to sea by the tide when, fortunately, a sharp-eyed RAF fireman spotted him floating past in the darkness.

About three weeks later, on 8 November, I was conducting a night dual check on a student pilot. It was a particularly dark night. We were the first aircraft to take off and the first to return to the airfield for some visual circuits with touch-and-go landings on Chivenor's westerly runway. The student flew a nice circuit and I was feeling pretty relaxed in the back cockpit. Rolling wings level on the final approach at 130 knots, with only the approach and runway lights visible through the pitch darkness ahead, the blackness was suddenly punctuated with white shapes hurtling towards us, illuminated by the landing light in the aircraft's nose. For a split second, I didn't know what they were, but then, 'Thump, thump, thump', on the airframe, and I realised that these were seagulls and we were experiencing a multiple bird-strike on short finals.

Fortunately, none of the birds smashed the windscreen or canopy and none went down the intakes into the engine. I immediately took control, informed air traffic that we had suffered a multiple bird-strike and would be converting our planned 'touch and go' landing into a 'full-stop'. We landed without further incident, rolled to the end of the runway, turned off and shut down on the taxiway. As there had been little warning of our emergency, the crash vehicles took some time to get to us and we climbed out and inspected the damage with our torches. There seemed to be bits of seagull stuck all over the aircraft, on the wing leading edges, underwing pylons and in the landing gear. Miraculously, and probably because we were quite slow when we hit them, there appeared to be no significant damage, to the aircraft that is; these seagulls had definitely flown for the last time. We had been very lucky; this could easily have been a repeat of what had happened three weeks earlier; if the engine had been damaged, we would have ejected too.

An investigation into the causes of these night-time bird-strikes concluded that recent heavy rainfall had raised the water table at the airfield so much that large numbers of earth worms had been forced out of the soil and onto the runway to avoid drowning. This had provided a flock of local seagulls with an irresistible midnight feast until some dirty great machine with a headlight in the nose came hammering down towards them, forcing them into unwanted and chaotic night flight.

There was an amusing sequel to this incident a few weeks later when we were having a rehearsal at Chivenor for a forthcoming Royal visit. The part of the Royal visitor was being played by the Senior Air Staff Officer (SASO) at HQ 11 Group, Air Commodore Peter Collins AFC, who had been my station commander at Gutersloh and knew me well. He was there to ascertain that all the preparations for the visit were properly in hand and he was being followed around by the station commander and an entourage of admin people. The staff pilots, including me, were lined up by our Hawk aircraft on the aircraft servicing pan at Chivenor. The SASO was supposed to just walk along the line at a distance, but when he spotted me, he veered off towards me, unscripted, with the entourage following, wondering what he'd noticed. He stopped in front of me; I saluted and he saluted back. Then in a voice louder than necessary and with a mischievous smile under his moustache he said, 'Hello Clive, I understand you've been having trouble with worms.' I could only say, 'Yes, Sir.' The entourage, who were not aware of the details, didn't know what to make of it. (Peter Collins retired as an Air Vice Marshal with a CB. He died in April 2017, aged 87.)

VIP Pilot

In January 1983, because of my qualifications as a Hawk QFI, Tactics Instructor (TI) and Instrument Rating Examiner (IRE), it was decided that I should become the personal VIP pilot to the RAF Inspector of Flight Safety, Air Commodore Tom Stonor. He was an experienced RAF fighter pilot with a background on Hawker Hunters and the SEPECAT Jaguar. He had commanded 31 Squadron when it was equipped with the Jaguar and had also been station commander at RAF Coltishall during its time as the base for the UK Jaguar Force. He was also an absolute gentleman. His duties as the Inspector of Flight Safety included visiting RAF bases around the country and he had decided that, whenever possible, he would arrive in a camouflaged Hawk. He needed a TWU staff pilot to collect him from Abingdon, the airfield nearest to his Oxfordshire home, to fly with him to the various stations around the country (having prepared low-level navigation route maps for him) and to return him to Abingdon afterwards.

My time as 'chauffeur' to Air Commodore Stonor did not start auspiciously. On 17 January 1983 I flew a Hawk from Chivenor to Abingdon to collect him. We then flew an instrument flying practice sortie for the air commodore from Abingdon to St Mawgan in Cornwall, as he wanted to be instrument-rated on the Hawk, and needed to go to St Mawgan for a visit. Whenever I arrived anywhere in a Hawk with the air commodore on board we were met and marshalled in by white-suited ground crew, specially kitted out for a VIP. The station commander would be on hand to meet him with his car, flag flying and star plate fitted, ready to whisk him away, leaving me to sort out the aircraft and the luggage. I left the air commodore at St Mawgan for his flight-safety visit and flew back to Chivenor on my own. The next afternoon I was scheduled to collect the Inspector from St Mawgan and bring him back to Chivenor.

At this time I was working up for a forthcoming QFI A2 confirmation of category sortie on the Hawk which would be flown with an examiner from the Central Flying School (CFS). I had previously held a QFI A2 category on the Bulldog and, although I didn't need to, I wanted to upgrade from being simply 'Competent to Instruct' on the Hawk to holding a full category. I knew that the CFS examiner would be sure to take a particular interest in my handling of a simulated engine failure after take off, with a practice 'turn back' onto Chivenor's single runway. The only options for an engine failure after take off in the single-engine Hawk were ejecting if the speed was less than 250 knots, or above that speed attempting to convert speed to height and use the aircraft's excellent gliding performance to either 'teardrop' back onto the reciprocal runway or to fly all the way round to land in the same direction as take off. These Hawk practice 'turn backs' proved to be particularly dangerous over subsequent years with several accidents and some fatalities whilst practising them. The Chivenor Flying Order Book at the time stated that if the headwind component was more than 25 knots the 'turn back' should be flown as a circuit onto the in-use runway, as the tailwind would be too great to land on the reciprocal.

With these things in mind I set off that afternoon to fly solo from Chivenor to St Mawgan to collect the air commodore with the opportunity to do some staff continuation training general handling en route. I decided to start with a simulated engine failure after take off for a practice 'turn back'. The headwind was exactly 25 knots so I elected to fly the 'turn back' onto the in-use runway, as I believed that was what the CFS examiner would expect me to be able to demonstrate in those conditions on my impending confirmation of category sortie.

I took off and probably flew a rather shallow climb-out, which I had become accustomed to doing, so the speed reached 250 knots at a lower height than it might have done. Then I chopped the throttle to idle and initiated a practice 'turn back' via the downwind leg. Abeam the upwind end of the runway I was below the normal gliding keys for both height and speed, but, determined to prove to myself, as if to the examiner, that I could fly the advertised procedure, I pressed on. As I approached the end of the downwind leg, I was significantly below the normal gliding height key and tight to the runway, but I was at the correct gliding speed and I thought I knew a trick or two for the final approach. I turned finals early, planning to land at the famous one-third down the runway point. To help me get round the tight finals turn I lowered full flap early, accepting the increased rate of descent for the extra turning ability. In retrospect I think I realised at this point that I was flying right on the limits, but I didn't consider throwing the approach away by applying power and going round. I crossed the edge of the runway at about twenty feet, still with about 60 degrees of bank and with about 30 degrees to go to the runway heading. The last ten feet of the approach involved rolling wings level (nearly), applying a boot full of left rudder to swing the nose round to get it pointing down the runway, and flaring into buffet to cushion the landing. If there had been any doubts in my mind up to this point, it was now very apparent how close to the limits I was flying. The aircraft landed firmly on the left wheel and rolled onto both wheels. I seemed to have got away with it. I breathed a sigh of relief, cursed myself for being so stupid, applied power and lifted off. As I became airborne again, a fellow staff member, who was waiting to take off at the holding point, called me on the radio to say that he thought I had touched my left wingtip on the runway. My head swivelled rapidly to the left; the wingtip seemed slightly turned up. I didn't remember it looking like that during my previous 600 hours on Hawks. I turned equally rapidly to the right to compare the other wingtip; it wasn't curled up.

The next ten minutes were a nightmare of embarrassment. I received a visual inspection from another Hawk, which confirmed what I could see. I carried out a low-speed handling check and, not forgetting the VIP nature of the sortie, I contacted the squadron and asked them to send another aircraft and pilot to collect the air commodore. I kept thinking to myself that if I was going to be a prat and have a self-induced flight safety incident, why did I have to do it on a sortie when I was supposed to be collecting the Inspector of Flight Safety himself? After an uneventful landing I taxied in to be met on the pan by the Squadron Commander.

As far as the aftermath was concerned, I was as lucky as I had been in the air. The damage to the aircraft was confined to the bent port wingtip and a scraped port aileron, both of which were easily (although probably expensively) replaced. The Boss listened to my honest confession sympathetically, the station commander wanted me 'hanged', but the highly-respected Wing Commander OC Flying, Wing Commander George Lee, was a complete star and, recognising my contrition, he fended him off. Later he wrote that he believed that it was completely out of character for me to do such a thing. The senior officers who protected me from punishment must have realised that I had learned a valuable lesson; one, in fact, that I was never going to forget.

The flight safety incident report I submitted was a masterpiece of understatement and, with appropriate phrases referring to gusty conditions and wind shear on the approach, a reader could have been forgiven for thinking that the incident was unavoidable. Of course, it was totally avoidable. I am not the least bit proud of what happened that day and I still feel profoundly embarrassed about it. I had learned that there is a form of so-called 'press-on-itis' caused by professional pride, which if not kept in check can result in exceeding the normal warning bells to back off. If this had been a real engine failure after take off, my flying so close to the limits might have been justified; I might even have been a hero for getting the aircraft down. However, for the sake of a simulated emergency and my own pride, I made a complete fool of myself and it could have been even worse. I had been extremely lucky. This was the only time in my entire RAF flying career that I ever damaged an aircraft as a result of my own silly mistake.

When I met the air commodore in the officers' mess bar later that day, he naturally asked me why it hadn't been me who collected him from St Mawgan as planned. I told him the complete truth. I never heard any more about it and, gentleman that Tom Stonor was, he was happy to fly with me again the next day when we completed his instrument rating test on the Hawk and flew a low-level navigation route to take him back home to Abingdon. I night-stopped at Abingdon ready to take him to Cottesmore via another low-level navigation route the following day, with a night stop there, before returning him back to Abingdon and continuing home to Chivenor on my own.

*****

In February 1983 I collected the air commodore from Abingdon and flew with him on a low-level 'navex' to Binbrook, home of the Lightning Force, where we night-stopped whilst he carried out his flight-safety inspection. The next day we flew another low-level navex from Binbrook up to Church Fenton in Yorkshire, where No. 7 Flying Training School was located with their Jet Provost trainers. We were planned to night-stop there too and I had agreed to give a presentation in the officers' mess anteroom after dinner about the Tactical Weapons Units and what we did. Whilst we were in the bar before dinner the Station Commander confided in the Inspector of Flight Safety that, as a joke, one of the student pilots had been told that he had been nominated for a 'practice ejection' from a Jet Provost at low level over the airfield the following day for the air commodore's delectation. Apparently, the student thought this was probably a 'wind up' but, if the Inspector would talk to him about it, he might begin to think it was true. Much to my surprise, Air Commodore Stonor was more than happy to go along with this prank and, when the student was brought over to talk to him, he asked him pertinent questions about such things as what height and speed the ejection would be occurring at. The student's face was a picture as his worst fears now seemed to have been realised. Fortunately, he was 'put out of his misery' fairly quickly and told it had been a joke all along.

Air Commodore Stonor eventually retired from the RAF as an Air Marshal with a KCB having been Controller of the National Air Traffic Services, before leaving the service for a successful career in Industry.

I passed my Hawk A2 QFI confirmation of category sortie on 1 March 1983.

Hawk Mid-Air Collision

On a glorious Friday afternoon on 29 July 1983, two Hawks from Chivenor were involved in a mid-air collision. I was preparing to go flying and already fully kitted, wearing my life preserver and carrying my flying helmet, when the station tannoy broadcast a 'State One', the most serious aircraft crash message, saying that a Hawk aircraft had crashed near Bude and both of the crew had ejected. This was followed almost immediately by a 'State Two' broadcast, stating that a Hawk was recovering to Chivenor for a visual inspection. It was not difficult to put two and two together and guess they had been involved in a mid-air collision.

The two Hawks, flown by pilots of 151 Squadron, had been conducting a tail-chase exercise over North Devon. The lead aircraft was flown by the very experienced and capable Royal Navy instructor, Lieutenant Commander Pete Sheppard, in the front seat, with Flight Lieutenant 'Pablo' Mason, who had just completed the TWU course, in his rear seat. He had scrounged the flight for extra flying whilst waiting to be posted to the Tornado GR.1. The 'chasing' Hawk was being flown by an Iraqi air force student pilot, Lieutenant Hameed (at the time the RAF was training Iraqi pilots on a routine basis) with instructor Flight Lieutenant Mike Phillips in the rear seat. Mike had been one of my instructors during my advanced flying training course on the Hunter at Valley in 1973 (the one who constantly berated me to speed up with, 'You'll never make a fighter pilot, Rowley').

During the tail chase the Iraqi student pilot overshot the lead aircraft and pulled up in front of it. The tail of the overshooting aircraft hit the nose of the lead aircraft, wrecking both. With no pitch control, Mike Phillips and Lieutenant Hameed had no choice other than an immediate ejection, which they both survived. Pete Sheppard's Hawk lost its entire nose section including the nose wheel, the cockpit canopy was shattered and the main undercarriage fell down. The crew radioed a 'Mayday' message and returned to the airfield for a visual inspection. Another Chivenor Hawk formed up with them at a respectably safe distance, as pieces were still falling from it, to provide an airborne visual inspection.

We all hurried outside to watch the spectacle unfold. It was an absolutely amazing sight to see as the Hawk flew slowly by. It had a blunt flat nose, with nothing ahead of the windscreen at all; the front four feet or so of the aircraft was simply missing and pipes and cables were flapping wildly in the airflow from the battered bulkhead. The main wheels appeared to be locked down (apparently the crew had the two green lights to confirm it was), but the nose wheel was missing along with the nose.

As Pete Sheppard's feet were now right at the front of the aircraft, any attempt to land with him still in it, without the nose and nose wheel, would almost certainly have caused him serious injury. It was decided that Pablo Mason should fly the aircraft from the rear cockpit and position out over

Barnstaple Bay whilst Pete ejected. Then if he still had control, Pablo could carry out a slow-speed handling check and, if that was successful, he could attempt to land the Hawk. We watched the Hawk position over the bay in the distance and we saw Pete eject and his 'chute open to drift down into the water. Unexpectedly though, this was almost immediately followed by Pablo ejecting and we saw his 'chute open, too. The first ejection had caused the engine to flame out, it wouldn't relight and, in Pablo's words, 'the aircraft was transformed into a mechanical bucking bronco'. He had no choice but to eject as well.

We had just lost two Hawks and had four pilots eject. It suddenly didn't seem like a day to go flying anymore and, as I stood there in my life preserver, holding my bone dome, I said so and headed back inside. A third Hawk from No. 1 TWU at Brawdy was lost that same day after a bird strike caused the engine to fail over the sea. The pilot ejected safely and was rescued. All Hawk flying was cancelled for the rest of the day, but we were all back flying again on the following Monday, quite happily.

In a sequel to this incident Pablo's Iraqi assailant that day was part of the Iraqi Air Force during the First Gulf War in 1991, when Pablo, by then a squadron leader, was flying Tornado GR.1s on bombing raids against Iraqi airfields. Pablo had saved the 'lucky' red Coca-Cola T-shirt that he had been wearing when he ejected from the Hawk in 1983. It was peppered with little black holes from the miniature detonating cord that exploded the canopy on ejection. His wife had tried to throw it out many times but he always saved it, sometimes in the nick of time, and it became his lucky talisman during the war. It had saved him once before and now he hoped it would do so again. It did.

'Aggressors'

The reputation of the Chivenor TWU Hawks and their staff pilots for providing valuable aggressor-style training to front-line units had spread throughout the RAF and in 1983 I was involved in several such exercises.

In March 1983 we deployed four Hawks to Lossiemouth on the Moray Firth in Scotland for a week to provide training to a Jaguar squadron working up for a RED FLAG exercise in the USA. We mainly worked with USAFE F-15 Eagles as a Mixed Fighter Force against the Jaguars who flew at low, sometimes ultra-low level, loaded up with a representative number of dummy 1,000-pound bombs. The F-15s were superb to work with as they could do it all, find the targets on radar at long range, take long-range missile 'shots' before the merge and then mix it in a visual dog fight. The MFF tactics worked extremely well with the F-15s leading us into fights. On a few sorties we flew visual low-level combat air patrols on the Jaguars' planned route without any other support. It was also interesting to see the Jaguars' tactics. Without any real way of defending themselves they were very impressive with their low flying, using terrain for concealment and, as a last resort, popping up to simulate dropping a bomb in your face. It was particularly nice to see how the RAF ground crew we took with us on this deployment were so enthusiastic and became really involved in what we were doing. They would quiz us on landing about what 'kills' we were claiming and even took to stencilling temporary kill markings on the noses of our Hawks.

*****

In November 1983 we were asked to provide four Hawks as external 'aggressors' for the final sortie of the NATO Tactical Leadership Programme (TLP) course held at Jever airbase, in Northern Germany. I was given the task of leading the 'show'. We were supposed to be working with RAF F-4 Phantoms from Wildenrath, using MFF tactics. On the day of the sortie, Wildenrath was in fog and the F-4s could not take off. We found ourselves as the only opposition against the now highly-trained TLP 'package', which consisted of twelve fighter-bombers, flying at low level, with five escorting fighters, F-15s and F-104s. We would be four Hawks versus seventeen. We were told only roughly where the package would be heading and, of course, we knew where they were starting from. Beyond that the plan for our part was left to me. I decided to 'put all my eggs in one basket', chose a spot on the map that I thought was a likely point the package would route through and set up two-low level (250 feet) visual CAPs one behind the other (in depth) at 90 degrees to the likely direction of approach, with two Hawks on each. It transpired I had chosen the initial point for their attack run, a good guess. As we were so few in number, the TLP staff allowed us to take as many AIM-9L missile 'shots' and gun 'kills' as we could, without being concerned about weapon expenditure. Much to everyone's surprise we fared extremely well; we spotted the package approaching at range, survived against the F-15s to the visual merge; we co-ordinated well between each other on the radio and claimed numerous 'kills' in the subsequent low-level combats. Back on the ground afterwards, our gunsight film was carefully analysed by the TLP staff to confirm our 'kill' claims. In the debrief I was required to recall everything that had occurred from our point of view, where we had taken 'shots', against whom, and what we were claiming. It was an extremely successful day and at the end of it I felt elated.

The following month I was in one of four Hawks which deployed to RAF Machrihanish on the Kintyre peninsula in Scotland for a week, to act as 'aggressors' during a RED FLAG work-up for another Jaguar squadron. This time we worked with both F-4s and F-16s against the low-level Jaguar formations; once again we were carrying the AIM-9L sidewinder acquisition rounds on our wing pylons. I flew eight sorties in four days.

*****

Our aggressor work was not restricted to fast-jet operations. We also sometimes flew against helicopters to provide their crews with experience of countering attacks by fighters, particularly on their qualified tactics instructor courses. I operated against Royal Navy Wessex helicopters and also against RAF Pumas. Far from being 'meat on the street', as I remember one RN helicopter crewman telling me that he thought he would be, it was not at all easy for us to locate and 'kill' a helicopter. They were extremely difficult to spot in the first place at ultra-low-level against the ground, with their crews finding the best backgrounds to hide and even hover against. Then it was equally difficult to retain tally on them as we manoeuvred around them, pitching into dives to attack and pulling out steeply, looking back over our shoulders trying not to lose them. When we pitched into a dive against a helo they would initially run straight towards us to steepen the dive, which was disconcerting, and then, at exactly the correct range, they would break onto the beam to present a crossing target and to upset the sighting solution (and later to point a door-mounted gun at you). We had to be extremely careful not to fly into the terrain. We taught the helo crews that if they could avoid detection in the first place, which they often did, or survive for about ten minutes against fast-jet attacks, the jets would probably give up through lack of fuel or because of other higher priority tasks.

Course Commander

During 1983 I began to make the right noises, as far as my superior officers were concerned, regarding a career in the promotion sense. In truth, I had discovered that several pilots I knew, who had been promoted to squadron leader, had been allowed to cross over to Specialist Aircrew terms of service, retaining their rank, but giving up any chance of further promotion in return for being allowed to stay flying. I still hankered after spending my entire RAF career in flying posts and, if that was now possible as a squadron leader, being promoted no longer meant that the 'Spec Aircrew' world was closed to me. So, I agreed to take the necessary professional exam – the so-called C exam – that was required to be promoted to squadron leader, although it actually took me a while to get around to it. The result was that where some positions on the unit had been reserved for those who were 'career minded' and had been closed to me up until now, I was now allowed to be considered for them. I was made a course commander and deputy flight commander on 63 Squadron.

As a course commander I was responsible for the progress, counselling and monitoring of seven or eight student pilots on a TWU course. The deputy flight commander role gave me responsibility, in part, for some of the operational and administrative aspects of the squadron. The first course that was 'mine' began in April 1983 and consisted of seven ab-initio student pilots of varying ability, plus an older experienced squadron leader, Sam Toyne, who was posted to Chivenor to be the Squadron Leader Operations Wing for his final tour before retirement from the service.

I think it would be fair to say that I became friends with the students on the course and we socialised together as well as working together. All the students passed the TWU course and succeeded in their subsequent RAF careers. At the end of this course Squadron Leader Sam Toyne wrote a lovely letter about me to the RAF Chivenor station commander, and he gave me a copy, which I kept for posterity. It was very good of him to do so. He wrote:

> I would like to bring your attention to No. 28 course's high regard for the Course Commander, Flight Lieutenant Rowley. Throughout the four-month period he has consistently demonstrated a genuine regard for our welfare and success, and it was largely due to his encouragement that certain officers maintained the will to pass the course. He is an excellent instructor and has that rare ability to promote confidence. His maxim that every mission, however unsatisfactory, has something to commend it, is possibly the key to this ability. Having flown with Flight Lieutenant Rowley on a variety of

sorties, including the bulk of those he flew during the recent Exercise PRIORY, I consider his overall performance to be amongst the best I have ever seen.

The second course I led began in August 1983. It was made up of more experienced pilots who were either crossing over to fast jets or were going to be joining the TWU staff. A mixed bunch, they included a Royal Navy pilot, an Armée de l'Air pilot who was starting an exchange tour as a TWU instructor and a pilot who had flown helicopters with the Rhodesian air force but had now joined the RAF and went on to fly F-4 Phantoms. Flight Lieutenant Guy Bancroft-Wilson was on this course, prior to becoming a fellow staff pilot on 63 Squadron with me, having previously flown F-4 Phantoms. He subsequently became the Strike Command Hawk display pilot in 1986 and then flew with the Red Arrows from 1987 to 1989. He left the RAF and became an airline pilot with British Airways, but sadly was killed when the sixty-year-old Bell P-63 King Cobra warbird he was flying at an air show at Biggin Hill crashed in June 2001. He was only 43 years old when he died.

*****

Towards the end of October 1983 we were deeply saddened to learn that former 63 Squadron TWU instructor Flight Lieutenant Ian Dixon had died flying a 617 Squadron Tornado GR.1 from Marham. Ian was an ex-Lightning pilot who had been on the staff of 63 Squadron with us at Chivenor until being posted to the Tornado. He was flying at low level over the sea, ten miles north of the Norfolk coast, near Sheringham, when he became unresponsive in the front cockpit. An unknown medical condition was subsequently considered the most likely cause of his incapacitation. His navigator, having failed to rouse him, ejected at only ninety feet above the water, with the aircraft rolling. With the command eject lever set to 'Both' the pilot would have been ejected about one second later. The navigator suffered major injuries, but was rescued some three and a half hours later, deeply unconscious and suffering from exposure. He survived. The pilot's ejection seat was subsequently recovered from the sea bed and it was determined that it had functioned correctly and that the pilot, together with his parachute, had successfully separated from the seat, but possibly with insufficient height for his parachute to deploy fully. Ian's body was never found.

On 28 November I flew in a Hawk from Chivenor to Marham with Flight Lieutenant Pete 'Stoney' Stone on board to attend Ian's memorial service. All the RAF funerals or memorial services that I have sadly had to attend over the years have been reunions of old friends and colleagues, all pleased to see each other but with, of course, a very sad reason for being there. I remember that Ian's wife, Jane, was incredibly dignified, calm and stoic, and pleased to see us all there to pay our final respects to her husband and the father of her children. We flew back to Chivenor at the end of the same day, in the dark, taking the opportunity for me to give Stoney a night-flying dual currency check.

Sadly, Stoney was also to die young, in June 1989, when he ejected too late from a two-seat Harrier T.4 at RAF Gutersloh. Stoney was one of life's characters. He had flown Lightnings with 92 Squadron at RAF Gutersloh during the same period as my tour in Germany and we had both been bachelors living in the officers' mess. He had met his lovely girlfriend Claudia, a local German girl, during his tour at Gutersloh and they had subsequently married. At Chivenor Stoney had become a highly-respected pilot, weapons instructor and flight commander, but he could undo months of good professional work in a moment with misbehaviour at a mess dining-in night.

After Chivenor, Stoney went on to fly Harriers and returned to Gutersloh, his wife Claudia's home town, now as a squadron leader and due to become a flight commander on IV Squadron. On 20 June 1989 he was flying a T.4 Harrier with an Army Air Corps pilot passenger in the rear seat and was attempting to establish the hover over a landing pad on a hot day. There was insufficient power for the circumstances and, despite his best efforts he lost control, the aircraft continued to descend and started to roll right. Stoney ordered his passenger to eject, which he did. He survived. Stoney ejected as the aircraft hit the ground with about 70 degrees of bank applied. This was beyond the ejections seat's capabilities and he was killed. It was truly tragic.

Back to the Front Line

With the end of my two-and-a-half-year tour as a TWU instructor at Chivenor looming, I spoke with my posting desk officer to see what he had in mind for me. It seemed that there was only one option. I was going back to flying Lightnings, this time at RAF Binbrook in Lincolnshire. The RAF had decided that it was going to form a third operational Lightning squadron at Binbrook; it had sufficient aircraft in storage to equip the squadron but needed Lightning pilots to man it. I had set my stall out to be posted to the new Tornado F.2, the air defence variant of the swing-wing (variable-geometry) jet fighter, not least because that might offer the opportunity to stay flying as a fighter pilot for many more years into the future. My desk officer promised me that if I went to Binbrook for a short tour I would be at the front of the queue for Tornado F.2 slots, as and when they became available. In the event, the third Lightning squadron was never formed, but my posting stood.

With a posting notice in hand I had to consider moving my family. I didn't know Lincolnshire at all, having thus far never been based in the county. I looked at a road atlas and found a town called Horncastle that was about two thirds of the way between Binbrook and Coningsby, twenty miles from Binbrook and ten miles from Coningsby. If a future posting was going to see me flying Tornado F.2s at Coningsby that seemed like a good place to buy a house. Elaine and I drove over, tested the drive from Binbrook to Horncastle over the Lincolnshire Wolds and spent a full day in the town with estate agents, viewing properties. We found nothing that we liked or that fitted our needs. Back at Chivenor I contacted the Binbrook Families Officer, a warrant officer, to request a married quarter. Apparently, there were no officer married quarters available and no private 'hirings' either. I explained that we had sold our house in Barnstaple, that we would soon be homeless and asked what I was supposed to do with my family. Astonishingly, he had very little sympathy, suggesting that my wife and daughter stayed with her parents and that I could live as a 'singly' in the officers' mess. I was, indeed I still am, appalled at this lack of official support for me and my family. The end result was that I managed to rent a property in Horncastle, despite there being a long list of applicants for it, because the landlady thought an RAF family would be trustworthy and careful with it. That was to be our home for the next six months until we did find a property to buy.

*****

My final reports from my tour as a TWU instructor were good. I was rated well above average as a TWU Hawk QFI, TI and IRE. In my final interview with the station commander, Group Captain Jerry Saye, he complimented me on my work and the results of my tour at Chivenor and said that there were student pilots 'who would forever have the name Clive Rowley engraved on their hearts'. I thought that was nice.

On 3 February 1984 I was dined out from the Chivenor officers' mess at a mess kit (black tie) dining-out night. As a leaving guest, even though I was only a flight lieutenant, I was seated in the rarefied atmosphere of the top table, but it turned out there was another reason for that too. No. 2 Tactical Weapons Unit had an Instructor of the Year award, with a model of a camouflaged Hawk being presented to the winner each year by British Aerospace. Much to my total surprise I was the No. 2 TWU Instructor of the Year for 1983 and I was presented with the trophy by British Aerospace aircraft designer Doctor John Fozard.

Chapter 8

Binbrook Lightnings

Binbrook

In February 1984 I started the Short (Refresher) Course with the Lightning Training Flight at Binbrook, initially with the ground school and simulator phase. The Lightning Force had shrunk considerably since I was last part of it and was now based entirely at Binbrook, with the last two operational Lighting Squadrons, 5 and XI, and the Lightning Training Flight (LTF).

RAF Binbrook was situated near the northern end of the Lincolnshire Wolds, a range of rolling hills and steep valleys that make up a designated area of outstanding natural beauty, not at all like the flat fens that many people associate with the county. The Lincolnshire Wolds run roughly parallel with the North Sea coast, from the Lincolnshire Fens to the Humber Estuary. The highest point of the Wolds is 550 feet above sea level. Binbrook airfield was 250 feet above sea level and it was said that the next highest point of land to the east of Binbrook was in the Ural Mountains in Russia. In the winter it sometimes felt that the easterly winds bringing snow to Binbrook came directly from there. My twenty-mile drive from Horncastle to Binbrook each day on the Caistor High Street over the Wolds followed the path of an old Roman Road. The drive could often be affected by poor weather in the winter with fog, snow and ice.

The two operational Lightning squadrons at Binbrook worked a fairly strict regime of day and night shifts on alternate weeks, with one flight on days and the other on nights. The day shift started at 08:00 each weekday with a mass station Met and air traffic brief in the main briefing room, with the station commander and all the execs present. It usually ended at 17:00 when the bar opened in the officers' mess. Meanwhile, the night-shift flight's pilots arrived around 15:00 to deal with any secondary duties, before a Met and air traffic brief at 16:00. They then flew into the evening, in daylight and in the dark, usually finishing at about 23:00, at which point all the pilots from both squadrons and the air traffic controllers on duty retired to the officers' mess. The bar would be shut, but cans of beer were available on an honesty basis and an RAF chef had stayed on to cook everyone who wanted it a 'night flying supper' of bacon, eggs and chips. I would usually get home soon after midnight from a night shift.

The day and night shift working regime between the two flights on the squadron meant that each shift of pilots on the squadron would never be more than seven, perhaps with the addition of the Boss on the day shift. With people away on leave, on courses and so on, it was sometime fewer. It was quite common for the pilot nominated as the duty authoriser on the ops desk, who might also be the duty pilot for the base, to be the only pilot left on the ground. This lack of human resources was and still is something that single-seat fighter squadrons have to contend with.

On Friday afternoons flying ceased, to allow the engineers to recover aircraft ready for the next week, whilst the pilots of both flights got together for ground training until 'Happy Hour'.

This working regime became very acceptable; you could plan weeks in advance whether you were on days or nights and you became used to working with the same people on your shifts, including the air traffic controllers.

Binbrook held a Quick Reaction Alert (QRA) (South) commitment for much of the year, shared with the F-4 Phantoms at Coningsby. So, when Binbrook was on 'Q', the station operated on a twenty-four/seven basis, with two fully-armed Lightnings, two pilots and half a dozen ground crew on readiness in the 'Q Shed' until called into action. Most of the QRA activity against Soviet aircraft was covered by the QRA (North) F-4 Phantoms based at Leuchars in Scotland, as they were closer to the part of the UK Air Defence Identification Zone where the Russian aircraft tended to appear. Occasionally though, there were scrambles for the QRA (South) fighters, with air-to-air refuelling tanker support.

Despite its somewhat bleak location on top of the Lincolnshire Wolds, Binbrook was a very happy station. There were only about forty Lightning pilots on the base and around 200 officers in all. Everyone knew each other, it was a very social station and the officers' mess bar was filled every evening after work, especially for the Friday evening 'Happy Hour'. There was a terrific esprit de corps amongst the Lightning pilots who, without exception, were proud to be amongst something of an elite and to be part of the final years of the mighty beast.

Lightning F.3, T.5 and F.6

The operational squadrons at Binbrook operated the F.6 version of the Lightning which had the large ventral fuel tank and cranked wings. The squadrons also had one or two of the T.5 two-seat trainer variants with the small ventral fuel tank. The Lighting Training Flight (LTF) operated T.5s, F.3s and one F.6 which had no guns and the full fuel load to act as a radar target.

All these marks of Lightning were powered by two Rolls Royce Avon 301R reheated jet engines producing 12,690 pounds of thrust each in un-reheated 'dry' power, and 16,360 pounds of thrust each in reheat. The maximum thrust, with both engines in reheat, was therefore 32,720 pounds, which was roughly the same as the weight of the aircraft with minimum fuel.

The weapons system centred around the Ferranti AI 23C mono-pulse radar, which was an improvement on the AI 21 radar of the earlier marks of Lightning that I had previously flown, but was still a simple pulse radar with a fairly limited detection range against smaller fighter-size targets, and limited capability looking down into ground or sea radar clutter. These later marks of Lightning could carry either two Firestreak infra-red (IR) homing missiles or two Red Top IR missiles. The Red Top had a slightly improved capability in terms of aspect off the target tail and could be used head-on against supersonic targets, homing onto the skin heat generated at supersonic speeds, and set to fuse instantaneously for a head-on kill. The AI 23C modifications allowed the missile seeker heads to be slaved to the radar hand controller so that they could be pointed at the target off boresight without locking the radar and alarming the target aircraft's radar-warning receiver. Until this modification it was necessary to point the aircraft and the bore-sighted missiles at the target; bunting down on a high-speed, low-level target at night took some courage.

The later marks of Lightning had originally been designed without guns but, when it was realised that there was a need for them, the F.6 version was retrofitted with a gun-pack containing two 30mm Aden cannon, fitted at the front of the 600-gallon ventral fuel pack at the cost of seventy-five gallons of fuel. The gun-pack also contained a reduced quantity of fuel, so these were literally 'fuel-cooled guns'. For gun aiming, the F.6 was fitted with a relatively simple and basic gun-sight, the light fighter sight (LFS), which applied gravity drop calculations only in the vertical on the assumption that the guns would not be fired with bank applied. As a result, academic air-to-air gunnery scores were often poor.

With the gun-pack fitted, the Lightning F.6 carried 9,700lb (4,400 kg) of fuel, which allowed sorties of over an hour if flown carefully. The minimum landing fuel was 1,600 lb (727 kg), enough to divert to the crash diversion airfield with just twelve minutes of flying time on one engine. Such crash diversions were fairly commonplace and constituted a real short-of-fuel emergency on a 'Pan' call.

The cockpits of these later variants of the Lightning were largely familiar to me from my time flying the earlier marks and they were just as cramped as ever. One difference was the combined strip air speed indicator and Mach-meter in place of the analogue clock instruments. It reminded me of the strip speedometer in a Hillman Imp. The Lightning's scheduled out-of-service date had been revised numerous times over the years and it had outlasted most of those revisions. This meant that there had been little investment in updating the aircraft and its systems because it was always close to impending retirement. A radar altimeter to give an accurate height above the surface below 5,000 feet was about all that had been added to the cockpit. It still did not have a radar-warning receiver, any self-protection counter-measures or any improvement in its weapons systems in terms of number of missiles or their capability. Just integrating the all-aspect AIM-9L Sidewinder missiles, as fitted to the Hawk T.1A during my previous tour, would have made the Lightning much more capable in its final years but such things were never to be.

Lightning Training Flight Short Course

The Lightning Training Flight (LTF) Short Refresher Course was really intended for pilots with previous experience of UK operations who were returning to the UK Lightning Force after a tour away. In my case it had been over seven years since I had last flown the Lightning, I had not previously flown the F.3, F.6 and T.5; I was not familiar with the weapons system and I had not operated in the UK air defence environment.

I completed the ground school and simulator phases without difficulty, learning the differences from the earlier marks of Lightning that I had been used to. When I started flying in mid-March, my initial dual sorties in a T.5 were flown with the two LTF QFIs who happened to be friends of mine from my days with the Lightning in Germany. Paul Cooper had been on 19 Squadron with me and Pete 'Boots' Boothroyd had been on 92 Squadron at Gutersloh, so we knew each other well. The officer commanding the LTF was Squadron Leader Ces Ilsley, who had also been on 92 Sqn at Gutersloh during my time there. It was nice to be back amongst old friends.

After five dual trips in T.5s, amounting to two hours and forty minutes flying, I went solo in a Lightning F.3. The duration of most of these sorties in the small ventral tank Lightning T.5 and F.3, as noted in my logbook, were only thirty to thirty-five minutes. One early dual sortie of maximum rate turns, with much use of reheat, was only fifteen minutes. After five hours thirty-five minutes of flying I passed the instrument rating test, which was always split into two sorties to achieve all that was required. I flew the first of those at night, in the dark, which ensured no cheating by sneaking a peek outside. It was pleasing to be awarded a Master Green instrument rating, the highest category of instrument rating, at the first attempt.

Unlike the two-seat Lightning T.4 which I had flown earlier in my life, the T.5 had a refuelling probe and could conduct air-to-air-refuelling (AAR). During the conversion phase of the course I took fuel from a Victor tanker on two sorties and found that I hadn't lost the necessary skills. Even with topping up to full from the tanker these sorties were only one hour in duration. There were often tankers on the North Sea AAR towlines and the Binbrook Lightning pilots routinely boot-legged fuel by asking the controller on the radio if there was any fuel available and then just turning up at the tanker. The crews were always happy to off-load fuel and get home sooner.

During the weapons phase of the course I had to learn how to operate the weapon system with its different displays, particularly for visual identification (visidents), and with the Red Top missiles, which were also new to me. There was a much greater emphasis on radar, 'head-down' work for the all-weather and night environment that UK Lightning pilots operated in. I found the totally head-down visident procedures particularly challenging, having previously been used to the Lightning F.2A's pilot attack sight head-up display for visidents. Closing to the minimum radar range of 300 yards on a target in cloud, or at night with its lights off, focusing entirely on the radar B scope and the instruments, and not looking out at all until stabilised at minimum radar range, just felt wrong. It also took some very accurate instrument flying.

Many of my dual sorties on the Weapons Phase were flown with LTF weapons instructor, Flight Lieutenant Neil 'Clachy' Maclachlan. Clachy was an Ulsterman, a fighter pilot through and through, and a popular member of the Binbrook Lightning Force. He went on to become a Red Arrow, joining the team in October 1987. Tragically he was killed in a flying accident on

25 January 1988 whilst training with the Red Arrows, practising a roll back over Scampton airfield. At the time of his death he was 32, married with a two-week-old child. His funeral took place at St Mary's Church, Binbrook, where he was laid to rest in the churchyard.

Towards the end of the LTF course, I was able to fly a couple of sorties in the big ventral tank F.6 'owned' by the LTF, providing a radar target for other students and allowing me to familiarise myself with the version I would be flying on the squadrons. In terms of handling it was very much like the F.2A version I had flown in Germany, but needed the flaps down for take off.

At the end of May, two and a half months after starting to fly the Lightning again, and with just thirty-seven hours flying under my belt at Binbrook, the Short Course was over. My course report pointed out that this had been a demanding course for me as I was given no extra allowance of flying over that allowed by the Short Course, despite my lack of recent and relevant Lightning experience. The report said, 'Although not a natural pilot, Flight Lieutenant Rowley makes up for any deficiency by hard work and careful preparation.' It appeared that, having got used to being told that I had plenty of natural flying ability over the previous seven years, now I was back in the Lightning world I was once again deficient and once again making up for it with hard work.

XI Squadron

In June 1984 I was posted to XI Squadron, operating from the hangar next to the LTF's. The squadron boss was Wing Commander (later Air Commodore) John 'Boss Spon' Spencer, who had been my flight commander on 19 Squadron in Germany and knew me well. He was a well-liked and somewhat feared squadron commander, and he was still very much the fighter pilot. I flew an arrival check with him in the squadron's T.5 the day that I arrived. We had last flown together in an aircraft more than eight years previously when he gave me the Lightning night close-formation dual check that I have never forgotten. My flight commander was Squadron Leader John Danning, who had also been on 19 Squadron at Gutersloh with me. My mentor for my squadron work up to Limited Operational (QRA qualified) and then to Combat Ready status was to be Flight Lieutenant Alan 'Porky' Page, who had been one of my University Air Squadron students on the Bulldog at Woodvale in 1977-78. How the world turns.

Ten days after I arrived on the unit, I was sent to RAF Valley as part of a small team from XI Squadron on a missile practice camp (MPC). The same day I fired a 'war round' Firestreak missile at low level against a Jindivik drone target on the Aberporth Range, the second of many air-to-air missiles I was eventually to fire.

During my first month on XI Squadron I also moved house for the final time. We had purchased a new-build bungalow on the outskirts of Horncastle, which became our home for far longer than we ever expected at the time. I was now well placed for a posting to Coningsby if it ever happened. I had been promised a short tour at Binbrook before moving on to the new Tornado F.2 but that wasn't how it turned out.

*****

On 13 July 1984 Binbrook suffered a tragedy and lost one of its own. Two 5 Squadron Lightnings and their pilots were deployed to Jever in Germany to participate in the NATO Tactical Leadership programme. During a sortie operating against four USAFE A-10s, which were evading hard at low level, one of the Lightning F.6s, flown by Flight Lieutenant Dave 'Frosty' Frost, flew through high-tension electricity cables. There was a bright blue flash as the Lightning hit the live cables and almost immediately a fireball as it hit the ground about five miles east of Bremen. There was no time for Frosty to eject and he was killed instantly. Everybody at Binbrook was much saddened by his loss, everyone knew him; he was well liked and much missed. His funeral was held at St Mary's church in Binbrook village and he was laid to rest in the churchyard there. His grave is marked with a military headstone.

Six days after Frosty's accident, a Lightning T.5 was returning to Binbrook from Jever flown by a 5 Squadron pilot with an engineering officer passenger who was part of the board of inquiry into the accident. On landing at Binbrook the T.5's starboard undercarriage collapsed through no fault of the pilot and as a result of a mechanical failure. Spectacularly, the aircraft swung off the runway and skidded across the airfield, through a fence, ending up on its belly in a field, with no damage to the crew. This incident resulted in a temporary restriction that the T.5s could only be flown with the undercarriage locked down, with ground locks in, until modifications had been carried out.

*****

My squadron Combat Ready work-up continued apace with numerous practice intercept (PI) radar sorties flown by day and by night, in all weathers. My logbook shows numerous sorties of low-level PIs, medium level PIs, supersonic PIs, 'high flyers', intercepts against radar jamming (ECM) Canberra T.17s of 360 Squadron, and so-called 'Opexs' where it was pretty much anything goes in simulation of the real air defence scenarios you might face operationally.

In August 1984, during a sortie of head-on supersonic intercepts in which we refuelled from a VC10 tanker to stretch the duration to one hour fifty minutes, I suffered an engine problem. On cancelling the reheats and throttling back at supersonic speed there was a brief staccato machine-gun-like noise from the engines. I immediately put the throttle back to an intermediate setting, recognising this as a probable engine surge. Checking the engine instruments, nothing seemed to be untoward and there were no unusual indications. One engine was perhaps indicating very slightly hotter than the other, but otherwise it was impossible to tell which engine had the problem. I wasn't confident enough of my diagnosis to shut down either engine in case it was the wrong one. I decided to recover to Binbrook for a precautionary landing with the slightly hotter engine at idle, flying on the other engine, but able to swap at any stage if necessary. After landing it was discovered that my assessment of which engine had surged was, in fact, correct. Not only that, the Rolls Royce Avon had lost twelve rows of its fifteen compressor blades from the axial-flow compressor at the front of the engine but it had continued to run without any obvious problems, although there must have been a significant loss of thrust. The Avon was a remarkable jet engine. Other Lightnings had been lost due to fires caused by engine surges like this, but I was lucky and the engine just chewed up the blades, spat them out and the failure was contained. A few days later, after an engine change, the Lightning was back on the 'line'.

*****

Cyprus and Air-to-Air Gunnery

In October 1984 XI Squadron deployed en masse to RAF Akrotiri in Cyprus for a month for the annual armament practice camp (APC), principally to conduct air-to-air gun firing against a towed sleeve banner target. These APCs were routine annual events in the calendars of the UK air defence squadrons.

The banner target was only six feet (1.5 metres) high and, although it was thirty feet (9 metres) long, because you were attacking it at an angle of around 15 degrees off its tail, the aspect made it appear to be a very small target to aim at from around 400 yards. The banner was towed at 180 knots by a Canberra target tug from 100 Squadron and the Lightning attacked at 360 knots with 180 knots of overtake. When the banner sleeve targets were returned, the number of coloured holes in it made by the painted cannon rounds was checked and scores were based on a percentage number of hits against the number of rounds fired.

The Lightning T.5 had no guns, so air-to-air gunnery dual checks were impossible. With the undercarriage restrictions in place on the T.5s, we didn't even take one to Cyprus. After several air-to-air gunnery cine sorties in the single-seat F.6s, with nothing more dangerous than film, the squadron weapons instructors cleared me 'hot'. The 'gunsight time' gained from all the weapons work I had done as an instructor on Hawks at the Tactical Weapons Unit seemed to pay dividends and my air-to-air gunnery scores were not bad.

The ceremony of marking the banner was one of the traditions of a fighter squadron's APC that was attended by all the available pilots, all keen to see how others had scored. The rules set by the intercept weapons instructors (IWIs) were strict: no-one was to tread on the banner after it had been laid out, there was to be no harassing the IWI doing the marking and, like a rugby referee's, their decision was final. Anyone breaking the rules was likely to be 'sent off'. The IWIs also assessed the cine film from each gunnery sortie and scores could be scrubbed for getting too close to the target or firing with too low an angle-off, which could be dangerous to the target tug.

I hit the banner with my coloured 30mm ball rounds on every sortie, sometimes more than on others. On two sorties one of my cannon shells hit the metal shackle that connected the banner to the tow line and I shot the banner off. That was never popular and inevitably another pilot, firing different coloured rounds at the same banner, would claim that, had the banner been returned, they would have had a brilliant score. It did mean I was hitting the target but it could also be dangerous. During an air-to-air gunnery sortie from Cyprus in January 1987, a 5 Squadron Lightning pilot, Flight Lieutenant Dave 'Kato' Chan, hit the wheel on the banner post with one of his cannon shells. The wheel broke off and flew down the Lightning's intake, causing the No. 1 engine to seize and also damaging the other engine. During the single-engine recovery to Akrotiri, the remaining

(No. 2) engine lost power and Kato was forced to eject on the approach at only 250 feet and 150 knots. The aircraft crashed and was written off. Kato was flying again the next day.

After three 'hot' gunnery sorties my scores really began to pick up: 30 per cent, 28 per cent and 38 per cent. Then one banner came back covered in holes of my colour. The first count was over 90 per cent. The Boss appeared and took over the marking. His first move was to get a check on the number of rounds my aircraft had been carrying. That proved to be as expected. Then he set to with some of the harshest marking I have ever seen, insisting that several of the holes were 'stitched' by the same round. Of course, I had to remain silent and couldn't complain. When he had finished his marking, the score was still a confirmed 80 per cent. The IWI assessment of my film showed steady and consistent ranging and tracking and no busting of the minima. The score stood and I believe it to be the highest score ever achieved in academic air-to-air gunnery by a Lightning pilot.

*****

To mark the end of our month at Akrotiri, the Boss, Wing Commander Spencer, decided to fly an eight-ship formation, the maximum number he was allowed to put together without special permission from Group HQ. Those of us asked to be part of it felt honoured to be chosen. Boss Spon was a brilliant close-formation leader, as I knew from my earlier acquaintance with him but he took no prisoners. We found ourselves being wheeled around in tight eight-ship diamond formation, pulling 4G, with the bumpy conditions in the heat making it very hard work. I was on the outside left of the diamond with another Lightning bouncing around between me and the Boss. After landing we were all wrung out; the Boss started the debrief by asking us, 'Did you enjoy that?' Everyone looked at each other and no-one answered; we'd been working too hard to actually enjoy it, but were still glad to have been part of it.

I flew home from Cyprus in a four-ship of Lightnings led by the Boss. We were supported by a tanker on the route back home, prodding several times to keep the fuel topped up, and the flight home took just over five hours. As we got close to Binbrook we were above eight-eighths cloud. The details of the recovery hadn't actually been part of the sortie brief and I was surprised when Boss Spon called us into close formation with 'Box four. Go'. A more normal cloud penetration would have been two close pairs in radar trail. I was number four and we penetrated thousands of feet of cloud with me hanging on at the back of the box four. When he was talking to Binbrook Tower it became apparent what the Boss's intentions were, as he asked if the visual circuit was clear and then announced that we were for a four-ship flypast. In fact we flew around the airfield in tight box-four formation for several minutes, making a number of passes, once again pulling 4G, to announce that XI Squadron was back. The trust that Boss Spon placed in those of us in the formation to complete our parts in this completely unbriefed arrival, safely and neatly, was typical of him. Equally, of course, we had total faith in him as our leader.

Another One Down

Only nine days after arriving back at Binbrook we lost another Lightning, this one an XI Squadron aircraft, with the pilot, Flight Lieutenant Mike 'Sid' Hale, ejecting over the sea. I was on the night shift that day and arrived at the squadron to find it almost deserted, with only the WRAF Corporal Ops Assistant on the ops desk running the show. It seemed that the pilot who was the duty authoriser was the only one left on the ground and, as he was also the duty pilot, he had been called to the air traffic control tower when news of the accident reached him. Then Sid Hale's wife, Anne, turned up. She was the WRAF Catering Officer on the Station. She had heard the station tannoy announcing the crash and had found out it was her husband. At this point we did not know whether Sid was alive or dead and she wasn't in a good frame of mind. I spent the next several minutes comforting her and information gradually came back that Sid had ejected, and then that he had been picked up by a search and rescue helicopter (SAR) from Leconfield.

It transpired that Sid had suffered a series of failures after take-off in his Lightning F.6. First the electric pitch trimmer ceased to operate and he found he was having to apply a constant push force to the control column to maintain level flight. He aborted the sortie and orbited over the sea off Spurn Head to burn off fuel. When he began to route back for a straight in approach to Binbrook, the 'Fire 2' warning caption illuminated. He shut down the engine and turned out to sea. Then the 'Reheat 1' fire caption lit up on the warning panel, quickly joined by 'Reheat 2'. Other failures were also apparent and the pilot of another chase Lightning alongside reported that he could see smoke from the No. 2 jet pipe and that there appeared to be a fire between the two jet-pipe nozzles. Then Sid noticed the controls beginning to stiffen, both powered flying control systems failed and the controls seized solid. He ejected as his Lightning dived towards the sea. It crashed ten miles off Spurn Point.

When Sid landed in the sea he was dragged by his parachute and became entangled in the lanyard that connected him to his dinghy. He used his dinghy knife to cut the lanyard and, in doing so, lost his dinghy and damaged the seal of his immersion suit. When he was picked up by the SAR helicopter, he had been floating in the water for twenty-five minutes and was hypothermic. He subsequently recovered well.

Combat Ready

In November 1984 I was declared fully combat ready on the squadron after completing an 'Op Check' with the Boss. To be allowed to wear the squadron badge on my flying suit I had to complete the XI Squadron tradition of drinking the 'op pot', a two-handled tankard containing four-and-a-half pints of Batemans real ale. This had to be done in the bar at the next happy hour without removing your lips from the tankard once started. I was never entirely comfortable with the concept that to be a real fighter pilot you had to be able to drink large quantities of alcoholic beverages as well as being able to fly and fight.

Just as I seemed to be getting established on XI Squadron, I was posted to 5 Squadron, the other operational Lightning squadron at Binbrook, which needed a deputy flight commander and squadron QFI. I fitted the bill.

5 Squadron

I arrived on 5 Squadron immediately after the Christmas and New Year break and flew my first sortie with my new unit on 2 January 1985 with no other arrival checks or procedures and no fuss.

I immediately slotted into the deputy flight commander duties. Working for my flight commander, Squadron Leader Chris Jones, I became responsible for planning and running the flying programme for the flight, ensuring that continuation training and currencies were maintained and also, generally, for authorising the junior pilots on the flight for their sorties. We had a spirited bunch of junior pilots, 'JPs', on the flight, some of them in the process of working up to combat ready status. Whilst the JPs could be great fun they did need some supervision and sometimes needed rescuing from difficulties. My previous experience actually meant that I didn't find any of this particularly difficult and, overall, my working life was great fun.

Lightning Qualified Flying Instructor

In February I was given a very short course at the LTF to become a Qualified Flying Instructor on the Lightning. The course was just two weeks long and consisted of a total of nine dual sorties in T.5 Lightnings, amounting to four hours and thirty minutes of flying. As an instructor in the Lightning T.5 it was necessary to fly in the right-hand seat, which meant that, because of the arrangement of the controls, you flew with your left hand on the control column and your right hand on the throttles and the radar controller, the opposite to the single-seat Lightning cockpits. Some pilots had difficulty adapting to this. I would never claim to be ambidextrous but I had considerable experience of flying with my hands that way round in the Bulldog which seemed to stand me in good stead and I had no difficulty with it. I flew a close-formation sortie and also an instrument-rating test in the right-hand seat, which was a separate requirement and, as was standard, took two sorties to complete.

I flew the QFI course sorties with Flight Lieutenant Pete 'Boots' Boothroyd, who was the Central Flying School (CFS) Agent for the Lightning, authorised to award QFI tickets on type. He was also an extremely experienced Lightning pilot, renowned for being able to do things with the aircraft that no one else could do, particularly at slow speed. It was he who taught me how, in a slow speed 'flat scissors' with another aircraft during air combat manoeuvring, it was possible with the Lightning's incredible nose-up pitch authority to unload slightly for a little extra speed and then, with the wings level, to pitch up suddenly to the vertical, using the rote after-take-off technique, before unloading again to 'float' over top of the vertical climb. This certainly surprised pilots of other types, even the USAFE aggressor pilots in their F-5Es, who couldn't follow this manoeuvre, and it gave you the chance to either re-engage with advantage or to bug out from an optimum nose-down head-on pass.

On one of the QFI-course sorties Boots asked me if I had ever spun the Lightning. Intentional spinning was prohibited, as it took many thousands of feet to recover and there had been instances of Lightnings failing to recover from spins, leading to the pilots ejecting. Our normal training consisted of watching a cine film – *Ten Seconds is a Long Time* – about test pilots spinning the Lightning, with advice on how to recover; this was an annual training requirement. The recovery drill was pretty standard and so we also practised spinning in visiting Jet Provosts from CFS on occasions. I told Boots proudly that I had never lost control or entered an inadvertent spin in a Lightning. He apparently felt that this was a gap in my experience as a Lightning QFI and announced that in that case we would do one. He got me to set the aircraft up at 28,000 feet at slow speed, close the throttles to idle and maintain level until the speed reduced further. Then he talked me through applying full rudder – I went left – and full back stick. The Lightning reared up and rolled slowly into a spin to the left, settling into a stable, relatively slow spin with just a slight 'nod', just like a big Jet Provost. Then I went through the standard recovery drill; the aircraft roll rate speeded up as it began to recover from the spin, it pitched more steeply nose-down and then recovered quickly. All no drama at all and an experience which I appreciated him letting me have, as he was taking a risk in doing so.

The following day we were doing slow speed recoveries from a steep to vertical climb. Boots set one up and gave me control in a steep climb. I applied full dry power, rolled the aircraft so that it was on its back and then centralised the controls to let it fall out. After recovering to level flight, Boots said that you didn't have to roll inverted; you could push out and the aircraft would not stall or 'flick' as you would be at zero G and generating no lift. I wasn't convinced but he set up the same steep low-speed climb again and, this time, when he gave me control he told me to push out. As I did so with full forward stick, the nose very gradually started to come down but not as fast as the air speed was decaying. 'Keep pushing,' said Boots, 'It won't spin. Keep pushing.' As we approached the level attitude the speed was lower than I had ever seen it in flight in a Lightning and the aircraft began to wing rock and to the nose began to slice, classic signs of a Lightning spin entry. 'Keeping pushing,' said Boots, 'It won't spin.' The aircraft suddenly flicked into a spin. 'Bugger,' said Boots, 'It's spinning', stating the obvious and leaving me to recover from it, something I'd practised just the day before. Those are the only two occasions I ever spun the Lightning and, whilst I benefited from the experience, it wasn't something that personally I would ever do deliberately.

I was awarded a competent to instruct QFI ticket on the Lightning and returned to 5 Squadron as the unit's squadron QFI, responsible for all dual-handling checks and for ground training on the aircraft systems.

Life (and death) on a UK Lightning Squadron

The flying during the year I spent on 5 Squadron was varied and fun. By night, on the alternate-weekly night shifts, the sorties were generally limited to practice interceptions at medium and low level over the sea, including visidents (sometimes with a lights-out target), supersonic interceptions and intercepts against the radar-jamming ECM Canberra T.17s of 360 Squadron. By day there was plenty of fun flying to be had. We flew so-called Opexs, sometimes with control provided by the Avro Shackleton AEW. 2s of 8 Squadron. In addition, we flew plenty of air combat training and dissimilar air combat training sorties, as well as numerous low-level affiliation sorties, mostly against Tornado GR.1s.

In February 1985 I was part of a small detachment of four Lightnings from 5 Squadron which deployed to the Royal Navy Fleet Air Arm (FAA) airfield at Yeovilton, in Somerset, for a few days, to conduct dissimilar air combat training against the Sea Harrier FRS.1s based there. I flew a 4v2 and several 3v3 dissimilar air combat sorties and the SHARS proved to be formidable opponents. The skill and aggression of the FAA pilots impressed us, as did the manoeuvrability of the Sea Harrier, especially when the pilots used the vectored thrust nozzles to VIFF (vectoring in forward flight) to get their noses on in a hard turn, at the expense of losing energy, to take missile shots with the Sidewinder AIM-9L missiles.

*****

Back home at Binbrook we suffered a tragedy on 6 March 1985. I was on the night shift that day and, before leaving for work, I received a telephone call at home from my flight commander. He said, 'Clive, it's Chris Jones. I'm sorry to tell you we've lost "Tetley".' It took a moment to sink in. I asked him what had happened and he explained what he knew.

Tetley was Flying Officer Martin Ramsay, a first-tourist Lightning pilot on 5 Squadron. He was a 26-year-old bachelor who was well liked on the squadron. That morning he had been flying a 1v1 air combat training sortie against another Lightning pilot from the squadron. During the second engagement his aircraft was in a right-hand turn at 11,000 feet when it sliced left and entered a spin. Tetley transmitted that he was spinning and the pair's leader advised him to check his height for ejection. The minimum recommended height for ejection from a Lightning in a spin was 10,000 feet. Tetley was below that when he called that he was ejecting. By this time the

Lightning was descending at a high rate and it hit the sea approximately ten seconds later, about twenty miles north-east of Skegness. The leader, who must himself have been shocked by this, put out a Mayday call and then descended to low level, to find Tetley floating face down in the water about fifty metres from some aircraft debris. A search and rescue helicopter recovered the pilot's body from the water about thirty-five minutes later and it was discovered that his parachute was still in its pack.

In an example of the sort of irresponsible journalistic reporting that sometimes occurs, a newsflash went out on national radio within minutes of the crash. Tetley's mother heard the news of a Binbrook Lighting crash and, with some sort of premonition that it was her son, she telephoned the station to ask for details before the next-of-kin informing process could be activated.

Despite being told that I didn't need to go into work that afternoon, as flying was cancelled for the day, I wanted to be with my friends and colleagues; we all did, and we gathered in the squadron and then held the usual RAF wake in the officers' mess bar, buying drinks on the dead pilot's bar book as his debts would subsequently be written off. It was a time-honoured RAF way of grieving quickly as we would be flying again the next day. Indeed, I was.

Subsequently, there was a funeral service for Tetley in the church in Binbrook village, when we met his mother, father and sister. I think his family were comforted to some degree that Tetley had another, RAF, family who were also grieving his loss.

A significant amount of the Lightning's wreckage, about 85 per cent, was recovered from the sea, including the ejection seat. The subsequent board of inquiry could not reach a conclusion as to why the Lightning had entered a spin and, whilst pilot mishandling could not be ruled out, the possibility of a structural failure or a malfunction with the flying-control system could not be discounted. The inquiry also focused on why the ejection had not been successful. We were subsequently briefed by the president of the board that, whilst there was still some conjecture, they felt it likely that the ejection had been at relatively slow speed with considerable side force being exerted by the yaw rate in the spin. This may have caused the drogue parachute on the seat to deploy at an angle and that, in turn, could have prevented the automatic separation from functioning as they proved that the ejection seat 'scissor shackle' would not open with a side force being exerted on it. Tetley may have been trapped in a tumbling seat until he managed to operate the manual separation handle, which evidence suggested he had, but by then there was insufficient height and time for his parachute to open.

A few months later his mother and father commissioned a bronze statue of their son, about two feet high, with him depicted wearing full Lightning flying kit. The sculptor did a brilliant job and it really looked like Tetley. It was presented to the squadron for perpetuity in his memory and always appeared at dinner nights in the officers' mess at Binbrook and later at Coningsby when 5 Squadron became a Tornado F.3 unit based there. Those of us who had known Tetley had developed a tradition of stroking his head when we passed the statue, something I was still doing several years later when just about everyone else was unaware of the significance of the bronze statue of a fighter pilot.

*****

In July 1985 we deployed four Lightnings to Rheims, in the Champagne area of France, for a week of dissimilar air combat training (DACT) with the Armée de l'Air Mirage F1 squadron based there, *Escadron de Chasse* 2/30 Normandie-Niemen. We were led out as a four-ship of Lightnings by the other flight commander on 5 Squadron, Squadron Leader 'Furz' Lloyd, who had been one of my instructors on my original operational conversion unit course on the Lightning at Coltishall in 1973. On the evening of our first day at Rheims we were welcomed by the French pilots with their own-label champagne – very nice, too.

Before we commenced flying with the French, we received a briefing on the area and local procedures. Then, along with the French pilots, we were briefed by the French squadron commander, a very Gallic moustachioed colonel. He really laid down the law about the combat rules which were to be complied with, including a minimum altitude for combat of 10,000 feet, 5,000 feet higher than I was used to and probably to the advantage of the Mirage F1 pilots. The colonel gave us the impression that 'busting the floor' was a 'hanging offence'.

My first DACT sortie was a 1v1 against the very same colonel. After some time turning against each other with neither gaining an advantage – he wasn't bad as a combat pilot – we reached the 'floor' of 10,000 feet, where I levelled off, in accordance with his strict briefing. To my surprise he continued to use height below me to low yo-yo in an attempt to gain the advantage. Clearly the rules were for the guidance of wise men and the obedience of fools, so I followed suit. Neither of us could beat the other.

Subsequently, I flew several 2v2 DACT sorties against the Mirage F1s with radar-to-visual splits. The Mirage F1 was a more modern aircraft than the Lightning and its very professional and aggressive French pilots proved to be tough opponents. At high altitude the Mirage probably had a slight advantage in turn rate against the Lightning, which was perhaps the better below 15,000 feet. The Lightning also had more power and could utilise the vertical to advantage. At slow speed there was not much between the two types. The Mirage could carry the Matra Super 530 semi-active short-to-medium range air-to-air missile which could give us a problem in surviving to the visual merge. It couldn't be ignored and we needed to employ some defensive tactics on the way to the merge to defeat it or the Mirage radar lock – their Thompson-CSF Cyrano radar had only limited look-down capability – and to cause confusion. Our bracket split with an altitude change worked quite well. The Mirages' R550 Magic IR missiles were also more capable than our old Red Tops in the visual fight. Overall, though, at the end of the week, we felt that honours were roughly even and it had been great fun.

*****

On 19 September I was on the night shift with 5 Squadron. I was on the ground as the squadron duty authoriser and I was also holding the responsibilities of duty pilot. The weather was good, so I didn't need to be in the air traffic control tower, just on the end of the phone. It was around 18:00 and still daylight when our 5 Squadron Ops Corporal answered the telephone and called me through from the crew room to take the call. I asked her who it was and she said 'Flight Lieutenant Shanley, Sir.' Liz Shanley was one of the Binbrook air traffic controllers and was the duty ATC supervisor that evening. Our conversation went something like this:

'Hello, Liz. Clive. I haven't seen you to talk to for a while. How are you?'

'Oh, I'm fine. How are you?'

'Yes, fine too. What can I do for you?'

'Craig Penrice has ejected.'

There we were doing small talk and she wanted to tell me we'd had an aircraft crash and a pilot eject. I rushed to the air traffic control tower to play my part in the proceedings as duty pilot. Wing Commander Simon Bostock, officer commanding XI Squadron, which Craig Penrice belonged to, soon appeared in the tower, too, and information trickled in.

Craig was found and rescued from the North Sea, fifty miles off Flamborough Head, by a Wessex SAR helicopter from Leconfield, about fifty minutes after he had ejected. Fortunately, it was still daylight, as the Wessex did not have a night auto-hover capability. Craig was initially flown back to Binbrook and taken to the station medical centre. Later that evening he was airlifted to the RAF Hospital at Ely in a SAR Sea King helicopter after it became apparent how serious his injuries were and once his acute hypothermia was arrested and he was stable enough to be moved. It had been a nasty accident and a very high-speed ejection.

He had been flying one of a pair of XI Squadron Lightning F.6s on a medium-level practice intercept sortie. When he reached recovery fuel, he rolled his aircraft to the left to turn left towards base at about 27,000 feet. As he did so the control column moved of its own accord to fully left, causing the Lightning to roll rapidly to the left and to keep rolling. Craig was unable to move the control column from its fully-left position and each time the aircraft passed inverted the nose dropped further until it was in a near vertical high-speed spiral dive. Craig turned off the auto-stabilisation system, but that had no effect. Having put out an initial radio call to his leader saying that he had a control restriction, he now ejected without any further R/T call. The Lightning was rolling rapidly in a steep descent, it had entered cloud and the speed was transonic, around Mach 0.95 (500 mph of wind blast), when Craig ejected at about 18,000 feet, having lost around 9,000 feet in seconds. He pulled the ejection seat-pan handle with just his left hand, with his right hand still on the control column.

Craig was not wearing an immersion suit for this daylight sortie because the sea temperature was 13 degrees centigrade, three degrees above the sea temperature at which the wearing of immersion suits was mandated. When he was located and winched into the SAR helicopter he had been floating in the sea for almost an hour, unable to completely disconnect himself from his parachute because of his injuries and not able to board his dinghy fully. He was seriously hypothermic when he was found.

Craig's injuries were serious and largely caused by the high speed of his ejection. His right arm had flailed and been broken against the elbow joint. His left knee had been pushed outwards by the control column, which was deflecting fully to the left when he ejected, and had also been broken. He also dislocated his left index finger, probably because he had tried to hold on to the ejection-seat handle when separation occurred. His face was puffed up and he wasn't a pretty sight.

The board of inquiry concluded that the accident had been caused by a failure of the aileron powered flying control unit which had jammed the aileron and the control column to full deflection, possibly due to an unknown loose article.

Craig's recovery to fitness to be allowed to fly again took the best part of a year and was aided by some expert medical care, some very sympathetic RAF doctors and his own fierce determination to fly again. He had orthopaedic surgery to fix his broken left knee and right elbow with assorted nuts, bolts and screws, and he had to have a nerve transplant which had to regrow to allow him to regain full use of his right hand, fingers and eventually his thumb, to be able to operate the aircraft controls. It was a long battle to get back in a Lightning cockpit, but get back he did. Subsequently, he flew an exchange tour with the USAF on F-15s and became a test pilot. He was the first RAF pilot to fly the Eurofighter Typhoon. A second ejection from a privately-owned Hawker Hunter on his way home from an air show in 2003 damaged his back so severely that his flying days had to come to an end.

Although I find it hard to believe today, my logbook records that, having dealt with the ground fallout from Craig's accident at Binbrook that night as duty pilot, I then went flying in a pair of Lightning F.6s of 5 Squadron on an Opex 3 with broadcast control, before some night close formation, totalling fifty-five minutes of night flying, as if nothing had happened.

*****

Saudi Lightnings

In January 1986 I passed the milestone of 1,000 hours flying on Lightnings. There are many Lightning pilots who have many more hours on type than this, several with more than 2,000 hours and at least one, Dave Carden, with over 3,000 hours. My 1,000 hours paled into insignificance against their achievements, but it still meant a lot to me to be able to wear the 1,000 hours Lightning patch with pride on the shoulder of my flying suit.

Just days after passing that milestone, many of the fully-qualified Lightning pilots from the two operational squadrons, me included, were involved in a special operation, which was classified at the time because of the impact on the readiness of the Lightning Force in UK, and which was described as being in support of 'UK Ltd'. Named Operation DOHNANYI, it was a two-stage affair to recover twenty-two Royal Saudi Air Force (RSAF) Lightning F.53s and T.55s back to the UK. British Aerospace had sold Tornado GR.1s and F.3s to the Saudis and had agreed to take the Lightnings back in part exchange.

The RSAF Lightnings had been delivered to the kingdom between 1968 and 1969. That was also the last time that the aircraft had conducted air-to-air refuelling (AAR) and they did not have refuelling probes fitted. Refuelling probes were removed from Lightnings at Binbrook and sent out to Saudi, where they were fitted to the F.53s and T.55s. Fuel was then pumped into the Saudi Lightnings through the refuelling probes, on the ground, from a bowser and we were told they would be fine for air-to-air refuelling, despite not actually having done it for more than fifteen years. We weren't that convinced but, in fact, there were no AAR difficulties at all during the operation. This was just as well as we were told that turning back to Saudi would not be welcome, to the point of being engaged by surface-to-air missiles, as we would be heading back from an area potentially hostile to them.

We flew out to Tabuk air base, in the north-west desert of Saudi Arabia, where the RSAF Lightnings were based, in some of the RAF VC10s that would be our tankers for the flights home to British Aerospace's site at Warton. We were well hosted by the British Aerospace ground personnel who had supported the Lightnings in service with the RSAF. We all had a simulator ride to get used to the few minor differences with these marks of aircraft. The most significant difference was that whereas all the RAF T-birds – T.4s and T.5s – had the small ventral tank, the RSAF T.55s had the large ventral tank and the same fuel capacity as the F.6/F.53. As it happened, I was to fly two T.55s back to UK, the first one solo on 14 January (with the right-hand seat strapped up) and the second one, on 22 January, after having been returned to Saudi by VC10, with my flight commander, Chris Jones, in the other seat. The two flights, with multiple AAR 'brackets', took six-hours-fifty-five minutes and six-hours-fifty minutes respectively. Seven hours is a long time to be strapped into an ejection seat in a cramped cockpit.

We found the RSAF Lightnings to be in completely brilliant condition. They had obviously been extremely well looked after by the British Aerospace engineers; everything worked and the Lightnings looked absolutely beautiful in their polished silver metal finish although we would have preferred not to have had the Arabic markings for the flight back across the Mediterranean.

The circumstances were very unusual as these were not RAF aircraft; in fact it wasn't particularly clear who owned them at that point. Certainly the RSAF had finished with them and lost interest. For the only time ever in my

RAF flying career I flew sorties which were not authorised on the normal RAF authorisation sheets; we just got on and did it.

With the first twelve aircraft we were told to depart without fuss, which we did. On arrival at Warton from that transit, the wind was gusting to 55 knots, well above any limits we would normally fly to in peacetime. We may as well have put the safety pins in the ejection seats as a parachute descent following an ejection would certainly have been injurious and may not have been survivable. We landed quietly at Warton and had a hairy ride back to Binbrook in an RAF Andover transport aircraft. This was almost the most dangerous part of the whole thing with a huge crosswind for its pilots to contend with on landing back at Binbrook.

When we left Tabuk for the last time on 22 January with the final ten Lightnings we were briefed once again to leave quietly. Since we hadn't been authorised for the sorties anyway and since this was the end of an era, especially for the British Aerospace engineers, many of whom had worked on these aircraft for the last fifteen years, that just didn't seem right. The pilots of the various formations of Lightnings came up with different and impressive ways of departing. Some took off in close stream into the Lightning's famous rote, snapping into a vertical climb before flying past the line low and fast and then pulling up and away in reheat. Some took off as pairs and split immediately into defensive battle formation, very low, as the undercarriages were still travelling. We called this a 'playtex' departure, named after a well-known brand of lady's bra which was advertised as 'lifting and separating'. When my turn came, leading Flight Lieutenant Steve Bridger as a pair, we did a 'playtex', splitting as we lifted off and then turning about to run back down the aircraft servicing pan in front of a hangar low and fast in tactical formation. I flew past the open hangar doors below the level of the roof at over 600 knots and, as I committed to that, Steve was on my left. In the subsequent steep reheat climb I was surprised to find him in battle formation on my right. Apparently, he had crossed underneath me over the pan.

When we got back to Warton just under seven hours later it was lunchtime and the workforce was out on the airfield in force to watch our arrival. Some of them had built these very same Lightnings fifteen years before. As each formation of Lightnings arrived they proceeded to beat up Warton airfield in right royal fashion. I led our pair into the circuit for a fast, low run-and-break. I overshot from the first approach to the runway, brought up the undercarriage and flaps and lit the reheats. From 180 knots my T.55 accelerated like a dingbat. I wound my way around the control tower and along the pan in front of the hangars, past the assembled workforce, at about 100 feet. In full reheat the speed was increasing so rapidly that when I passed the far end of the pan I had to throttle back and pop the airbrakes out to avoid going supersonic. Slowing down to land from the ensuing circuit proved to be quite difficult.

Sadly, those wonderful Lightnings never found a buyer and they never flew again.

Promoted

In February 1986 my tour with 5 Squadron came to an end. I was finally posted to the Tornado F.2/F.3 at Coningsby as an instructor on the operational conversion unit, over a year after I had originally expected to be. I started to hand in my Lightning flying kit and to visit various sections around the station at Binbrook to get my clearing card signed. On 9 February I received a telephone call telling me to report to the station commander's office that afternoon for an interview. I assumed it was my leaving interview.

The station commander was Group Captain (later Air Vice Marshal) John May who had been a flight commander on 19 Squadron at Gutersloh when I was a junior Lightning pilot on the squadron. I was ushered into his office in the station headquarters at Binbrook with my hat on. I saluted and he invited me to sit down. Then, worryingly, he asked me if I wanted the good news or the bad news. I feared the worst regarding my posting and I was right. The bad news was that my posting to the Tornado F.2/F.3 was cancelled. The good news was that I was promoted to acting squadron leader tomorrow and had better get the correct rank braid on my uniform. In five days I would be taking command of the Lightning Training Flight (LTF). I wanted neither and said so in no uncertain terms. He gently pointed out to me that this wasn't a request; there was no one else but me for the job and no alternative. I guess they had scraped to the bottom of the proverbial barrel and found me. I was to move to the LTF and start the staff work-up immediately. The station commander also suggested that I might telephone the squadron leaders' postings desk officer who might have some further good news for me in the way of a future promise. I should have been pleased about being promoted; after all I had only recently taken and passed the necessary promotion exam — the C exam — but the loss of my posting really took the gloss off it.

I telephoned the fast-jet-pilot squadron leaders' desk officer, Squadron Leader Pete Hitchcock, straight away. He had been my personal instructor when I completed my advanced flying training at Valley on the Hawker Hunter in 1973. He understood my disappointment at having my posting to the Tornado cancelled at such short notice and said that, as the LTF was due to disband in only eighteen months' time and that didn't really count as a full executive flying tour, he would put me forward for a flight commander post on one of the new Tornado F.3 squadrons. That would mean that I would still get to fly the new aircraft and would also get more than one executive flying tour. Normally, experience dictated that you should never trust what a poster told you but I knew Pete and trusted him more than most, so I was somewhat placated. Anyway, the military is not a democracy and I would just have to get on with it.

Officer Commanding Lightning Training Flight

I started with the Lightning Training Flight (LTF) the very next day. Literally overnight I had moved from peer to senior officer with the experienced flight lieutenant instructors on the LTF which might have proved difficult and awkward. It would be more normal to be posted away to a new job on promotion, but that could not happen in this instance. In fact, all the junior officers, my friends, at Binbrook were very accepting of the situation and I didn't stand on ceremony, so it wasn't actually a problem. On the LTF, after I took over command from Ces Ilsley on 14 February 1986, I was usually addressed as 'Boss' rather than 'Sir'. In fact, I learned that if someone called me 'Sir' it was generally going to be followed by something I didn't really want to hear.

In just over three weeks, sometimes flying three or even four times a day, I completed the staff instructor work-up to become a Lightning operational conversion unit qualified flying instructor and tactics instructor. As such, I was cleared to instruct all the sorties on the LTF Long and Short Course syllabus to student pilots.

*****

As the new Officer Commanding the LTF (OC LTF), I had suddenly found myself, as a brand-new squadron leader, in command of a decent size flying unit, at the age of 35. The LTF engineering team, working directly for me, consisted of eighty-seven men, with a flight lieutenant engineering officer in charge. I also led six pilot instructors – two qualified flying instructors, two weapons instructors and two tactics instructors – whilst the student pilot population on the flight was generally around twelve to fourteen. We had ten Lightning aircraft on strength, a mixture of F.3s and T.5s plus the single F.6 with no guns and the large ventral tank full of fuel to act as a target for radar intercepts. My admin staff consisted of one leading aircraftman registry clerk, straight out of training. He did what I directed him to do but the administration on the unit was largely down to me. Having, until now, been in charge of nothing more than a handful of pilots, I was suddenly commanding an entire unit.

Early in my tenure as OC LTF I had several visitations from the Officer Commanding Engineering Wing (OC Eng. Wing) at Binbrook, Wing Commander Blackman, who was concerned about the standards of engineering on the Flight. Apparently, it had recently failed a quality-assurance inspection and there were other aspects that he thought did not measure up to the required standards. As I was OC LTF he expected me to sort it out. I identified the weak points in the flight's engineering team and, with the help of OC Eng. Wing, we restructured. The LTF engineering officer was about to be posted away and he was replaced by Flight Lieutenant Al Greenbank, a superb engineering officer, who really got a grip of things. Some years later Al was the Wing Commander OC Eng. Wing at Coningsby and, when he was posted away at the end of his tour, I was able to give him a passenger ride in a Tornado F.3. We had a new flight sergeant posted in. Flight Sergeant Herring was relatively young, he was a hard man who took no nonsense and he really knocked the team into shape. The final piece of this engineering management team reshuffle took a little longer to organise and that was to establish a new post for a warrant officer. This was done much more quickly than was usually the case and Warrant Officer Edmundson became the third member of the LTF engineering senior management team.

From then on, despite the ageing aircraft and a shortage of spares, the engineers on the flight worked wonders in generating aircraft for us to fly. The Lightning was never an easy aircraft to work on; everything was crammed together inside the fuselage and no job was straightforward or easy. There were no more complaints from OC Eng. Wing and whenever the flight's engineering standards were inspected it passed with flying colours.

The engineering management team kept me, as an inexperienced commanding officer, on my toes too. Warrant Officer Edmundson came to me one day and told me he thought I should address the ground crew who he would gather together in the hangar at shift changeover in a couple of days' time.

'What do you want me to say to them?' I asked him. 'That's up to you, Sir,' he said.

The eighty-plus ground crew were duly assembled in the hangar and a box was provided for me to stand on. Having given it a bit of thought, I told them how pleased and proud I was of all their hard work and how well we were doing with the flying task. I balanced that by telling them that we were approaching a difficult time, explaining the details, and that it would need some hard work to get through it. The sea of faces gave me no inkling of their reaction to my words and when I asked if there were any questions at the end of my speech there were no takers and they were dismissed. I caught up with Warrant Officer Edmundson, who was hurrying off, to ask if what I had said was alright. I got only a non-committal response of 'Yes, fine, Sir', so I was none the wiser. Subsequently, I noticed an improved sense of morale and a renewed pulling together from the ground crew. I realised that Warrant Officer Edmundson knew, with his much greater experience, that just getting the whole team together to be spoken to by the Boss was all that was required. It probably mattered very little what I actually said to them. That was not the only time that I used the Boss's talk to the ground crew to draw the team together and to communicate. I learned from that.

As I was the only squadron leader on the LTF, I was the senior subordinate commander for disciplinary matters. The flight lieutenant engineering officer, as the junior subordinate commander, had limited powers of punishment and sometimes disciplinary charges were referred to me. Having learned how to run an orderly room and hear a charge during officer training some fifteen years earlier, I had never needed to do so since, but now suddenly I did.

I mention these things just to illustrate how all-encompassing commanding a unit like this was. As the officer commanding, I was responsible for the flying operations and training output, for the engineering, disciplinary and administrative aspects; everything in fact. Even in 1986 it was rare for a squadron leader to find themselves with such wide-ranging responsibilities and to be in command of a flying unit this size, operating a front-line type. I wouldn't find myself in a similar position again until I took command of the Battle of Britain Memorial Flight (BBMF) in 2004, although those aircraft had long ceased to be front-line.

Missile Firings

As the Lightning Force neared its disbandment there was a surplus of Firestreak missiles that would have no use after the aircraft had been retired. As a result, there were increased opportunities to fire them.

Someone realised that in all the years that the Lightning had been operating there had never been a missile fired from the aircraft at night and the effects on the pilot's vision were a complete unknown. The LTF was tasked with firing two Firestreak missiles over Aberporth range in the dark, against the normal flare target towed by a Jindivik drone, but with two pilots in each of two T.5 Lightnings. One of the pilots in each T.5 was supposed to shut his eyes to protect his vision and could then take over if the flying pilot was blinded when the missile was fired.

I was in the right-hand seat of the LTF Lightning T.5 that fired the first ever air-to-air missile at night from the type, on the night of 12 March 1986, as the safety pilot. One of the LTF intercept weapons instructors, Flight Lieutenant Ian 'K9' Howe, was flying our aircraft from the left-hand seat when we launched the war-round missile fitted with a full warhead. Needless to say, I didn't shut my eyes. The rocket motor on the missile burned red as it shot off towards the towed flare in the darkness, having no effect on our vision at all. What we hadn't anticipated was that when the rocket motor burned out, before the missile reached the target, everything went black and there was nothing to see for a few seconds. Momentarily, we thought it had failed, but then the warhead exploded in a huge ugly orange-and-black fireball. It was quite a spectacular firework show.

Having fired our missile, we held at the 'gate' for the range over Bardsey Island, off the western end of the Llyn Peninsula, at about 20,000 feet and observed the second Lightning T.5 firing their Firestreak from some miles away, whilst listening to proceedings on the Aberporth Range frequency. The other T.5's flying pilot called, 'Firing. Firing. NOW' and there was a streak of red from the missile rocket motor as it shot across the night sky at Mach 2.0. The rocket motor burned out and there was nothing but blackness for a few seconds, then that orange fireball. I realised that if there ever was an aerial war at night this was how it would be fought.

*****

In May 1986 we were asked to fire two Firestreak missiles from ultra-low-level over the sea in Aberporth range. The firings were intended to prove that the Firestreak could be fired from as low as 100 feet against a higher target and that the missile would not hit the sea. This had never been tried before. The lowest we were normally allowed to fly was 250 feet, but now we were told to go and practise the missile firing attack profile at 200 feet and then 100 feet over the sea off the Lincolnshire coast.

Having completed the necessary practices, we deployed several Lightnings to the Strike Command Air to Air Missile Establishment at RAF Valley for the missile firings in Aberporth range. On 6 May I fired 'my' Firestreak from a Lightning F.3 at 200 feet above the sea and it performed perfectly. Then Chris Allan fired a Firestreak from 100 feet, also with complete success.

When I returned to Binbrook later that day in a T.5 Lightning, flying solo with the right-hand seat strapped up, I experienced a reheat Fire 2 fire warning, which resulted in me having to shut down that engine and to put out an emergency radio call. It turned out to be spurious, caused by an electrical fire-wire problem.

Mildenhall Air Fete 1986

The LTF was asked to provide a tactical set-piece demonstration display for the Mildenhall Air Fete air show in May 1986. The idea came from the air fete co-ordinator and commentator, Roger Hoefling. He had somehow managed to gain official approval from an appropriately high level within the RAF for the LTF to be tasked with providing it. He and I discussed what he had in mind and I turned the ideas into something that would work in front of a crowd. We wanted to present a demonstration of an airfield defence low-level visual combat air patrol (CAP) with two Lightnings engaging two 'bandits' played by Hawks.

The plan was to launch two Lightning F.3s with a pair's reheat take off to 'playtex' into an airfield defence low-level visual CAP over the airfield. The two Hawks playing the bandits were from one of the tactical weapons units. As they ran towards the airfield in defensive battle formation about 1,500 yards apart, at 250 feet, head on towards the display line and the crowd, the Lightning pilots – me leading, with Flight Lieutenant Ian K9 Howe as wingman – would 'spot' the bandits and turn in behind them. As the Hawks reached the display line, they would react to the Lightnings attacking them by breaking hard right, defeating the simulated missile shots. It was obvious that taking simulated missile shots from a mile away would not be very impressive to the crowd, so we needed to simulate very close gun kills. I would be behind the right-hand bandit as they broke and, as I would be in danger of being sandwiched, I would engage full reheat and pull out vertically, leaving K9 to engage the rear of the two bandits. We worked out that the Lightning F.3 could hold 4G at 300 knots in full reheat using buffet to avoid accelerating, so we got the Hawks to 'tow' at that speed and G, following each other around a figure-of-eight pattern in front of the crowd. This was much slower than we would be flying for real, but it would keep it all nice and tight in front of the crowd with the Lightnings in full reheat for maximum noise effect. After I had disengaged and whilst K9 tied up the bandits in a role play of 'free and engaged' tactics, I would then re-engage from head on to the other Hawk which was not under threat from K9, converting in behind it as it continued to turn. All four aircraft would then carry out a noisy tail chase for a few minutes with the two Lightnings in full reheat, until the Hawks were 'claimed' as guns kills.

My plan received approval and we practised it over Binbrook airfield on 12 and 13 May with the two Hawks and with the station commander observing us. Then, having refined a few details, we flew the tactical set-piece demonstration display in front of the Air Officer Commanding (AOC) 11 Group, Air Vice Marshal Mike Stear, on the 14th and he granted his authorisation to fly the display in public at the Mildenhall Air Fete. Roger Hoefling, having been involved throughout, would provide an explanatory commentary, if the crowd could hear him. The sortie duration for our two Lightning F.3s on these sorties, landing with minimum fuel, was generally ten minutes. Effectively we were turning fuel into noise.

We deployed several Lightnings from Binbrook to Mildenhall for the air fete. These included the singleton Lightning F.3 display aircraft flown by the Lightning display pilot from the LTF, Flight Lieutenant 'Big John' or 'BJ' Aldington, the two F.3s for the tactical set-piece demo, which included my personal Lightning F.3 XR749, tail letters DA, and some Lightning F.6s from the two Binbrook squadrons for the static display. Across the weekend the air fete drew a crowd of more than 100,000 spectators.

On the Saturday of the air show our tactical set-piece demonstration display went perfectly. We even impressed some of the Red Arrows pilots who said it looked like we were having fun. Indeed, we were.

That evening I spent some time chatting in the bar with the two Central Flying School (CFS) Vintage Pair pilots, Flight Lieutenants Andy Potter and Dave Marchant, who were flying the vintage Gloster Meteor and DH Vampire at the show. I had known them during my time as an instructor with CFS at Leeming. The following morning, Sunday 25 May, I met up with them again at breakfast and sat next to them at the pilots' briefing for the air show that day. Later that morning, I was outside the pilots' tent with my Lightning colleague, K9 Howe, watching the Vintage Pair display. He wasn't paying much attention to them when I nudged him with my elbow and said, 'They've hit each other. They're going to crash.'

I had watched the Meteor, flown by Andy Potter, leading the Vampire, flown by Dave Marchant, around a relatively slow-speed barrel roll with the Vampire in close formation. As the aircraft came down out of the roll the Vampire seemed unable to remain behind the Meteor. It overshot underneath it and pulled up in front, its tail hitting the port-engine intake cowling of the Meteor. The Vampire pitched up violently but, more horrifyingly, the Meteor, probably with the left engine out and full power on the right engine at low speed, rolled uncontrollably to the left and the nose dropped into a vertical dive. It impacted the ground seconds later, just outside the airfield, exploding in a ball of fire and a mushroom-shaped cloud of smoke. The Meteor T.7 did not have ejection seats and there was no chance for the crew to get out. I had just watched two men die, the pilot Andy Potter and his RAF ground crewman, Corporal Kevin Turner, who was flying with him because they were travelling on to another show. The Vampire 'waffled' away with catastrophic damage to its starboard fin, rudder and tail plane. Then one of its occupants, it turned out to be the pilot, ejected and his parachute deployed, to be followed a few moments later by his ground crewman. The Vampire crashed in a field further from the airfield. It was shocking to watch.

The commentator, Roger Hoefling, no doubt following a planned course of action and because the crashes were off the airfield, immediately switched to the next act of the air show, which carried on with hardly a pause. Not long afterwards it was our turn to strap into our Lightnings and to fly our display. It was one of the hardest things I'd ever had to do, ignoring what I had just witnessed, suppressing any emotions and concentrating on the job in hand; it actually took some courage. Our display went well.

I was subsequently called to the board of inquiry into the Vintage Pair accident as an expert witness. I had a very clear and detailed recollection of what I had seen and what had occurred. After giving my evidence to the board, I was asked to leave the room and wait outside which seemed unusual. Several minutes later I was called back in and given an explanation. The board had access to several videos of the accident taken by various spectators from different parts of the crowd line. They had also interviewed many of those civilian witnesses to the crash and as a result their interpretation of the videos had been skewed by that evidence. I was the first witness they had interviewed who described it the way I had so they had gone back to the videos and seen that my recollection was in fact the correct version of events.

Later I also had to attend the coroner's inquest into the deaths which was a sad affair with the dead crew's families present along with the surviving pilot. It was rather daunting to have to repeat my evidence for the coroner.

TACEVAL

In July 1986 RAF Binbrook underwent a NATO TACEVAL. On that exercise I flew six sorties in Lightning F.3s plus one in a squadron F.6.

During this TACEVAL, Flight Lieutenant Bob Bees, one of the experienced students who was on the weapons instructor course on the LTF, was temporarily back with XI Squadron, flying their F.6 Lightnings for the exercise. On 15 July, after refuelling from a Victor tanker, he and another Lightning attacked a pair of Tornadoes, after which Bob accelerated his aircraft to 580 knots in order to catch a pair of F-16s at low level over the North Sea. At 580 knots he deselected reheat and continued accelerating to 600 knots using maximum cold power. Reducing power to maintain 600 knots he manoeuvred the Lightning to obtain a position for a simulated gun kill on one of the F-16s. As he turned away the audio attention getters sounded and a Reheat 1 fire caption illuminated. He shut down the affected engine and headed the aircraft to the east away from the coast and initiated a climb, declaring an emergency and asking for a visual inspection from the pilot of the second Lightning. This confirmed that he did have a fire. Things deteriorated rapidly from there and, when the control column seized solid, Bob throttled back the other engine and ejected at 10,000 feet and 280 knots. I remember him telling me later that he had his eyes open during the ejection (there was no miniature detonating chord in the Lightning canopy, so Lightning pilots were not trained to close their eyes on ejection). When he was ejected at more than 30G, he rolled forward in his harness and saw his aircraft flying away beneath him. The Lightning crashed into the sea about seven miles north of Whitby and Bob was rescued from the sea by SAR helicopter a short while later, none the worse for wear. His flying boots were subsequently added to the growing collection nailed to the ceiling of the bar in the officers' mess on the station, all boots owned by pilots who had ejected whilst flying from Binbrook. Bob was back flying very quickly.

Training Lightning Pilots

Meanwhile, the real job of the LTF, training pilots to fly and operate the Lightning, continued.

We graduated one Long Course of ab-initio pilots and the final Royal Australian Air Force (RAAF) exchange pilot to fly the Lightning, Flight Lieutenant Dick Coleman. Dick had flown Mirage IIIOs with the RAAF. We were not to know it at the time but he was also to become the last pilot to eject from a Lightning after joining XI Squadron when, on 11 April 1988, not long before the Lightning Force disbanded, he suffered an in-flight engine fire and was forced to eject. He was rescued from the sea and was back flying very quickly. This was the seventy-sixth and last Lightning to be destroyed in RAF service from the 280 delivered.

In September 1986 Group Captain John 'Spon' Spencer arrived to take over command of RAF Binbrook from Group Captain John May; he joined the LTF for a short refresher course. I now found myself working for him for the third time in my career; he had been my flight commander on 19 Squadron as a squadron leader, my squadron commander on XI Squadron as a wing commander and now he was to be my station commander. He was a massively experienced Lightning pilot and weapons instructor and still very much the fighter pilot. I flew some of the dual sorties in the conversion and the radar phases with him in T.5s and my logbook shows a 1v1 air combat training (ACT) sortie against him in two F.3s with the note 'kill' beside it, meaning I had shot him down. He was probably out of practice, but a 'kill' against Spon was not to be sniffed at and I had got my own back for the complete thrashing he had given me on a 1v1 ACT sortie when I was a junior pilot on 19 Squadron in 1974.

The LTF had a special trick it reserved for one student on every course on their first solo in a Lightning. The ground crew had become so adept at fitting a new brake parachute that they could do so before the student pilot climbed out of the cockpit after his first solo on type. (To put this into context, when pilots had to turn round their own aircraft it probably took about fifteen minutes to fit a new brake parachute.) Flushed with excitement and with their brain somewhat befuddled by the overwhelming experience of a first solo on the Lightning, the student pilot would be greeted by the ground crew scurrying around with fire extinguishers and putting asbestos blankets over the wheels, whilst pointing out to the pilot that he hadn't pulled the brake parachute on landing and now the brakes had overheated and the wheels and brakes would need to be changed. A glance at the rear of the aircraft would confirm the brake parachute fully stowed with the doors shut. Most would say that they thought they had pulled the brake parachute, but in the excitement of the moment, they couldn't be sure. A 'rocket' from the Boss would follow, until they were put out of their misery later on and told it was a spoof.

One of the students on the Long Course around this time, on whom we played this trick, was Flight Lieutenant Ian Black, who was unusual in that he had previously been an air defence navigator on F-4 Phantoms, but had been allowed to cross-train as a pilot. His father, George Black, had been a renowned Lightning pilot and reached the rank of air vice marshal before retiring from the service to work in the defence industry. Ian had a serious incident on only his third solo sortie on the LTF course in a Lightning F.3 on 22 October 1986. Somewhat fortunately, as it turned out, it was a very short sortie of maximum-rate turns with considerable use of full reheat. When he landed the brake parachute failed and, having stopped and cleared the runway using the wheel brakes alone, he shut down to await the fire crews. It was found that a large hole had been burned in the rear fuselage by the lower jet pipe and there were other indications of a serious in-flight fire, which had burned through the brake parachute cable. It was subsequently discovered that the cause of the fire was a broken fuel pipe at the rear of the aircraft; the leaking fuel had been ignited by the reheat. The fire had been so severe that the fire-detection wire had been burned through so that there had been no fire warning in the cockpit. We nearly lost another Lightning to an in-flight fire that day and Ian came close to having to eject very early on in his time with the aircraft. The Lightning F.3, XP751, was not repaired after this incident and never flew again.

Ian had no difficulty with the radar phases of the course with his navigator background and, as it transpired, he was the last pilot to complete the LTF course and to qualify to fly the Lightning operationally. His compatriot on the course was suspended – 'chopped' – from Lightning training as, sadly, were the five ab-initio students sent to the Lightning after him. The unfortunate students each tried their very best and their failure was more a reflection of inaccurate assessment in earlier training and of inappropriate role disposal than of any lack of effort on their own part. Two of them subsequently did well on the F-4 Phantom and another eventually succeeded on the Tornado F.3.

These student pilot suspensions were a final confirmation, if any were needed, of the difficulties which had always existed in flying and operating the Lightning and of the requirement for successful Lightning pilots to possess a very high cockpit workload capacity. Over the years this was the downfall of many pilots who failed to make the grade at the Lightning conversion unit and were sent off to fly something less demanding. The cockpit workload in the Lightning could be extremely high. The radar took skill and dexterity with the hand controller to operate, to find the target and to optimise the picture. As there was no automation, a radar intercept took considerable amounts of mental arithmetic and capacity to complete successfully. Doing this whilst flying the aircraft at high speed, possibly on instruments, in cloud or at night, sometimes at low altitude, worrying about where you were and how much fuel you had, created a considerable cockpit workload. This ramped up further if things started to go wrong, which they frequently did. The Lightning was a rather dangerous aircraft that could bite even the wary.

Twice the Speed of Sound

In October 1985 I had the opportunity to take a Lightning to M2.0, the only time I ever did. I was conducting an engine air test on the LTF Lightning F.6 XR726, which had the ventral gunpack removed and so carried the most fuel. The air test required a high-speed run to M1.6 but, as I had the fuel and the inclination, I let her keep accelerating whilst I gently climbed to allow the Mach number to increase against the indicated air speed. Eventually, I saw that magic M2.0 indicated on the strip Mach-meter, twice the speed of sound. There was, of course, no impression at high altitude of the fact that I was travelling at over 1,500mph and this was the only time in my RAF fast-jet career that I ever saw that speed.

*****

In December I took the opportunity on my annual dual check to fly with the Lightning Central Flying School Agent and LTF QFI, Flight Lieutenant John Fynes, so that he could confirm my category as an A2 instructor on the Lightning. I had now held the A category as a QFI on the Bulldog, the Hawk and the Lightning.

On 1 January 1987 my acting rank of squadron leader was made substantive. The station commander, Group Captain John Spencer, wrote in his letter of congratulation to me: 'Just because you are no longer an acting Squadron Leader does not mean that you can stop acting like a Squadron Leader.'

Having received this news, I contacted the fast-jet squadron leader pilots' desk officer, my poster, to discuss my future posting. Pete Hitchcock, whom I had spoken to about it when I was first given acting rank, had moved on and his replacement claimed to have no knowledge of the promise I had been made about being put forward for a flight commander post on a Tornado F.3 Squadron. However, he agreed to look into it after I had explained. In due course I was 'boarded' for a flight commander 'slot' with 5 Squadron, which was due to re-equip with the Tornado F.3 at Coningsby shortly after the LTF disbanded in the summer. In the interim, a decision was taken to 'fold' the LTF in April 1987, sooner than had originally been planned. It didn't affect my selection for the Tornado F.3 flight commander post but did mean that an 'out of area' four-month posting became inevitable. I was posted to RAF Mount Pleasant in the Falkland Islands as the squadron leader operations for four months from May to September, but then subsequently on to the Tornado F.3 at Coningsby, commencing the conversion course in November. That was all for the future though; I had to finish the job at Binbrook first.

Lightning Swansong

With the LTF now due to disband before the 1987 air-show season started, Flight Lieutenant Barry Lennon from 5 Squadron was selected to be the Lightning display pilot for the year. The display needed to be flown in a Lightning F.3 to save fatigue on the operational F.6s. Because the squadrons did not have F.3s on their strength, Barry commenced his work-up using an F.3 borrowed from the LTF.

On a beautiful spring morning on 19 March, Barry took off early, before the rest of the station commenced flying, to practise his display sequence in the Binbrook overhead, in LTF Lightning F.3 XP707, with a minimum height of 5,000 feet. I was at the main Met brief in the station briefing room, with the station commander and executives in the front row and the doors open to the outside world, as it was pleasantly warm. During the briefing we heard an ominous 'thump', immediately followed by the sirens of fire trucks. This was quickly followed by the sound of running feet and one of my LTF tactics instructors, Flight Lieutenant Andy 'Spock' Holmes, who had been watching the Lightning stunting overhead from outside the LTF, burst into the briefing room without ceremony, obviously out of breath and flustered. Pointing at the station commander, then at OC 5 Squadron and then at OC Operations Wing he said, 'Sir. Sir. Sir. Come quick,' and then disappeared as fast as he had appeared, without further explanation. The station commander calmly suggested that we had better stop the briefing and go and find out what had happened.

What had happened was that Barry Lennon had ejected from one of the LTF's Lightning F.3s. During his practice display the ventral tank fuel feed was slow to keep up with the demand of the engines in reheat, so the aircraft had developed an aft centre of gravity. During a slow roll the nose had begun to drop and Barry pushed hard and rolled faster with the application of aileron and rudder. The resulting manoeuvre, a negative-G tuck into an inverted spin, had never before been demonstrated in a Lightning. We were all much relieved that he survived the subsequent ejection and parachute landing on the airfield with nothing more than a pair of bruised heels to show for it. The aircraft crashed onto the airfield, conveniently near the fire dump. Within twenty minutes of the accident Barry telephoned me from 5 Squadron and said, 'That aircraft is u/s, Sir. Can I have another one?' My answer was in the negative, accompanied by appropriate expletives, but then I did inquire after his health.

Subsequently, Flight Lieutenant John Fynes was selected as the Lightning display pilot for 1987; he became the last ever Lightning display pilot.

*****

The end for the LTF was now looming and I managed to persuade my direct Boss, Wing Commander Jake Jarron, OC Operations Wing at Binbrook (who subsequently took command of XI Squadron up to the unit's disbandment with the Lightning), that we should fly a Lightning F.3 with its ventral tank removed as a thank-you present to all the LTF instructors. He agreed as long as he could have a go himself. Without its ventral tank, the F.3 carried only 5,000lbs of fuel at start-up and weighed in at just over 32,000lbs. With the engines rated to produce 32,720lbs of thrust this promised to be interesting.

On 14 April 1987 LTF Lightning F.3 XR716 was towed out onto the pan ready to fly with no ventral tank fitted. All the LTF staff instructors had a flight in this cigar-shaped 'rocket ship'. The rotation 'rote' take offs were spectacular in terms of how high the aircraft went in the vertical from such a low-speed pull-up after take off. However, when viewed from outside we all felt that the aircraft did not 'square the corner' in the same spectacular way that the Lightning normally did with the ventral tank fitted. On my sortie I also explored the low-level acceleration from 300 knots to 600 knots.

It took fifteen seconds. I then discovered that it was possible to sustain 6G at only 300 knots at low level in full reheat. Then it was all over; I had used all the fuel, having spent most of the time airborne in reheat, and it was time to return to Binbrook to break into the circuit and land. My sortie was logged as ten minutes. Whilst the performance was fantastic, this was obviously not a useful operational aircraft in the ventral-less configuration.

*****

The last flights by the LTF were on 16 April 1987 when we flew a final disbandment flypast at Binbrook and then had a party although the unit did not finally disband until the end of the month. I led the eight aircraft off, in five-second stream, each of us doing 'rote' take offs, before we joined up in an eight-ship close formation. After an eight-ship formation flypast, with two box-fours joined together in line astern, we then split into two separate four-ships for a couple of synchronised formation flypasts before we arrived back in two echelon fours to break and split into individual aircraft for 'rotes' and low, fast flypasts. It was quite a beat up and will always have a special place in my memory.

My time flying the Lightning was over. It was a sad day when we finally stopped flying on the LTF and, for me, it ended an association and a love affair with the Lightning that had begun in 1973. Like all the pilots who were fortunate enough to fly the Lightning in operational service with the RAF, I feel truly privileged to have had the experiences that the aircraft and the Lightning Force gave me. Lightning pilots felt that they were part of an elite band and, in truth, there were never that many of them even after over thirty-five years in service. I'm very glad that I was one of them.

In the four years from the start of my tour with the Lightning Force at Binbrook until its disbandment in the spring of 1988, no fewer than eight Lightnings were lost with two pilots killed and six being forced to eject. It was a rather dangerous aircraft and my wife was relieved when I stopped flying it.

Falkland Islands

I was now looking forward to flying one of the newest aircraft in the RAF inventory, the Tornado F.3, but before that I was to spend four months in the Falkland Islands, 7,000 miles away from home, spending the UK summer in a South Atlantic winter. It felt a very long way from home and a long time away from my family but it undoubtedly broadened my experience in many ways.

I worked closely with the British Army and the Royal Navy as well as elements of the RAF, which I had no previous experience or much knowledge about. I formed a good working relationship with the British Army resident infantry company from the Devonshire and Dorset Regiment and fired their SA80 rifle. I worked with the RAF Regiment Rapier squadron at Mount Pleasant and spent a day with them firing general-purpose, belt-fed machine guns, mounted on poles at model aircraft drones, practising light anti-aircraft defence. I flew in the back of an F-4 Phantom and I visited all three of the mountain radar sites – Mount Kent, Mount Byron and Mount Alice – that provided fighter control for air defence of the Falklands. I flew in Chinook and Sea King helicopters, even acting as a survivor in a dinghy in the sea for the Sea King crew to rescue me, because one of my roles was to act as the Rescue Centre Co-ordinator for real rescues. I also flew in a Chinook to Sea Lion Island to see the elephant seals close up and travelled by Land Rover to find penguin colonies.

As the Squadron Leader Operations, I was not only responsible for the station's central operations centre and for QRA, but I was also the station Intelligence Officer and the station Navigation Officer. It was intense and hard work with hardly any days off and I was permanently on call for a variety of reasons for the entire time that I was at Mount Pleasant.

Contact with home in those days was limited mainly to the free airmail letters – 'blueys' – as there was no Internet, no e-mail, no mobile phones and the telephone had about a minute delay on the line and conversations were stilted and virtually impossible. The mail was a major morale booster and if the Tristar didn't get in each week and the mail didn't arrive it was a big disappointment. I was glad to get back home in September for some well-deserved leave, before starting on the Tornado F.3.

Chapter 9

Tornado F.3 Squadron

Tornado F.3

The Tornado Air Defence Variant (ADV), which became the Tornado F.3, shared 80 per cent commonality with the interdictor-strike (IDS) Tornado GR.1. It was the cheapest and most politically acceptable option available to fulfil the Air Staff Requirement, although at £25 million each it was not exactly a 'snip'. The requirement was driven by the Cold War scenario of intercepting and engaging Russian heavy bombers over the North Sea, an environment where there would be no surface-to-air threats, nor the need to counter enemy fighters, so self-defence counter-measures and air-to-air combat capability were not deemed relevant to its role.

During its early years of service with the RAF the Tornado F.3 was barely capable of achieving even the original limited requirements as a bomber interceptor. It took time, and a considerable amount of work by the Tornado F.3 Operational Evaluation Unit and the squadrons, to convince the RAF hierarchy of the aircraft's deficiencies and the need to rectify them. Then later, as the aircraft had been developed to face new threats and had been improved beyond all expectations it took many years to shake off its early bad press. In fact, over the twenty-five years it was in service, the Tornado F.3 became a first-class interceptor, ultimately equipped with state-of-the-art avionics and a world-class weapons system.

*****

The Tornado F.3 was powered by two RB199 104 engines with extended reheat, which together produced 18,200 pounds of thrust in dry power (the same as the Tornado GR.1) and a respectable 32,800 pounds in full reheat (seven per cent more than the GR.1). These figures show a much greater difference in thrust between dry and reheated power than earlier pure-jet engines. The relatively-small RB199 engines were three-spool high-bypass ratio turbofan engines optimised to provide most power at lower altitudes with good fuel economy, ideal for the low-level role of the Tornado GR.1 but less so for operating at high levels as the F.3 frequently needed to do. In dry power the aircraft could struggle when manoeuvring at medium level and even in reheat it was always short of power at higher altitudes, something that was never rectified during its service.

The Tornado's RB199 engines included thrust reverse for stopping on the runway after landing – always used because the wheel brakes were not up to much – and this provided significant benefits over the Lightning and F-4 Phantom's brake parachute systems.

In keeping with the electronic and complex aircraft that it was, the throttles on the F.3 had no direct or mechanical connection to the engines. They were effectively just electrical rheostats that fed the pilot's demands to the digital engine-control unit, which then controlled the engines and their acceleration or deceleration, taking into account altitude, airspeed and angle of attack. This provided carefree throttle handling, meaning that the pilot could slam the throttles in any flight condition and the engines would react at an automatically controlled rate that would prevent them from surging. The digital engine-control unit was just one of nineteen computers which controlled various systems.

The Tornado F.3's fuselage was slightly longer than the GR version, with a small plug inserted aft of the rear cockpit to make the underbelly long enough to accommodate four medium-range air-to-air missiles, slightly staggered on their launchers. This increased length had a number of beneficial effects apart from making the aircraft appear sleeker. The F.3 was certainly a good-looking aircraft. The rear cockpit was moved forward, giving the occupant, usually the navigator, a better view forward and down. The extra space behind the cockpit accommodated the so-called 'O' tank, a fuel tank that held an additional 600 kilograms of fuel. The lengthened fuselage, along with the longer nose radome and the extended 68-degree swept-wing-root glove fairing, also endowed the aircraft with some aerodynamic advantages, including better transonic and supersonic acceleration with reduced supersonic drag. Going supersonic at any altitude, even at very low level, was completely without drama and very easy to do. The Tornado F.3 was normally operated to a maximum airspeed of 725 knots in RAF service, but it was capable of speeds up to 800 knots at low level. At low level, acceleration from 300 knots to 600 knots took about twenty seconds, the same as a Lightning F.6. You could chase most other aircraft types down at low level and nothing was going to outrun you. At high altitude the aircraft was capable of M2.0, although I never saw it, but I frequently and routinely pushed it to M1.6.

The Tornado was, famously, a variable-geometry, swing-wing, aircraft and there was an additional lever in the cockpit beside and inboard of the throttles for the pilot to play with, to sweep the wings. It worked in the natural sense, forward for wings forward and rearwards for wings back. The F.3 wing-sweep lever had notches for five wing-sweep settings: fully forward at 25 degrees for speeds below 350 knots, 35 degrees, which was never actually officially cleared for use but was useful for range cruising, 45, 58 and 67 degrees, the fully-swept setting being for high speed and supersonic flight.

The Tornado F.3 was supposed to have an automatic wing-sweep-and-manoeuvre devices system and new aircraft were delivered from the factory at Warton with the system fitted and activated. I flew a brand-new Block 14 Tornado F.3 from Warton to Coningsby in 1990 with the system activated and working perfectly. I thought it was marvellous. However, the RAF engineers in their wisdom believed that the system could not be supported in service and so de-activated it on arrival. That was the only time that I flew with the system functioning. The lack of it meant that pilots had to remember a whole bunch of numbers for airspeeds and Mach numbers for the different wing-sweep settings and then move the wing-sweep lever and operate the manoeuvre flaps and slats to keep within the limits. If you got it wrong the aircraft would generally tell you by buffeting. If you did it correctly you would have a distinct advantage in a turning fight against another Tornado F.3 pilot who didn't. Meanwhile, the Tornado F.3s in service with the Royal Saudi Air Force operated with the automatic system in place without any difficulty.

The control system in the Tornado F.3 was light and relatively responsive – it was designed to be about 30 per cent lighter in feel to the pilot than the GR version – although the aircraft was so stable that it could take a significant initial control input to get it moving. The aircraft had a fly-by-wire electronic control system, with a complex command stability augmentation system (CSAS) along with a spin and incidence limiting system (SPILS). Together they offered carefree handling and, as long as you flew within the angle of attack and G limits, which were not automatically limited, you could do whatever you liked with the control column and the aircraft would not depart from controlled flight. The corollary to this was that it could be quite disconcerting to realise that your controls were not directly connected to the aircraft.

In some configurations the Tornado F.3 was a 7 G aircraft; so whilst it was never a dogfighter it would be wrong to think that it couldn't pull high G forces.

The Tornado was flown largely by reference to angle of attack (AOA); there was a physical instrument beside the head-up display (HUD) and AOA indications in the HUD. For me, this was the first time I had flown using AOA 'units', but it was something I quickly became used to although I never lost my grounding in cross-referencing the airspeed.

The HUD was a brilliant addition to anything I had experienced before and was very much the main source of reference for the pilot rather than the head-down instruments. With an old-fashioned attitude indicator instrument there is no telling what indicated attitude will be required for level flight at various speeds and aircraft configurations. With the HUD all the pilot had to do was to put the aircraft symbol on the horizon bar and the aircraft would fly level at any speed, configuration or wing weep. The F.3 also had so-called specific excess power (SEP) bars in the HUD that looked like equal signs. If you moved the throttles to put the SEP bars level with the wings of the aircraft symbol then the aircraft would not accelerate or decelerate, which made holding a given speed very easy. In addition to displaying the necessary flight instrument indications for attitude, speed, altitude, heading, G and AOA, the HUD also presented all the necessary weapon and weapon-aiming symbology, including a target detection (TD) circle which overlaid the target being tracked by the radar, making it easier to gain a visual tally by looking through it.

The Tornado cockpit was a comfortable place to be, quiet even at high speed, with an excellent air-conditioning system and with good all-round vision. The voice-operated microphones in the oxygen masks meant that the intercom was silent and devoid of breathing noises, until either the pilot or the navigator spoke. The Martin Baker Mk 10 rocket ejection seats were comfortable, at least as much as any ejection seat can be; they had a zero-height and zero-speed capability and in the Tornado the crew were provided with double leg restraints – at the ankle and above the knee – and with arm restraints to prevent limbs from flailing in the event of a high-speed ejection.

*****

The Tornado F.3 weapon system and its development merit a book in its own right. Suffice it to say here that it centred on the AI 24 Foxhunter radar, a main computer and synthetic single-colour displays. There were two TV tabs in the rear cockpit for the navigator, who usually selected the radar display on one and the 'god's-eye-view' tactical plan display on the other. The pilot could select a repeat of either of those on his electronic head-down display and switch between them. The displays could be recorded on video for subsequent training value in the sortie debrief.

The radar had good detection range and provided a track-while-scan capability which meant that the crew were offered the same detailed information on any one of several radar tracks whilst still tracking others and being able to switch between them without alerting a target's radar-warning receiver by locking the radar on. Earlier radars gave that detail for only one target when locked onto it and blind to all others. There were numerous problems with the AI 24 Foxhunter radar in the early years of the Tornado F.3's service with the RAF and it took many years to resolve them, but resolved they eventually were. Initially though, the radar lacked much in the way of automation and took skill and attention by the navigator to operate.

A software-driven radar-homing-and-warning receiver provided accurate and detailed threat warnings to the Tornado F.3 crew. Twin inertial navigation systems provided accurate navigation information, much improved later in the aircraft's life when replaced by twin laser inertial navigation systems with an embedded global position system (GPS). A main computer looked after a number of aspects and integrated them onto the displays, including information on the fuel required to a destination.

Eight air-to-air missiles – four semi-active Skyflash missiles with beyond visual range capability and four Sidewinder AIM-9L infra-red-homing short-range missiles – provided a substantial punch. The Tornado F.3 also had a single 27mm Mauser cannon.

The pilot had hands-on-throttle-and-stick (HOTAS) controls on the throttles and control column which was improved quite early on in the aircraft's life with a new stick top similar to that fitted to the F-18. This allowed the pilot to select and fire the weapons and to take control of the radar for various close-in visual radar-lock modes without taking his hands off the controls.

This then, as it transpired, was to be 'my' aircraft and the principal focus of my working life for the next sixteen years. I flew the Tornado F.3 continuously from 1987 to 2003.

Squadron Conversion Course

When I arrived on the Tornado F.3 Operational Conversion Unit – No. 229 OCU – at Coningsby in November 1987, it had been operating the Tornado F.2 and F.3 for more than three years, slowly building up, training its own OCU staff and then converting the first squadron aircrew to type. The first operational Tornado F.3 unit, 29 Squadron, also based at Coningsby, was about to be declared operational that month. No. 5 Squadron (Designate) was in the process of forming as the second operational Tornado F.3 unit, also based at Coningsby, to take over the squadron number plate and identity from 5 (Lightning) Squadron.

No. 5 (Tornado F.3) Squadron was initially formed with ten pilots and ten navigators, all with previous experience of air defence on the Lightning, the F-4 Phantom, or both. Some of these crews had begun the Squadron Conversion Course on the OCU ahead of me and I was in the second batch of 5 Squadron crews to be trained.

The ground school phase took a month to complete which was hardly surprisingly for such a complex aircraft. There was no full mission simulator at this time, just a cockpit emergencies procedure trainer which didn't 'fly' as such, and some other basic training systems. These were sufficient to allow us to learn the procedures, cockpit checks and emergency drills.

The flying phases of the course began for me with my first conversion flight in a Tornado F.3 on 3 December. After four dual sorties in 'two-stick' trainer Tornado F.3s, I flew a 'single-sticker' with an OCU staff navigator in the rear cockpit. The conversion phase was completed that month with a total of fourteen hours of flying.

In the New Year I completed the basic radar and combat phases during a deployment by the OCU to RAF Akrotiri in Cyprus for better winter weather. By mid-February my course was over with just thirty-three hours of flying on the new type. The rest of the work up to become fully combat ready would take place with 5 Squadron, which was to self-train all ten of its first crews to combat-ready standard before being declared operational.

Apart from learning the new aircraft and its plethora of systems, my previous background meant that, unlike the majority of pilots coming to the Tornado F.3 who had experience of semi-active, beyond-visual-range 'Fox 1' (Skyflash) missile tactics from the F4, I was not familiar with the tactics and procedures for front-hemisphere missile attacks. It was all new to me and took me a while, even on the squadron, to become familiar with it all.

No longer did the tactics involve only stern conversions to kill bandits with stern missile shots, now you could shoot them in the face.

In addition, I was having to learn to work and co-operate with a navigator, something that my single-seat mindset didn't initially find easy. Making full use of what the 'nav' had to offer, keeping him informed of what I was thinking tactically and what I was going to do with the aircraft, and working together as a team, took quite some time to get used to. This was very important as poor crew co-operation would reduce the fighting effectiveness of the aircraft and could even be dangerous. There were many more aspects to this than first met the eye but it was something that I think I eventually mastered, although you would have to ask the navigators that I flew with later in my time on the Tornado F.3 to see if they agreed. I know that I came to enjoy the mutual understanding that could develop in the cockpit between pilot and navigator, with inter-cockpit communication minimised, if you flew together regularly. I also learned that flying with a weak nav actually increased your workload as the pilot.

On Parade

Whilst much of my focus during this time was on getting to grips with all that the Tornado F.3 had to offer, I was also one of the two flight commanders on the nascent 5 (Tornado F.3) Squadron with numerous responsibilities in setting up the unit's headquarters and its operational functionality. One of the tasks that fell to the new squadron whilst we were still completing the conversion course on the OCU was to take-over the 5 Squadron Standard from the disbanding 5 (Lightning) Squadron, with a parade at Binbrook.

An RAF squadron Standard is a light-blue embroidered silk flag, fringed and tasselled in gold and blue, mounted on a staff surmounted by a gold eagle, with the unit's Battle Honours emblazoned on it. When squadrons disband, their standards are laid up and when they reform the standard is handed over. The standards are treated with great reverence, respect and ceremony; they are always guarded when in public and are paraded on special occasions.

The ceremony to take over the 5 Squadron Standard took place in a hangar at Binbrook with a full parade of airmen NCOs and officers of the new 5 Squadron in front of an audience of their families and with the Air Officer Commanding (AOC) 11 Group, Air Vice Marshal (later Air Chief Marshal) Roger Palin, as the reviewing officer. As a former Army officer with the Parachute Regiment and the Royal Green Jackets, he would have a critical eye for our parade drill. We had practised extensively for the parade at Coningsby, with the new OC 5 Squadron, Wing Commander Euan Black, as the parade commander. He had to learn the lengthy script of drill commands, whilst the rest of us had to remember how to march and drill, in my case as a flight commander with sword drawn, leading one of the two flights on the parade.

On the day, in the hangar at Binbrook, the parade went well until just before the 'advance in review order'. It was necessary for the parade commander to call 'Shoulder arms' to get the parade to shoulder their rifles before 'Advance in review order. By the centre, quick march'. Everyone then marched fourteen paces forward and halted without command, before a 'General salute. Present arms'. Unfortunately, the Boss forgot the all-important 'Shoulder arms' command. I hadn't actually noticed. When I had marched my fourteen paces forward in front of my flight, with my eyes firmly to the front and as unaware as the Boss of what was going on behind, I was slightly disconcerted to hear far less crashing of rifles at the 'present arms' than was normally the case. The Boss, as parade commander, then marched forward to the dais on which the AOC was standing, waved his sword in salute and asked for permission to carry on. The AOC returned the salute and said words to the effect of 'Sort that fxxxxxx lot out Black!' The Boss saluted back with his sword, about turned and for the first time saw the shambles that had ensued. Some of the airmen, believing that you couldn't march with the rifle butts on the ground at the 'order', had remained where they were. Some had marched forward with their rifles dragging on the ground. Some, but not many, had invented a new drill movement and managed to present arms from the 'order' which had ended with their rifles shouldered. So, some were fourteen paces ahead of others, some had their rifles at the order and some had them shouldered. I could see none of this behind me, but I could see that the Boss was looking horrified and somewhat lost, trying to work out how he was going to get out of this. He also seemed to be trying to catch my eye, as if I could help. I kept my eyes firmly forward. Eventually, the Warrant Officer who had drilled us all to perfection before this marched on to the parade and, with a few commands, got everyone where they were supposed to be. The rest of the parade, including the march past, went off without further incident.

We subsequently climbed onto the coaches for the trip back to Coningsby, where an all-ranks beer call was planned to end the day in the newly set up squadron bar on the dispersed site that was to be 5 Squadron's new home.

When we left that morning, the bar didn't have a name. When we returned it had a brand new pub sign outside and had been christened 'The Shoulder Arms'. This was a name it was to keep for many years, long after those who knew the original significance had moved on.

5 Squadron

The new 5 Squadron equipped with Tornado F.3s officially 'stood up' in February 1988. We then had less than three months to complete the remainder of the squadron work up and to get the first ten crews, all with previous air-defence experience, up to fully combat-ready status so that the squadron could be declared operational on schedule. This period culminated in a NATO TACEVAL.

We settled into our new hardened accommodation in the second of the two dispersed sites at Coningsby. The aircraft were all accommodated in dispersed hardened aircraft shelters (HASs), with one or two aircraft in each, rather than lined up on an aircraft servicing pan. The squadron aircrew and ground crew were, therefore, operating daily just as they would in war. The aircrew walked or were taken by minibus to the HAS where their allocated aircraft was resident, strapped in and started up inside the HAS with the doors open front and back and taxied out with the wings swept back until clear. At the end of the sortie, the aircraft was winched back into the HAS with one engine running and with the wings swept back to ensure good clearance, before sweeping the wings forward and shutting down in place ready for the next sortie. The squadron operations and briefing rooms were also in a hardened bunker, known as the pilot briefing facility (PBF), which was resistant to bomb damage, with filters and air locks to permit continued operations if the outside environment was contaminated by nuclear fall-out or chemical agents. The PBF also contained a windowless dormitory, which we called 'the submarine', with tiers of bunks packed into it where air crew and ground crew 'hot bunked' in order to get sleep during exercises, just as they would have to do in war. Next door to the PBF was the 'soft', a normal building with the day-to-day aircrew crew room and all the necessary offices, including the squadron and flight commanders' offices.

Over the next several weeks we conducted more esoteric practice intercepts, such as against high-flying supersonic or low-flying targets. Night flying saw us become qualified to operate at 1,000 feet over the sea in the dark and cleared crews to conduct night visidents against targets at both medium and low level with their external lights on or off. We deployed aircraft to RAF Valley for a short missile practice camp, during which some crews fired live missiles. I photo-chased and observed a Sidewinder AIM-9L firing. Back home we practised Quick Reaction Alert (QRA) procedures in preparation for taking over QRA (South) duties. We also conducted some dissimilar air combat training against Lightnings and against Dutch F-16s. There were also major exercises during which we practised wartime procedures. It was all very intense with no time to waste.

On the ground, meanwhile, I was settling into my new role as the unit's flight commander operations, responsible for all operational aspects of the squadron, including the plot for managing our aircrew resources with leave and courses balanced against the task, overseeing the structure and content of the flying programme, which was put together daily by the junior officer programmers, planning our part in all exercises and for QRA operations and rostering. Meanwhile, in the air I needed to build my credibility as a fighter pilot and leader whilst myself learning the new aircraft. I won't pretend it was easy.

On 1 May 1988 No. 5 Squadron was declared to NATO as the RAF's second fully-operational Tornado F.3 squadron. There was no let-up in the pressure though, as the next day we started our first stint of QRA, requiring two crews and two fully-armed aircraft on a high alert state in the 'Q Shed' twenty-four/seven. In addition, the squadron received four new ab-initio crews – four pilots and four navigators – straight from the OCU, to work up to combat-ready status to make the full complement of fourteen crews on the squadron. Then it was straight into a NATO TACEVAL, which went well.

Tornado F.3 Air-to-Air Gunnery

In July 1988 the squadron deployed to RAF Akrotiri, Cyprus, for its first Armament Practice Camp (APC) to fire the single Mauser 27mm cannon in the Tornado F.3 at a banner target towed by a Canberra. I flew one of the aircraft out to Cyprus non-stop with air-to-air refuelling from a VC10 tanker, the transit taking five hours.

It was a fun detachment, giving the chance for all the squadron's aircrews and indeed the whole squadron to bond together. It was extremely hot in Cyprus that July, often plus 40 degrees centigrade or more, and we found ourselves pushing the limits that the Tornado F.3 was cleared to in terms of operating temperatures at that early stage of its service. The aircraft skins were sometimes too hot to touch and we were grateful for the excellent air conditioning in the Tornado cockpits. The ground crew, meanwhile, had to work outside in those temperatures and the blazing sun all day long.

Firing the 27mm Mauser cannon, which was mounted on the right side of the Tornado F.3's nose, was good fun and very satisfying. It made a classic loud machine-gun noise, 'drdrdrdrdrup', the vibration was pronounced and then you could smell cordite in the cockpit from the spent cartridges. We found that, with the radar locked on, the gun and sighting system in the Tornado F.3 was really very accurate and there were some good results. I scored over 50 per cent on some shoots; my best score on this APC was 58 per cent.

At that time, we were only permitted to fire with the radar locked to the target giving the locked gun-sighting picture in the HUD. This presented an unwinding range circle as the range to the target reduced, giving very accurate range, and also accurate prediction of the necessary 'lead' and gravity drop for the shells to hit the target. ('Lead' is the term for how much the aircraft needs to be pointed ahead of a moving target in order for shells from the fixed gun to hit it. The amount of lead required is proportional to the crossing speed and angle of the target.)

The Tornado F.3 had an alternative gun-sighting system for attacks without the radar locked, but at the time it was not cleared for use. The continuously computed impact line (CCIL), shown in the HUD as a line of sixteen dots spreading back from a fixed gun-sight cross, purported to show the predicted impact point of the first sixteen shells from the gun. It stretched like an elastic band when G was increased and waved when the bank angle was changed. Some pilots referred to it as the 'wiggly worm'; others said that attempting to track a target with it was like trying to 'shove wet spaghetti up a wild cat's arse.' It was certainly difficult to use, but was eventually improved along with the pilots' abilities to track with it and it became a fully-cleared gun-sighting system. For now, however, it was not an option.

On my first 'limited academic' live shoot we had problems with the radar lock tenacity, a typical weakness with the early versions of the Foxhunter radars we were using at the time. On a 'lim ac' shoot, once the pilot had called in 'hot' the first time, he had to fire out all his rounds at the banner over a maximum of four passes. If he didn't and returned with rounds still on board, the score would still count from the number of rounds carried rather than the number fired (none fired, equalled zero per cent). On this shoot, on the first three passes from calling in hot, despite the very best efforts of my navigator, Tony Evans, in monitoring the radar lock and trying to hold onto it, our radar lock failed each time I approached firing range. I hadn't been able to fire at all and now with only one pass left I knew that I might well be heading for a zero score.

With little confidence in the radar lock for the final pass, I selected the standby sight in the HUD, telling Tony what I was doing and that I would shoot using it to aim if the radar lock failed again. He didn't object. The standby sight showed red in the HUD and was simply a fixed sight, similar to what Spitfire and Hurricane pilots would have used in the Battle of Britain, meaning that the range, lead and gravity drop had to be assessed visually by the pilot.

As I had feared it would, the radar lock failed at the critical moment on the final pass. With all the 27mm rounds we were carrying now needing to be fired in one long burst, I opened fire at longer range than usual with the fixed sight held deliberately high – a high line – to compensate for the additional gravity drop and placed well ahead of the target as a guess at the necessary lead. Keeping the trigger pulled, I allowed the fixed cross to slide back and down slightly towards the banner to reduce the lead as the range reduced. The gun ceased firing, out of rounds, and I broke out, making the trigger safe. I wasn't at all confident that I'd hit the target at all.

Back on the ground one of the squadron's qualified weapons instructors (QWIs) debriefed my HUD film before the banner was returned. The QWIs had some *gizmos* that allowed them to assess the range and angle-off at trigger press and cease fire. I had opened fire at 700 yards, much further out than normal, with a safe, if slightly high angle-off. The QWI's gizmo allowed him to assess the amount of lead required at the open fire range. Amazingly, it seemed I had guessed it perfectly. He thought that my line seemed rather high and didn't like the sight sliding back as the range reduced. He thought most rounds would have missed high or off the back of the target, although I might have got a couple on. I had ceased firing before breaking the minimum range or angle-off, so whatever my score was it would stand.

As we left the windowless video debriefing room, we could see that the banner had just been returned and was being unrolled outside. There seemed to be a considerable number of holes of my colour. The QWI looked at me and Tony and said firmly, 'Don't tell anybody how you did this. We don't want anyone else trying it.' When the holes were counted, I had hit the banner with 54 per cent of the rounds fired, with the fixed standby sight. It seemed I was developing an eye for the dark art of air-to-air gunnery.

At the end of the four-week detachment to Cyprus, having flown several ground crew passengers in the back of Tornado F.3s as a thank you for all their hard work, we transited back to UK on another five-hour sortie, 'tanking' from a VC10.

QRA Russian Intercept

Quick Reaction Alert (QRA) duties were shared at Coningsby with 29 Squadron. One of the two units would hold the commitment for a period before handing over to the other. The two QRA HASs, each housing a fully-armed and ready Tornado F.3, were on the 29 Squadron dispersal. The QRA building where the on-duty crews and ground crew lived was next to the QRA HASs. The aircrew tour of duty was for twenty-four hours from 09:00 and I did my fair share, especially at weekends. The aircraft and aircrews were on a high alert state, expected to get airborne in less than ten minutes if scrambled. In most circumstances only one aircraft would be scrambled. During the day it was possible to get some paperwork done whilst wearing all the kit and being ready to go. Food was brought to us in 'hot locks' from one of the Messes and we watched videos and TV. Full and proper sleep wasn't really possible, partly due to the beeping from the 'Telebrief' system from which the scramble order would emanate, also because we were partly dressed and because you didn't let yourself sleep deeply just in case. After twenty-four hours on 'Q', the aircrew generally had a twenty-four-hour stand-down which was actually needed. I quite liked doing Saturday QRA because that way my stand-down day was on a Sunday and I didn't miss any of the Monday to Friday flying and action on the squadron.

One day in early September 1988 I was scrambled from QRA, with first-tourist navigator Dave Thomas, to intercept two Russian Tupolev Tu-95RT four-engined maritime reconnaissance and electronic-intelligence-gathering aircraft, known to NATO as Bear Deltas, inside the UK Air Defence Region, well north of Scotland. At that time we were sitting QRA with our Tornado F.3s armed with eight live air-to-air missiles and a loaded gun but without any underwing fuel tanks fitted, so we needed the VC10 tanker support that was provided for the mission which lasted over six-and-a-half hours.

When we intercepted the Soviet Bears, we took over shadowing them from USAF F-15s out of Keflavik in Iceland. I asked one of the F-15 pilots on the radio to take a photo of our Tornado F.3 alongside one of the Russian aircraft; the colour photo which resulted has hung in my house ever since. My nav photographed the Bears in detail for our intelligence analysts. I dare say that the Russian crews were just as interested in the new Tornado F.3 and its radar emissions, as well as photographing us in return, not that the 'rear gunners' seemed very friendly. Perhaps they were just irritated that, ever since they entered NATO airspace without filing a flight plan and without permission, they had been shadowed by Norwegian, American and British fighters.

The Bears were flying fairly high, around 30,000 feet, at an altitude and speed combination that was quite challenging for the Tornado. I was also surprised that we could actually feel the vibration from their propellers through the air as we flew alongside in loose formation. This was due to the fact that these were one of the few aircraft ever designed which had supersonic propeller tips.

Shortly after this we began to fly with the large 2,250-litre underwing fuel tanks and that became the standard QRA fit along with the full load of missiles. It made the Tornado F.3 feel very heavy and imposed some significant G limitations on the airframe – if you needed to fight, the tanks would have to be jettisoned – but sorties over three hours without air-to-air refuelling were then easily possible.

Air Combat Training in Sardinia

When all the crews on the squadron had reached the required level of training and combat readiness, the sorties we routinely flew became more demanding. We frequently flew as tactical four-ship formations and we conducted affiliation and dissimilar air combat training against increasing sizes of target formations of various RAF and NATO aircraft types.

In February 1989 the Squadron deployed en masse to Decimomannu for two weeks to utilise the Air Combat Manoeuvring Instrumentation (ACMI) range that had been set up for air combat training (ACT) over the sea off the Mediterranean island of Sardinia. I hadn't been back to Sardinia and to 'Deci' since we had used the range for air-to-air gunnery with Lightnings from Gutersloh fourteen years earlier. Nothing had changed much and it all seemed very familiar.

The ACMI system allowed very realistic training and superb debriefing facilities for ACT. Each aircraft carried a missile-shaped instrumentation pod on a missile station so that all aircraft could be accurately tracked, they could be 'controlled' from the cabins on the ground and their flight parameters were recorded for the debrief when the combats would be replayed in three dimensions on large video screens. The system also permitted live and accurate assessment of whether missile 'kills' were achieved. An aircraft that was 'shot down' had a coffin appear around it on the screen in the ground cabin in real time and the pilot/crew would receive the dreaded call, 'You're dead.'

We conducted dissimilar air combat training (DACT) with RAF Harriers and USAFE F-15s, with various scenarios up to 4v4. The weaknesses in the Tornado F.3's 'Z-list' versions of the Foxhunter radar we were using at this stage of its life could be frustrating to say the least. You could fight hard to get to a point where you could take a shot, only for it to be foiled by the radar losing the lock or the plot, degrading the crew's situational awareness. We also suffered from the Tornado F.3's lack of high-level performance.

On one 4v4 DACT sortie against four experienced USAFE F-15 pilots we found ourselves totally outranged by their AIM-7M upgraded Sparrow missiles, which could achieve even greater range when fired from the very high altitudes that the Eagles could easily reach. The F-15s came towards us in a line abreast 'wall' with the highest at one end at 50,000 feet and the lowest at the other end of the wall at 5,000 feet. The F-15 at 50,000 feet fired an AIM-7M and 'killed' one of our Tornado F.3s in our four-ship formation at what seemed like an unbelievably long range to us before we had even started manoeuvring to defend against it. A second 'fight' against the same four F-15s with more limited weapons, with kill removal and regeneration to 'feed the fight' was much more fun; we fared surprisingly well in the ensuing dogfights and even got some kills.

Overall, the ACMI detachment provided some very useful training and proved to be great fun, even if it did highlight some of the areas of the Tornado F.3 that needed to be improved.

Tactical Fighter Meet Husum

In April 1989 we deployed several of our Tornado F.3 aircraft and crews, myself included, to the Luftwaffe air base at Husum in Schleswig-Holstein, northern Germany, just south of the border with Denmark, for a NATO Tactical Fighter Meet (TFM). The Meet was organised by NATO's Allied Forces Northern Europe and involved several different types of fighter and fighter-bomber aircraft from various NATO air forces. The Luftwaffe contributed RF-4E 'recce' Phantoms, F-4F Phantom fighters and Alpha Jet light-attack aircraft, whilst the *Marineflieger* (German Navy air arm) provided Tornado GR.1s. The USAFE sent F-4 Wild Weasels, F-15s and F-16s. From Denmark there were F-16s and Saab Drakens, whilst Norway sent F-16s and F-5s. The RAF was represented by SEPECAT Jaguars and our Tornado F.3s.

The TFM saw some large missions. Sometimes our Tornado F.3s operated as fighter sweep and escort to 'mud-moving' packages, clearing a path through defending fighters for them to attack ground targets and then sweeping the route back out. Sometimes we provided fighter defence opposition for the escorted ground-attack packages. Three of the missions I flew were leading or as part of a four-ship of Tornado F.3s acting as a fighter sweep, leading a package, or 'gorilla', of twenty-four aircraft at low level around Denmark against twelve defending fighters. On one mission, when we were the defenders on fighter combat air patrols, we were fourteen versus forty-plus attackers. We also flew some alternate fill-in sorties of DACT against F-16s and F-4s, 2v4, 4v6 and 4v10. It was extremely good training value to be involved in sorties with such large numbers of aircraft and great fun, too. The Tornado F.3 radars and weapons systems stood up well in the environment and with much of the 'fighting' at low level the aircraft performance was not lacking either. We were able to hold our heads high and feel pride in the results.

There was fun to be had on the ground too. The Danish pilots seemed to be direct descendants of hellraising Vikings and there was some good socialising between us all.

On Target – Armament Practice Camp Cyprus

In June 1989 the squadron deployed en masse to Akrotiri in Cyprus for another annual armament practice camp (APC) of air-to-air gunnery. The transits to and from Cyprus were flown with the big underwing tanks fitted to our Tornado F.3s, but still with air-to-air refuelling (AAR) from VC10s on the way out and Victor tankers on the return just over three weeks later. Both transit sorties were just over five hours.

We were now becoming used to the accuracy of the Tornado F.3 gun and sighting system and the resulting high scores. That said, I was 'chuffed' with the 70 per cent score from my first academic air-to-air gunnery shoot and a subsequent 57 per cent on a limited academic shoot. After two of each of those, we moved onto the so-called 'op shoots'. For these the Canberra towing the banner target would begin turning on a 'commence' call from the 'shooter'. It would turn through 540 degrees and then roll out, at which point firing had to cease. If well flown, the shooter could make three firing passes in that time, pitching in, firing a burst, breaking out, re-positioning and dropping in again three times, in what was a relatively realistic operational scenario. Like the limited academic shoots the score was from the number of rounds carried rather than the number fired.

On my first op shoot, with my navigator Rich Sanderson, it went well in the air and the subsequent gunsight video film showed consistent ranging and steady tracking, with no busts of the minima. We sat and waited for the banner target to be returned. It was a windy day, so when it was delivered it was unrolled inside the hangar next door rather than outside our building as usual. Rich went off to find it and came back to get me, insisting that I came to see it and refusing to tell me why. When I had followed him into the hangar and saw the banner laid out on the floor I understood his excitement. It seemed to be covered in holes of our colour. When our holes had been counted officially by one of the QWIs, the score was an official 100 per cent. Every single round I had fired had hit the target, unbelievable as that seemed. As far as I know, no other Tornado F.3 pilot ever repeated the feat of a 100 per cent score on an op shoot. My second op shoot was less impressive, but still a score of 49 per cent, so over two op shoots I averaged 74.5 per cent hits.

First Tornado F.3 Fatality

At the end of that week the Tornado F.3 Force suffered the loss of its first aircraft, tragically with the death of ex-Lightning pilot Flight Lieutenant Steve 'Alf' Moir. He had been one of the ab-initio students on the Lightning conversion course when I was the Officer Commanding the Lighting Training Flight, so I knew him well. Like me, he had transitioned from the Lightning to the Tornado F.3 and was now on 23 Squadron at RAF Leeming.

On Friday 21 July 1989 Steve, or Alf as we knew him, was part of a low-level 2v2 intercept training sortie over the North Sea, thirty-five miles north-east of Newcastle. Bugging out of an engagement from low speed with a simulated enemy F.3 behind him, he lowered the nose to 20 to 25 degrees from an altitude of 4,000 feet, accelerating down and away into a haze layer over the sea. At 1,000 feet, still not going particularly fast, he swept the wings back to 67 degrees (fully swept) and then began to slowly bring the aircraft's nose up. His navigator, Flight Lieutenant Dave Sully, who had been looking back over his shoulder at the bandits behind, became aware of the height decreasing through 300 to 400 feet with a steeper than normal nose down attitude for the height. He shouted a warning to the pilot as the radar-altimeter audio warning, set to 200 feet, sounded. The aircraft struck the sea in a slightly nose up attitude and was immediately engulfed in a fireball. The navigator pulled his ejection-seat handle just before the tail hit the water. His ejection was successful although he suffered minor burns as he passed through the fireball. With the command eject set to 'both', Alf was ejected half a second later, during the impact. However, he had sustained multiple injuries, including a very severe head injury that would have caused instant loss of consciousness. Once in the water he made no attempt to carry out any survival procedures and was found to have drowned. His body was picked up by a fishing boat. The navigator, Dave Sully, was winched out of the sea by a search-and-rescue Sea King helicopter after forty minutes in the water. He recovered well.

The subsequent board of inquiry suggested that the pilot had probably not appreciated the significant loss of lift, caused by sweeping the wings fully back at too low a speed, which compromised his attempt to level off. In addition, the smooth sea and haze may well have given him insufficient visual cues. This was the first of fourteen Tornado F.3s that were lost in the aircraft's twenty-five years of service and also the first of four to be lost to what is termed 'controlled flight into terrain' (CFIT).

I flew a Tornado F.3 to Leeming to attend Alf Moir's funeral in a local church and the wake in the officers' mess before returning home later the same day. It was a very sad occasion; he was buried in the graveyard of the church where he had been married only a couple of weeks before his death. His new wife was clearly shattered but immensely stoic. After his coffin had been lowered into the grave, all his RAF friends and colleagues in uniform marched up to the grave in pairs, saluted and turned away. It was quite unscripted and most moving, as we all said our unspoken farewells to him.

As a result of this tragic accident the Tornado F.3 OCU introduced a conversion sortie sequence which taught the correct technique for bugging out, sweeping the wings back only as the limiting speeds in each configuration were reached. I later taught that sequence many times to OCU students and often thought of Alf and the reason why we were doing it.

Greek Exchange

In August 1989 I was part of a team from 5 Squadron which deployed to Tanagra Air Base in Greece on a NATO squadron exchange (this one a one-way affair) for ten days. With air-to-air refuelling from a Tristar tanker the transit from Coningsby to Tanagra was flown in just under four hours.

We were royally hosted by the Greeks during our stay and there were plenty of parties as well as good flying to be had. Tanagra is about forty miles north of Athens and we had the opportunity to visit the various tourist sites in the city at the weekend and take in some culture. The taxi ride back to Tanagra from Athens in a BMW taxi with a local taxi driver, often hitting 120 mph and overtaking on blind bends, sticks in mind as being particularly dangerous.

The Hellenic Air Force's (HAF) 331 Squadron based at Tanagra flew the Dassault Mirage 2000-5. The pilots impressed us with their professionalism and their attitude and they also seemed keen to learn from us. It appeared that they would occasionally find themselves engaging in unbriefed and fairly serious mock dogfights with Turkish F-16s over disputed areas of the Aegean Sea and islands.

We flew some visual 1v1 DACT sorties against the Mirage 2000s and we were surprised that we were able to hold our own against them better than we expected, despite the delta-wing Mirage's ability to 'bat turn'. It was as well that we didn't have to fight at higher levels against them. On one sortie I flew with a HAF Mirage 2000 pilot in the rear seat of my Tornado F.3 two-stick trainer and we engaged in 1v1 DACT, with him flying my aircraft against a two-seat Mirage 2000, being flown from its rear cockpit by one of our squadron pilots. The Greek pilot in my aircraft appeared to be more used to totally carefree handling than the F.3 allowed, the risk of a mid-air collision was high and, all in all, it was one of the more dangerous things I ever sat through in an aircraft. In fact, it was a close-run thing as to whether this or the Greek taxi ride from Athens was the more life threatening.

A week into the deployment we were offered an Aegean cruise to the island of Limnos, which is geographically closer to Turkey than to mainland Greece. Some of us flew out to the island in a HAF C-130 Hercules whilst others flew our Tornado F.3s in company with Greek Mirage 2000s. We all had a splendid lunch in a *taverna* on the island and then swapped places for the return flight, in which I flew a Tornado F.3 two-sticker with one of the Greek pilots in my rear seat, in company with a Mirage 2000, for a return Aegean cruise back to Tanagra.

Supersonic Sidewinder Firing

In late November and early December 1989 I took part in an unusual Missile Practice Camp (MPC) working from RAF Leuchars, in Fife, Scotland, to fire air-to-air missiles over the North Atlantic in the Hebrides Range, to the west of Benbecula on the Outer Hebrides. The range extends over 7,000 square miles and provides the space needed for supersonic missile firings.

There had, so far, never been a Sidewinder AIM-9L missile fired from a Tornado F.3 at supersonic speed with the wings swept fully back. This brought the missile on the underwing launch rails closer to the engine intakes, increasing the risk of the engine ingesting rocket gases, potentially causing an engine surge. Also, the rocket-motor efflux was very close to the taileron at launch, the leading edge of which was protected to resist the heat that would be generated. This, then, was to be a test firing and a first.

These Sidewinder missile firings were to be against supersonic targets provided by expendable Stiletto rocket-powered drones launched from a Canberra. For my firing, the target would be at 30,000 feet flying at Mach 1.6 and I was to be in a steep climb from 15,000 feet at Mach 1.3 for a head-sector AIM-9L Sidewinder war-round shot. The Stiletto had a 90-second flight-time and it would then self-destruct, so the set-up and launch ranges had to be perfect and would be controlled from the ground.

My supersonic missile firing would be photo-chased by a clean (no external fuel tanks fitted) Leuchars-based F-4 Phantom, which would film the launch and missile flight. The selected pilot for the F-4 photo-chase happened to be Pete McNamara, who had been one of my students at the Tactical Weapons Unit at Chivenor. It wasn't an easy profile to fly and we practised it several times, with air-to-air refuelling support from a VC10 tanker on each sortie to ensure we had sufficient fuel to fly the profile and transit back across Scotland to Leuchars. I needed to fly smoothly and predictably for Pete in his F-4 to stay with me, even during the required 4G pull up into the steep climb.

On the day of the actual firing we gained a good long-range radar contact on the Canberra that was going to launch the Stiletto. We had suggested that it might be best if we called the launch at the correct range but the ground controllers wanted to keep control and thought that they could do better. The profile was going well and we were established in the climb doing M1.3 with the wings swept fully back. The Stiletto was launched and my first-tourist nav, Flight Lieutenant Clive Duance, locked the radar to the drone. We were well set up with the missile dot centred, so that we would be firing the missile on a collision course, to give it the best chance. The Sidewinder, slaved to the radar, acquired the infra-red source from the target and 'growled' in our earpieces; the noise changed to a 'chirp' when I pressed the button on the control column to uncage the missile seeker head to confirm that it had a good lock-on. Calling 'Firing. Firing. NOW', I pulled the trigger. There was a whoosh and the missile shot off the port wing with a plume of white smoke trailing behind it. I broke away hard to starboard, pleased to discover that there were no adverse effects on the aircraft or the engines and then, as soon as I could, I reversed to observe the effect of the missile. It wasn't exactly what I had expected to see. The trail of white smoke from the missile left in the sky had a distinct kink in it where the missile had suddenly changed course and at the end of it was a large doughnut-shaped explosion. It transpired that the Stiletto had been launched fractionally too early and when it self-destructed after ninety seconds it was only halfway through the Sidewinder missile flight time. Pleasingly though, the Sidewinder had adjusted its course and detonated on the fireball from the drone. The photo-chase F-4, flown by Pete, barrel rolled over the explosion and got some impressive film.

We had proved what we set out to do and considered the whole thing to be a success – the first supersonic missile firings from Tornado F.3s.

Far East Foray

On 28 February 1990 the UK Minister of State for Defence Procurement, Mr Alan Clark, made a statement in the House of Commons. Included in it was this announcement:

> This year, Royal Air Force aircraft will again be deploying to the Far East to take part in a major exercise under the five-power defence arrangements. Those arrangements bring United Kingdom forces together with those of Malaysia, Singapore, Australia and New Zealand. Royal Air Force participation will include Tornado F.3 and GR.1 aircraft, together with tanker support, and underlines our continued commitment to the arrangements and the importance that we attach to the area.

The Tornado F.3s he referred to were ours. We were off to the Far East to participate in an integrated air defence system (IADS) exercise over the jungles of the Malaysian peninsula, operating from the Royal Malaysian Air Force (RMAF) air base at Butterworth. Our task was to deploy four Tornado F.3s, whilst 27 Squadron from Marham would send a pair of Tornado GR.1s. Our trail out to Malaysia would be supported by Tristar tankers which could also carry many of our squadron personnel and some of the equipment. In theatre we would be supported by two VC10 tankers. The Royal Australian Air Force was deploying a squadron of F-111 attack aircraft to Butterworth, whilst the RMAF was operating its A-4 Skyhawks on the exercise. We would be away for just over two weeks with twelve days in Malaysia.

The deployment of the F.3s to Malaysia was an epic in itself. If the exercise proved nothing else it showed that we could deploy combat aircraft to the area in just a few days if it was ever required. We flew the 6,500 miles to Malaysia in three legs over three days, setting off on 4 March, with air-to-air refuelling from Tristars and with the same four crews flying every leg. I flew with navigator Gary Simm. On the first day we flew from Coningsby to Akrotiri in Cyprus, a five-and-a-quarter hour sortie. The next day it was Cyprus to Seeb, in Oman, which took four and a half hours and where we were accommodated overnight in a fabulous hotel. Then on the third day it was the long flight across the Indian Ocean from Oman to Butterworth, Malaysia. This took seven and a half hours. Somewhere mid-Indian-Ocean, flying in autopilot about a mile from the Tristar with height, heading and speed set and with nothing to see but sea from horizon to horizon, I dozed off to sleep. I don't know how long I was asleep for, but I woke with a start and a quick check in the rear-view mirrors showed Gary slumped in the rear cockpit. We had both been asleep. I woke Gary and then searched frantically for the tanker, which was only just visible well ahead of us. It took several minutes to catch it up.

The Air Officer Commanding No. 1 Group, Air Vice Marshal 'Sandy' Wilson, was in the cockpit of one of the two Tristars which led us and refuelled the two pairs of F.3s on the flight across the Indian Ocean. It had been decided that, on arrival at Butterworth, we would form up as a box-four of Tornado F.3s behind the Tristar with the Air Vice Marshal in the cockpit, for a flypast over the airfield to announce the RAF's arrival in style. After a flight of seven and a half hours, having been strapped into an ejection seat for eight hours it was the last thing we really wanted to be doing, but we were outranked. The first flypast behind the Tristar was uncomfortable at slow speed in the bumpy conditions but, as the Boss peeled the box-four away and the speed increased, the wings went back to 45 degrees and the

G increased, it all felt much better, even if having the G-suit squeeze my bladder wasn't really what I wanted at that point. Nor was the bottle of beer I was handed on climbing out of the aircraft after landing; I just wanted to relieve myself first before rehydrating. By the time we landed at Butterworth I had flown seventeen hours and fifteen minutes in just three days.

How you coped with the problem of having a 'pee' in the confines of a fast-jet cockpit on a long sortie was a matter of personal choice. We were issued with 'pee bags' which were strong polythene bags shaped rather like a hot-water bottle, although smaller, with a small sponge inside and with a method of fastening the neck once it had been filled. In order to use the pee bag it was necessary to put the safety pin into the ejection seat-pan firing handle, unstrap, find a way into all the flying clothing and then use the bag. My personal preference was to dehydrate myself before flying a long trip and to hold on; I never used the pee bag, although I always carried one just in case. My nav on this trip was much more used to dealing with the pee bag and did so several times, sometimes with too much joyful commentary for my liking.

Our accommodation during the detachment in Malaysia was the rather wonderful Orchid Hotel at Batu Ferringhi on Penang Island; it was a splendid place to stay and lived up to its name with a fresh orchid laid on the pillow when the bed was turned down each night. Off duty we had the chance to be tourists, visiting some magnificent Buddhist temples and some offshore islands. We also enjoyed the varied cuisine on offer, such as the Chinese wok-cooked street-corner offerings, and you haven't eaten a proper curry until you've done so with your fingers from a banana leaf.

With only four aircraft and all the squadron aircrew on the detachment, the flying needed, quite rightly, to be shared around. Personally, I flew only three sorties over Malaysia during the exercise, refuelling from a VC10 tanker on each one and amounting to a total of seven hours flying. It was a different experience to fly low over the top of the jungle canopy which stretched for miles and miles. We all hoped that nothing would force us to eject into the jungle because, as far as we had been told in the pre-detachment briefings, it was full of creatures that wanted to bite us: snakes, creepy crawlies and even tigers.

The return trip home, twelve days later, was the reverse of the flight out, taking three days with AAR from Tristars but staging through Bahrain. The sortie from Butterworth to Bahrain took eight hours and twenty-five minutes, the longest flight I ever made in a Tornado F.3. Overall, it took sixteen hours and forty-five minutes to fly home. During the month of March, I flew forty-five hours in total.

Tornado F.3 Qualified Flying Instructor

Around this time, it became apparent that we were going to lose the squadron's only QFI on posting and that no replacement was immediately available for him. This would leave the squadron without the ability to carry out the necessary periodic dual checks on pilots, so I volunteered to become rear-seat qualified and to ratify my QFI ticket on the Tornado F.3. I also knew that this could be a useful qualification to have in the future.

I was converted to flying in the rear seat by the outgoing squadron QFI. This also meant learning how to operate all the equipment, such as the inertial-navigation systems, the radar and the displays, which could only be done from the back cockpit, usually by the navigator. Effectively, it meant being able to do the jobs of both the pilot and the navigator. In addition, flying the aircraft from the rear cockpit and, in particular, landing it from the back seat, presented challenges due to the restricted forward view and lack of a head-up display.

On 22 March 1990 I flew a sortie with the Tornado F.3 Central Flying School Agent from the OCU and he awarded me a 'competent to instruct' QFI ticket on the Tornado F.3.

*****

I was now reaching a point where I could choose to leave the RAF or to remain. I was seriously considering my future and took the opportunity for a career interview at the Personnel Management Centre at Innsworth, a 'palm-reading' session, as we called it. The wing commander who 'read my palm' was commendably frank with me. He explained that if I remained in the RAF, I could expect to have to complete a squadron leader staff tour or two as my next postings and that I would need to attend Staff College; I might get promoted to wing commander if things went well. I could expect at best one more flying tour as a wing commander, perhaps as a chief flying instructor at a flying training unit or Tactical Weapons Unit. After that, promotion to group captain was a faint possibility with staff jobs the only option.

The prospect of spending most of the rest of my career as a staff officer did not appeal to me. I asked what would be the reaction if I requested to transfer to 'Specialist Aircrew' terms of service, giving up any chance of further promotion but retaining my squadron leader rank and being employed in flying or flying-related jobs. The wing commander virtually bit my arm off at this suggestion, saying that it would be no problem at all to transfer to Spec Aircrew as long as I didn't expect to leave the fighter world where my experience would be put to best use.

I left very happy with that as a future plan and, after discussions with my wife, I decided that I would far rather stay in the RAF on those terms than become an airline pilot as so many of my friends and colleagues chose to do, even if that did mean that, ultimately, on eventual retirement, I would probably be worse off.

The die was cast. At the end of my tour with 5 Squadron I would be transferring to Specialist Aircrew terms of service and remaining in the Tornado F.3 Force. It meant I would continue flying in the RAF as I had always intended to do. Meanwhile though, there was still plenty to be done as a flight commander on 5 Squadron.

Goose Bay

In June 1990 No. 5 Squadron deployed a number of Tornado F.3s to Goose Bay in Labrador, Canada, for multi-national low-level flying training. Goose Bay is a strange and remote place with no road links to the outside world, supplied solely by air and, in the summer only, by sea. The surrounding 114,000 square miles (294,000 square kilometres) of tundra provided a fantastic training area, ideal for low-level and ultra-low-level flying training. As a result, the base hosted permanent detachments from the Royal Air Force, the Luftwaffe, the Royal Netherlands Air Force and the Italian *Aeronautica Militare*, in addition to temporary deployments from several other NATO countries. In the summer, when the weather was good, the area was an unrestricted playground for fighter pilots and crews. Whilst we were there in June 1990 there were F-4s, F-16s, Alpha Jets and Tornado GR.1s in residence to play with. My first sortie, for example, was as part of a four-ship of Tornado F.3s against six Luftwaffe F-4s, with four F-16s, eight Alpha Jets and four Tornado GR.1s.

One snag with the location of Goose Bay was that off-duty entertainment was hard to come by. We had discovered that whilst we were deployed there was to be an international air show at the Canadian Forces Base (CFB) Trenton, on the shores of Lake Ontario, not far from Toronto. This offered the opportunity for a weekend escape for a couple of crews if the air show could be persuaded to accept a pair of RAF Tornado F.3s as static exhibits. In fact, we took three aircraft and three crews for what turned out to be an excellent weekend away, with a NATO beer call on the Friday, an excellent air show on the Saturday and a spectacular hangar party on the Saturday night. The Canadians in the air show crowd were all pleased to see the Tornado F.3s. Many wanted to know why we had a maple leaf on the fin. The answer was that it came from the squadron's association with the Canadian Corps on the Western Front in the First World War and had been incorporated into the 5 Squadron badge.

On the Monday morning, with the normal strict instructions not to beat up the airfield on departure ringing in our ears, we strapped into our F.3s and fired them up for the return flight to Goose Bay. My aircraft was ready to go, but the other two both had snags and had to delay their departures. Despite the instructions to depart normally, I took off in combat power, held my Tornado low along the runway and pulled up into a near-vertical climb at the far end, showing that in its clean state with no underwing tanks the F.3 had some sort of fighter performance.

Unfortunately, without underwing tanks, the F.3 didn't have that much fuel and after we levelled off at altitude from the reheat climb, it became apparent to me and my nav, Flight Lieutenant Steve 'Spit' Pittaway, that fuel was going to be tight for the long flight back to Goose Bay. A more conservative departure might have been wiser. When we then hit some strong headwinds en route, the computer indicated that we weren't going to make it back with sufficient reserves of fuel and we needed a plan B.

There weren't many options, but CFB Bagotville in Quebec was not far off track and seemed to offer the chance of a stop-off for a fuel top-up. When we were close enough, we gave them a call. The Bagotville air traffic controller explained that the base was on stand-down for the day, but that the airfield was open, the tower was manned and the visiting aircraft section could provide fuel.

We duly landed at Bagotville and were met by a marshaller from the visiting aircraft section who parked us up on the aircraft pan in front of the air traffic control tower. He was surprised but happy to see us and called for the fuel bowser. My navigator, Spit, offered to go and sort out the flight plan with air traffic control (ATC) whilst I conducted the refuel and the turn-round on the aircraft. This seemed a fair and logical split of duties. When Spit returned from the control tower, he told me that the ATC people were quite pleased to have some trade on what would have been a boring day for them, with the base on stand-down, and that 'the price of the refuel is a fly-by'. Now, I have to admit that, although I was a flight commander with responsibilities and an example to set and I was no longer the young 'rip shit' I had been in earlier years, the devil's horns on my head were kept only barely retracted and given half a chance they would readily pop out again. A request for a fly-by was not something I was going to refuse.

We fired up and taxied out to the runway and when I called for take off I asked for a 'closed pattern and fly-by before departing vertically and then as per flight plan'. Bagotville ATC sounded slightly surprised at this but didn't deny my request. I took off and we turned downwind, accelerating all the while. The voice from the back cockpit asked exactly what I was planning and I explained my intention to fly along the aircraft servicing pan, past the control tower, low and fast with the wings fully swept back, before pulling up into a vertical reheat climb. Spit seemed content with that plan.

Even if I do say so myself, the beat up was a good one. As I went past the control tower I was level with the windows of the visual control room, accelerating through Mach 0.9 (about 600 knots) in full reheat, with the wings swept fully back to 67 degrees and with 90 degrees of bank on to present a top side to those watching from the tower. I had been aware when planning this little show in my head a few minutes earlier that the shape of the airfield and its perimeter was such that not far beyond the tower at the end of the pan were some married quarters. Unfortunately, travelling at a mile every six seconds, by the time I had rolled the wings level and pulled up at 7G to the vertical, I had overrun the airfield and was over the top of said married quarters. The residents got the full benefit of the many decibels created by a Tornado F.3 in full reheat as we rocketed vertically up to 28,000 feet. Rolling inverted to level off at the top of the climb, I felt quite pleased with myself and the voice from the back cockpit said, 'Nice one, Boss.'

We landed back at Goose Bay uneventfully, one hour and ten minutes later.

A couple of hours after my departure from Trenton, one of the other Tornado F.3s of the squadron got going and took off, following the same profile that we had done and getting into exactly the same pickle with shortage of fuel, diverting in turn to Bagotville for a refuel. This F.3 was crewed by our Australian exchange-officer pilot, Flight Lieutenant Jim Eaglen, with navigator Flight Lieutenant 'Cocky' Cochrane, who was on my flight and therefore worked for me. As soon as they landed at Bagotville the navigator was called to the telephone to take an extremely irate call from a Canadian Air Force colonel who wanted to know who that idiot pilot was who, a couple of hours before, had flown his Tornado 'through my barbecue'. He wanted the pilot's name, rank and number, along with the squadron commander's as he planned to make a formal complaint. The navigator knew straightaway who was responsible and with commendably quick thinking told the colonel that the pilot was 'only a young lad on his flight' and that he would deal with him personally when he got back to Goose Bay; there was no need to involve the squadron commander. The colonel was persistent but the navigator was more so; his argument won the day and he was left to deal with the recalcitrant pilot personally.

When this second Tornado F.3 landed at Goose Bay, the crew had plenty of 'ammunition' to expend on me, their flight commander; it took several days to expire and cost me many rounds of drinks. During this aftermath, which fortunately for me was nowhere near as serious as it could have been, my navigator Spit, who had told me that the Canadians at Bagotville had requested the fly-by, disclosed that, actually, they had not done so at all and, in fact, it had all been his idea.

Operation GRANBY (DESERT SHIELD)

At the end of July and into August 1990 I was on holiday with my wife and daughter in Mallorca. Whilst I was on leave, 5 Squadron was deploying to Akrotiri, Cyprus, for the annual armament practice camp and I had permission to join them a few days late. On 2 August the news reached me in Mallorca that Saddam Hussein's Iraqi forces had invaded and annexed Kuwait. I told Elaine that I thought I knew what was going to happen next. The 5 Squadron Tornado F.3s in Cyprus, already halfway to the Middle East, would be deployed to Saudi Arabia, which also operated the type, in a move that would not be seen as provocative because the aircraft's role was defensive. I was proved correct.

When we got home from Mallorca, even though I was still supposed to be on leave, I immediately went into RAF Coningsby and to the Operations Centre to get the latest information. Things were certainly getting serious. No one knew whether the Iraqis would stop at annexing Kuwait or whether they would continue southwards into Saudi Arabia to take control of the Saudi oilfields – the world's largest oil reserves – which would allow them to hold the world to ransom. The rest of the world had condemned the Iraqi actions and the United Nations Security Council had passed a resolution declaring Iraq's annexation of Kuwait to be illegal. Plans were being made by the British government and the Ministry of Defence to send the Tornado F.3s in Cyprus to Saudi Arabia.

I found myself going home to pack and leave, potentially to go to war. The next day I was booked onto a VC10 to Cyprus. When I left home it was difficult and emotional. Both Elaine and I appreciated how serious this was and so did our daughter, Suzanne, who was now almost ten years old. She cried and said that she didn't want me to go. I told her that I had to; it was my job.

At the airfield things were taking an unexpected turn towards a war footing. I got an update on the situation from the Operations Centre and, when I reported to Air Movements, I was surprised to find that we were all being issued with real wartime nuclear biological and chemical (NBC) kit and respirators and we were not required to sign for it. Now if the military give you something without you having to sign for it, it's serious. Some of the young airmen and airwomen on the booked flight to Cyprus for a sun and fun detachment were beginning to become very unsettled. I realised that I was the most senior officer on the flight and, with permission from the 'Movers', I decided that I had better explain what I knew to them all about the situation as some knowledge might be better than the fear of the unknown. I don't remember exactly what I said, but I certainly explained the seriousness of the situation. I may have laid it on a bit thick as, by the end, some of the WRAF airwomen were in tears.

After arriving in Cyprus, the plans to deploy operationally to Saudi Arabia were accelerating, although it seemed that some on the squadron were having trouble shaking off the Cyprus holiday mindset and putting on their 'war heads'. Weapons were delivered so that we could fly into Saudi Arabia fully armed with eight missiles and a loaded gun. It was not clear whether we would actually have to fight our way in past the Iraqi Air Force. Exactly where we were going and how we would be accommodated was also uncertain. On 9 August the British government publicly announced its intention to send forces to support Saudi Arabia in response to their request. We were told that we were going to Dhahran, 190 miles (306 km) south of the Kuwait border, just down the road really, and where the Saudi F.3s were based, but we were told this was highly classified and we were not to tell anyone, including our wives, precisely where we were going. The British operation was named Operation GRANBY (the Americans called this phase DESERT SHIELD).

The night before we deployed from Cyprus to Saudi Arabia I was walking back to my room in one of the accommodation blocks from the officers' mess deep in thought. I suddenly realised that I was really quite scared. I gave myself a 'talking to', telling myself that I couldn't take the Queen's shilling for all the years I had and then get upset when asked to do my job for real. In any case, this is what I had trained for, over many years. I wasn't to know that my small part in the conflict would not be life threatening; at this point in time it seemed quite possible that I wouldn't be going home. Once I had come to terms with that possibility, I felt much better and I can honestly say that I suffered no nerves at all after that, but I suppose that I had once again dipped into that finite well of courage.

On the early morning of the 11th I flew one of the first six fully-armed Tornado F.3s, carrying the large 2,250-litre drop tanks, taking off from Akrotiri in the dark, for the four-hour flight to Dhahran. We joined up with a VC10 tanker and watched the sun rise over Egypt, before crossing the Red Sea into Saudi Arabia, air-to-air refuelling en route. We didn't meet any opposition and didn't have to fight our way in.

Initially, we deployed twelve Tornado F.3s to Dhahran with double the complement of combat-ready crews drawn from both 5 Squadron and 29 Squadron, which had been in Cyprus when 5 Squadron arrived. The combined unit was dubbed 5 (Composite) Squadron because the Officer Commanding 5 Squadron was given overall command. After clearing the airspace co-ordination aspects with the Saudis and the USAF, whose F-15s had, impressively, arrived after fourteen-hour non-stop flights from the States a few days previously, we were flying combat air patrols (CAPs) over Saudi Arabia in boxes up by the Iraqi and Kuwaiti border from the following day. The CAPs were permanently manned, twenty-four/seven, by fighters of the Royal Saudi Air Force (RSAF), the USAF or the RAF. Our presence undoubtedly had the effect of maintaining the confidence of friendly nations and perhaps limited any ambitions the Iraqis may have had for further expansion.

There was much to be done on the ground to set up a functioning squadron headquarters, engineering and ops facilities, with some accommodation shared with 29 Squadron RSAF, which operated the Tornado F.3. Suddenly, after decades of the Cold War, planning to fight from hardened fixed bases, the RAF found itself involved in deployed expeditionary operations that it had not anticipated. Dhahran was an extremely impressive sight during the coalition build-up that quickly began to take shape during our time there. Numerous huge USAF transport aircraft, C-5s, C-141s and C-130s disgorged hundreds and hundreds of troops; helicopters of all sorts were unloaded and assembled before being flown off and, in their sun shelters, fully-armed F-15s and Tornado F.3s held alert or waited to be flown.

Domestically, we were accommodated in a compound in Dhahran city which, in normal times, provided married quarters for British Aerospace (BAe) personnel who maintained the Tornados under contract for the RSAF. All but one of the BAe men's wives had been evacuated to the UK and we lived comfortably in the married quarters within the compound, sharing rooms as constituted crews, a pilot and navigator together. The compound offered a delightful open-air swimming pool and a community centre which also became our mess and dining room. Off-duty crews were to be found swimming or sun bathing by the pool, with their respirator and loaded personal weapon – a Walther PP pistol – in case of a surprise attack. It was a strange way to go to war. I was very surprised to get a landline telephone call in the house where I was staying, on the first evening, from Elaine. I thought no one was supposed to know where we were. She had attended a briefing for wives at RAF Coningsby and been given the phone number. I found myself talking to her about problems with the washing machine when I had my war head on.

When we left the compound to go to work at all hours of the day and night there could hardly have been a greater contrast. We flew lengthy sorties mounting CAPs up to the Iraqi or Kuwaiti border in fully-armed aircraft, always carrying our loaded pistols in shoulder holsters under our life-jackets.

On the first sortie I flew in daylight, the temperature at Dhahran was plus-45 degrees centigrade and, as always, we were fully loaded with eight missiles and the large 2,250 litre underwing fuel tanks. On take off, roaring down the runway in combat power, acceleration was notably sluggish in the high temperature. When I raised the nose wheel at 150 knots we actually seemed to slow down and it took much more runway than I expected to get airborne. The highest daytime temperature we experienced was plus-49 degrees centigrade.

Most of the CAP sorties I flew were unrefuelled and generally of around two hours. I conducted air-to-air refuelling from a Victor tanker on only one, which then lasted almost four hours. We generally operated as a pair or four-ship formation by day and as a pair at night.

On one early sortie, shortly after making radio contact with the USAF E-3 AWACS aircraft which was going to provide us with radar control, there was something of a flap. The AWACS was already controlling two USAF F-15s on the same frequency and reported two Iraqi fighter aircraft heading south towards the border with Saudi Arabia at high speed. The AWACS controller became increasingly concerned, apparently beginning to wonder if they were the target for the Iraqi fighters, and the F-15s moved to defend it. The AWACS controller then called 'retrograde', which I had never heard before, but which I subsequently came to understand meant that the AWACS was running away in a descent. We were obviously very interested in what was going on and where the Iraqi aircraft were with relationship to us. Then suddenly the AWACS controller called something like 'Going Green', which again we'd never heard, and then they were gone, along with the F-15s. We no longer had any RT contact, control or picture of what was happening. For the first time, we realised that our aircraft were not well-equipped for the scenario we now found ourselves in. The Americans had frequency-hopping jam-resistant 'secure' HAVE QUICK radios. We didn't. Shortly afterwards HAVE QUICK radios were delivered to us and fitted to our aircraft, unfortunately with very little in the way of instructions on how to set them up and use them. It took some trial and error to get everyone on the net.

This was just one example of the lack of appropriate equipment for the situation. Another was the lack of the latest type of military secure Mode 4 IFF (Identification Friend or Foe) equipment. We also knew that we were not well placed with regard to self-defence ECM, which had never been a requirement in the original Tornado F.3 design. Later, infra-red flare dispensers were 'scabbed on' to the engine-bay doors underneath the rear of the aircraft to decoy infra-red missiles. In the interim, we felt that one of our best defences against attack by Iraqi fighters, apart from killing them first, would be to run away fast and as low as possible.

The rules of engagement which we were given at this stage of the conflict before the war had begun, issued directly by 10 Downing Street, were very restraining. It was obvious that the government didn't want us provoking anything. Penetration of Saudi airspace by Iraqi aircraft wasn't a reason to shoot them down. In essence, we were going to have to be fired at, even have one of our aircraft shot down, before we could shoot back and if we did shoot down an Iraqi aircraft it was essential that it crashed in Saudi territory. We certainly could not cross the border into Iraqi or Kuwaiti airspace.

The Iraqis did test the coalition air defences during these early stages by running pairs or more of fighters from Iraqi or Kuwaiti airspace towards the border with Saudi Arabia, even sometimes slightly over it, before turning back. The Iraqi Air Force had some potent fighter aircraft including Dassault Mirage F1s, Sukhoi 'Fitters', MiG-21 'Fishbeds', MiG-23 'Floggers' and MiG-29 'Fulcrum' fighters, the latter being our biggest concern. They also operated some Su-24 'Fencers', which could have provided an effective attack aircraft. Our hope was that the Iraqi pilots would be less well trained than the coalition pilots, with more regimented soviet-style closely-controlled tactics and less autonomous thinking. I think that was eventually proven during the war. It meant that the Tornado F.3 was having to counter a fighter threat that it had never been designed to take on. However, we had trained for this and felt confident in our abilities to deal with it.

Some of the CAP sorties that my nav, Rich Sanderson, and I flew were late at night. If I needed to get up to go to work at 02:00 I would go to bed eight hours before that, regardless of what time of day that was. I had an uncanny ability to sleep whenever required but I did need eight hours sleep to feel sharp. Sometimes when we went to work at that time of night it was so humid at Dhahran that it was foggy. We occasionally took off in very poor visibility, hoping that it would clear by the time we landed. It always did. A number of the sorties we flew saw us taking off in the dark and returning at dawn. Sunrise over the desert can be exceedingly beautiful and invariably seemed at odds with what we were doing.

At the end of the month we learned that we were soon to be replaced by a new contingent of eighteen Tornado F.3s and their crews. These F.3s had been newly and specially modified in a number of ways, under an urgent operational requirement and with the direct involvement of the Tornado F.3 Operational Evaluation Unit (OEU) as well as the British defence industry. They would have the latest and much improved Stage 1 Plus version of the AI24 Foxhunter radar, would be fitted with the flare dispensers on the engine-bay doors and could carry a Phimat chaff dispenser on one of the Sidewinder rails. The Radar-Homing-and-Warning Receiver (RHWR) display in the rear cockpit had been moved up on top of one of the TV Tabs with the buttons for dispensing chaff and flares. In addition, these aircraft would have some radar-absorbent tiles and paint to help in reducing the Tornado's large radar signature. Meanwhile, the new crews had been given the chance to work up specifically for the task that faced them. We were, mostly, torn between being relieved to be going home and wanting to stay to be involved in the forthcoming action.

After a short period of handing over to the new Tornado F.3 crews and flying together with them in their newly-modified aircraft, we left Dhahran to fly home on 17 September. With a Tristar tanker refuelling our pair of Tornado F.3s – we were the last to leave – the nonstop flight home to Coningsby took seven hours and forty-five minutes. Leading our pair

Above: Scottish Aviation Bulldog T.1s, the aircraft in which the author completed the Central Flying School course in 1977 to become a Qualified Flying Instructor.

Below: Clive & Elaine Rowley's wedding in 1978. The uniformed friends and colleagues in this photograph provided an archway of swords. Tragically, Chris Jones, on the far right, was killed in a flying accident in an F-4 Phantom just over two months later.

Above: Hawk T.1 of 63 Sqn, No. 2 Tactical Weapons Unit (TWU), Chivenor, in 1982, with an Aden 30mm cannon pod on the centreline and practice-bomb carriers under the wings.

Below: 63 Sqn TWU staff instructors at Chivenor in 1983. The Hawk T.1A behind them is loaded with a centreline gun pod and a Sidewinder AIM-9L acquisition training-round missile under each wing. The author is second from the right. Sadly, two of the pilots in this photograph lost their lives in flying accidents subsequently. Pete 'Stoney' Stone (back row centre) was killed flying a Harrier T.4 in 1989, and Guy Bancroft-Wilson (second from left) was killed displaying a P-63 Kingcobra warbird at an air show in 2001.

Above: The specially marked Lightning F.3, XR749, DA of the OC Lightning Training Flight, with the author's name, 'SQN LDR C M ROWLEY', under the cockpit in 1986.

Right: Officer Commanding Lightning Training Flight in the cockpit of the second of his personal aircraft bearing his name, Lightning F.3 XR718 DA in 1987. (*Chris Allan*)

SQN LDR CM ROWLEY

The author as OC LTF (in green flying suit) with the Flight's engineers outside the LTF hangar at Binbrook in 1987 with Lightning T.5 XS456 DX.

Above: The author in a fully-armed 5 Sqn Tornado F.3 shadowing one of the two Russian Tupolev Tu-95 Bear Deltas intercepted north of Scotland on 8 September 1988.

Below: The author (left) and his 5 Sqn navigator, Flt Lt Rich Sanderson, during an APC in Cyprus in 1989. The pair flew together during Operation GRANBY in 1990.

Above: A Tornado F.3 of 5 Sqn, fully armed with eight missiles and the large 2,250-litre drop tanks, starts up for a combat air patrol sortie in one of the sun shelters at Dhahran, Saudi Arabia, during Operation GRANBY (DESERT SHIELD) in August 1990.

Below: The author welcomed home from operations by daughter Suzanne and wife Elaine, after a flight of 7 hours and 45 minutes from Saudi Arabia, on 17 September 1990.

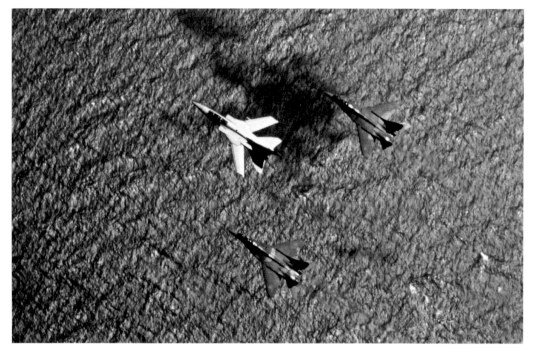

Above: The author, in a Tornado F.3 of the Operational Evaluation Unit (OEU), leading two Luftwaffe MiG-29s – former foes – back to Decimomannu, Sardinia, in 1991.

Below: Tornado F.3 of the F.3 OEU, dropping infra-red decoy flares over the China Lake ranges in the Californian high desert, in February 1992 during a trial.

Above: Walking away from an OEU Tornado F.3 in Cyprus, with navigator John Prescott.

Below: Squadron Leader Gordon 'Scotty' Scott and the author with the then highly-classified Tornado F.3 Towed Radar Decoy (TRD) pod during trials at Eglin AFB Florida in 1995.

Above: Tornado F.3s of 1435 Flight in the Falkland Islands. The author flew with the Flight over the Islands on a number of detachments to Mount Pleasant Airfield. (*UK MoD*)

Below: With wife Elaine and daughter Suzanne after an investiture at Buckingham Palace to receive the MBE from HM The Queen in 2002.

Above: The author in the rear cockpit of a Tornado F.3 of 56(R) Sqn with the Chief of the Air Staff, Air Chief Marshal Sir Peter Squire, in the front cockpit in April 2002.

Below: The Tornado F.3 Operational Conversion Unit – 56(R) Sqn – photographed here with its aircraft, ground crew, staff instructors and students in March 2003, prior to moving from Coningsby to Leuchars. The author is in the third row, eighth from the right. (*UK MoD*)

Above: The author flying BBMF Hurricane IIC PZ865 in 1996 during his first display season with the Flight.

Below: The author in BBMF Spitfire Vb AB910 before his first public Spitfire display.

Above: The author flying BBMF Spitfire Vb AB910 in May 1997, photographed from the BBMF Lancaster rear turret. (*UK MOD*)

Below: The BBMF fighter pilots for the 2000 display season. Left to right: Gp Capt (later Air Marshal) Peter 'Ruddles' Ruddock, Sqn Ldr Ian 'Shiney' Simmons, Sqn Ldr Paul 'Major' Day (OC BBMF), author, Wg Cdr (later Air Cdre) Nick 'Watnik' Watson.

Above: The author airborne in the cockpit of BBMF Spitfire Vb AB910 in 2002. (*UK MoD*)

Below: Officer Commanding BBMF in 2004, with the Lancaster and a Hurricane behind and a Spitfire in the foreground. (*UK MoD*)

Above: BBMF Lancaster, Hurricane and Spitfire over Buckingham Palace in July 2005 for the sixtieth anniversary commemorations of the end of the Second World War, immediately prior to the Lancaster dropping one million paper poppies from its bomb bay. The author was flying Spitfire IIa P7350 on the left. (*UK MoD*)

Below: The author, in a Spitfire, leading two Eurofighter Typhoons for a flypast over the AOC's salute at Coningsby's Annual Formal Inspection in September 2005. (*UK MoD*)

Above: The author's last Spitfire display at the end of the 2006 display season and after 11 years with the BBMF. Some observers said that he flew between the trees and rocked the light stanchions with his propwash, but that must have been an optical illusion!

Below: End of an era. Clive Rowley with an appropriately marked Spitfire PR XIX in September 2006, at the end of his 11 years flying with the BBMF.

Above: Recalled for a special appearance at the BBMF's fiftieth anniversary air show at Duxford on 5 May 2007. The author flew Spitfire AB910 on the left of this picture. (*Mike Cook*)

Below: The author as a volunteer reservist Flight Lieutenant, relieved at having performed a successful forced landing in a farmer's field, off the airfield at Cranwell, in August 2012, in a Grob Tutor, after one propeller blade disintegrated at only 500 feet. (*Paul Smith*)

was the Squadron Qualified Weapons Instructor Leader, Squadron Leader Howard 'Padre' Prissick. When we got back to Coningsby we arrived very low and fast over the squadron's dispersal in tactical fighting-wing formation. The Station Commander, Group Captain Martin Widdowson, was outside the PBF with our squadron commander when we flashed over, and he apparently said, 'I didn't see that, but I will if they come back.'

It was great to be back home and, best of all, Elaine and Suzanne were there to meet me when I climbed down from the cockpit of my Tornado. Suzanne had been given a special afternoon off school to go to the airfield to meet her Dad, who according to her had 'almost been to war'.

Gulf War Roulement

Shortly after we returned to Coningsby, the Officer Commanding 5 Squadron, Wing Commander Euan Black, was posted out and replaced as the Boss by Wing Commander Al Lockwood, who immediately showed a more relaxed and trusting style of leadership. For the next three months, whilst the military build-up in the Gulf continued, we settled back into the normal peacetime existence for a fighter squadron, catching up with the training of non-operational aircrew, which had been on hold for a while. It seemed strange, because other members of the Tornado F.3 Force and the entire RAF were about to engage in the first war for many years and certainly for our generation of aircrew.

On the night of 16/17 January 1991 the First Gulf War began with the 'shock and awe' of a massive aerial bombing campaign, which continued for forty-two consecutive days and nights. The same day, we on 5 Squadron were told to commence a work-up to go back out to the Gulf. At this point no one knew quite how long the war would go on for and the RAF has long believed in the importance of 'roulement' for front-line crews to keep everyone fresh and sharp and to avoid battle fatigue. It was thought that there would be a need for fresh crews to be sent out to replace those already involved. It seemed we would be going back into the war unless it ended first. I should have been posted away from the squadron at about this time; indeed, my replacement as flight commander had already arrived on the squadron, but it was decided that I needed to stay because of my experience.

Our first step was to start flying as constituted crews. My navigator was now Flight Lieutenant Dave 'Harry' McBryde, an experienced ex-F-4 nav who had been with 5 Squadron since its early Tornado days. (Harry later became a squadron leader and eventually achieved his long-held ambition to cross-train as a pilot.) Having the same pilot and navigator flying together all the time, as a constituted crew, confers all sorts of benefits in terms of easier and more effective crew co-operation with a greater understanding between the two. We also flew as constituted four-ships with experienced crews as leader and number three and with less experienced crews as the wingmen. Harry and I led our four-ship. These constituted four-ship formations quickly became effective fighting units.

We began the work-up straightaway, both on the ground and in the air, with 2v2 and 4v4 dissimilar air combat training (DACT) against our friends from 323 Squadron Royal Netherlands Air Force in their F-16s. We made full use of the North Sea Air Combat Manoeuvring Instrumentation (ACMI) Range. The North Sea range offered the same training facilities as the ACMI range in Sardinia; it had been set up and was operated by BAe with ground cabins at Coningsby and Waddington. It offered excellent training value, as did our Dutch F-16 friends. We also flew 2v2 and 4v4 DACT sorties on the North Sea ACMI Range against Harrier GR.5s and against Jaguars, which was beneficial to their pilots as well as to us. In addition, we flew multiple aircraft low-level affiliation sorties against Sea Harriers, with RAF F-4 Phantoms against Tornado GR.1s, and 4v4 against RAF Harrier GR.5s.

Another aspect which we had long been keen to avoid, but which now seemed something well worth doing, was flying wearing the aircrew nuclear biological and chemical (NBC) protective equipment and AR5 respirator. It was thought that the Iraqis might use chemical weapons against the Coalition forces, as they had previously done in the war against Iran. The squadron had one pilot who was specially trained as the NBC Officer; now, suddenly, his expertise and advice were much appreciated by us all, instead of being dreaded. Donning and wearing the NBC gear was unpleasant and tiring; flying in it was not normally allowed in peacetime, but now we were allowed to, as long as it was in a two-stick trainer with a rear-seat-qualified pilot in the back cockpit as a safety pilot. We flew a number of sorties, mostly 1v1 air combat training sorties because, although these were hot and sweaty, they were at least short. I flew as safety pilot on one AR5 sortie and flew in the kit twice myself.

On 24 February the Allied Coalition in the Gulf commenced the ground assault. In just 100 hours Kuwait was liberated and coalition forces had advanced into Iraqi territory. A ceasefire was declared on the 28th. The war was over and 5 Squadron was stood down; we hadn't been needed.

End of Tour

I saw out my tour as a flight commander on 5 Squadron during March 1991 with the squadron returning to normality. Most of the sorties that month were routine training but I flew for the first time at night wearing night-vision goggles (NVGs). This was quite an experience. The goggles were attached to the front of the flying helmet and could be swung down in front of the eyes when needed. You looked under the goggles into the cockpit and through them outside. It would be unwise to eject with the weight of the goggles on your head as it would probably damage your neck, so they were fitted with a system that blew them off on ejection. We called it the 'exploding head mod'. The NVGs allowed the wearer to see lights or infra-red sources miles away and suddenly you could see just how many aircraft were in the night sky. Looking through the NVGs everything was monochrome green and speckled, there was little depth perception and it was like looking through two toilet tubes. However, I never tired of flying in close formation with another Tornado F.3 with his lights off, quite comfortable that I could see him through the goggles, although I had to move my head more to take in the whole aircraft. If I lifted my head and looked under the goggles it was just black, although there was actually another aircraft there just feet away.

My final sortie on the unit was my choice; I led a 1v1v1 air combat training mission on the North Sea ACMI Range with kill removal and regeneration to feed the fight, and with each of the aircraft armed only with either a Fox 1, Fox 2 or guns-only capability drawn from a hat. It was fun.

At the age of 40 I was now transferring to Specialist Aircrew terms of service to keep flying, remaining a squadron leader but with no prospect of any further promotion. I had managed to organise the best possible specialist aircrew posting that I could think of; I was posted across the airfield at Coningsby to the Tornado F.3 Operational Evaluation Unit (Tornado F.3 OEU) as a trials pilot. I had been with 5 Squadron as a flight commander for almost three and a half years. Adding my fifteen months as Officer Commanding the Lightning Training Flight to that, I had been fortunate enough to have over four and a half years flying as a squadron leader in executive appointments. I for one was not complaining and I was very much looking forward to the future.

Chapter 10

Tornado F.3 Trials Pilot

Tornado F.3 Operational Evaluation Unit

The Tornado F.3 Operational Evaluation Unit (the F.3 OEU) was formed in 1987 as an element of the Central Trials and Tactics Organisation (CTTO), which became the Air Warfare Centre (AWC) in 1993. Based at RAF Coningsby, the role of the F.3 OEU was to conduct operational testing and evaluation of existing, new or modified equipment, systems and weapons for the Tornado F.3. The unit also developed tactics hand-in-hand with testing and evaluation so that operating instructions, procedures and tactical advice could all be provided to the front line along with new equipment.

As a small specialist unit the F.3 OEU had only four or five Tornado F.3s on strength. The aircraft were modified to the latest operational standards and were often fitted with equipment, systems and software still under development. The OEU's small engineering team consisted of about thirty-five technicians led by a Squadron Leader Senior Engineering Officer. The technicians, especially the electricians and avionics specialists, were real experts in their field.

There were only eight aircrew – four crews – on the unit. When I arrived, the Boss, who had recently taken command, was Wing Commander Ray Hodgson. I had known him since we both flew Lightnings with 19 Squadron in Germany. He had subsequently flown F-4 Phantoms, F-15s on exchange with the USAF and been a flight commander on a Tornado F.3 squadron. The F.3 OEU flight commander was a squadron leader navigator and RAF Aerosystems Course graduate. This post was filled by David Lewis until December 1992, when Gordon Scott took over. There were also two qualified weapons instructors (QWIs), one a pilot and the other a navigator on the unit, an electronic warfare officer (EWO) and another pilot – me – later known as the Senior Pilot. In addition, there was a staff crew of two squadron leaders, a pilot filling the role of Trials Management Officer and a navigator staff officer. These two were theoretically on ground tours but, in fact, with only three other crews on the unit, they flew almost as much as the others. The OEU aircrew were all experienced fighter pilots or navigators, highly-qualified experts with strong characters and opinions. The collective level of knowledge and technical understanding amongst the OEU aircrew was immense and they were all dedicated to improving the Tornado F.3 to the best possible operational standard.

It was a privilege and a challenge to be joining this impressive team. I saw several other pilots and navigators posted in after me and all were initially a little daunted by the expertise and knowledge that existed on the unit. Such a small unit could not carry any passengers and it was necessary to hit the ground running on arrival. The OEU crews spoke a different language, rattling off trial names, code names for classified equipment and the designations for main computer software editions, such as 'OFP 3C BT3', radar data processor software, such as 'PS4.2C', and radar-warning-receiver pre-flight message designations. This level of detail was important to the job and you had to catch up on it all very quickly to become familiar with the nomenclature and to understand the implications.

The F.3 OEU worked closely with co-located and visiting scientists, engineers, trials specialists and experts from industry, from the Ministry of Defence Procurement Executive and Operational Requirements Staff (MOD (PE) and OR). Some of the trials flying conducted by the OEU was planned by the industry specialists with practical inputs from the unit's aircrew.

The OEU definitely punched above its weight and its advice and opinions were respected and sought at high levels. We became used to dealing directly with senior-ranking officers without necessarily going through the normal chain of command.

As a specialist aircrew squadron leader, I was filling a flight lieutenant post. I was specifically tasked with the planning and running of the flying programme and I was also responsible for all the aircrew training requirements both on the ground and in the air to maintain the mandated currencies. From time to time, I took on the planning of specific trials, including some overseas deployments. Inevitably, on such a small unit there were all sorts of other little tasks that needed to be done, with few officers to complete them, and many of these came my way too. Then, of course, there was the flying: trials flying, tactical flying and, as the unit's Qualified Flying Instructor (QFI), conducting the necessary periodic dual-handling checks on the other pilots. I also became an instrument rating examiner on the Tornado F.3 so that I could conduct the annual instrument rating tests on the unit's pilots as well. I generally spent an average of about twenty hours in the air each month.

The flying on the OEU was a roughly equal mix of trials flying – dedicated to trialling various software, hardware, equipment, systems and weapons – and tactical flying, needed to ensure that the aircrew retained their skills and to facilitate the evaluation of the equipment and tactics in realistic scenarios. Some of the trials flying could be relatively mundane, although it required very accurate flying. All the flying was demanding and some of it was exciting and fun. It was a particular pleasure for me to be crewed with some of the finest navigators in the F.3 Force, who could work magic with the radar and the equipment so that I had the best possible situational awareness, and as crews we could be very effective.

There was a fair amount of written staff work involved in the job on the OEU which I was happy to do. However, the introduction of personal computers was new to me; I had been used to writing everything by hand and getting the unit typist to type up my words. That was now a thing of the past; unit typists were no more. We had to produce our own printed or electronic documents and I rapidly had to learn how to use a computer. With very little instruction available I was self-taught, but I eventually mastered the various programs and applications.

Much of the trial activity was concurrent, with several different trials ongoing during any given period. We could find ourselves flying on these different tasks on consecutive days or in the same week. During my time on the Tornado F.3 OEU the principal trials that I was involved in were related to the long-running development of the Tornado F.3's AI 24 Foxhunter radar, improvements to the radar-homing-and-warning receiver (RHWR), the integration of the Link 16 data-link Joint Tactical Information Distribution System (JTIDS), defensive counter-measures – including infra-red decoy flares and the towed radar decoy ECM 'jammer' – and some weapons trials including gunnery and missile firings. Much of this was driven by the requirements of the Tornado F.3 Force on the front line. The lessons learned from the urgent operational requirements that generated temporary modifications to the F.3s for Operation GRANBY – the Gulf War – needed to become formally-approved modifications and, from 1993, Operation DENY FLIGHT over Bosnia drove some operational requirements. Working with the kit that no one else in the Tornado F.3 Force yet had access to was exciting, fascinating and a privilege. In addition to the long-running trials there were other short or one-off trials to add to the interest.

Tornado F.3 versus MiG-29

The first week of my new tour with the Tornado F.3 OEU saw me flying that classic mix of OEU sorties with trial sorties for a new radar tracker, and tactical flying including low-level affiliation sorties against Harriers and Jaguars, and dissimilar air combat training against F-18s on the North Sea ACMI range.

The next week the F.3 OEU deployed to Decimomannu, Sardinia, for a special classified trial against Luftwaffe MiG-29 Fulcrums. My transit to 'Deci', with QWI navigator Colin 'Wiki' Wills, didn't go quite according to plan as our aircraft suffered a failure of the left hydraulic system and we were forced to divert into Boscombe Down. After getting the problem fixed, we were able to continue on the direct transit flight to Deci with the big 2,250-litre underwing fuel tanks allowing us to do it in one hop.

After the fall of the Berlin Wall in November 1989 and the re-unification of Germany in October 1990, the Luftwaffe took over the remnants of the East German air force. Former East German MiG-29s were integrated into the Luftwaffe, flown by a mixture of West German and former East German pilots. As the MiG-29s were now being operated by a NATO air force, it gave us the first opportunity to test the Tornado F.3 and its weapon system against one of the most significant threat aircraft at the time.

The German MiG-29s did not have an IFF that was compatible with western air traffic control and so we had to lead them in formation from Deci to the ACMI range over the sea, and back to the airfield on each sortie. It seemed very strange to have the MiGs sitting in close formation with me on my wing tips, when I had long thought of them as enemy. I treasure a photograph I have kept, taken from another of our Tornado F.3s, of me leading a pair of MiG-29s – former adversaries – in tight close formation back to Deci.

As this was a trial with specific aims, the set-ups on the range were somewhat 'canned' and did not allow free-for-all fights. We already knew how foolhardy it would be to get into a close-range dogfight with a Fulcrum in a Tornado F.3 and that needed no additional evidence. The MiGs did manoeuvre hard on some occasions when we were behind them and it was very impressive. We also got the MiGs to deploy their infra-red decoy flares against our Sidewinder AIM-9L acquisition training missiles. The MiGs' flares were unusual to us in that they were ejected upwards from the rear fuselage, were quite smoky and not very bright. However, they were very effective and would easily deny Sidewinder shots if the MiG pilot knew you were shooting at him.

What was encouraging and quite surprising was that we could use our radars and beyond-visual-range (BVR) tactics to very good effect against them, especially when the MiG pilots employed Soviet tactical doctrine. The Soviet doctrine relied on close control and, if that was denied, the MiGs' systems were not ideal for autonomous BVR scenarios as the pilots did not have the best situational awareness. We found we could take semi-active Skyflash missile shots, Fox 1s, against them, 'crank' away the maximum amount to keep outside their radar scan during the missile time of flight, then re-commit from outside of the MiGs' limited 'Slotback' radar coverage to take an unseen Sidewinder shot. We were surprisingly successful in the BVR arena and I got quite a kick out of shooting down MiG-29s. The Fulcrum was also blatantly short of fuel and obviously very much a short-range, point-defence fighter.

On the ground we were able to get up close up to a MiG-29, take a good look around it and sit in the cockpit. It was built like a battleship with little finesse and the cockpit was relatively basic by fast-jet standards of the time.

Radar Trials

For all of the four and a half years that I spent with the Tornado F.3 OEU we were involved in various trials and development work to improve the Tornado F.3's AI24 Foxhunter radar, ultimately bringing it up to a truly excellent standard.

For much of my time on the unit we were working on improving the Stage 1 radar that was now the standard equipment for the Tornado F.3 Force. This work involved incorporating the temporary modifications made to a limited number of radars for the Gulf War – the so-called Stage 1-plus and Stage 1G modifications – and developing an improved radar tracker known as the Stage 1AA tracker. Later, in 1993, it became necessary to make improvements to the radar to suit it better for the tactical environment found over Bosnia during Operation DENY FLIGHT. All of these trials were conducted in conjunction with industry and the MoD and, as can be imagined, many aspects were classified.

Every radar trial sortie required targets and, whilst these were sometimes provided externally, in many cases we flew the target profiles with our own Tornado F.3s. These radar trial target profiles did not necessarily make for the most exciting flying, but they required care, attention and very accurate flying so that the subsequent analysis of the trial radar video could be compared with known target behaviour. Typical target profiles would involve manoeuvring in a set manner at specified ranges and perhaps as a pair of targets crossing over to test how a radar tracker coped. It also meant that all the crews involved in the trial sortie were present in the brief and debrief and kept abreast of developments and problems.

Our QWI navigator, Colin Wiki Wills, who was a New Zealander, had a particular scathing way with words when the latest industry software or hardware didn't measure up. Many was the industry engineer whose months or years of work behind the scenes was crushed with Wiki's much-used summary, 'It's about as much use as zips on socks.'

*****

Coincident with the development and trials work on the Stage 1 radar, the Tornado F.3 OEU became increasingly involved in the development work for the next, Stage 2, version of the Foxhunter radar and its Stage 2G and Stage 2H follow-on improvements. Initially, the majority of this work was conducted by GEC Marconi with BAe at their Warton airfield, and we sometimes provided targets for their specially-instrumented Tornado F.3 radar test-bed aircraft. In January 1992 the MoD Procurement Executive decided, in an unprecedented and bold move, that faster progress could be made on the Stage 2 radar development if the specially-instrumented Tornado F.3 was moved from Warton, along with the radar industry trial specialists, and operated instead by the Tornado F.3 OEU at Coningsby.

Tornado F.3 ZE756, also known as AS 54, had the ability to record everything that the main computer and radar was doing on wide-band tape for subsequent analysis. In all other respects ZE756 was a standard Tornado F.3. This special trials aircraft served with the F.3 OEU for the next three and a half years, until I delivered it to Boscombe Down in July 1995. As a special one-off instrumented aircraft, ZE756 placed an additional burden of responsibility on the Tornado F.3 OEU and its crews, which we definitely felt. We also knew that we needed to show that RAF Operational Evaluation Units could conduct flight trials that had previously been the exclusive realm of the test pilots in the defence aviation industry and at the Aeroplane and Armament Experimental Establishment (A&AEE).

*****

The Tornado F.3 OEU's involvement in the Stage 2 radar development spawned an interesting 'UK Ltd' attempted sales pitch to the Royal Saudi Air Force (RSAF) in October 1994. The Saudis had been operating the Tornado F.3 with the Stage 1 radar and, even though trials and development of the Stage 2 radar were not complete and it was still somewhat immature, BAe invited some Saudi aircrew over to the UK to fly with the F.3 OEU to experience the new version of the radar. The RSAF aircrew team was led by a Saudi lieutenant colonel and also included two Saudi Tornado F.3 QWIs, a pilot and a navigator. We were told by the MoD to be as honest as possible with the Saudis about the current state of the Stage 2 radar, without actually bad-mouthing it. This was direction for which we were grateful as we didn't see ourselves as salesmen.

The interesting aspect for me came about because it was decided that the Saudi QWI pilot, Major Ayish, needed to fly in the front seat of one of our Tornado F.3s, but no-one was prepared to let him fly an RAF aircraft solo with an RAF navigator in the back seat. It was, therefore, decided that the three demonstration sorties would be flown in our two-stick training aircraft, fitted with a Stage 2 radar, with me occupying the back seat as safety pilot whilst also acting as the navigator. The first demonstration sortie was a relatively straight forward introductory 1v1 with a manoeuvring target, but the other two sortie profiles were quite challenging. The second was against a jamming Falcon 20 to demonstrate the ECCM capabilities of the radar, and the third was against a pair of low-level hard-manoeuvring Hawk targets and four low-level Tornado GR.1s, which would break onto the beam and use chaff to 'trash' the radar lock and then re-commit. These target manoeuvres would present challenges to some fully-qualified Tornado F.3 navigators; for me, as a pilot, less used to operating the radar from the rear cockpit, it was quite intense. In addition to operating, instructing and commentating on the radar, I had also, of course, to monitor Major Ayish's flying. I also flew one sortie with the Saudi colonel to show him the Stage 2 radar. The weather was particularly poor that day, requiring an instrument approach to land back at Coningsby, something the colonel was not used to having to do back home, so I flew the approach and landing from the back seat. It all proved to be challenging and rewarding, although in the end the RSAF did not purchase the Stage 2 radar.

*****

The radar developments we worked on were tested in tactical environments as well as the 'canned' trials. The Stage 2 radar was eventually formally

'Opevaled' by us in July 1995 and entered service with the front line soon after that, some five years after it was originally scheduled to do so. Around that time we were already planning the changes to automation and to the displays, which would eventually become the Stage 3 radar. I remain proud of what the Tornado F.3 OEU achieved in developing the radar during that period and I am also proud of my own small part in it.

Flare Trials

In late 1991 I was given the lead to set up a short-notice trial in the United States to employ our Vinten infra-red decoy flares against a range of threat missile systems, operating from the US Naval Air Weapons Station at China Lake in the Californian high desert. I flew across to the US, initially to Washington DC, in an RAF VC10 with a wing commander from the Central Trials and Tactics Organisation, to make all the necessary arrangements both from an operational and trials point of view and also domestically. When we had completed our planned meetings in Washington we flew across the States to Los Angeles, where we hired a car to drive the 150 miles to China Lake in the western Mojave Desert. Discussions with the American missile and counter-measures experts revealed that we would need to make a significant modification to the interval at which our decoy flares were ejected if we hoped to have a successful outcome against the sophisticated and clever infra-red counter-counter measures (IRCCM) fitted to some of the missiles we would encounter. Not that any would actually be fired at us. I also arranged the working accommodation and our domestic accommodation in a local hotel in the small township of Ridgecrest on the base's doorstep.

Back home the necessary modifications were incorporated and we then deployed two Tornado F.3s, an additional crew and many of our ground crew, with VC10 tanker support, to the USA. On 10 February 1992, I and QWI navigator Wiki Wills flew a Tornado F.3, fitted with the 2,250-litre underwing fuel tanks, across the Atlantic to Goose Bay in north-eastern Canada. This was a six-hour sortie, air-to-air refuelling several times en route. The other F.3 was flown by the Boss, Wing Commander Ray Hodgson – whose experience of operating in the US airspace as an exchange officer was going to be useful – with navigator Squadron Leader David Lewis. As we passed south of Greenland the ice floes in the sea below made the thought of having to eject most unpalatable. The next day, after a night stop at the very cold Goose Bay, we planned to fly direct to China Lake in California, taking the last fuel top-up from the tanker near Denver, where the VC10 would land. We would then complete the route to China Lake unescorted. It didn't go according to plan.

First my aircraft suffered a double inertial-navigation system failure, leaving us without the normal navigation information and without the attitude and heading information in the head-up display. I wasn't too bothered about this as I could simply follow the VC10 and the other Tornado. Then, just over six hours into the flight, after topping up to full fuel from the VC10 near Denver, Colorado, and setting off on our own as a pair of Tornadoes across the Rocky Mountains, an OIL P warning illuminated in my cockpit, indicating low oil pressure on one of the engines. The drill required straight and level flight, which I was already doing and, if after ten seconds the warning did not disappear, close down the affected engine. Keeping 'Wiki' informed, that was what I did. I also informed my leader, the Boss, who duly announced an emergency on my behalf to the American air traffic controller. In a Tornado F.3 carrying the big underwing fuel tanks full of fuel and flying on one engine, the only way was down and I was forced to descend to maintain a reasonable airspeed. The Boss was doing a good job keeping air traffic informed as we turned back towards Buckley Air Force Base, an Air National Guard airfield about fifteen miles south of Denver International Airport, on the eastern edge of the city. Buckley airfield is 5,500 feet above sea level; the Rocky Mountains we were flying over had peaks up to 14,000 feet. This was very much on my mind as we descended through some thin cloud, fortunately regaining sight of the surface soon afterwards. However, as I flew towards Denver City we were running out of height and speed over the mountains. I considered jettisoning the underwing tanks, which would certainly have improved the situation flying on one engine but I felt that 'bombing' the USA with full fuel tanks before I'd even arrived or cleared customs would not endear me to the locals and would likely involve reams of paperwork, so I rejected the idea. Fortunately, before we ran out of height and speed altogether, the eastern edge of the Rockies came up and we were able to descend further above the Denver plain. The aircraft was quite a handful, being so heavy and with the power of only one engine, but six hours and thirty minutes after taking off from Goose Bay we touched down at Buckley Air National Guard Base. I was more than a little relieved to have got down safely. The Boss, having escorted me to Buckley, overshot and went on alone to China Lake, leaving me and Wiki to sort out our problem.

As soon as we climbed out of our aircraft at Buckley, we were met by various uniformed Americans who seemed quite friendly. One of them was a military police lady, small in stature but with a big gun. She followed us everywhere we went and it eventually dawned on me that we were foreign aliens who had not entered the country as advertised and, whilst we weren't exactly under arrest, we were being carefully escorted. Fortunately, the VC10 had landed up the road at Denver International with some of our ground crew on board. We managed to get in telephone contact and arranged for ground crew and equipment to make their way to Buckley to look into the loss of oil pressure on our aircraft. In the meantime, we were stuck for the night in Denver. Having shaken off our police escort we met up with the VC10 crew in a hotel in the city and were royally looked after by them.

The next day our aircraft had been declared serviceable by our brilliant ground crew. It seemed that the engine had consumed the oil rather than losing it, and with a re-fill it would be okay to continue for the two-hour flight to China Lake. We duly took off, only to find that the undercarriage would not retract (the problem was later found to have been caused by the nose-wheel steering failing to centre the wheel). I found myself flying a visual circuit in a very heavy Tornado F.3, at low speed, with the undercarriage down, around an airfield that was at an elevation of 5,500 feet. This turned out to be quite difficult. The aircraft didn't want to fly at such low speed so heavy and so high. I needed reheat on both engines around the finals turn and Wiki later confided that he had his hand on the ejection-seat firing handle. There's confidence for you. Once again, we landed safely and by now it was apparent that we were becoming something of a nuisance.

After another excellent night enjoying Denver City, with the VC10 crew's hospitality and a meal in a local restaurant, the nose-wheel centring problem was also fixed by the hard-working ground crew. We took off the next day and successfully made it to China Lake, arriving two days behind schedule.

The flying area around China Lake was amazing and vast. The two main ranges extend over 1,740 square miles (4,500 square kilometres) and include the Sierra Nevada mountains in the west with Mount Whitney, California's tallest peak, 14,500 height above sea level, and Death Valley in the east, 280 feet below sea level. The area is largely undeveloped and consists of arid mountain ridges and valleys coloured by the minerals they contain. The US Navy uses the facilities for weapons and armament research, development, acquisition, testing and evaluation. Unusually for us, supersonic flying was permitted overland in the area at any height.

Whilst we were settling in at China Lake, we flew several dissimilar air combat training (DACT) sorties, 1v1, 1v2, 2v1 and 2v2, against F-18s operated by VX5, the US Navy's Operational Evaluation Unit. Apart from being able to fly supersonic overland at any height, we were also surprised to find that the 'floor' nominated for these combat training sorties was set above sea level, which with the elevation of the terrain meant that you could actually terrain mask behind mountain ridges during air combat. With these factors in our favour we fared well against the F-18s and it was enormous fun.

On one sortie I flew a US Marine Corps F-18D back-seater weapons-system operator, Major Henry Bless, in the rear cockpit of a Tornado F.3 for his experience. The sortie included some 1v1 ACT against another of our Tornadoes and I also had the opportunity to demonstrate to him the low-level acceleration and supersonic capability of the Tornado F.3. He was surprised at how manually intensive operating the radar was in the Tornado without the level of automation he was used to. He was also very impressed with the low-level acceleration and 700 knots demonstration. After landing he summed it up by saying, 'Gee that baby really hauls the chilli.' Which I gathered meant it went very fast.

The infra-red counter-measures (IRCM) flare trial started with some academic and mundane flying over the range area. We had to fly along fixed lines, which we loaded into the Tornado's navigation kit, so that the infra-red signature of the aircraft could be mapped at various aspects and different power settings. Then we started to deploy flares against the threat infra-red missile systems to ascertain whether they were effective in decoying the missiles' seeker heads.

The system we were playing with was quite something. It looked like a large motor home, or RV as the Americans call them, which was driven out to the range area each day with the scientists on board. The back section opened up to expose what looked like a Lancaster rear gunner's turret on which were mounted the threat missile-seeker heads. The vehicle was full of electronic recording equipment from which the behaviour of the missile-seeker heads against our flares could be analysed. At the end of each sortie we took the opportunity to give the scientists on the ground a very low high-speed fly-by to say thank you and because we could.

I also flew several sorties from China Lake across to the Nellis ranges in Nevada to work with a special F-16 carrying one of the more sophisticated threat missile-seeker heads with excellent IRCCM capabilities. On these sorties we were able to fly in a much more tactical manner and at low level, employing our flares with tactical manoeuvring and power settings as we would do for real. It was pleasing to establish that the flares proved effective against all the threat missiles.

During the six weeks that we were away in California we took every opportunity at weekends to visit as many of the state's attractions as possible, driving hundreds of miles and staying away on Friday and Saturday nights, sometimes at US military establishments where we were welcomed. We explored the surrounding desert, including the must-have road trip to Death Valley, where even in February it was seriously hot; we also found a gold-mining ghost town to wander around. We visited various wineries in the Napa Valley and also explored San Francisco. We drove the Big Sur coastline on Highway One from San Francisco southwards through Carmel and Monterey and we also visited Santa Barbara and San Diego. We made a trip to Sequoia National Park, in the Sierra Nevada mountains, to see the giant sequoia trees which are amongst the tallest, widest and longest-living organisms on earth. With snow on the ground around them at that time of year they were quite magical. It was good that some years later I was able to repeat much of this tour of California with Elaine. It never seemed fair that I was getting to do all these things when she was stuck at home and it was really she who was more the avid traveller than me.

With the trial complete we returned home via Goose Bay in Canada, supported by a Tristar tanker. The flight to Goose Bay took six and a half hours; it was dark when we arrived there and the base and the small township were the only lights in an otherwise completely black wilderness. The eastbound flight across the Atlantic to Coningsby the following day took four hours and forty minutes. Fortunately, the return flight was without any of the dramas of the outbound one six weeks earlier.

*****

The China Lake deployment was not the only infra-red counter-measures (flare) trials that I was involved in during my tour on the Tornado F.3 OEU. For example, in June 1994 I took a single Tornado F.3, with navigator Gordon Scott, to operate over the Luce Bay sea range from the Defence Research Agency's West Freugh airfield, near Stranraer in Dumfries and Galloway, Scotland, for a week, on a trial to test new types of flares.

Initially, we deployed our standard flares as a baseline against which to compare the new ones. One of the issues concerning the use of flares to decoy the seeker-heads of infra-red-homing missiles is that if the missile has clever IRCCM it might be able to spot the increased sightline rate of flares falling behind an aircraft and 'blink' or jump ahead to maintain a lock-on to the real target. The rate at which flares fall away is, therefore, critical: too fast and they may be ignored, too slow and they may still attract the missile towards the aircraft. The new trial flares we were to deploy actually contained rocket propellant so that, as well as burning as a flare, they would chase the aircraft and drop away less quickly. These advanced trial flare 'fireworks' were, not surprisingly, considered to be quite dangerous and we had to land at RAF Machrihanish on the Kintyre Peninsula of Scotland, which was by now largely deserted, to have the rocket flares loaded and, if necessary and if we hadn't used them all, unloaded. Should any be fired accidentally on the ground at Machrihanish any damage would be minimal. We were not about to walk behind the aircraft once it was loaded though and treated it with great care all around. Firing these flares on the range was initially quite startling as I could see them chasing us in the rear-view mirrors. We were the only aircraft operating from West Freugh that week and, on returning to land from each sortie, I arrived low and fast over the airfield with the wings swept fully back to flash past the control tower before breaking downwind to land.

High-Value Asset Attack

A deployment to Leeuwarden in the Netherlands in June 1991 provides an example of the tactical flying that the F.3 OEU undertook, in this case to take part in an exercise to attack a defended so-called 'high value asset', specifically an E-3D AWACS aircraft.

Sixteen Royal Netherland Air Force F-16s defended the AWACS whilst a large package of mixed NATO combat aircraft types attempted to break through the defensive fighters to attack it. The F.3 OEU was given the lead on one particular mission and we employed many of the attacking aircraft to cause confusion and as a distraction to the defending fighters, whilst some dedicated attacking fighters, including our pair of Tornado F.3s, tried to get at the AWACS. We broke away from the rest of the attack package and descended rapidly to low level to skirt around the defensive fighters. We were flying at 700 knots, M1.1, at low level over the sea and looking across at the Boss, a mile and a half away in line abreast battle formation,

I could see the 'bow wave' and 'rooster tail' produced by his supersonic shockwave on the water. It was a very impressive sight and I guess my aircraft was doing the same. Our tactics worked and sadly for the AWACS it didn't escape and was claimed by us. This sort of exercise would help us to refine the Tornado F.3 Tactics Manual.

Tornado F.3 to Woodvale

In September 1991 I took a Tornado F.3 to RAF Woodvale, where I had been an instructor on the university air squadrons (UASs) some 12 years earlier. The airfield was frequently used as an operating base for aircraft involved in the Southport Air Show and they were happy to have static aircraft to add to those involved in the flying display. Even though the main runway at Woodvale was only 5,000 feet long, this was adequate for a Tornado F.3 with its thrust reverse, and so a plan was hatched to take one of our aircraft over on the Friday, spend the weekend in Southport and return home on the Monday. I was accompanied by navigator Wiki Wills.

I wanted to arrive in style and briefed air traffic control at Woodvale that I would arrive at high speed and low level from the west to overfly the airfield west to east, avoiding the built-up areas, before joining the circuit to land. They were happy with that. As we approached the airfield from over the sea, I gave them a 'one-minute' call and then a 'thirty-seconds' call on the radio. I ducked down below the level of the conifer trees on the edge of the airfield as I swept in over the sand dunes and then popped over the trees to flash past the tower at about fifty feet, doing Mach 0.92 with the wings fully swept and the throttles back at idle for a whispering arrival. It worked, because the ATC controllers did not see me until I was upon them, despite being given my direction of approach and a 'thirty-seconds' call. As I pulled 4G to pull up into a climb the pressure wave produced a 'wumpf' that shook the roofs and windows of the UAS buildings. What I didn't know until after I landed was that two of the UAS instructors were walking back to their HQ building from ATC as I flew over the top of them. One of them was Rod Newman, whom I had known for many years (he had actually awarded me my A2 QFI ticket on the Bulldog in 1979). He later explained that he was walking and talking to his Boss when he noticed some sort of 'fluff' on the top of his head, that was me and the transonic 'fluff' around my aircraft. A fraction of a second later there was the 'wumpf' as I flew over and pulled up, which caused them both to throw themselves to the ground.

Everyone, especially the UAS students, took a great interest in the Tornado F.3, which we spent some time showing to them, with plenty of them getting to sit in the cockpits.

Skyflash Missile Firings

In November 1991 the F.3 OEU visited RAF Valley on Anglesey for a short missile practice camp with several trial Skyflash missile firings over Aberporth Range.

One of the most significant drawbacks of a semi-active missile like the Skyflash was that, in maintaining a radar lock to provide the continuous wave illumination needed to guide the missile to the target, the shooter would be dragged closer to the bandit, probably into visual range. This could rapidly turn a BVR engagement into a potential visual merge, to the disadvantage of the F.3 against agile opponents. There was a theoretical option for the Skyflash firer to turn away after launching the missile, whilst a second fighter in trail behind the firer provided the necessary radar lock and continuous wave illumination to the missile, hence increasing the stand-off range from the target when the missile arrived. This was known as a 'co-operative firing' and it took considerable co-operation between the fighters and some skill by the navigators. For our first missile firing of the week my aircraft was the illuminator for a co-operative Skyflash missile firing against a target towed by a Jindivik drone. It was successful.

Later the same day I fired my first ever Skyflash, against a jamming electronic counter-measures (ECM) target. A Skyflash missile firing from the Tornado was quite dramatic. There was a seemingly endless delay, actually only a fraction of a second, after trigger press and before the missile fired, which made a misfire seem a possibility. Then there was a pronounced thump as the launcher rams ejected the missile away hard from underneath the belly of the aircraft and reached full extension. This was immediately followed by a bang as the rams retracted equally rapidly back into the aircraft, and the whoosh of the missile as it shot away. It was quite exciting, probably quite expensive and was also a successful shot.

Even later on the same day I fired another Skyflash, in the dark, wearing night-vision goggles (NVGs), which were unaffected by the missile. I had fired two Skyflash missiles in the same day and I now knew what to expect with the various sound effects.

The following day I was the photo-chase aircraft for a Skyflash fired from another of our F.3s at low speed and high angle of attack (AOA). The firing aircraft was at 21 units AOA, the maximum permitted, with manoeuvre flaps and slats deployed. I sat alongside in fairly close formation. It was interesting to watch the Skyflash missile being thrown off to seemingly stagger away initially, until it picked up speed. Again, it was successful.

I was subsequently to fire three more Skyflash missiles in trials over Aberporth range in May 1993, to bring my personal count of air-to-air missiles fired to a total of ten. Most RAF fighter pilots are lucky if they get to fire one missile on a full tour. To fire ten is probably fairly unusual. The combined cost of these missiles must have been huge and it was a good thing we didn't have to pay for the experiences.

Operation DENY FLIGHT

The Bosnian War began in October 1992. A United Nations Security Council Resolution was quickly passed, prohibiting military aircraft from flying over Bosnia. It was obvious that there might be a need to enforce the UN Resolution in the future and that the RAF and Tornado F.3s in particular could become involved. The F.3 OEU was directed by the CTTO to start brainstorming and planning for any upgrades that might better suit the aircraft to the tactical environment over Bosnia and Herzegovina should it be called into action there.

Various modifications and equipment were considered and the processes were started, some of them as urgent operational requirements. Amongst these considerations were the tactics and equipment to operate effectively against helicopters.

The Tornado F.3 OEU already had considerable experience amongst its crews of operating against helicopters, gained from previous tours and also because the F.3 OEU was often called upon to provide fighter opposition for the RAF helicopter Qualified Tactics Instructor (QTI) courses. In October 1991, for example, we had operated against Puma helicopters whilst deployed to Chivenor in Devon. In December 1992 we had another opportunity to look at fighter-versus-helicopter operations when we deployed to Chivenor for a week to operate against RAF Puma and Chinook helicopters as part of their QTI course. Most of the sorties were 2v2, but towards the end we flew two missions with a pair of Tornado F.3s against three pairs of Puma, Chinook and Royal Navy Wessex helicopters.

The sorties confirmed what we already knew about the use of the Tornado F.3's Foxhunter radar against ultra-low-level helicopters and the difficulties, although not impossibilities, of getting kills against them with either Skyflash or Sidewinder AIM-9L missiles. Most of the kills we did achieve were gun kills, using a technique that was effectively air-to-ground strafe. We were also reminded just how difficult it is to keep tally on ultra-low-level helicopters, especially after pulling off from an attack. Our pairs free-and-engaged tactics helped enormously, as you could regain tally by watching the other fighter pitch into an attack. I thought that our navigators were particularly brave to sit helplessly and with complicity in the back cockpit as we pilots hurled the aircraft in steep dives at the helicopters and the ground. There wasn't much margin for error, especially in more difficult terrain.

*****

The anti-helicopter flying brought one particular factor into focus which was that, whilst the Tornado F.3 had a perfectly acceptable sighting system for air-to-ground strafe gunnery, this mode of attack was not cleared for use. Clearly, if strafe could be included in the weapons options available to F.3 crews it could be of considerable benefit, so the F.3 OEU commenced trials. We had some previous air-to-ground experience amongst the aircrew on the unit, including from exchange tours and, in my case, as an instructor at a Tactical Weapons Unit.

In January and February 1993 we began air-to-ground strafe trials on the range at Donna Nook, close to RAF Coningsby. Initially, we were restricted to 'dry' cine attacks only, to prove the system and techniques. When we started live, hot strafe gunnery we immediately began to achieve some decent scores with more than 30 per cent of the rounds hitting the strafe target panels. The initial attacks were in shallow 10-degree dives, but we quickly moved on to attacking in steeper 20- and 30-degree dives with equal success. This would obviously provide excellent training to front-line Tornado F.3 aircrew for anti-helicopter operations and other possible operational scenarios. We had developed the techniques and managed to get a clearance rushed through.

In April that year I had the unusual experience for a Qualified Flying Instructor (QFI) of flying in the back seat of one of our two-stick trainer Tornado F.3s with a front-line squadron Qualified Weapons Instructor (QWI) in the front, flying from RAF Leeming to teach him the strafe techniques on Donna Nook range. We then flew a second sortie with him in the back cockpit so that he would feel confident in passing the instruction on to his squadron pilots. The QWI happened to be an ex-Lightning pilot colleague of mine, Flight Lieutenant Derek 'Grinner' Smith. It was not normal for a QFI to be teaching a QWI a weapons event.

*****

In April 1993, in order to enforce the no-fly resolution over Bosnia, which was being frequently ignored, NATO began Operation DENY FLIGHT. At the time, the Leeming Tornado F.3 squadrons held the NATO Joint Rapid Reaction Force commitment, being held at very high readiness, and the Leeming Wing provided part of the first RAF deployment to the Italian air base at Gioia del Colle in support of Operation DENY FLIGHT.

We were having a Tornado F.3 OEU officers' dinner in a local hotel on a Friday evening. During the pre-drinks Group Captain Mal Gleave, from the CTTO, took me aside and told me that he wanted me to go to Leeming to deploy to Gioia del Colle on Sunday. I had tonight to enjoy, tomorrow to pack and then off to Italy the following day. He wanted me to be the eyes and ears on the ground at Gioia and to feed back to the CTTO what was happening and how the organisation could assist.

The flight from Leeming to Gioia in an RAF C-130 Hercules was interesting as I was one of few passengers in an aircraft fully loaded with live air-to-air missiles. At Gioia the eight Tornado F.3s from Leeming had not long arrived and there was an understandable level of organised chaos. I was eventually given a ride to a rented private house in the town which gave me a room for the night.

The next day I found my way back to the airfield and to the area where the RAF was setting up its operations. One of the first people I bumped into was the RAF Leeming Station Commander, and ex-Lightning pilot, Group Captain Phil Roser who was the detachment commander. We knew each other and he greeted me with words to the effect of 'What the f... are you doing here?' I explained quickly and succinctly and was much relieved when he immediately saw the value of a CTTO liaison officer and invited me to all his future execs' meetings.

For the next three weeks I was a fly on the wall for the initial Operation DENY FLIGHT missions. I fed back daily reports and information on specific requirements to CTTO and was even able to offer some guidance and advice to the crews involved. Whatever time of the day or night that crews briefed and debriefed for missions over Bosnia, I was there. I felt a fatherly concern for the crews putting themselves in harm's way, 'going sausage side' as they called it, quoting from *Blackadder Goes Forth*, and I also felt a tinge of guilt that I wasn't personally sharing that risk. I attended a briefing from an American Combat Search and Rescue (CSAR) helicopter crewman who would be one of those to try to rescue any downed aircrew. It immediately became apparent that the RAF did not have the equipment the Americans expected, such as personal radios or infra-red beacons. I fed that back and it was rectified. We also quickly got combat waistcoats to carry the necessary kit, to be worn under the lifesaving jackets. The accommodation and domestic arrangements settled down and I moved into the Hotel Svevo in Gioia town, which became the RAF officers' mess for the duration; so I was now living with the squadron aircrew who, of course, I knew.

Due to their capabilities and the night-vision equipment carried in the Tornado F.3s the contingent got more than its fair share of night tasking over Bosnia. One night I attended the brief for a four-ship of Tornado F.3s and, after they had launched, I went back to the hotel to get my head down before intending to drive back to the airfield for their return. When I walked out of the hotel in the dark at 01:00 I was shocked to find thick fog, which had not been in the forecast. To cut a long story short, we very nearly lost four Tornado F.3s that night. Two managed to divert to Sigonella in Sicily and were talked down on an instrument approach in very bad weather with very little fuel remaining. The USAF air traffic controller was subsequently given a flight safety award. The other two F.3s, with insufficient fuel to make it to Sigonella, managed to land in very poor visibility at nearby Bari airport on the coast, which wasn't properly open, again with very little fuel remaining.

After three weeks at Gioia I was replaced by another squadron leader from the CTTO and allowed to go home and back to flying. My annual report that year included some words from Group Captain Gleave, which amused and pleased me in equal measure:

> Every O.C. should be issued with a Rowley to maintain his faith in the human race, to raise his spirits when low and to do all the jobs that others would find irksome or difficult, with enthusiasm, right first time, every time.

I was also delighted to be assessed that year as 'Exceptional' as a pilot for the first time. There is no higher accolade for a pilot in the RAF. This was the standard to which I had aspired and striven for very many years. In achieving an 'Exceptional' rating I had reached the peak of my profession as a fighter pilot, but I also knew that the problem now was staying there.

Towed Radar Decoy

The major threat to NATO aircraft over Bosnia was not from Serbian aircraft but from the numerous surface-to-air-missiles (SAMs), some of which were mobile systems. To prove the point, Captain Scott O'Grady USAF was shot down in his F-16C by a mobile SAM 6 (SA-6) missile over Bosnia in June 1995. (He ejected into Serb-controlled territory, evaded capture for six days and was rescued by a US Marine CSAR helicopter crew.) The Tornado F.3 did not have an electronic counter-measures (ECM) self-protection jammer to defend itself against SAMs. It had never been anticipated in the original design and specification that the aircraft would be operating in a SAM-threat environment. This was obviously an urgent requirement that needed to be addressed to protect the Tornado F.3s and their crews, flying daily over Bosnia on Operation DENY FLIGHT.

GEC-Marconi had been working on a prototype towed radar decoy (TRD) jammer for some time. It was now proposed that its development into an operational system could be accelerated under an Urgent Operational Requirement with the Tornado F.3 OEU conducting the flight trials. I became the lead pilot for the TRD programme, with Squadron Leader Gordon Scott – the F.3 OEU flight commander – as the lead navigator. He was ideal for the job as a qualified electronic warfare officer with a great technical understanding of radars and ECM. I brought a pilot's input and a tactical mind to the team.

The GEC-Marconi towed radar decoy was mounted in a hollowed out BOZ pod (the electronic-counter-measures pod from the Tornado GR.1/GR.4). The pod contained all the clever electronics, including the receiver for radar threats and the processor, which was reprogrammable to deliver jamming specific to the threat. At the rear of the pod was the decoy, which transmitted the jamming signals; it could be streamed and towed approximately 100 metres behind the aircraft on a cable containing fibre optics – 'clever string', as we called it. When the jamming signals were transmitted they, therefore, emanated not from the aircraft but from the decoy some distance behind it. The jamming alone might be sufficient to break the lock of the guidance radar and defeat the SAM but if the missile was sophisticated enough to 'home on jam' it would be guided towards the decoy and not the aircraft. Once streamed the TRD could not be wound back into the pod; instead it could be dropped over the airfield, as part of the recovery procedure, from a low height and speed, with a small parachute retarding its fall. The device could then be refurbished and re-used. This was important because the decoys were not cheap and were available only in limited numbers.

The Tornado F.3 had only two underwing pylons, one under each wing, to carry fuel drop tanks and the four (two per pylon) Sidewinder missile launchers. The Tornado GR.1 had been designed with four wing pylons, two per side, which was its normal fit. When the Tornado F.3s were assembled, the hardware for the outboard pylons was not deleted and so it was relatively easy to re-activate and fit outboard pylons to one of our Tornado F.3 OEU aircraft, ZE968. This allowed the carriage of fuel tanks and missile launchers on the inboard pylons, the TRD pod on the port outboard pylon and a Phimat chaff-dispenser with a balance weight on the starboard outboard pylon as a counterbalance. The increased weight and drag of the full fit were immediately apparent to me as the pilot and was always the most significant drawback to the system, especially if operating the Tornado F.3 at medium to high altitudes or if manoeuvring hard.

Gordon and I first flew with the TRD pod in November 1993. On the first three sorties the decoy remained stowed in the pod whilst we operated against SAM threat radars on the Spadeadam Range, the RAF Electronic Warfare training facility on top of the Pennine hills in Cumbria, to test the pod electronics. We flew with the 1,500-litre underwing fuel tanks fitted and the sortie durations for these flights were between two hours ten minutes and two and a half hours. On our fourth sortie with the TRD, flown in December, we had tanker support from a VC10 and we streamed the decoy for the first time, in straight and level flight, over the sea in case it fell off. It streamed successfully and for the first time but, by no means the last, I was aware of this little dark object, visible in the rear-view mirrors, dancing around behind us on its tow cable. It didn't fly in a stable manner but rather described a conical path and would be upset further when I manoeuvred the aircraft. We operated on Spadeadam range, tanked to full once again and then dropped the decoy at the range as no one was prepared to let us fly back home with it at that point. This first drop was without the parachute, but the soft peat meant that the decoy survived intact anyway. This was a five-hour sortie.

We flew another similar four-hour sortie in January, with VC10 tanker support, operating over Spadeadam Range. This time we were allowed to bring the decoy home, flying south over the sea, minimising the overland track to the airfield at Coningsby and, of course, avoiding built-up areas. We dropped the decoy over the airfield at Coningsby using the parachute which deployed automatically as soon as the cable and the electrical supply were cut. This was the first time that this had ever been done and we had no real idea of how long the decoy would spend in the air under the parachute and therefore how far it might drift. The result, with a crosswind that day, was that it drifted right past the air traffic control tower and landed on the road behind it, nearly knocking a WRAF airwoman off her bicycle. We learned from that, lowered the drop height and amended our calculations for drift in a crosswind.

*****

With just five TRD trial sorties under our belt we now moved the trial to the United States. On 15 January 1994, Gordon and I took ZE968, fully fitted out for the TRD trial, to Lajes in the Azores with a Tristar tanker carrying our ground crew and equipment and providing us with fuel top-ups for the four-hour flight. The next day we flew on to Bermuda (it's a tough life, I know) for another night stop with the Tristar refuelling us on route. This was a five-hour trip. Then on the third day we routed with the Tristar to Eglin Air Force base on the western 'panhandle' of Florida. The Tristar crew was impressed that on every single 'plug' for a fuel top-up during the three-day transit, thirteen in all, I never missed and always connected the probe with the refuelling drogue first time. In truth, in a two-seat fighter, this was a crew effort and the navigator provided the pilot with a commentary from the back seat to help with plugging in.

Eglin Air Force Base was home to the USAF Air Warfare Centre and was also a USAF development, test and evaluation centre, particularly for weapons. The base area was enormous, larger than the Peak District National Park, and the over-sea range area even bigger. The number of combat aircraft based at Eglin seemed to outstrip the entire assets of the RAF. In addition, the ranges boasted excellent simulations of Soviet SAMs and anti-aircraft-artillery (AAA) threats, against which we were planned to work.

Domestically, all of the Tornado F.3 OEU personnel and the accompanying scientists and industry experts were accommodated in apartments in a condominium on the beach front at Fort Walton Beach, a short drive from Eglin Air Force base. I shared an apartment with Gordon; there was a swimming pool below the balcony, the beach beyond that and you could often watch brown pelicans flying along the water's edge from the lounge. Even in January and February the weather was pleasantly warm. We didn't get much time for being tourists as we worked at weekends, too, although we did visit the US Naval Air Museum at Pensacola and the battleship USS *Alabama* in Mobile Bay. We ensured that the team, including the civilians, socialised together in the evenings, which was something new to most of them, but enjoyed by us all and which made us a better and closer-knit team. It appeared that those who had been on trials of this type before, with other aircrew, found that they didn't take much interest in the trial beyond the flying and didn't socialise with the rest of the team. We could not have been more different in those respects.

During the three weeks that we spent at Eglin we operated against SA-3, SA-6 and SA-8 SAM simulators and also against the ZSU-23-4 radar-guided anti-aircraft-gun system. Inevitably, the trial profiles were slightly 'canned' to begin with. Some runs were made with no jamming at all, some with just chaff, some with the TRD streamed and jamming, some with both TRD jamming and chaff. The effect of dropping chaff whilst jamming with the decoy was to magnify the effects as the jamming signals bounced off the chaff, known as chaff illumination or 'Chill'.

As far as the Americans were concerned our towed-radar decoy programme was not just highly classified, it was a so-called 'black' project. We were there to utilise the threat simulators and data-recording-and-analysis facilities; they were providing us with these facilities on the basis that they would 'exploit' the British technology and learn more about the capabilities. The black nature of the trial meant that we were kept in a quiet corner of the base and we were not allowed under any circumstances to bring the TRD back to Eglin airfield. It had to be dropped on a range just inland from the coast where a wide and very long avenue had been cut in the trees. If we were unable to drop the TRD on the range we had to land with it at another airfield within the range area.

We had a tricky time dropping the TRD on the range on the last sortie when, as we finished working with the ZSU-23-4 system, some very low cloud, which was not forecast, quickly rolled in off the sea, covering the coast and the range where we had to drop the decoy. This led to a powerful demonstration of the trust that had developed between Gordon and me. He fixed the 'nav' kit to ensure its accuracy, backing it up with his handheld GPS, and provided me with a picture to line up with the range beneath the low cloud. I descended gingerly into the murk, knowing that the trees were the highest obstacles around. We worked closely together, checking on each other and monitoring the height with the radar altimeter as I descended. We popped out of the murk, very low, into the avenue in the trees, just in time to drop the TRD. The Chief Technician armourer on the ground on the range, with his radio to call the 'Cut', didn't see us coming until the last moment. We cut the TRD off and climbed back up into the cloud. I'm not sure that I would have done that with any other navigator and he may well not have trusted any other pilot to do it.

A strong bond had developed between Gordon and me, which was reinforced on this and other detachments that we completed together. We could not have been more different as characters. He was quiet, studious, very intelligent, with a dry sense of humour, studying for an Open University degree in his spare time, liked listening to classical music and ran to keep fit. I wasn't any of that. However, we worked brilliantly together as a team, both on the ground and in the air. It was one of the best pilot-and-navigator teams that I ever experienced. In the cockpit we worked together with very little talking, almost seeming to know what the other was thinking. Gordon and his wife Alison became good friends with Elaine and me, and we continued to socialise long after we stopped working together. Gordon eventually retired from the RAF as a wing commander with an OBE. I was very sad when he died suddenly of a heart attack in 2017, aged just 62.

With the first stage of the TRD trial complete, the return flight from Florida back to the UK was a reverse of the outbound route with one exception. On the day of the planned Bermuda to Lajes leg, the weather in the Azores was not suitable and we had a full day off in Bermuda. Gordon and I hired mopeds and toured the island (tough life).

*****

With various aspects of the TRD needing to be addressed by the experts and industry, it was December 1994 before flight trials re-commenced, initially from Coningsby to operate on Spadeadam Range. The urgency of the operational requirement had increased and Gordon and I flew twenty-three TRD-trial sorties up to the end of April 1995. It had become standard to stream the TRD over the sea and to bring it back to Coningsby for a drop at the end of the sortie. I even carried out a night drop at the end of one sortie. Some of the sorties were double-length with air-to-air-refuelling.

Later we moved the trials work to Aberporth range and, to avoid having to drag the streamed decoys all the way back to Coningsby overland across the width of Wales and England, we started to drop them at Llanbedr airfield on the west coast of Wales. Unfortunately, during these trial sorties there were some TRD failures. Those failures were critical as it was becoming increasingly likely that the available resources would not allow operational Tornado F.3 crews to pre-emptively stream the TRD and check its serviceability before entering a threat area. The first time they were going to find out if it stayed on and worked was when they streamed it as part of a defensive SAM break, having been targeted. If it failed or fell off at that point they would probably get shot down.

The operational need to stream the TRD whilst manoeuvring defensively against a SAM radar lock meant that the original clearances and limitations, which restricted us to streaming the decoy only in straight and level flight, were not tactically acceptable. We were keen to develop tactics that started with the TRD stowed and, when targeted by a SAM-threat radar, involved manoeuvring hard to put the threat radar on the beam, whilst deploying the TRD and dropping chaff. I made this point strongly and eventually I was told to increase the parameters at which we could stream the decoy. This would perhaps normally have been a task for a qualified test pilot, but it fell to me. I gradually increased the amount of positive G, the roll rate and the manoeuvres at which we streamed the decoy, with another aircraft observing and filming the results. We eventually reached an operationally realistic set of parameters, which were accepted as the new clearance.

During this period Gordon and I found ourselves briefing the Commander-in-Chief of Strike Command, Air Chief Marshal Sir William 'Bill' Wratten, on the TRD system during one of his visits to Coningsby. He was naturally keen to get the equipment operational as soon as possible for Operation DENY FLIGHT, but was not necessarily being given all the best and most helpful information and advice by the staff chain. We were told to rectify that. The C.-in-C. had a reputation for being a hard man who would see straight through any waffling or lack of clarity. However, we were fighter boys, we knew our stuff and we were confident about it. We briefed him on how the resources issue affected the operational and tactical employment of the TRD system, which was currently not as reliable as it needed to be. He was convinced, our credibility was intact, perhaps even increased, and more time was granted to sort out the problems.

*****

In May 1995 we deployed again to Eglin Air Force Base in Florida for more TRD trials, this time with two aircraft modified for the TRD system.

The transit out to Eglin was flown using the northerly route via Goose Bay in Canada, as it was summer and the chances of surviving an ejection into the North Atlantic were that much greater. With a Tristar tanker supporting us and carrying the ground crew and equipment, the two-day transit to Eglin took almost eleven hours flying time.

Over the next six weeks at Eglin, Gordon and I flew fourteen TRD trial sorties on the electronic-warfare range working against SA-3, SA-6 and SA-8 SAMs. The tactical and operational employment of the system gradually came to the fore and we were able to start each trial session with a realistic SAM break against whichever system was locked onto us, manoeuvring hard in an overbanked break turn to put the threat radar on the beam whilst descending to maintain speed, streaming the TRD to jam the threat and punching out chaff to produce the chill effect. The effects were very successful against the SAM systems.

There were two amusing distractions during the trial at Eglin. The first began one day when we were at the food hall on the base buying some lunch, when we were approached by a USAF colonel who asked us if we were the 'Brits' doing a trial there. Having confirmed who we were, he told us that Air Chief Marshal (he may have said 'General') Wratten was visiting Eglin that day and wanted to get in touch with us. We were to telephone him. It transpired that the Air Chief Marshal was part of a visit by NATO air force chiefs and wanted us to update him on the TRD project. As the next day was a Saturday, he suggested a breakfast meeting at his hotel further down the Florida coast. We duly met with him at his hotel, he bought us breakfast and we provided him with an informal update over the breakfast table. It was rather surreal. He clearly trusted our knowledge and opinions; he asked many pertinent questions and also asked how he could help the trial in any way. We suggested a couple of things that he could influence at his level. The following week we were amused to receive several telephone calls from various senior staff officers back in the UK, who had discovered that the C.-in-C. had received a face-to-face briefing from 'the coalface' and were desperate to know what we had told him, lest they be blindsided.

On Sunday 4 June 1995 Hurricane Allison (uncannily named after Gordon's wife) was approaching the coast of Florida and we were told to evacuate our two Tornado F.3s to Kelly Air Force Base at San Antonio in Texas. Hurricane Allison was the first named hurricane of the 1995 season. We had been operating two Tornado F.3s on the trial at Eglin, with Gordon and me as the only crew. Fortunately, a second F.3 OEU crew arrived on Saturday 3 June, intending to spend the last week of the trial getting a handover of the

TRD project from Gordon and me, as we were both due postings. We had not anticipated the need to fly the aircraft out of Eglin on the Sunday and so had spent Saturday evening with the other crew ensuring some 'detachment first night madness'. We were therefore rather shabby when Gordon received the call on Sunday morning telling us we had to evacuate the aircraft to Texas that day. We flew both aircraft to Kelly Air Force Base in Texas and spent that night in San Antonio town, famous for the Battle of the Alamo, along with most of the USAF fighter pilots from Eglin. The worst of the hurricane made landfall further east down the Florida coast and, fortunately, there was no significant damage at Eglin where our ground crew had been forced to remain. We flew our aircraft back later the next day. Unfortunately, the other Tornado F.3 had an oil over-temperature problem after take off and the crew had to declare an emergency and land back at Kelly. We continued back to Eglin and had to send ground crew over to Texas to rectify the problem with the other aircraft; we didn't see them again for the rest of the week.

With the trial complete, our transit home, six weeks after we had departed, followed the reverse route with a VC10 tanker via Goose Bay in Canada for a night stop, before the eastbound Atlantic crossing.

*****

The towed radar decoy was deployed operationally with the RAF Tornado F.3s flying on Operation DENY FLIGHT over Bosnia in December 1995. The TRD pod and the cockpit control panel were rather Heath Robinson, as we had taken a prototype and turned it into an operational system as an urgent operational requirement. However, it provided the F.3s with a state-of-the-art self-protection jammer with world-leading technology and effectiveness against SAM systems and with equal utility against radar-guided air-to-air missiles. The technological advances achieved in the process were fed into the Typhoon Defensive Aids Sub System. In addition, many current US aircraft types are now fitted with similar towed radar decoy ECM systems. I am proud of the small part that Gordon Scott and I played in the development of the TRD for the Tornado F.3.

Cyprus Display

In May 1994, during a gap in the trial flying for the TRD and other equipment, the Tornado F.3 OEU deployed two aircraft to RAF Akrotiri in

Cyprus for two weeks, for an air-to-air high-angle gunnery trial. At least that was the excuse.

RAF Akrotiri was holding an open day air display during the time that we were to be there. With the Red Arrows completing their pre-season work-up flying and public display approval at Akrotiri, they would also be displaying. We were asked if we could provide a Tornado F.3 display with our pair of aircraft. The Officer Commanding the Tornado F.3 OEU was now Wing Commander Stu Black, a navigator, who had taken over as the first navigator Boss of the F.3 OEU in October 1993. He turned to me as the 'Senior Pilot' to come up with something. I designed a display that was effectively a series of linked flypasts to show off some of the characteristics of the Tornado F.3, including the capabilities of the aircraft's navigation kit. I would lead with Gordon Scott in my back seat; the No. 2 would be the unit's Trials Management Officer, Squadron Leader Paul 'Gandhi' Willis, with the Boss, Stu Black, in his back seat. The plan was that we would arrive together in echelon formation to complete the first curving flypast, showing topsides. As we reset for the second pass, within sight of the crowd, Gandhi would move into close line-astern formation. I would have the wings set to fully forwards and he would set his fully back, thus showing the different plan forms. Whilst flying along the display line showing the undersides, we would both simultaneously swing the wings on my command, so that mine moved from fully forward to fully back and his went the other way. The Tornado flying-control system allowed you to do this in close formation with no significant trim changes and it showed off the swing-wing capability. After this we would split for two synchronised passes. On the first I would be at the slowest possible speed and maximum angle of attack, with the undercarriage and flaps down and the refuelling probe out. Gandhi would pass me at crowd centre at 600 knots with the wings fully back, demonstrating the opposite ends of the speed range of the aircraft. Achieving this took good co-ordination between the navigators, using the time-to-go indications in the nav kit. That applied even more on the last pass, which was a head-on synchronised pass with both of us at 600 knots, pulling up to the vertical at maximum G as we crossed at crowd centre, to climb vertically in full reheat, carrying out two vertical rolls and levelling off at 28,000 feet.

The plan was approved and we flew three practice displays over the airfield at Coningsby to gain the necessary public display approval to fly the display at Akrotiri during their open day air show.

We flew the aircraft out to Cyprus, staging through Sigonella in Sicily to refuel. At Akrotiri, in the days before the weekend air show, we flew a couple of practice displays. On all the practices we flew we never quite managed to achieve the crossover at the centre point on the final pass with both aircraft doing 600 knots (a closing speed of almost 1,400 mph). The Boss said that if we did it on the day he would buy a barrel of beer.

On one of our practice displays in Cyprus, not long after take off, Gordon's voice came up on the intercom, sounding more concerned than normal, with what seemed a strange question to pose considering the task in hand.

'Clive, how do you feel about wasps?' he said.

Dismissively, I replied, 'I'm not bothered about them. Why?'

'Because you have an enormous hornet sitting on your right shoulder.' Glancing to my right I saw he was absolutely correct. The thing was huge. It must have been about two inches (five centimetres) long. It was the biggest wasp I'd ever seen. Gordon had obviously been concerned that, if I was terrified, I might eject, taking him with me. I was wearing my sleeved life-saving jacket over my flying suit and it was sitting on that, so I felt fairly safe and anyway we had a job to do. I ignored it and got on with the display. When we landed the hornet was nowhere to be seen. I told the ground crew to be careful and to look out for it. They found it, dead, under the ejection seat; either it couldn't take the G or the altitude. It was presented to me in a plastic bag as a souvenir.

On the day of the air show, the display went perfectly and for the first and only time we managed to cross exactly at crowd centre on both synchro passes, including the 600 knots final head-on pass. The Boss bought the beer.

Data Link Trials

It is no exaggeration to say that the Link 16 Joint Tactical Information Distribution System (JTIDS) data-link system was an absolute game changer. The F.3 OEU commenced trials of the JTIDS on the Tornado F.3 in September 1993, trials that ran concurrently with those for the development of the radar and the towed radar decoy.

The introduction of JTIDS provided a high-capacity secure data link that was highly resistant to jamming and which allowed the real-time sharing of the tactical air picture with all assets on a network, as well as providing a secure voice and messaging facility, and friendly and hostile identification. GEC-Marconi developed the JTIDS in the UK, with involvement from the USA. The Tornado F.3 was the first UK combat aircraft to be equipped with the system and the first fighter outside the US inventory to operate with it.

Before the advent of JTIDS, situational awareness (SA) in the Tornado F.3 cockpit was limited to what you could see with your own sensors (radar and RHWR) or eyes and the mental picture you could build from radio transmissions. With JTIDS the tactical air picture was displayed visually on the existing tactical Plan display, both in the front and rear cockpits, using shared information from other friendly assets, such as other JTIDS-equipped fighters, AWACS aircraft, fighter-control agencies and air defence capable ships. This provided not so much a step-change but more of a quantum leap in SA.

The JTIDS-equipped fighter crew now knew the position and status of all other assets on the network. You could see where the other members of your formation and your wingmen were, whether they were in front, alongside or behind you, even if they were beyond visual range, or in cloud, along with their fuel and weapons status. You could also see any targets that were being tracked by the radars of friendly fighters on the network. In addition, you knew where the JTIDS-equipped AWACS and tankers were and, best of all, you could see any targets being tracked by the AWACS's powerful long-range radar, beyond the fighters' radar range.

*****

On 8 September 1993, with navigator Gordon Scott, I flew the first-ever sortie by an RAF Tornado F.3 equipped with JTIDS. Not surprisingly, there were some technical and software problems to sort out initially but we very quickly learned what the system had to offer and how to exploit it. A week later I flew three tactical trial sorties with JTIDS during the large air defence exercise ELDER JOUST. The following week I flew for the first time with an E-3D AWACS providing us with its radar picture by data link. From there on we flew both dedicated trial sorties and tactical sorties with JTIDS, including dissimilar air combat training (DACT) sorties 2v2 and 4v4 against F-16s, F-15Cs and F-15Es and low-level affiliation sorties against four-ships of Tornado GR.1s and Jaguars.

We also flew with the JTIDS functioning between our own OEU aircraft on routine sorties, including those when we provided targets for radar trials. We found that the SA provided by the system allowed us to operate together in cloud or at night in tactical formations that would previously have required us to be visual with each other, because we could see each other on the tactical Plan displays. Clearly, the system was going to lead to changes in the tactics we could employ in those conditions.

*****

In August 1994 we deployed several aircraft, along with aircraft and crews from No. 5 Squadron – the first front-line Tornado F.3 squadron to be equipped with JTIDS – to Mountain Home Air Force Base, Idaho, USA, to participate in a tactical trial with USAF F-15Cs, US Navy F-14Ds and an RAF E3-D AWACS, all equipped with JTIDS. Once again, the transit out to the USA was via a night stop at Goose Bay in Canada, with Tristar tanker support and with a total flying time of eleven hours and forty-five minutes.

Mountain Home Air Force Base was home to the 366th Fighter Wing of the USAF Air Combat Command, nicknamed the 'Gunfighters'. The Wing was the USAF's premier Air Intervention composite wing, a complete air force comprising a variety of aircraft types, including F-15Cs and F-15Es, F-16Cs and even B-1B Lancer bombers, with their own support aircraft and tankers and a large deployable headquarters with air planning staff and all the necessary support staff. The wing was held at high readiness and would be the first to deploy rapidly to anywhere in the world for contingency operations, able to deliver integrated combat power wherever it was needed. Its 390th Fighter Squadron's F-15Cs were the first USAF combat aircraft to be equipped with JTIDS. US Navy F-14D Tomcats were also beginning to be equipped with JTIDS and two F-14Ds deployed to Mountain Home during the trial so that we could include them in the network. The Americans hoped that the trial results would prove inter-operability and add weight to their push to get funding for more JTIDS equipment, not least because it could massively reduce the possibility of so-called friendly-fire incidents.

During the three weeks that we were at Mountain Home we flew numerous tactical sorties, with our Tornado F.3s working alongside the F-15Cs armed with AMRAAM, and sometimes with the F-14s added. Mainly we flew in the defensive counter-air role, but we also flew offensive counter-air and high-value asset (AWACS) defence sorties. We operated against enemy forces provided by the wing's F-16Cs, simulating being armed with the Russian AA-10A and C 'Alamo' long-range semi-active air-to-air missiles and AA-11 'Archer' short-range infra-red missiles. Fighter control and the data-link picture was provided by the RAF E-3D AWACS on every sortie. The number of aircraft in the sorties was gradually increased to add to the complexity. We had more crews than aircraft, so I didn't fly on every sortie, but I flew nine sorties over the Mountain Home ranges which were in an area that looked like something from a Wild West movie, with canyons and rocky, mountainous terrain. I flew with the Boss, Wing Commander Stu Black, as my navigator. Beginning with a pair of F.3s teamed with a pair of JTIDS-equipped F-15s versus four F-16s, the numbers built up until the final sortie was four Tornado F.3s with four F-15s versus eighteen F-16s. The trial was a success, proving the system and the tactics and also the interoperability between the RAF and the USAF (and US Navy). The flying was also great fun.

*****

I flew on a Controller Aircraft Release to Service approval sortie for JTIDS in February 1995 and the equipment was fully cleared for operational use with the front-line Tornado F.3s shortly afterwards. I was very pleased to have experienced the future.

Posted

At the end of August 1995, after four and a half years with the Tornado F.3 Operational Evaluation Unit, my tour came to an end and I was posted to 56 (Reserve) Squadron, the Tornado F.3 Operational Conversion Unit, at Coningsby, as an instructor. This was a posting that would make full use of my experience with the aircraft. I now had over 1,800 hours on type, and I had been flying the Tornado F.3 for almost eight years. It would also mean that I would continue fast-jet flying for several more years yet. The posting was sugar-coated because, in addition, I had been selected to fly Hurricanes and Spitfires with the RAF Battle of Britain Memorial Flight (BBMF), also based at Coningsby, as a secondary duty. More of that later.

My extended tour with the F.3 OEU, during which I had flown more than 1,000 hours on the F.3, had been one of the best I ever had. I had enjoyed every moment of it. Much of the work had been highly technical, as may be gleaned from my brief descriptions of it, but I had immersed myself in those aspects and, as a result, found it all very interesting, even fascinating, and rewarding too. I had also developed what was described in an official report as an 'unparalleled level of knowledge of the Tornado F.3's systems, operating procedures and limitations'. There had been some brilliant tactical flying that had been enormous fun and which, I felt, had further advanced my experience and expertise as a fighter pilot. The Group Captain Tactics and Trials at the Air Warfare Centre commented on my final report: 'Rowley is truly a "specialist" within the aviation world.'

Chapter 11

Tornado F.3 Instructor

Tornado F.3 Operational Conversion Unit

The Tornado F.3 Operational Conversion Unit (OCU), based at RAF Coningsby, was the largest of all the RAF's Tornado F.3 squadrons, with some twenty-four aircraft, forty aircrew instructors, over 250 engineers and a student aircrew population of up to sixty. From August 1992 the OCU carried the shadow squadron 'number plate' of No. 56 (Reserve) Squadron. The job of the OCU was to train ab-initio pilots and navigators to fly and operate the Tornado F.3 to a standard where they could be posted to front-line squadrons. In addition, the unit ran short refresher courses for experienced aircrew returning to the aircraft after tours away, plus the post-graduate qualified-weapons-instructor (QWI) courses. It also trained qualified flying instructors (QFIs) for the Tornado F.3 and produced instrument-rating examiners (IREs). It was a large busy and impressive operation.

The OCU instructors – staff pilots and navigators – were all experienced Tornado F.3 operators with at least one tour on a front-line squadron behind them. They were a dedicated bunch who routinely started work early in the mornings and worked ten or eleven-hour days. On arrival at the OCU the new instructors had to complete a staff work-up for each phase of the course before being allowed to instruct it. More experienced instructors formed the staff work-up team to provide the training to the new instructors.

I arrived on 56(R) Squadron in late September 1995 and completed the staff work-up training for the basic radar-intercept phase in the first week. I then immediately began instructing students on the basic radar techniques, procedures and tactics. I was, of course, already a Tornado F.3 QFI and an instrument-rating examiner (IRE) but I had to learn the specific sequences taught on the OCU conversion sorties. That was completed in a single sortie, with air-to-air refuelling, in November and, from then on, I was cleared to instruct as a QFI on the conversion phase. The same month I completed the staff work-up for the advanced phases of the course.

Tornado F.3 STANEVAL

In November the Officer Commanding the conversion unit, Wing Commander Steve Ayres, called me into his office and asked me if, despite my time-consuming secondary duty of flying with the Battle of Britain Memorial Flight, I thought I would be able to cope with the demands of being a member of the Tornado F.3 Standards and Evaluation (STANEVAL) team. This was a small unit within the OCU with a squadron leader officer commanding, who was either a QWI or a QFI. He led a team which consisted of two flight lieutenant QWIs (one a pilot and the other a navigator), two QFIs, who were also the Central Flying School (CFS) Agents for the aircraft, and the Command Instrument Rating Examiner (IRE) who trained and checked all the Tornado F.3 IREs.

The STANEVAL team was responsible for the standards of pure and tactical flying within the Tornado F.3 Force. It was tasked with maintaining all aspects of Force standardisation by producing briefing notes, maintaining the content of the *Aircrew Manual* and flight reference cards (FRCs), and publishing Force Standard Operating Procedures (SOPs). One of the specific tasks which fell to the team within this remit was the regular, approximately annual, two-week STANEVAL visits to each Tornado F.3 squadron. Every pilot within the F.3 Force was required to fly a dual-check sortie with one of the two STANEVAL QFIs at least once every two years; so, when possible, these dual checks were carried out during the visits to their units. In addition to the QFI dual-handling-check sorties, the Team's QWIs conducted assessments on the squadrons' pilots and navigators in the tactical arena. These checks included the planning, briefing, flying and debriefing of realistic training missions. As well as providing individual assessments, the STANEVAL team produced a written report, with an assessment and grading of the squadron as a whole, for the officer commanding and HQ 11 Group.

I was pleased to have been asked to join the STANEVAL team so early in my time as an instructor at the OCU and accepted without hesitation. In retrospect it was an inspired move by the Boss to offer the opportunity to me. He gained an experienced Tornado F.3 pilot and QFI on the team, with recent experience of the latest kit from the F.3 OEU, who was comfortable in the rear seat of the operational aircraft, and who he knew would be willing and able to do all the necessary staff work. From my perspective I gained an additional focus that I felt made good use of my experience and abilities. It placed me in a role where, once again, even as specialist aircrew, I felt I had influence and could make a difference for the Tornado F.3 Force.

I had previous experience of the role from my time as the Officer Commanding the Lightning Training Flight at Binbrook, almost a decade earlier. That experience led me to push for changes in the way that the Tornado F.3 STANEVAL team operated. When I joined the team the QFI and QWI elements were located in different offices, rarely spoke with each other and operated independently even on the visits to squadrons. I believed that the team should be much more integrated and that we should work together more, including running the STANEVAL visits quizzes with a joint realistic operational scenario, rather than separate QFI and QWI lists of questions.

Shortly after I joined the team, Squadron Leader Bill Vivian was posted to 56 Squadron as the Officer Commanding STANEVAL. He was a QFI who had taken over from me at the Tornado F.3 OEU when I was posted to the OCU. He had then been promoted and this was his first job in his new rank. Bill was an extremely capable pilot, instructor and officer, and a thoroughly nice person who was very easy to get on with. He was also ambitious and keen to make an impact, and immediately bought into my ideas. From then on, the whole STANEVAL team occupied one office, with the QWIs and QFIs together providing a useful synergy. I led the introduction of the joint QWI and QFI scenario quizzes, which were introduced on the next visit to a squadron. I also suggested that the traditional singleton dual-handling checks, when a squadron pilot might be asked to 'show me your aeros', which was not something that the operational pilots ever practised, were not very relevant to their role. Instead, I proposed that we flew as a pair, with a formation brief by the lead squadron pilot, a pair's close formation take off and some close-formation manoeuvring, checking the pilots' abilities to lead and fly in formation. Then we would fly some 1v1 air combat training starting from line-abreast one mile apart at only 300 knots, with an inwards turn to commence the fight. This forced the pilots into low speed, high angle of attack (AOA) handling in a realistic combat scenario, which allowed us to check their limit handling in a competitive environment. Subsequently, we split up for some individual handling, such as high AOA manoeuvring with the spin and incidence limiting system (SPILS) turned off, followed by a simulated emergency recovery to base and a mixture of different types of visual circuits, including flapless, simulated single-engine and low level. These suggestions were also accepted by Bill and incorporated into our dual checks on visits to squadrons. These changes significantly increased the credibility of the STANEVAL team within the Tornado F.3 Force.

Disproving the 'Big Sky Theory'

Some pilots believe in the concept of the 'big sky theory' to prevent mid-air collisions on the basis that the odds of two aircraft arriving in exactly the same piece of the sky, in three dimensions at the same time, must be incredibly high. On 10 January 1996 two crews and aircraft of the Tornado F.3 OCU proved that the theory is not to be relied upon.

Three Tornado F.3s of 56 Squadron took off from Coningsby that morning to fly a short-course syllabus 2v1 air combat training (ACT) sortie. Apart from the experienced short-course student pilot who had recently returned from an exchange tour, all the other aircrew involved in the sortie were OCU staff instructors. Once established in the operating area at medium level, the singleton 'bounce' aircraft engaged the pair of Tornadoes from head-on to the No. 2, which was flown by the student pilot, with both aircraft at M0.9. The crew of the No. 2 aircraft had a radar lock on the singleton bandit and the student pilot descended below his sanctuary altitude block, despite not having visual contact (tally) with the bandit. The pilot of the singleton aircraft – the bandit – was tally with the No. 2 aircraft of the pair, but over-estimated the range and did not break away with sufficient urgency to avoid a collision. The two aircraft collided head on with a closing velocity of over 1,000 knots. The singleton bounce aircraft, ZE166, lost three to six feet of its right wing and began rolling uncontrollably. The other aircraft, ZE862, lost two-thirds of the right wing and two to three feet of the right taileron. It, too, began rolling uncontrollably and extremely rapidly. All four crew members ejected at high speed, with the pilots initiating command ejection. The two aircraft crashed, creating impressive craters, approximately eight miles west of Coningsby, one only fifty yards from the Sleaford to Lincoln railway line (aircraft wreckage blocked the line for five hours) and the other into a farmer's field near Sleaford. I had flown ZE862 on its previous sortie the day before and now it had been destroyed.

Back on the ground at Coningsby we were shocked when news filtered back about the collision. The news that all four aircrew had ejected was better. In fact, three of them had only the usual relatively minor ejection injuries, although the injuries to the pilot of ZE862 were categorised as major. The navigator of ZE862, Flight Lieutenant Dave 'Wibble' Weaver, had been ejected when the aircraft was rolling at an estimated 450 degrees per second. His head was displaced by the high rate of roll and was not in the ejection-seat head box when he was ejected. He was rendered unconscious immediately, his head was ripped backwards and his flying helmet pulled from his head, breaking his neck (at the same point as Superman actor Christopher Reeve who became quadriplegic as a result). Wibble also suffered a frontal lobe brain injury, a smashed shoulder and severe chest injuries. The automatics on his ejection seat worked as they should; he separated from the seat at 10,000 feet and his parachute deployed for the descent. After landing he was found face down in the mud, unconscious, by a local farmer who had chased his parachute across the fields in his four-by-four vehicle. He kept him alive until an RAF SAR Sea King helicopter arrived and took the navigator to hospital, where he was unconscious for the next nine days. Wibble spent the next year in and out of hospital and then another year at home recovering, but made a miraculous recovery to near normal life, albeit with life-changing injuries that prevented him from ever flying again and led to his medical discharge from the RAF.

Although both pilots had made human factor mistakes which contributed to the collision, we all felt it was rather 'there but for the grace of God go I'. The fact that no one died was a tribute to the remarkable Martin Baker Mk 10 ejection seats, with their double leg restraints and arm restraints preventing limbs from flailing. The crew of ZE166, which included navigator Mark 'Skids' Richardson, presented a photo to the squadron of them standing deep in the crater left by their crashed Tornado, with the caption 'Never trust the big sky theory.'

Tornado F.3 OCU Instructor

By February 1996 I was trained and qualified to instruct on all phases of the OCU course as a Tactics Instructor. As a QFI, I confirmed my A2 category on the Tornado F.3 in March, so that I had now held an A category QFI ticket on the Bulldog, Hawk, Lightning and Tornado F.3. Later I became a rear-seat combat instructor, qualified to teach the early sorties of the basic fighter manoeuvring phase which were flown dual in two-stick aircraft.

I had by now become quite a useful asset to the OCU. I was a QFI, IRE, Tactics Instructor and rear-seat combat instructor, qualified to instruct all phases of the course, part of the staff work-up team and a member of the STANEVAL Team as one of the two CFS Agents. This was all very deliberate on my part and involved no small amount of hard work. I thought that if I could make myself virtually indispensable I would be allowed to stay on the OCU and stay flying.

Falkland Islands

The Tornado F.3 OCU routinely deployed one staff crew to 1435 Flight in the Falkland Islands for five-week detachments to Mount Pleasant Airfield (MPA), to fly the Flight's Tornado F.3s and hold QRA duties 'down south'. Every OCU instructor's turn would come around every so often for the detachment to the South Atlantic.

Because my secondary duty, flying with the Battle of Britain Memorial Flight (BBMF), prevented me from being rostered for the Falklands during the spring BBMF work-up and the summer and early-autumn display season, I volunteered to take my turn in the Falklands during the winter periods, sometimes at times that most others would want to avoid, such as over Christmas and New Year. It seemed only fair. In all I deployed to the Falklands for three separate five-week stints, the first in January 1997, the next over Christmas 1998 and into the New Year, and the third in January 2001.

I was familiar with the Falkland Islands: bleak, windy, four seasons in one day and a long way from home. I was less familiar, at least on the first detachment, with flying over and around the islands, which was actually great fun. The Tornado F.3 had taken over the air defence presence from the RAF's F-4 Phantoms in the Falklands in 1992 and held it for seventeen years until the Typhoon took over. No. 1435 Flight had a proud history as a unit raised in Malta during the Second World War. The Flight's Tornado F.3s, like the F-4s before them and the Typhoons afterwards, were named after the three famous Gloster Sea Gladiator biplane fighters that defended Malta in 1940: Faith, Hope and Charity. The fourth Tornado was named 'Desperation'. The 1435 Flight aircraft carried the initials of these names: F, H, C and D on their tail fins. Armed Tornado F.3s and their crews held alert on QRA duties twenty-four hours a day, 365 days a year in the Falklands, as a deterrent against any aggression from Argentina. A VC10 tanker was also based at MPA to support them.

One of the aspects of detachments to the Falklands that I least enjoyed was the trip out and back. It usually took something like thirty-six hours in total, with sixteen hours flying in an RAF Tristar. The first part of the flight was from Brize Norton to Ascension Island where the passengers were temporarily unloaded and held in a sort of 'prisoner of war cage' on the airfield whilst the Tristar was refuelled and a fresh crew took over. Then the second part of the flight was the seven or eight hours to the Falklands. On arrival, suffering from sleep deprivation, the new F.3 crew was met by the crew they were replacing, who were keen to go home on the same Tristar. The new crew was taken straight to the Flight's working accommodation and given the theatre brief. This was later changed to the following day, after some rest, as it was realised that the content of the brief didn't necessarily register.

*****

On my first two Falklands detachments I was crewed with navigator Flight Lieutenant Tony 'Bat' Smith. This was actually somebody's idea of a joke as it was thought that we wouldn't get on at all and one of us would probably kill the other. We actually got on famously, hence our second detachment together. Bat was highly intelligent, talented and slightly mad, with a well-developed sense of humour that was not to everyone's taste. He could be quite scathing and was a master of one-line put-downs. He also had a penchant for practical jokes and I found his humour funny even when it was directed at me.

I enjoyed flying with Bat and I think he did with me. He might have expected me to be a boring fuddy-duddy and rule-bound old flying instructor but soon discovered that I wasn't at all like that in an aircraft. There was considerable flair and élan to my flying and whilst I knew all the rules regulations and limitations, letter and verse, they were for the obedience of fools and the guidance of wise men, weren't they?

There was generally a reasonable amount of flying to be had with 1435 Flight in the Falklands. The serviceability of the four Tornado F.3s varied at the end of a long supply chain but the Flight's RAF engineers were always brilliant in providing the best possible serviceability. It was relatively rare to fly all four aircraft together, although I was involved in several four-ships, but pairs and sometimes three-ship sorties were quite normal. I averaged about eighteen hours flying during each of my three detachments to 1435 Flight despite the Falklands weather.

On approximately half the sorties we would conduct air-to-air refuelling from the VC10 tanker. On the first detachment with Bat in my back seat he quickly realised that I wasn't really paying much attention to his commentary as I approached the refuelling basket and plugged in. I was just doing it the way I had on single-seat Lightnings. He could tell because there would be a little 'jiggle' as I looked at the basket to put the probe in. He suggested that we had a competition between us. On alternate prods I would do exactly what he said and on those between he would say nothing and leave me to do it my way. We would see who was the more successful. There was a bet involved and I took him on. I missed once on my own and not at all following his commentary. So, he won. Obviously, he rubbed it in.

The Falklands airspace was largely unrestricted for us and low flying over the islands was particular fun. Every RAF fighter pilot who has flown over the Falklands has flown low along 'A-4 Alley', the valley between two ridges running parallel to the Falklands Sound, imagining what it must have been like for the Argentine fighter pilots during the Falklands War in 1982, knowing that when they popped over the ridge into the Falkland Sound they would be met by a hail of gunfire and missiles.

We carried out most of the various types of practice intercepts, overland and over the sea, including supersonic intercepts, high-fliers, and with targets running at low level. We also flew air combat training sorties against each other.

Each week when the Tristar came in from Ascension Island we would send one or two Tornado F.3s to intercept it as it entered the Falkland Islands zone and escort it towards Mount Pleasant Airfield. This gave us another interesting target to intercept and for the passengers on the Tristar, almost all servicemen and women about to commence a four-month or six-month tour of duty in the Falklands, it demonstrated the air defence of the islands in action. Having intercepted the Tristar we would fly in close formation on its wingtips so the passengers could see us. When it got closer to MPA we would depart in style, perhaps with full reheat accelerating rapidly away. On one occasion I rolled upside down and held formation inverted for a moment before pulling down and away. I wonder what the passengers thought.

Many sorties ended with a 'Fiery Cross' over the airfield at MPA. This exercise was intended to give the RAF Regiment Rapier missile crews, who defended the airfield, some practice against fast low-flying jets. It also gave us the chance for some licensed hooliganism and to beat up the airfield. We often tried to approach using terrain masking, perhaps from behind the rocky lump of Mount Pleasant itself but, in truth, we knew from the radar lock indications on our radar homing warning receiver that we were always targeted and 'shot down'.

Another fun exercise was known as 'Measles', the codename for overflying any of the three mountain-top ground-control-intercept (GCI) radar sites at Mount Kent, Mount Byron and Mount Alice. In those days all the personnel needed for each GCI site were located and lived on the mountaintops in accommodation mainly built from ISO containers. It was inhospitable, cold, windy and austere. I had visited all three of the mountain sites on the ground during my four-month tour as Squadron Leader Operations in the Falklands and I thought that those who lived there, men and women, seemed to me to be a pretty tough and resilient lot. (Later most of the personnel were re-located to MPA after it became possible to 'pipe' the radar picture from the mountain-top sites.) Originally, the 'Measles' exercise had been intended to simulate attacks on the mountain sites so that the personnel on the ground could practise air-raid procedures and local air defence. By the time the Tornado F.3 took over, the original reasons for 'Measles' had largely been forgotten and they were a morale-boosting flypast for those who lived the lonely existence on top of the mountains. It was, therefore, great fun. We always warned them we were coming and spoke with them on the radio as we approached, so there would be a small crowd outside to see us overfly. Mount Alice was my favourite because it sat on top of a pyramid-shaped mountain in the extreme south-west of West Falkland. You could approach from very low towards the base of the mountain, engage full reheat to climb steeply up the side and then roll inverted to pass over the people on top, upside down, before pulling down the other side of the mountain and then rolling the right way up. The first time I did this with Bat in the back seat there was some harrumphing from the rear cockpit on the intercom afterwards.

On my third Falklands detachment with navigator Flight Lieutenant Neil Crawley, inevitably known as 'Creepy' Crawley, we did many of these things on one sortie and as he sat in the back cockpit he came up on the intercom and said, 'This is just a big playground for pilots really, isn't it?'

*****

Aside from the flying in the Falklands we sat our fair share of alert duty in the QRA Shed, on high readiness to scramble in minutes, by day or night, if required. Live QRA scrambles were unusual but in January 2001, during my third detachment, with Creepy Crawley as my nav, 1435 Flight had three in one day.

First, 'Q1' was scrambled to intercept and identify what was believed to be an Argentine air force aircraft which was operating over the sea to the north-west of the Falkland Islands and which was continually infringing the Falkland Islands Protection Zone (FIPZ). The Q1 crew gained a radar contact on the aircraft, but as they approached it turned away, outside the FIPZ and beyond visual range. The crew was unable to identify it but they remained on station inside the zone, which we were not allowed to leave, until their fuel state dictated a return to the airfield.

Not long afterwards, with the Tornado having left the area, the Argentine aircraft began to infringe the protection zone again. Creepy Crawley and I were scrambled as Q2 to intercept and identify. We flew out to the position, now on the western edge of the zone, at high speed and gained a radar contact on the aircraft. I asked Creepy to lock the radar to it and then, using the target detection (TD) circle in the head-up display, I was able to get visual with it. I identified it from about six miles as a four-engine Lockheed P-3 Orion maritime patrol aircraft. As soon as we locked the radar onto the P-3 it turned tail and ran out of the area. Although I wasn't close enough to see its markings, it was Argentinian. We then noticed a grey naval ship sailing southward right on the western edge of the zone. We descended to a lower altitude and flew past its port side, noticing a civilian cargo ship sailing in the same direction near to it. We were just inside the zone, something we could easily ensure with the F.3's navigation display, and the naval vessel was just outside. It was an Argentinian Meko 140 destroyer and, as we flew past, it locked us up with its surface-to-air-missile-system radar, triggering a warning on our radar homing warning receiver. This seemed rather unfriendly but, to be fair, we had just locked our weapon system to their colleagues in the P-3 Orion. We reported what we had found on the radio and remained on station monitoring the Argentinians, who remained outside the protection zone, until fuel dictated a return to the airfield.

Soon afterwards, the P-3 Orion, as we now knew it to be, began infringing the zone again. This time we scrambled a third Tornado F.3 using 'silent procedures', something we sometimes practised. This third F.3 was piloted by Flight Lieutenant Paul 'Vossers' Carvosso, a first tourist. He was the son of Ken Carvosso with whom I had gone through officer and flying training, right up to and including the Lightning OCU in 1973. When Ken's son had arrived as a student pilot on the Tornado F.3 OCU in July 1999 I suddenly felt very old. The silent-procedure scramble meant that there were no radio transmissions and all electronic emissions from the F.3 were turned off until the fighter controller gave a 'Punch' call. The P-3 Orion's electronic-surveillance-measure (ESM) equipment therefore gave no warning to its crew of the approaching F.3. When the 'Punch' call came, Vossers and his nav were already visual with the large Orion, so they remained silent and just slid up on his wing, some miles inside the zone with the nav taking video with the hand-held camera. The P-3 ran away to the west but not before he had been captured on video. There were no further infringements that day.

As to what the Argentinians were doing, we were subsequently told that they were escorting a ship carrying nuclear waste, a perfectly reasonable and internationally useful task, although they should have respected the Falkland Islands Protection Zone.

There was a sequel to this story on the Friday of that week. After the Argentinian P-3 Orion had spent a couple of days at an airfield in Tierra del Fuego, the southernmost part of Argentina, it set off northwards back to its base. I'm sure that it could have flown quietly up the coastline but instead, at about 17:30, it penetrated the western edge of the Falkland Islands Protection Zone. Our Q1 Tornado F.3 and crew were scrambled. The rest of us were in the officers' mess bar for Friday 'Happy Hour'. The Q2 crew, who were not drinking due to being on duty, were brought to readiness and dashed back to the QRA Shed. Most unusually, a Q3 was called to readiness and not long afterwards I found myself sitting in an armed Tornado F.3 at cockpit readiness, having drunk a pint and a half of beer. Fortunately, I wasn't required to fly. By the time that the Q1 F.3 got to the western edge of the FIPZ the Argentinian aircraft was gone. That Argentinian P-3 crew knew exactly what they were doing and where the RAF fighter pilots on the Falklands would be at 17:30 on a Friday. Despite the inconvenience and the interruption to our drinking, we rather appreciated their thinking and their mutual understanding.

*****

During my third Falkland Island detachment, in January 2001, I celebrated my 50th birthday on QRA duty on a Saturday. The 'boys' got me a birthday cake which was presented to me in the Q Shed. It was not perhaps the ideal 50th birthday; I had to wait for the family celebrations until I got home in February. However, if a crystal ball had told me when I was 20 and starting my RAF flying training that thirty years later I would be a squadron leader specialist aircrew fighter pilot, flying jet fighters operationally, and Hurricanes and Spitfires during the summer months, I think I would have been very happy, if somewhat disbelieving. To still be flying operationally on fast jets with the RAF, at the age of 50, was a dream come true.

Evolving the Training

As emerging technology and weapons were incorporated into the Tornado F.3 and tactics evolved on the front line, the training offered by the OCU also had to be updated. It was obviously essential that new crews were trained in the techniques, procedures and tactics they would be using on their squadrons.

In May 1999 we introduced the Stage 2G-star radar and weapons system, which I had spent so many years and hours in the air developing with the Tornado F.3 OEU. Then we introduced formalised training for executing surface-to-air-missile (SAM) breaks, both in visual conditions and on instruments. This was something I was well prepared for from my experience with developing the towed radar decoy against SAM threats.

Before my time with the OCU was over we also introduced the ASRAAM infra-red air-to-air missile as it was now replacing the AIM-9L Sidewinder on Tornado F.3s. The MBDA Advanced Short Range Air-to-Air Missile (ASRAAM) was another game changer. It was fast, with much longer range than the Sidewinder, it had excellent flare-rejection IRCCM capabilities and increased lethality. We found that when targets broke onto the 'beam' to attempt to break our radar lock and trash our Fox 1 Skyflash shots, we could simply acquire them with the ASRAAM and shoot them with the Fox 2 as they faced up, at ranges we wouldn't have dreamed of with the AIM-9L Sidewinder. They couldn't even flare off the shots. Things became very one-sided in our favour after that.

Tornado F.3 Force TACEVAL Team

In May 1998 the Tornado F.3 Force underwent a NATO TACEVAL with a simulated expeditionary operational deployment to St Mawgan, on the north coast of Cornwall near Newquay. There was a requirement from the NATO TACEVAL Team for a crew of airborne evaluators who were current and qualified to fly the latest standard of front-line Tornado F.3s, to be airborne observers on the sorties and to report back to the team with their assessments and evaluation. I was chosen, along with STANEVAL QWI navigator Al Gillespie, to deploy to St Mawgan for the task. The front-line squadron crews would be living in tents on the airfield in austere conditions, eating from field kitchens, dodging 'air raids' and wearing nuclear, biological and chemical (NBC) suits and respirators. We were exempt from all of that with our TACEVAL Team status and armbands and we were accommodated in the delightful Headland Hotel on the headland overlooking Fistral Beach, Newquay.

The front-line Tornado F.3s we flew were at the latest standard with the Stage 2G-star radar, 1,500-litre underwing fuel tanks and the JTIDS data-link system fitted. I hadn't worked with JTIDS since I had left the

Tornado F.3 OEU. It was every bit as good at providing enhanced situational awareness as I remembered.

We flew three sorties as airborne TACEVAL evaluators, the first as part of a four-ship formation, the second as part of a six-aircraft defensive-counter-air combat air patrol in the Southwest Approaches, and the third as one of eight Tornado F.3s on a high-value-asset attack mission. This last sortie was particularly memorable. It was extremely well planned, briefed and led by Mark 'Skids' Richardson, who had been one of the four aircrew who ejected from the two Tornado F.3s involved in the mid-air collision in January 1996. We took off from St Mawgan and flew to an air-to-air refuelling tanker towline over the North Sea, where we all filled to full from a VC10 tanker. The high-value-asset target was a NATO E-3C AWACS. The foreign-sounding controller who was providing us with the air picture was more than a little reticent with exact details about the target's position. We eventually realised that, although he was supposed to be on our side, he was actually sitting in the target and didn't really want to get 'shot down'. The AWACS was defended by eight US Marine Corps F-18s armed with AMRAAM active missiles. Up against their 'bigger stick' our eight Tornado F.3s had to employ confusion tactics and we were sometimes forced defensive, but with the JTIDS picture we could ensure that there were always some of our force facing 'hot' towards the 'enemy' and targeting them. Several 'kills' were taken against F-18s as we fought our way through their defensive screen. Al and I eventually skirted around the fighting at low level over the sea before climbing up towards the AWACS target which we had on radar. We were beaten to the 'kill' against it by another of the F.3s. Then we had to fight our way out and, as there had been no kill removal, there were still eight F-18s impeding our exit. Once again, the situational awareness provided by JTIDS was of great benefit and I claimed an unseen Sidewinder AIM-9L 'kill' against an F-18 during the egress. We then re-grouped and flew back to St Mawgan, landing three hours and twenty-five minutes after take off.

It was great fun to be involved in these operational training sorties, it was good to find that this ageing flying instructor could still hold his own as a fighter pilot and it did no harm for the credibility of STANEVAL with the Tornado F.3 Force.

Tragedy Strikes

On 15 June 1998 a 29 Squadron Tornado F.3 failed to return to Coningsby from a routine training sortie over the North Sea. The aircraft and its crew were reported as 'missing'. The pilot was my friend and former OC STANEVAL, Squadron Leader Bill Vivian, who was now a flight commander on 29 Squadron. His navigator that day was Flight Lieutenant Des Lacey. News of the accident filtered through to us and we learned that there had been no indications of the crew having ejected. The missing aircraft had been working with another Tornado F.3, 2v1 against a Hawk target, with radar control provided by an AWACS, when radio and JTIDS data-link contact was lost and the aircraft disappeared from radar some thirty miles off Flamborough Head on the Yorkshire coast. It seemed probable that both crew members had been killed.

Despite a communication black-out on the station, I managed to make another of those, 'It's not me' phone calls to Elaine. She was always relieved but also concerned to get one of these calls, which were to pre-empt anything that might appear on the news, and she knew not to ask me what had happened or who had crashed. I would tell her that later. It also meant that she could assure our daughter Suzanne that it wasn't her dad if she picked anything up. Suzanne was very aware, even at a young age, of the risks her father's job entailed and, if she heard something about a Tornado crash, she would immediately ask, 'Is it daddy?' Elaine also knew I was likely to be late home. The strain on a military pilot's family is not something that is always recognised, but it is most definitely something that they have to live with.

As the day wore on, with no good news forthcoming, we all accepted that the missing crew had been killed, although at that stage we didn't know how or why. We were shocked and saddened by the loss. At the end of the day we all retired to the officers' mess bar to drink to our lost friends on their bar books – debts which would be written off – in the finest tradition of the RAF. It was a typically sad but wild occasion with so much alcohol consumed that, later, an extraordinary general mess meeting had to be held to vote money to cover the cost. It was noticeable to me how badly affected some of the younger aircrew were by the two deaths. RAF fast-jet flying had become considerably safer, or at least less dangerous, in recent years; accidents, especially fatal ones, were far less common than earlier in my career. Some of these young aircrew had suddenly had their own mortality brought into sharp focus and realised that 'there but for the grace of God go I'.

The next day we were all back at work and ready to carry on as usual. I received a telephone call to report to the station commander's office along with my fellow STANEVAL QFI, Squadron Leader Roy Lawrence. We duly reported together to see Group Captain Al Lockwood, who had known me since he took command of 5 Squadron for the last six months of my tour as a flight commander. The RAF always provided an officer to assist the widow of anyone killed on duty and he had decided that Roy and I were to be the Assisting Officers to the newly-widowed wives of Bill Vivian and Des Lacey. I was to assist Jude Vivian. We were given our terms of reference and told to go and introduce ourselves individually to 'our' widows straight away. I was horrified, but this was an order not a request. Typically, officers were expected to carry out these Assisting Officer duties with absolutely no training for it. It was to be, emotionally, the toughest thing that the RAF ever asked me to do.

I met Jude Vivian at her home later that same day, still only the day after the accident. She was being supported by friends from Bill's squadron and was obviously still coming to terms with the death of her husband; she was naturally still shocked and upset. Although I had met her previously, it was still a difficult and awkward introduction. Jude was only 30, she had a son, Michael, who was 6, and she was six-months pregnant with a baby girl that would now never know her father. Jude had met Bill when she was just 17 and they had been married for nine years. It was completely tragic.

In order to do the job that I did as a pilot, with the risks involved, I had always cut myself off from the emotional fall-out as much as possible. When a friend or colleague was killed, we held the wake in the bar, and then went back to flying the next day. Later, there would be a funeral or a memorial service to attend to pay our respects. But that was it; you couldn't really allow yourself to become too emotional or too involved with the family tragedy.

Now I was drawn into the full domestic trauma and tragedy of Bill's death with high emotion on an almost daily basis, which tugged at my heart strings. I helped Jude for the next six months, effectively acting as a solicitor and financial advisor, initially seeing her most days, then perhaps weekly and later fortnightly. It was over a year before the full official accident report was delivered to her, with me beside her, and I could consider the job done. Throughout it all I kept telling myself that, in helping Bill's wife and family, this was one last thing I could do for him. Jude was actually magnificent in the way she behaved throughout it all; she was brave, resilient and practical, and determined to build a new life for herself and her family. Of course, there were difficult times and some tears, but I thought her resilience was admirable. She came to trust me and was able to lean on me. My wife, Elaine, was completely brilliant about this 'other woman' in my life, even when Jude telephoned me at home some evenings to talk about something. It helped that I told Elaine everything; we had no secrets and we had tremendous trust between us. It really was a very difficult thing to deal with over a prolonged period.

I was kept closely informed of news and progress with the inquiry into the accident. A massive air and sea search was launched immediately after the crash and the wreckage was located on the sea bed during a sonar search by an 819 Naval Air Squadron Sea King HAS.6 helicopter. Some small amounts of human remains were also recovered, but nothing that could be identified. Soon afterwards, the accident data recorder – the 'black box' – was recovered. The board of inquiry told me that this revealed, unbelievably and inexplicably, that the data and the cockpit voice recordings indicated that the aircraft had hit the sea in a controlled 15-degree dive from 11,000 feet at 540 knots. From 8,500 feet it had taken only twenty-five seconds to reach 500 feet. Of note, on the day of the accident there was layered cloud over the sea below 14,000 feet and extensive low cloud and sea fog below 2,000 feet, which meant that the surface of the sea was not visible. At 225 feet the radar altimeter low-altitude audio warning had sounded (it had been set to that altitude in accordance with the HQ 11 Group orders). Bill had made a rapid input on the controls to pull up, which altered the aircraft's attitude, but was too late to prevent impact with the sea.

There was no body as such to release for a funeral, which Jude understood, not least because she and her son Michael were swabbed for DNA to help prove Bill's death for the coroner. It was actually seven weeks before we were able to get a death certificate to allow things to move forward administratively. After a couple of weeks Jude decided that there should be a memorial service for Bill so that everyone could move on. It was held in a section of the 56 Squadron aircraft hangar at Coningsby, with a Tornado F.3 as a backdrop and Bill's bright yellow Triumph Daytona motorbike at the front. A very large number of people attended. I went in an RAF MT car to collect Jude and 6-year-old Michael from their home and then sat next to her to support her through the memorial service. At the end we moved outside through the hangar doors and watched a flypast by a Canberra, which Bill had flown before becoming a fighter pilot, followed by a four-ship of Tornado F.3s. As the F.3s flew over, one of them engaged reheat and climbed away steeply in a 'missing-man' display, which is always very moving. I had held it together quite well until then but, when young Michael said, 'That's daddy, isn't it?' as the Tornado powered heavenwards, it was almost too much to bear. (When Des Lacey's memorial service was held in a local church some days later, I flew the part of the 'missing man' in the Tornado four-ship flypast for him.)

Throughout all the months that I was involved as Assisting Officer, I still had my 'real' job to do and I continued to fly Tornado F.3s with the OCU and also to fly with the BBMF.

When the accident report eventually emerged over a year after the event, I sat with Jude going through it, page by page, as she wanted to do. The report recommended the fitment of a ground-proximity warning system (GPWS) to the Tornado F.3 and concluded that: 'This tragic accident has reminded us yet again how harshly unforgiving aviation can be of a momentary relaxation, and that even the most able, experienced and conscientious aircrew are vulnerable.'

Jude rebuilt her life. Baby Imogen was born three months after her father's death. Jude eventually remarried. Michael grew up wanting to be an RAF pilot like his father; he became an air cadet and did very well. I flew him several times in Grob Tutor aircraft at Cranwell after I had become a Volunteer Reservist pilot with the Air Experience Flight there. Michael then joined the RAF and was commissioned, but defence cuts saw the RAF with a temporary surplus of pilots in the training system, and his offer of pilot training was withdrawn. He subsequently joined the Royal Navy as a Fleet Air Arm pilot, completed his flying training and became a Wildcat helicopter pilot.

My Assisting Officer efforts drew praise in my annual confidential report, but I had not done it for that; I'd done it for Bill and for Jude. It was emotionally very difficult and I decided that if I was ever asked to do it again, I would refuse.

STANEVAL Projects

Throughout my seven years as a member of the Tornado F.3 STANEVAL Team I became involved in and sometimes led various projects to improve the safety and operational effectiveness of the Tornado F.3. They all required a significant amount of staff work for which my background and experience seemed to have prepared me well. Bearing in mind that I was flying almost as much as any other instructor on the OCU and that I also did my fair share of being the duty authoriser, running the squadron ops desk and the daily flying programme, and being the duty aircrew officer in the air traffic control tower, I don't know quite how I found the time. Working ten-to-eleven-hour days was very much the norm.

I was keen to become intimately involved, from its beginnings, with the project to fit a ground-proximity-warning system (GPWS) to the Tornado F.3. This was something that was close to my heart as it was felt that such a system might have prevented the accident and deaths of Bill Vivian and Des Lacey in June 1998. When the twin-laser-inertial-navigation system (LINS) with embedded GPS was fitted to the Tornado F.3, the addition of a GPWS became a more straightforward option. The Terprom GPWS with its highly accurate digital terrain map and predictive system was selected for fitting to all the RAF's front-line fast jets. In the Tornado it took account of many parameters, including the aircraft configuration and the wing-sweep position, as well as the aircraft's height, speed and attitude. I went to great lengths to ensure that the system was optimised for the dynamic nature of air defence operations. When the GPWS became available in the Tornado F.3 in 2001, I wrote the handling advice for aircrew and designed an airborne training profile that showed crews how the system worked without any unnecessary risk or getting too close to the surface. I felt considerable satisfaction that my personal crusade to get GPWS for the F.3 was successful.

VIP Pilot

From time to time I would be asked to fly VIP passengers in the Tornado F.3. These were always interesting sorties to be involved in.

In April 2002 I had the privilege of flying again with Air Chief Marshal Sir Peter Squire, who was now the Chief of the Air Staff (CAS). As a flight lieutenant he had been my flight commander on the Hawker Hunter squadron at RAF Valley where I completed my advanced flying training in 1972-73; whenever we met subsequently he remembered me. He was familiar with the Tornado GR.1, having been the station commander at RAF Cottesmore when it was home to the Tri-national Tornado Training Establishment, which trained Tornado GR.1 crews for the RAF, the Luftwaffe and the Aeronautica Militare. He had not previously flown in the Tornado F.3 and I was given the task of showing him the differences, with him flying in the front seat and me in the back, having given him a short ground school and an extensive briefing which I had provided to him in advance. It was a pleasure to do so.

The CAS wrote me a nice letter in which he said:

> It was a most pleasant surprise to be teamed up with you for
> my Tornado F.3 trip last Thursday and I much enjoyed flying

with you. I was delighted to have the opportunity to see the handling characteristics of the F.3 and how best to fly the aircraft at or about its limits. My thanks once again for your patient mentoring.

Clearly, there was no harm in having the Chief of the Air Staff as a supporter; his words also showed the emphasis we placed as fighter pilots on flying the aircraft to the limits.

MBE

In early June 2002 I received a letter through the post to my home address. The envelope was marked 'Honours in Confidence'. It was from The Air Secretary, Air Vice Marshal Ian Stewart, at the RAF Personnel Management Agency. It said:

> I am delighted to inform you that Her Majesty The Queen has been graciously pleased to appoint you as a Member of the Order of the British Empire in recognition of your selfless devotion to duty, exceptional skill and utter professionalism in combining the duties of full-time instructor on No. 56(R) Squadron, authoritative member of the Tornado F.3 Standards and Evaluation Unit and volunteer display pilot on the Battle of Britain Memorial Flight.

It went on to say, 'Your award will be published in a supplement to the London Gazette on 15 June 2002 but must remain confidential until then, so please keep this news to yourself and your immediate family.' I was astonished. I read it again. There seemed to be no mistake, this was me getting an MBE. I was delighted. I immediately told Elaine, who was equally surprised but pleased, and I also told my parents, which was a risk as my father was hopeless with secrets. I swore him to secrecy until 15 June.

On 15 June I was called to the Station Commander's office at Coningsby. The Station Commander was now Group Captain Phil Goodman whom I had known for many years. He thought he was going to surprise me with the news and was slightly disappointed when he found that I had already been informed. He was also an MBE and told me that I would have a wonderful day at Buckingham Palace for the investiture. He handed me a letter he had written to me in which he said:

This award rightly recognises your outstanding contribution to the Royal Air Force over the last 28 years, specifically, as an exceptional instructor and a highly gifted tactical pilot, and acknowledges the out of duty hours you have devoted to expanding the operational clearances for the front line. The award also recognises your immense contribution to the Battle of Britain Memorial Flight for the last six seasons where you have sacrificed much of your own time for the overall benefit of the Service. This award is richly deserved and I offer you my warmest congratulations.

I was allowed to start wearing the MBE medal ribbon on my best uniform jacket and the miniature medal on my mess kit straightaway but the investiture at Buckingham Palace was not until November when I was presented with the actual medal by HM The Queen in person. I cannot remember what she said to me, or me to her, and anyway you are not supposed to repeat such conversations but it was a wonderful day and a real honour. I took Elaine and our daughter Suzanne as my guests to the investiture and we made an occasion of it by stopping the night before in the RAF Club in Piccadilly. Suzanne was now at university and came down to London by train for the event on the promise of cocktails in the cocktail bar on the top of the Hilton Hotel, Park Lane, just around the corner from the RAF Club.

I was and remain extremely proud to have been made an MBE and to have had my efforts recognised in such a way.

'Elder Statesman'

I had by now become something of an 'elder statesman' on the OCU with more experience than most. During my time as an instructor on 56 Squadron I served under four different wing commanders. With each one of them there were occasions when I felt compelled to knock on the OC's office door, ask if he had a moment, enter, close the door behind me and tell the Boss something he probably didn't want to hear, usually about pushing too hard or some other flight-safety concern. I didn't over use the privileged position that I appeared to have as specialist aircrew and an 'elder statesman' and I only did this when it seemed really necessary. They were each gracious enough to give me the time of day and to listen to me, and none threw me out. In fact, they tended to comment positively on the unsolicited advice I gave them.

The OCU staff instructors sometimes sat Quick Reaction Alert (QRA) duties to help out the front-line squadrons at Coningsby, especially over holiday periods. For example, when it came to the millennium New Year on 31 December 1999 into 1 January 2000, when everyone else was out celebrating, I was sitting on duty in the Q Shed. We launched one of the Tornado F.3s early in the morning of the millennium New Year to prove that computers still functioned normally with three zeros in the year. On one QRA shift in early 2003 I found myself holding alert duties in the Q Shed almost twenty-nine years from the first time I had done so. At the age of 52 I was accepting of the fact that I wasn't quite as quick on my feet and the run to the aircraft in the event of a scramble might take slightly longer.

3,000 Hours Tornado F.3

On 19 February 2003 I reached the milestone of 3,000 flying hours on the Tornado F.3 on a simple routine OCU instructional conversion-phase sortie, flying as I so often did in the rear cockpit of a two-stick trainer F.3 with a refresher course student pilot. I was met on my return to Coningsby by the Officer Commanding 56 Squadron, Wing Commander Phil Storey, with a glass of champagne to celebrate.

When the Tornado F.3 was eventually retired from service with the RAF in 2011 there were only six pilots and three navigators who had achieved more than 3,000 hours on the type. Two of those, pilot Roy Macintyre and navigator Colin Wiki Wills, both of whom I had worked with on the F.3 OEU, had accumulated over 4,000 hours. I was one of the other five pilots with more than 3,000 hours. I had been flying the Tornado F.3 for just over fifteen years; I had seen it slowly become the interceptor it should always have been and I felt that I'd had a personal involvement in its long journey of development.

Tornado F.3 OEU Guest Pilot

During my time as an instructor at the Tornado F.3 OCU I was sometimes invited back to the F.3 Operational Evaluation Unit (F.3 OEU) to fly with them. I often flew routine dual checks and instrument ratings on the OEU pilots, in the back seat of their two-stick trainer. It was always a challenge for me because they would expect me to operate all the latest kit in the rear cockpit, including the secure radios, the new laser-inertial-navigation system with embedded GPS and the JTIDS data-link system, as well as whatever modification state the radar was at, all equipment that would not yet have reached the OCU aircraft and which I was not well-practised with.

From time to time, if they were short of a pilot, the F.3 OEU would invite me back to fly on trial sorties. So it was that in August 1999 I flew one of the OEU Tornado F.3s with modifications for the so-called 'Capability Sustainment Programme' (CSP). These modifications gave the F.3 the capability to fire ASRAAM and AMRAAM missiles with improved navigation equipment and radar, plus the Successor Identification Friend or Foe (SIFF) to allow the identification of aircraft by electronic means. It was a taste of how far the F.3 had come and a glimpse of the future.

In May 2001 I flew on an OEU trial sortie in an F.3 with ASRAAM and AMRAAM, conducting dissimilar air combat training (DACT) as a fighter sweep for four Harriers with two ECM-jamming Falcons, versus three F-16s with simulated AA-10C 'Alamo' missiles.

I also flew on a couple of trial sorties for the new active matrix-liquid-crystal display (AMLCD) TV Tabs for the Tornado, including one at night. These AMLCD colour TV Tabs were a 'drop-fit replacement' for the original monochrome displays, paving the way for a full colour upgrade and providing good readability even in full sunlight.

*****

In April 2003 No. 56 Squadron, the Tornado F.3 OCU, moved to RAF Leuchars in Scotland, making way at Coningsby for runway resurfacing and the building of new infrastructure required to welcome the new Eurofighter Typhoon. The Tornado F.3 OEU moved temporarily to Waddington and I became a fulltime BBMF pilot. However, I continued to make guest appearances with the F.3 OEU at Waddington and over the next six months I flew another sixty hours on the F.3. Trial flights concentrated on the CSP modifications, with the Stage 3 radar and ASRAAM and AMRAAM missiles.

With the Stage 3 version of the Foxhunter radar, the way the radar tracked a target was fundamentally changed. A new main computer and radar-data processor drove the system. Automatic track-while-scan was finally introduced, allowing the navigator to concentrate more on the tactical battle. A modern digital data-bus carried information between the sub-systems. The Successor Identification Friend or Foe (SIFF) and additional systems, which analysed the nature of a target response and could identify the aircraft type by its electronic characteristics, finally gave effective means of declaring targets hostile. This last stage of development for the Tornado F.3 allowed it finally to match the best in the world.

I was asked to fly in the back seat of an OEU Tornado F.3 two-sticker with the CSP modifications, with ex-Tornado GR.1 pilot Air Vice Marshal Andy White in the front seat, to demonstrate to him the Stage 3 radar, ASRAAM, AMRAAM, JTIDS and the GPWS. He was the Chief of Staff RAF Operations at the time. The same day, at the other end of the scale, I flew him in one of the BBMF Chipmunks.

It was simply wonderful to be involved in the final stages of development of the Tornado F.3, having struggled with its initial capabilities in the late 1980s, and to see it now having evolved into a first-class interceptor with state-of-the-art avionics and an enviable world-class weapons system.

*****

My last flight in a Tornado F.3 was on 22 September 2003, flying an AMRAAM trial as one of two F.3s against four Hawks. I didn't know it was to be my last Tornado flight. I wasn't actually on the strength of the Tornado F.3 OEU and the flying just dried up. So that was it.

Suddenly, although not completely unexpectedly, my days as an RAF fast-jet fighter pilot were over. It hadn't been a bad run; I was approaching 53 years of age. I had been flying fast jets since 1972 and I had accumulated just short of 5,200 fast-jet flying hours.

From now on I was going to have to continue my RAF flying on Spitfires and Hurricanes, as I took command of the Battle of Britain Memorial Flight (BBMF). That provided no small consolation.

Chapter 12

Battle of Britain Memorial Flight

I had harboured an ambition to fly with the RAF Battle of Britain Memorial Flight (BBMF) and specifically to fly a Spitfire since I first saw Ray Hanna displaying one of the iconic wartime fighters in 1972. It was not an ambition that I ever really expected to achieve but I had carefully positioned myself to have the best chance by getting myself based at Coningsby, co-located with the BBMF, and by becoming Specialist Aircrew. I had applied in writing twice, each time getting a letter back saying that, whilst I was well-suited, there were no vacancies for fighter pilots on the BBMF.

In May 1995 I learned that two of the BBMF's five fighter pilots were planning to leave at the end of the 1995 display season. I took the bull by the horns and requested an interview with the OC Operations Wing, Wing Commander Peter 'Ruddles' Ruddock (later Air Marshal CB CBE), who controlled the selection of BBMF pilots. I explained to him what I knew about the forthcoming potential vacancies for BBMF fighter pilots and restated my interest. He told me that he was considering the options to replace Squadron Leader Chris Stevens in particular, as not only was Chris a Hurricane and Spitfire pilot, he was also the Flight's Chipmunk QFI. What he needed, he said, was a Specialist Aircrew squadron leader of the right calibre and character who was a QFI and could become the BBMF Chipmunk instructor, and who was in a position to commit to flying with the BBMF for at least five years. There was only one name on his list, he said, and it was Clive Rowley. I said I would be delighted to accept his terms and that five years with the BBMF would be no problem. One slight snag was that I was due to be posted from the Tornado F.3 OEU to 29 Squadron at Coningsby. Experience had shown that flying with the BBMF and holding down front-line squadron duties with all the operational deployments was not really compatible. Could he get my posting changed to 56 Squadron, the Tornado F.3 OCU? Meanwhile, I was off to the Eglin Air Force Base in the USA for six weeks to conduct a Tornado F.3 towed-radar decoy trial, whilst he tried to sort out my posting.

When I returned in mid-June, it was all organised. I was to be posted to 56 Squadron as an instructor on the Tornado F.3 OCU in September 1995 and would begin flying with the BBMF as a secondary duty. I was delighted but didn't want to get ahead of myself as there were many hurdles to be jumped yet.

Chipmunk Training

The first stage of any fighter pilot's training with the BBMF is carried out in the Flight's de Havilland Chipmunk T.10, two-seat tandem-cockpit tail-wheel training aircraft. The 'Chippies' are used to teach, learn and practise tail-wheel ground handling, take off and landing techniques and other handling aspects relevant to the Hurricanes and Spitfires. As far as possible, the Chippies are used as 'airborne simulators' for the Hurricanes and Spitfires, with pilots being taught techniques that may not be needed on the Chipmunk but will be on the warbirds.

I had some previous tail-wheel experience with the Chipmunk, amounting to forty hours flying but had not flown one since February 1979, over sixteen years earlier. On 15 August 1995, when I flew with Chris Stevens, it was obvious that he was taking no prisoners in that regard. He expected me to complete the full Chipmunk Flying Ability Test on my first sortie, with spinning, stalling, aerobatics, simulated engine failure for a practice forced landing into a field and 'fighter circuits' back at Coningsby, with landings on the grass and main runway. I got the distinct impression that if I had not achieved solo standard and passed the full flying ability test on that first sortie then I was not the pilot that the BBMF was looking for.

Fortunately, I passed muster. I had remembered how to land a tail-wheel aircraft and Chris sent me solo straight away on the same day. I flew the Chipmunk solo twice more over the next two days and then subsequently continued to build flying hours and tail-wheel handling experience. The minimum requirement for fighter pilots new to the Flight was that they flew twenty-five hours on Chipmunks, with at least ten hours in the rear cockpit, before being allowed to fly the Hurricane. In my case, I was also required to become the Flight's Chipmunk QFI.

On 18 September Chris Stevens checked me out flying in the rear cockpit of the Chipmunk and also taught me how to fly simulated fighter practice forced landings. If you glided the Chipmunk with the throttle at idle and with an airspeed of 110 knots, rather than the Chipmunk's best gliding speed of 70 knots, the rate of descent and limited time available was similar to a Hurricane or Spitfire with an engine failure. The restricted view forward when landing the Chipmunk from the rear cockpit was similar to that in a Spitfire. After this I flew in the rear cockpit frequently, whenever I could get someone competent and qualified to occupy the front seat.

On 28 November 1995 I flew a QFI confirmation-of-category dual-check sortie with a Central Flying School examiner, Squadron Leader Peter Bruce, whose large frame in the front cockpit certainly blocked the view forwards almost entirely. He was content with my briefing, airborne instruction and rear-seat flying and awarded me a QFI ticket on the Chipmunk, the fifth aircraft type on which I had held a QFI qualification. I was now simultaneously qualified as a QFI on the Tornado and the Chipmunk, at opposite ends of the scale. I held the role of BBMF Chipmunk QFI for the next eleven years, conducting conversions to type and all the necessary dual checks on BBMF pilots.

The Chipmunk makes a perfect trainer for the BBMF. It is relatively easy to fly but difficult to fly well. It also teaches or reminds modern pilots to use their feet on the rudder pedals more to keep the aircraft in balance during flight. In common with all tail-wheel aircraft, it will bite if allowed to get away from you on landing. Many was the experienced and expert jet-fighter pilot who, on their first trip with me in a Chipmunk, did not give it the respect it deserved and needed my intervention from the back seat to keep us on the runway. It usually seemed that once they had found themselves beyond the limits of directional control on the ground they never went there again.

By the time I first flew a Hurricane I had achieved over forty-five hours flying on the Chipmunk with the BBMF, of which almost twenty-eight hours were in the rear cockpit, far more than the minimum requirement. It was an excellent grounding.

Flying the Harvard

Before flying the Hurricane there was one other important hurdle that had to be jumped, the requirement to fly two sorties in one of the Defence Evaluation and Research Agency's North American Harvard trainers at Boscombe Down.

The Harvard was the aircraft which many wartime pilots flew during their advanced flying training before moving on to Hurricanes or Spitfires.

It had vintage characteristics, it was considerably larger and heavier than the Chipmunk, and had a more powerful engine. The requirement was for new BBMF fighter pilots to fly one dual sortie in the front seat and one in the back seat of the Harvard to demonstrate that they could land the aircraft safely from both cockpits on both hard and grass runways. In some ways it was a sort of test to confirm that the new pilot had learned sufficient about flying and landing tail-wheel aircraft in the Chipmunk, to allow him to jump into a new vintage type and land it competently, just as he would have to do with the Hurricane without any dual instruction.

I managed to get hold of some information on the Harvard before I went to Boscombe Down and there I received an excellent briefing from test pilot Squadron Leader Paul Mulcahy, with whom I was to fly. It became apparent that even the test pilots treated the Harvard with great respect and didn't allow just anyone amongst their fraternity to fly it. It had an unforgiving 'bite' if mishandled or if the pilot didn't anticipate sufficiently at slow speed and on the landing roll. It certainly was a large and impressive aircraft, quite a climb up into the cockpit where it looked and smelt like a vintage aircraft and the view forward was mostly of engine cowling. Compared with the simple Chipmunk cockpit it had an imposing mass of fighter-style levers, dials and instrumentation. It was all rather daunting.

I flew in Harvard 2B FT375, which was painted bright yellow, as RAF training aircraft once were. Just starting the engine was an adventure and once it was running the noise was deafening, even at low power settings. At higher RPM the whole aircraft shook and the noise level was incredible.

During the taxi out to the runway at Boscombe Down, Paul demonstrated on a wide area of concrete just how easy it was to ground loop the Harvard, especially when the tail wheel was unlocked by moving the control around halfway forward. The resulting spin around was incredibly rapid. On that first sortie, with me in the front cockpit, we flew circuits and touch-and-go landings on the grass strip and main runway at Boscombe Down and on the grass airfield at Netheravon on Salisbury Plain. On the second sortie I flew in the back cockpit and we practised some stalls. The Harvard's stall characteristics were rapid and abrupt; it would drop a wing violently and could easily end up on its back. In this regard it was not dissimilar to the Hurricane. We also flew some practice forced landings at Netheravon, and circuits on the grass and hard runways with touch-and-go landings. At the end of the day, with two hours and twenty-five minutes flying in the Harvard, front and back seat, I returned to Coningsby with a report which would allow me to progress to the Hurricane.

The Battle of Britain Memorial Flight

In 1996 the BBMF had been in existence for thirty-nine years and had been based at Coningsby for the past twenty. The Flight had a slightly smaller number of historic aircraft than it later accrued, but was still an impressive and famous collection of iconic warbirds.

The Avro Lancaster B.1, PA474, was the undoubted queen of the fleet, although you would have to go a long way to find a BBMF fighter pilot who would admit it out loud. It was one of only two airworthy Lancasters in the world, the other being based in Canada with the Canadian Warplane Heritage Museum at Hamilton, Ontario.

The BBMF also operated Douglas C-47 Dakota ZA947 which had been with the Flight since 1993.

Of the BBMF's two Hawker Hurricanes, IIC PZ865 – 'The Last of the Many' – was the only one airworthy in 1996, which was also the year that it had dummy 20mm cannon fitted to its wings, funded by Lincolnshire's Lancaster Association, a charity that supports the BBMF. The other BBMF Hurricane, LF363, was still being completely rebuilt by Historic Flying at Audley End after it had crashed on landing with an engine failure at Wittering in 1991 and been largely burnt out. LF363 eventually returned to the BBMF, totally pristine, at the end of September 1998, ready for the 1999 display season. Until then though, the Flight had only one Hurricane to fly. The Hurricane was the first warbird that new BBMF fighter pilots flew as, although it is arguably slightly more difficult to fly than a Spitfire, it is more forgiving on landings and has a greater degree of directional control and rudder effectiveness on the ground with its wider track undercarriage and larger fin and rudder.

In 1996 the Flight had four Spitfires on its strength. The two Rolls Royce Merlin-engined so-called 'Baby' Spitfires were IIa P7350 – the world's only surviving airworthy Spitfire from the Battle of Britain in 1940 – and Vb AB910, a wartime veteran that had flown143 operations in the Second World War, including supporting the D Day invasion. In addition, the Flight operated two Rolls Royce Griffon-engined Spitfire PR XIXs – PM631 and PS915 – known as the 'Big Spits'. In November 1997 a fifth Spitfire was added to the BBMF fleet with the arrival at Coningsby of clipped-wing IX MK356. (The final addition to the BBMF Spitfire line-up was XVI TE311, which first flew in October 2012, some years after I had left the Flight.)

Squadron Leader Paul Day OBE AFC, known to all as 'The Major', took command of the BBMF in April 1996. He was the first fighter pilot

OC BBMF. The Major had joined the RAF in 1961 and had flown Hawker Hunters, F-4 Phantoms – including an exchange tour with the USAF where he picked up his nickname – and the Tornado F.3. He had joined the BBMF as a fighter pilot in 1980 and became the 'Fighter Leader' in 1982. He had, therefore, already displayed the Flight's Hurricanes and Spitfires for sixteen display seasons when he took over as the Officer Commanding. He commanded the unit for eight years, achieving over 1,000 flying hours on Spitfires in the process. He was to be my Boss and mentor on the BBMF until he retired after the 2003 display season. He was a brilliant pilot and was uncompromising in the standards he demanded of us all. He was very much the fighter pilot, but was also an excellent instructor. For the next eight years I was effectively an apprentice to the wizard and I learned much from him.

One thing that all BBMF pilots need to understand is that it is the aircraft that are the stars, not the pilots. The Major was always very keen to stress that there was absolutely no room for egos when flying these historic aircraft. The people in an air show crowd did not care less who was flying them; they had turned up to see the beautiful sight of the iconic aircraft in the air and to hear the evocative engine notes. The aim of the BBMF displays was, therefore, to present the aeroplanes to their best advantage rather than the supposed brilliance of the pilots. The Major would tell new BBMF pilots that 'the only way to become famous with the BBMF is to crash one'.

Another factor that very much influenced BBMF operations was the limited flying hours available on the historic aircraft, imposed to ensure their longevity. This meant that time in the air was never squandered and training needed to be completed with the minimum expenditure of flying hours and a consequential steep learning curve.

Hurricane Training

Before I first flew a Hurricane, I devoured the notes provided on flying it and learned the flight reference cards' drills and emergency actions. I spent time sitting in the cockpit of Hurricane PZ865 in the BBMF hangar on my own, learning the cockpit layout and practising the checks. Despite the relative simplicity of the controls in the Hurricane compared with modern jet fighters, they obviously hadn't invented ergonomics when this cockpit was designed. Controls, instruments and warning lights seemed to be scattered about in a most haphazard manner and some aspects were not user-friendly.

The Major took me through a short but thorough ground school on the Hurricane. The whole emphasis was on not over-complicating things but covering only what you really needed to know. After all, the BBMF fighter pilots, apart from the full-time Officer Commanding, were also flying the Tornado F.3 and with the Chipmunk, Hurricane, 'Baby Spitfires' and the 'Big Spitfires', they could be required to be current on five aircraft types at once. Part of the ground school involved physically looking over the Hurricane in the hangar to learn its features and the cockpit controls and sitting in it with the aircraft raised on jacks so that the flaps and undercarriage could be operated, pumped up and down with the hydraulic hand pump in the cockpit, whilst becoming familiar with the 'H' gate for the undercarriage and flap lever.

On 17 April the big moment came when I was to fly a Hurricane for the first time. I was as excited and nervous as could be. I was about to fly a precious 1944 Hurricane, in this case the very last Hurricane ever built, the famous 'Last of the Many', which was completely irreplaceable and I was going to do it without any dual instruction. The Major's pre-flight brief was perfect, succinct but thorough. I knew exactly what I was about to do.

As I walked out to Hurricane PZ865 I was struck by the aircraft's impressive shape, its hunched-back stance and height off the ground making it seem more imposing than other similar-sized aircraft; it looked purposeful and sturdy. It was difficult to suppress the feeling of excitement and slight disbelief that I was about to go flying in this truly classic and very rare warbird. She and I were about to share an experience and I hoped she was going to be good to me.

With the external checks completed, and after I had strapped in, the Major stood on the Hurricane's wing beside the cockpit as I started the monster 27-litre Rolls Royce Merlin engine for the first time. I primed it with fuel using the 'KIGAS' hand priming pump; I signalled for start clearance to the ground crewman and a confirmatory signal from him gave me clearance to start. The propeller turned very slowly and jerkily for three or four blades; then the engine kicked and the Merlin V-12 burst into life, with puffs of smoke from the exhaust stacks and a roar.

The effect was startling. At this time I had 5,300 hours of RAF flying; I was completely comfortable in the cockpit of a Tornado fighter jet, but this was something else. The smell, the cacophony of noise, the vibration, all assailed my senses and took me right out of my comfort zone. I hadn't felt like this since I was a young student pilot twenty-four years earlier. (Later on, after I became OC BBMF in 2004, I introduced a tied-down engine run for new BBMF fighter pilots, before and separate from their first flight, because I had seen the stunning effect that first firing up the Merlin had on pilots. It also gave new pilots the chance to open the throttle to take-off power to experience the noise and how far the throttle lever moved, before they did so on their first take off.) The Major was pointing around the cockpit to get me to re-focus and get the after-engine-start checks done. Then he patted me on the shoulder and jumped down off the wing, to race off to the air traffic control tower to monitor my first Hurricane flight. I was on my own. I took a moment to look around outside and to try to memorise the picture I would be seeing on landing, in terms of the height of my eyeline off the ground and the nose-up angle of the aircraft with the tail wheel on the ground. I hoped I would remember it in forty minutes' time.

When I had climbed to 7,000 feet and got a feel for the Hurricane – it felt nice – I carried out a clean stall, cautiously avoiding holding it in too far in case of the wing dropping and then flew a dirty stall with the undercarriage and flaps down. When I raised the undercarriage, it would not retract fully and I used the hand pump to lock it up. This was, in fact, I was to learn later, caused by a weak hydraulic pump that subsequently had to be changed. I thought I'd better tell the Major on the radio. He suggested trying the undercarriage again and this time it needed the hand pump to get it to lock down. That meant the sortie had to be curtailed and, instead of practising three circuits and landings as planned, I had to land from the first approach. Fortunately, that first approach and landing was a good one and I had survived my first Hurricane flight and my first minor Hurricane systems problem.

The Hurricane was not available for the next few days whilst the hydraulic problem was rectified by the ever hard-working and dedicated BBMF engineers. Then on 22 April, with PZ865 serviceable again, I flew it four times in the day, short sorties but including eight practice displays over Coningsby airfield at 500 feet minimum height, plus two displays at the absolute minimum height of 100 feet, once cleared down. Flying displays down to 100 feet was licensed hooliganism. I also completed ten circuits and landings that day. At the end of the day I was completely wrung out, having given my all. Satisfyingly exhausted, I fell asleep shortly after finishing my dinner.

The following day I flew two more Hurricane sorties, the first to complete three more practice displays at 100 feet and the second to fly close formation in the Hurricane for the first time. The Major led me in a Spitfire, having shown me on the ground the formation references I should try to maintain. We took off separately and then I joined into close formation, initially in echelon right. The Major was always keen to minimise radio transmissions and often used hand signals. When I had settled into what I thought was the correct close formation position on him, he waved his hand at me. I thought he was beckoning me to get closer, so I moved in tighter. He waved some more, so I moved in even closer, thinking that these BBMF boys really do fly tight formation. Then the Major's voice came up on the radio with a terse 'Hurricane you're too close. Move out.' He had, in fact, been waving me out all the time. After some close formation manoeuvring away from the airfield, we returned to practise so-called 'Bomber re-joins' with the Major simulating the end of the Lancaster display in the Spitfire, with the final gear-down pass at 110 knots and then turning away, cleaning up and accelerating slowly up to 150 knots as I chased him down and joined into close formation. We did that three times. The next time it would be with the Lancaster in front of an air show crowd.

I flew the Hurricane once more on 24 April on a dress rehearsal for the Public Display Approval the following day, with a single practice display at 100 feet. I then flew a Tornado F.3 the same day, because my real job as an instructor with the conversion unit still had to go on.

On 25 April all the BBMF pilots displayed for the Air Officer Commanding (AOC) 11/18 Group at Coningsby for his Public Display Approval. He thought us all safe and granted the BBMF his formal approval to display the aircraft in public. When I landed from my display for the AOC, I had four hours and ten minutes flying time on the Hurricane and now I was cleared to display at air shows around the country.

Flying the Hurricane

Being allowed to fly the Hurricane was always an enormous privilege and the achievements of the aircraft and its pilots during the Second World War were never far from my mind. Just as those wartime pilots wrote in their memoirs, the Hurricane was an aircraft that felt strong, robust and rugged; it inspired confidence.

The Hurricane was a very stable aircraft to fly and I could easily understand why the wartime pilots said it was a good gun platform. That said, stability is the antithesis of agility in aerodynamic terms, and the Hurricane needed larger control inputs to get it moving compared with other aircraft I had flown. The controls seemed to have a sort of dead spot in the centre, which was particularly noticeable when you wanted to pitch the aircraft. A small movement of the control column from the centre had negligible effect, so you naturally moved it further, which then had a greater effect than you intended so you were immediately backing off your input once the aircraft started to respond. In roll, the controls were lighter than in pitch, except when the speed was high when the ailerons became quite heavy, but the roll rate was rather sluggish.

When I became more experienced with the Hurricane, I often flew the so-called 'high-speed pass' of the display, which was usually flown straight and level, as a topside pass with bank and top (usually right) rudder applied to hold the nose up. I discovered that – for some aerodynamic coupling reason that I never fully understood – when you applied right rudder to do this, the nose would dip markedly. You needed to pull quite hard on the control column to hold the nose attitude, otherwise it could be quite disconcerting at 100 feet. The original wartime *Pilot's Notes* actually contained a warning that 'care should be taken not to let the aircraft yaw to the right [at higher speeds] as this produces a marked nose down pitching tendency'.

During displays I routinely flew with both hands on the control column spade grip, with the throttle set to display power (we used plus six inches of boost for displays) and the throttle friction clamped tight. (The throttle friction was a real 'gotcha' on take off, because if you did not set it tight enough the throttle would begin to close of its own accord when you took your left hand off it and swapped hands on the control column, to raise the undercarriage with your right hand.) The engine temperatures could get quite hot during a display and, as the radiator was located underneath the cockpit, that heat could be felt directly by the pilot. When a display had been completed it was good to cool down both the engine and the pilot. At display power settings the Hurricane was incredibly noisy. Much later in my time with the BBMF the RAF conducted noise-level trials on all its aircraft types. The sensors inside the earpieces of our modern bone domes detected noise levels of 120 decibels at display power in the Hurricane (the UK Health and Safety legal limit is 85 decibels). It is no wonder that my ears ring with tinnitus now. (Later still, the RAF introduced noise-reduction measures to keep the noise levels to within legal limits for pilots.)

The canopy on the Hurricane could be locked open for take off or landing, but could not be locked shut. The result was that it always worked open slightly and there would be a gap that let in the airflow and the rain if you encountered any. There were also *punkah* louvres that could not be closed, only swivelled, and if it rained the water found its way through them to hit the exposed areas of your face and your legs got wet. We flew the Hurricane only in relatively benign temperatures, although it could sometimes get very hot in mid-summer, but this was nothing compared with the freezing or tropical temperatures that pilots might have encountered in the Second World War in some theatres of operations.

When it came to landing the Hurricane, as the flaps were lowered there was a marked nose-down change of trim. Most conventional aircraft have a 'flaps down, nose down' pitch change, but in the Hurricane it was pronounced and, as the pitch control was relatively sluggish and heavy, you needed to be ready to catch it and add a significant amount of nose-up trim with the large wooden elevator trim wheel. Approaches to land were best flown steeper than modern aircraft, probably about a four-degree approach angle, with a trickle of power applied and nicely trimmed, using the 'crab' technique if there was a crosswind. In a crosswind it was important to get the aircraft straight before touchdown. It was wise to avoid closing the throttle sharply in the landing flare as that would cause the nose to drop and it wasn't possible to hold it up, resulting in a firm touchdown and a bounce, something that the Hurricane was prone to do. Once all three wheels were on the ground the Hurricane was relatively easy to keep straight, using the correct techniques of large pre-emptive rudder inputs, and the view forward over the sloping nose was quite good. The BBMF operated the Hurricane to a maximum crosswind limit of 15 knots for landings, which was quite comfortable, although pilots needed a minimum of fifty hours on the warbirds before being allowed to land in crosswinds of more than 10 knots.

Taxiing in after landing it was a good idea not to over-use the wheel brakes, despite the need to keep weaving to see around the nose and with directional braking being the principal method of turning. The wheel brakes would easily fade and become next to useless if over-used; BBMF Hurricane pilots were told it was best to assume that they didn't have any.

Some of my comments about what it was like to fly the Hurricane might perhaps sound rather negative but these things really just gave the aircraft a certain eccentricity. I always enjoyed it and I never forgot how privileged I was. You would be mad not to, especially at a time when there were perhaps only six or seven airworthy Hurricanes in the world (a number that has now more than doubled).

Hurricane Displays

My first public display in a Hurricane was flown on 4 May 1996, in company with a Spitfire, at an air show at the Shuttleworth Collection at Old Warden, before displaying at Duxford and landing on the grass runway at that famous old airfield. On 6 May we displayed again at Duxford, taking off and landing on the bumpy grass runway. Later that day on the transit home from Duxford to Coningsby I was one of four BBMF fighters that flew in close formation with the BBMF Dakota for an air-to-air photo shoot. Those first experiences of BBMF flying perhaps indicate just what pilots new to the Flight were expected to be able to cope with.

On 11 May I flew as a singleton Hurricane to the air display at North Weald where I was to join up with a BBMF Spitfire, flown by Flight Lieutenant Paul 'Shents' Shenton, who had been conducting flypasts elsewhere on the way to North Weald. The BBMF Dakota was already at North Weald and would be taking off into our display. As I approached the Stansted control zone, I started to dial up the Stansted radio frequency on the Hurricane's single VHF radio when one of the frequency-setting knobs just came loose and ceased to function. The radio was now stuck on a useless frequency and I had no radio contact with anyone. I skirted around the Stansted zone and found my way to North Weald where I spotted the Spitfire holding crowd rear as planned. Of course, I couldn't talk to him or anyone else. Much to Shents' surprise, my Hurricane suddenly slid up into close formation on his wing. I used the standard hand signals of pointing to my oxygen mask microphone and my ears, and giving a thumbs down, to indicate no radio transmit or receive. He nodded his understanding and then pointed at his wrist watch and gave a thumbs up, meaning display on time. So that is what we did. I knew that Shents would have been keeping North Weald air traffic control advised that the Hurricane had no radio; he displayed first and then I took over, as briefed, before we joined into close formation for a final pass and broke downwind to land, again him first. I assumed that I had permission to land behind him. The experience taught me what would be expected of me with the BBMF. Our ground crew had a spare radio in the pack on board the Dakota, and the radio was quickly changed ready for the display at North Weald the following day, after which we flew home.

Continuing the steep learning curve, on 25 May I flew my first BBMF display in a Hurricane with the Lancaster and a Spitfire – the famous

BBMF three-ship routine – at the Mildenhall Air Fete. My first ever close formation with the Lancaster was flown on the way to the air show and on arrival we went straight into the three-ship routine, arriving in close formation in front of a crowd of many thousands of people. I never tired of flying in formation with the Lancaster. It was such an amazing shape and it was always a thrill to sit in formation with it. When we were transiting from place to place with the Lancaster, we didn't generally fly in close formation with it, except for practice, for air-to-air photographs, or for flypasts. The Lancaster crew liked to fly at 1,000 feet as this was the best altitude to avoid the majority of light aircraft and gliders, of which there were very many flying around the UK at weekends. As our Hurricanes and Spitfires were single-engine, the fighter pilots wanted to fly much higher to give more time and options in the event of an engine failure, so we frequently flew at around 3,000 feet in a wide vic formation. The Lancaster's upper-surface camouflage was extremely effective when we were looking down on it against the fields below and it was very easy to lose visual with it.

Many people probably imagine that whilst cruising on a transit flight in a Hurricane the pilot can just sit and look around at the view and revel in the experience of flying a warbird. Nothing could be further from the truth. In the cruise I never relaxed for a moment. I was constantly monitoring the engine instruments for any hint of an engine problem and continually updating my plans for a forced landing in the event that it should suddenly become necessary. Where was the nearest runway and which field was the best within gliding distance for a wheels-up forced landing? Every few minutes I checked the fuel-tank contents by turning the fuel gauge button to the tank I wished to interrogate and pressing it. I also needed to keep a check on the navigation and keep a good lookout for other aircraft and gliders that might pose a collision risk. However, there were occasional moments when I could snatch a few seconds just to look out through the Hurricane's latticed canopy at the wingtips, twist round to see the tail, and imagine I was transported back in time.

By the end of June 1996 I had flown eleven public displays in the Hurricane at air shows and I had a grand total of fourteen hours and five minutes flying on type. The single Hurricane we had airworthy at the time – PZ865 – was now needed to train Squadron Leader Ian 'Shiney' Simmons, the other new fighter pilot to join the BBMF that year, who had been waiting his turn. It was time for me to fly a Spitfire.

An Ambition Fulfilled

Knowing that I would soon be converting to the Spitfire filled me with excitement and a fair amount of trepidation but I tried to approach it in as professional a manner as possible. I studied the notes for the Spitfire, learned the Flight Reference Card drills and spent time sitting in the cockpits of Spitfire P7350 and AB910 in the BBMF hangar to become familiar with the layout and to practise the checks. Then the Major took me through his ground school for the 'Baby' Spitfires, which followed a similar style to that for the Hurricane. Once again, he concentrated on what I really needed to know. The cockpit of the Spitfire actually had a simpler layout than the Hurricane with fewer controls. In addition, sharing a Merlin engine with the Hurricane, many of the engine controls, procedures and limits were the same or similar. Everything in the Spitfire cockpit fell easily to hand, with the only slight drawback being the need to change hands to raise the undercarriage after take off.

On 2 July 1996 the big day arrived; as far as I was concerned it was the culmination of years of dreaming that, one day, I might fly a Spitfire. I was told that my first-ever Spitfire flight was to be in what is probably the world's most precious and irreplaceable Spitfire IIa, P7350, the only airworthy survivor of the Battle of Britain. No pressure there then. Once again, the Major stood on the wing beside me as I started the engine, but I was by now used to the sounds, smells, noise and vibration and I felt less out of my comfort zone than on my first Hurricane flight. Taxiing out to the runway I could feel how light, lively and skittish the Spitfire was on the ground with its narrow-track undercarriage, 'a paper bag in the wind' as the Major would say. It was also obvious how much the Spitfire nose obstructed the forward view with the tail wheel on the ground and weaving was very necessary to see ahead.

My first surprise came on take off when, with the same engine power set as in a Hurricane, the acceleration on the runway was so lively that I didn't raise the tail in time and the Spitfire lifted off in a three-point attitude, almost saying to me, 'Come on, keep up.' As soon as I had raised the undercarriage and set the power for the climb, I could immediately feel how wonderful the Spitfire felt on the controls. It was light, sensitive and responsive, an absolute delight to fly. When I took it through some stalls at 7,000 feet, taking care to keep straight and balanced, there was no drama at all, no wing drop, just some buffet and a loss of lift as it 'mushed' down, and it recovered immediately when I moved the control column forward and applied power. In fact, those ellipsoidal wingtips are still flying quite happily even after the wing roots have stalled. The reduced drag from the wonderful and aerodynamically almost perfect wing shape was noticeable, especially when pulling 4G in a practice display at height. Then it was back to the airfield for a practice forced landing to overshoot, followed by three circuits and landings. The skittishness of the Spitfire on the runway was very evident and I had to work hard to keep her straight and under control, long after touchdown and right down to taxiing speed, but all my landings were okay and none raised my heart rate excessively on this sortie, as was sometimes to happen in the future.

I flew Spitfire P7350 once more that day, flying two practice displays over the airfield with a minimum height of 500 feet, and then a third at 100 feet, plus three circuits and landings. On the first practice display I had a heart-stopping moment during the so-called 'victory roll' at the end of the display. With the Hurricane's slow roll rate, I had become used to setting a steep climb angle and then rolling with full left aileron and a boot full of rudder. The Hurricane rolled so slowly that even with full roll inputs, by the time it had rolled through a full 360 degrees at 1G the nose would have dropped from the steep climb to a level flight attitude. When I flew my first victory roll over the airfield in a Spitfire, I set the same steep climb angle and then gave it full-left aileron and some rudder. It rolled through 360 degrees so rapidly that, when I stopped the roll, we were still in a steep climb with the airspeed rapidly reducing. I instinctively pushed the nose down and the negative G caused a rich cut of the engine, which momentarily went quiet. Heart thumping, I re-applied 1G and the Merlin engine picked up immediately. I learned the lesson: either roll more slowly or don't set such a steep attitude for a rapid roll in a Spitfire.

In the afternoon I flew the other of the BBMF's 'Baby' Spitfires, Vb AB910, another wartime survivor with an impressive pedigree. On this sortie I flew my first ever 'synchro' display as the leader of the pair of Spitfires, with the Major as the No. 2. We flew two synchro displays with a minimum height of 500 feet and one at 100 feet, and then once again I flew three circuits and landings. It was quite difficult to arrange the synchro crossovers to occur at crowd centre, compensating for the effects of the wind on both aircraft, but the 'close aboard' head-on crossovers were great fun.

At the end of the day I had flown three Spitfire sorties with six practice displays, including my first synchro displays, and nine landings, and I was beginning to feel at home in the aircraft. Amazingly, I could call myself a

Spitfire pilot. I went home feeling over the moon, completely drained and satisfyingly exhausted.

Two days later I flew another sortie in Spitfire AB910 with three practice synchro displays, this time as the No. 2. The Major now declared me Spitfire-qualified and ready to display in public, including synchro displays. I had two hours and ten minutes on Spitfires.

Flying the Spitfire

The thing about flying the Spitfire, quite apart from its beauty and charisma, which are magical, is that from a pilot's point of view it is the finest handling aircraft it is possible to imagine. It takes skill and finesse to fly it well, but once 'hooked up' with it the result is infinitely satisfying. Everything that has ever been written about flying the Spitfire, by wartime pilots and those since, is true: you really can become one with the machine. You just have to think about what it is you want to do, pitch or roll, bank, turn or climb, and with the slightest touch on the controls you're doing it. It's almost as if you are the machine's brain and you are built into it, as if your arms were extending up the wings and the interconnection between your hands and feet and the controls is almost superfluous. The Spitfire is so agile and pitches and rolls so rapidly that it is just wonderful to fly. It actually makes no aerodynamic sense, because with a conventionally-controlled aircraft, to make it respond more rapidly you need to move the control column further from the neutral position to deflect the control surfaces further. With the Spitfire it seemed that small but rapid movements of the control column produced a faster reaction and large control inputs were rarely required.

The Spitfire is virtually vice-less in the air; it tells the pilot when he is doing something wrong and has no unpleasant handling characteristics at all. If you pull too hard in a turn with the speed too low, it will buffet and then when the wing roots begin to stall and the wings lose lift it just 'mushes', which you can feel, but it is still quite controllable. For the same engine power from its 27-litre V-12 Rolls Royce Merlin engine as the Hurricane, the Spitfire is considerably lighter and less 'draggy', with livelier performance. The later Griffon-engined Spitfires, such as the BBMF's PR XIXs, are heavier aircraft but possessed of even greater power output from their 37-litre engines.

However, throughout the joyful experience of flying a Spitfire there is the nagging concern that you are going to have to land it at the end of the sortie. That is when the aircraft's vices will come to the fore and it will bite the unwary, or any pilot who does not give it sufficient respect. On the runway after landing, the narrow-track undercarriage does not aid the Spitfire in running straight – 'tramlining'. Meanwhile, the relatively small fin and rudder, especially on the early-mark 'Baby' Spitfires, do not endow the aircraft with much directional control, especially once the tail wheel is on the ground and the airflow over the fin is blanked by the nose and fuselage. In fact, the Spitfire possesses all the directional stability of a supermarket shopping trolley with three wheels. As soon as the wheels touch the ground on landing, a Spitfire can be totally unpredictable and can quite unexpectedly veer off in any direction it cares to take, rather than continuing to run straight. This can be exacerbated by crosswind, which might either try to weathercock the aircraft into wind, or get underneath the upwind wing to send the aircraft off in the other direction. Even heat off the runway surface might lift a wingtip and cause the aircraft to start to swing. In the Spitfire these effects are amplified because the wing tips are still flying long after the wing roots have ceased to do so. The landing roll requires great attention by the pilot to monitor what the nose of the aircraft is doing and to keep the wings level, applying instant, rapid and positive corrections with the rudder and the ailerons to keep it under control, otherwise a ground loop or worse is a likely outcome. Sometimes you were literally dancing on the rudder pedals. Meanwhile, of course, you cannot see where you are going over the nose of the Spitfire.

Spitfire Displays

My first public appearance in a Spitfire was as one of a pair, with the Major leading me, to conduct four flypasts at events in the local area, taking off and landing at Coningsby, what we called an 'out and back'. Then my very next sortie was to deploy with the Lancaster and a Hurricane to Fairford to display at the Royal International Air Tattoo. When I landed Spitfire P7350 at the end of the display, in front of a crowd of some 60,000 people, I bounced. My second landing that day, a second or two later, was fine. We displayed the classic BBMF three-ship again the next day for the huge crowd that the Tattoo always draws and then returned to Coningsby.

The following weekend I flew Spitfire Vb AB910 in company with the Lancaster and a PR XIX Spitfire to Belgium where we performed a synchro display at the air show at Ostend before landing there. This was the first time

I crossed the English Channel in a Spitfire. The next day, a Sunday, we flew a synchro display at the small Belgian airfield of Sanicole before landing at Kleine Brogel. Whenever we flew at the Sanicole air show, which was generally an annual event for the BBMF, we were invited to the post-air-show party at the Sanicole flying club where the Belgians were extremely welcoming and hospitable.

Over the weekend of 17/18 August I flew five Spitfire sorties in company with a Lancaster and a second Spitfire, taking in Exeter, Paignton air show, a flypast at Plymouth and a display at Eastbourne. After displaying there, I suffered another radio failure in Spitfire P7350 and the Lancaster led me to Biggin Hill where we landed and fixed the problem before continuing home. The weekend after that, I flew three more BBMF three-ship displays with the Lancaster and a Hurricane.

In two months, I accumulated almost twenty-two hours on the Baby Spitfires and I flew eight displays and several flypasts at events. The Major now decided that I should convert to the Griffon-engined Spitfire PR XIXs.

Flying the 'Big Spits'

It was and still is fairly unusual for a BBMF fighter pilot to graduate to flying the PR XIX Spitfires – the 'Big Spits' – in a first display season. The Major must have thought I was ready for it. Once again, I read all the notes, studied the Flight Reference Cards and sat in the cockpits in the hangar learning the layout and the checks. This time the conversion was a ground school briefing and a single sortie.

As I taxied out to the runway in Spitfire PR XIX PM631 on 6 September 1996, for some reason I immediately felt completely at home, despite the even longer nose in front of me and the growling Griffon engine sounding quite different from a Merlin. Perhaps it was because the aircraft felt slightly heavier and more planted on the ground, more what I was used to as a jet pilot, or maybe I was getting used to Spitfires.

The thirty-five-minute sortie included climbing to 7,000 feet for some stalls, a high-speed dive where it would have been very easy to exceed the BBMF never-exceed limit of 300 knots (345mph) – the XIX really picked up speed in a dive – two practice displays away from the airfield at 1,500 feet, one display over the airfield at 500 feet minimum height and one landing. That was it. I was qualified to fly and display the 'Big Spits'.

The very next day I took Spitfire PR XIX PS915 to display at the Farnborough International Airshow in front of a huge crowd, landing at Biggin Hill. The display at Farnborough was repeated the next day from Biggin Hill before returning to Coningsby.

*****

The Supermarine Spitfire was originally designed around the Rolls Royce Merlin engine. The Merlin is a 27-litre (1,650 cu. in.) capacity V-12, liquid-cooled (water/glycol mix), supercharged right-tractor aero engine (the propeller rotates clockwise when viewed from the cockpit). The Rolls Royce Griffon is 37- litre (2,240 cu. in.) liquid-cooled (water/glycol mix) supercharged V-12 left-tractor aero engine (the propeller rotates anti-clockwise when viewed from the cockpit). The firing order and valve timing of the Griffon engine is different from the Merlin which gives the bigger engine its distinctive 'Griffon growl'. The Spitfire PR XIXs are powered by two-speed two-stage supercharged Griffon engines, originally rated at 2,220hp.

On first acquaintance a Griffon-engine Spitfire looks and feels different from its Merlin-engine sisters. It is almost as if it is an entirely different aircraft, despite having fundamentally the same airframe. There is something rather intimidating about it, even to a pilot well versed in Merlin Spitfires. It has the classic lines of the Spitfire but a Spitfire on steroids, with its longer snout and huge propeller spinner, bigger fin and massive radiator pods under both wings housing the coolant radiators, the oil cooler and the supercharger inter-cooler radiator. It is bigger and heavier, almost 30 per cent heavier in fact, something that is bound to affect how the aircraft feels to the pilot on the ground and in the air.

Entering the cockpit requires a long stride from the wing over the high cockpit sill, necessary because there is no drop-down cockpit door due to the PR XIX originally having a pressurised cockpit. Inside the cockpit there are some notable differences from the Merlin-engine Spitfires, but it is still unmistakably a Spitfire, including the tight fit that makes the pilot feel part of the aircraft. The throttle quadrant has a longer 'throw', something that was introduced with experience from the early Griffon-engine Spitfires, giving a throttle movement virtually twice that of the Merlin Spitfires to make it easier for the pilot to control all the power available from that huge 2,000-plus-horsepower engine. The fuel priming pump is different from the Merlin-engine Spitfire's KIGAS pump. This one is a much larger T-handled stirrup-pump affair with a larger stroke and bore, heavier to operate and needed to prime that massive 37-litre engine with fuel prior to starting it. Most other aspects of the cockpit, including the undercarriage lever, are just pure Spitfire and instantly recognisable to a pilot who has flown Merlin-engine Spitfires.

The Griffon Spitfire feels heavier even just taxiing – less the 'paper bag in the wind' of the early Spitfires and instead feeling more 'planted' on the ground, a good thing in strong or gusty wind conditions. The longer nose really obstructs the forward view, making weaving and peering around the side of the windscreen even more necessary than with the Merlin-engine Spitfires.

All propeller-driven aircraft will tend to swing on take off (unless fitted with contra-rotating propellers), with tail-wheel aircraft displaying this tendency to a greater degree, and powerful warbirds even more so. The cause is often referred to as the torque effect but there are actually several factors at play. For a Merlin-engine Spitfire with the propeller rotating clockwise as seen from the cockpit, the aircraft will try to swing to the left on take off, requiring right rudder to keep straight. The rudder trim is set fully right for take off to assist with this. In a Griffon-engine Spitfire, with the propeller rotating the other way, the effects are reversed and the aircraft will try to swing to the right. The effects are amplified because of the enormous torque of the Griffon engine, the stiffness of the five-bladed propeller and the long moment arm caused by the elongated nose. The advice to pilots, therefore, is to open up the throttle slowly to a maximum of plus 7 inches of boost (less than half of the maximum boost available) and to be prepared to apply full left rudder pre-emptively as the throttle is opened. The rudder trim is set fully left for take off. It was obviously vital to remember which way it was going to swing. I have to admit to opening the throttle on take off in a Griffon Spitfire too quickly on a few occasions and, even with only plus 7 inches of boost set, full left rudder would not stop the aircraft veering right. The only way to keep straight was to reduce the power, which is counterintuitive on the take-off roll. As the tail lifts, another big stab of left rudder is required to keep straight. If the pilot had not realised it up to now, this is when it becomes apparent what a monster engine you are sitting behind.

In the air the Griffon-engine Spitfire is a noticeably heavier beast to pull around the sky and sometimes careful energy management is needed, although it will rapidly pick up speed when not turning and especially when going downhill. The Griffon engine is less smooth-running and its note is more guttural and snarly than the symphonic Merlin. It will complain even more loudly than the Merlin, popping and banging, it the throttle is closed to near idle, especially with high revs set. In this respect the Griffon behaves like a highly-tuned racing engine. The massive torque from the five-bladed propeller on the front of the 2,000-plus-horsepower Griffon engine, with a greater moment arm due to the longer nose, really yaws the aircraft with changes of power or speed and when pitching up. The pilot has to be very active with his feet on the rudder pedals to keep the nose pointing straight and to avoid out-of-balance side slipping.

That longer nose also gets in the way of the pilot's view when cruising at slower speeds; you really need to be going faster to get a half-decent view ahead. The Griffon Spitfires are obviously in their element cruising at 240 knots (275 mph) although this is not the most economical speed. Running into a typical flypast, the venue will disappear under that long nose about two minutes out and ideally needs to be approached in a dive to keep it in view. When the Spitfire PR XIXs were flown on photo-recce missions in wartime at high altitude, the aircraft's nose and wings would have obscured miles of ground features. It must have been enormously difficult to navigate accurately to pinpoint targets.

These minor inconveniences are more than made up for in other ways. This is still obviously a Spitfire and still feels delightfully responsive to control inputs, just with extra verve. When it comes to landing, the extra weight helps the PR XIX to sit better on the runway on touchdown, there is less skittishness than with the 'Baby' Spitfires and the large fin and rudder give more directional control, allowing it to cope with stronger crosswinds (15 knots maximum crosswind for BBMF pilots with sufficient experience). The PR XIX really is an ultimate Spitfire and a joy to fly. For me, they became my favourite Spitfires because of their sheer power and performance.

*****

For the remainder of the 1996 display season I exclusively flew Spitfire PR XIX PS915 with the BBMF, completing seven further public displays and nine flypasts. Then, suddenly, the display season was over. The BBMF aircraft were put to bed in the hangar for winter servicing and it would be six months before I flew one of them again. This was to become a familiar set of emotions: on the one hand feeling tired after a full display season and looking forward to some time and weekends at home; on the other hand, knowing that it would be six months before I could experience the joy of flying the BBMF's Hurricanes and Spitfires again. I had flown fifty hours on Hurricanes and Spitfires in my first display season. I had displayed the aircraft for the public at numerous major air shows from the south coast of England to Scotland and I had learned more in that time than I would have thought possible. During the display season I had continued with my primary duty as an instructor on the Tornado F.3 Operational Conversion Unit, flying eighty hours on the F.3 in addition to my BBMF flying. Now the OCU could have me back fulltime (well almost) for the winter.

BBMF Experiences

Over my next ten display seasons with the BBMF I flew hundreds of displays and flypasts in Spitfires and Hurricanes. Some of these had particular significance and created abiding memories.

Bentley Priory

One of the most revered venues for flypasts and displays in the minds of most BBMF fighter pilots was RAF Bentley Priory which had been the headquarters of Fighter Command during the Second World War, the place from which its commander-in-chief, Air Chief Marshal Sir Hugh Dowding, had masterminded victory in the Battle of Britain in 1940.

Situated in Stanmore on the northern edge of the Greater London area, Bentley Priory officers' mess was originally an eighteenth-century stately home. It had a large terrace at the rear which overlooked the extensive gardens and it was on the terrace that guests stood to watch flypasts and to view BBMF displays over the garden and the open space beyond.

Various important dinners and events were held in the mess at Bentley Priory, often involving the Chief of the Air Staff and other air-ranking officers. None were more important to us than the annual Battle of Britain Fighter Association event, attended by veteran pilots who had fought in the Battle in 1940.

Bentley Priory was not especially easy to find and I always swept in from the west, curving in low over the open area of a golf course and park, looking for the clock tower on top of the Bentley Priory building protruding above the trees and mindful of the difficult-to-see mast that stuck up out of the trees to the south west. I would try to arrive at the datum exactly on time to the second, in a roaring top-side pass. On more than one occasion that arrival was part of a sunset ceremony as the Chief of the Air Staff saluted. Then it was into a standard BBMF fighter display but often in the knowledge that there were men on the ground watching me who were my heroes, who had flown in anger the type of aircraft I was flying and who would be watching me with an expert eye.

Some of the sunset ceremonies, such as the first one I displayed at in May 1997, were literally at last light and I had to land at the nearest airfield, which was Luton airport, almost in the dark. On another occasion, in September 1997, we took a Hurricane, flown by the Major, with me as his No. 2 in a Spitfire PR XIX. The plan was to do a pair of singleton displays but, in the event, with cloud cover that evening it was so dark that the Major decided to make it a series of close-formation flypasts with me on his wing as he wheeled us around. It was sufficiently dark that I could see the flames from his Hurricane's exhausts and we landed at Luton practically in the dark.

*****

Displaying Spitfires and Hurricanes for surviving members of 'The Few' was not restricted to Bentley Priory but was also something we often did at the annual ceremony at the Capel-le-Ferne Battle of Britain Memorial. A thank-you letter I received after one of those displays pointed out that:

> We had more than 20 veteran aircrew present who flew in the Battle of Britain, as well as several hundred guests in addition to our Royal Patron, HRH Prince Michael of Kent. There wasn't a dry eye in the place when your Merlins roared over; the old boys particularly loved the sound. Amongst the guests were the current, the next and some former Chiefs of the Air Staff. So, if you ever feel short of high-level support this was a good place for you to be!

Ostend Air Show 1997

On Friday 25 July 1997, during my second display season with the BBMF, I flew Spitfire PR XIX PM631 to Ostend, Belgium, in company with a Hurricane and the BBMF C-47 Dakota, to display at the Ostend Air Show the following day.

The three BBMF aircraft were due to close the air show on the Saturday and we were taxiing out to the runway at 17:00 whilst the Royal Jordanian Air Force Falcons aerobatic formation team of Extra 300 aerobatic light piston aircraft were displaying. I was paying close attention to where I was going, weaving the long nose of my Spitfire to see ahead and I was only vaguely aware of the display going on overhead. I noticed the Falcons' singleton Extra 300 cross over the top of me in a descending series of flick rolls, heading towards the crowd line to my left and I thought, 'He's bust the display line.' Then I was aware of a mass of flames in the crowd area to my left. Immediately, the Belgian air traffic controller came up on the radio with a message that the air show was cancelled and we were to return to parking.

As we turned round to taxi back, I could clearly see that something horrific had occurred in that section of the crowd. In fact, the Jordanian Extra 300 had somehow crashed into the crowd barrier near a Red Cross tent, with burning wreckage being hurled into the crowd. The airfield was locked down for several hours whilst casualties were attended to, survivors were taken to hospital and initial investigations took place. I and the other BBMF crews waited in the Ostend Flying Club, where we had been hospitably hosted during the day, and harrowing stories of the fatalities and casualties filtered back to us. Nine people were killed, including the Jordanian pilot and a Red Cross volunteer, and fifty were injured, including some children. Many of the casualties were critically injured, some with severe burns and some had lost limbs. It was truly horrific and tragic. The reasons why the aircraft had crashed into the crowd area were never really ascertained. The after-effects of the accident were to reverberate through the Belgian air show scene for many years, with an initial ban on all air shows and then subsequent stringently increased limits on minimum heights and distances from the crowd line when displays re-commenced. The Ostend air show has never been held since and the tragedy is etched on my mind.

Duxford

During my time with the BBMF, Duxford was the epicentre of warbird operations in the UK and a mecca for enthusiasts, with three or more air shows every year, and numerous privately-owned warbirds maintained in airworthy condition at the airfield. Attending the Duxford air shows and displaying the BBMF aircraft there was always special, with the 'Flying Legends' air shows being particular highlights. The BBMF did not fly fighter displays as dynamic or as aerobatic as some of the privately-owned Spitfires and Hurricanes but no one else had an airworthy Lancaster, so the classic BBMF three-ship display was always well received. In addition, no one else flew the fighter synchro displays that we sometimes did. We always knew when displaying at Duxford that there was extra pressure with a knowledgeable and critical audience, as well as many experienced and respected warbird pilots watching.

At some Duxford air shows the BBMF fighters became involved in something extra special and different. A case in point and a real highlight of my eleven years flying Spitfires was the close formation diamond-sixteen of Spitfires at the air show in May 1998. Some people think that the BBMF will not fly in close formation with anyone else. That is a myth. The BBMF is just choosy about which pilots it allows to fly close to its precious aircraft and requires proven pilot skill and experience before recommending the mixed formation to the Group headquarters for the necessary staff officer approval. For the diamond sixteen, the Major led our four-ship of Spitfires with me as the No. 2 in Spitfire PR XIX PM631. He had agreed that he would see how the other twelve Spitfires settled into close formation and, if he liked the look of it, he would bring our box-four formation in to join at the rear. He liked it and we did join right in. As we ran in towards Duxford for the diamond-sixteen flypast, I sneaked a couple of glances forward and found that the view was simply full of gently floating Spitfires. It was an amazing thing to be involved in and certainly something I never thought I would do.

The day before the diamond sixteen we had flown a BBMF five-ship fighter display for the Duxford crowd and we did the same again in September 2000 to occupy the crowd whilst a twenty-two-ship of warbirds formed up to fly overhead.

In September 2005 I flew in Spitfire PR XIX PS915 as the tenth Spitfire in an eleven-aircraft tail chase over Duxford airfield. I had applied to the Group Headquarters for permission to do this, which was granted, although questions were asked afterwards as to who had approved it. It was the most enormous fun and took some fighter-pilot skills as well as flying skill. There were times at slower speed near the top of wingovers when I was caught in large amounts of prop wash from aircraft ahead and my Spitfire was trying to roll the opposite way to my control inputs.

Biggin Hill

Biggin Hill, or 'Biggin on the Bump' as it is sometime known because of its hilltop location on top of the North Downs in Kent, was an iconic airfield to display at because of its famous connections with RAF fighter operations, crucially during the Battle of Britain and subsequently during the remainder of the Second World War. Just landing a Hurricane or a Spitfire there, especially from an approach to the northerly-facing runway with the steep slope of the hill in the undershoot, is an experience, with the obvious hump in the runway. I flew BBMF Spitfires and Hurricanes at several air shows at Biggin Hill during my time with the Flight, especially at the Battle of Britain air shows which were held in September. Sometimes we also used the airfield as a base for a weekend, to display at air shows in the south-east of England, such as Eastbourne.

Three experiences in particular stick in my mind. In September 1997 I was flying Spitfire IIa P7350, the Battle of Britain Spitfire, in company with the Lancaster and a Hurricane. We conducted a special flypast at Biggin Hill with many other civilian-owned warbirds following behind. On completion I was the first to land there, with all the other aircraft coming in behind me. My landing was a nice one but, shortly after touchdown, the aircraft lurched and veered to the right quite unexpectedly, instant full left rudder wasn't enough to stop it and I had to apply a dab of brake which lifted the tail. The next few seconds were a blur of hands and feet in the cockpit as I fought to keep the precious Spitfire on the runway and, eventually, as we slowed down, it all came back under control. My heart was thumping and I had no idea what had happened. I parked up under the direction of my BBMF ground-crew marshaller, Corporal Clive O'Connell, shut down and climbed out, shaking. I said to Clive, 'I've just had the most horrendous landing. I nearly lost it. I've no idea what I did wrong.' Clive looked back at the Spitfire and then walked over to the right wing, which was sitting low; he bent underneath it and lifted it with his back. When he ducked down, it immediately dropped again. Then he checked the right undercarriage oleo leg and discovered that a seal had failed, allowing all the hydraulic fluid to leak out so that the oleo leg had collapsed on landing. That was what had sent me careering across the runway. I was relieved that it hadn't been caused by my incompetence and felt fortunate to have saved it. My logbook shows that I flew P7350 out of Biggin Hill three days later, after the hard-working ground crew had rectified the problem.

Another experience I particularly remember was at a Biggin Hill Battle of Britain air show in September 2004. I led a formation of two Hurricanes and eight Spitfires – I was in BBMF Hurricane PZ865 – on a simulated scramble and a flypast in tactical rather than close formation. As I curved in toward Biggin Hill, I looked back over my shoulder at a wonderful selection of warbirds following me over such a famous airfield and felt very privileged. It was a thrill to lead such a formation.

In September 2005 I was asked to fly Spitfire IIa P7350 in close formation with privately-owned Hurricane R4118, flown by BBMF pilot Squadron Leader Al Pinner, for the Biggin Hill Battle of Britain Air Show. This put together the only surviving airworthy Spitfire and Hurricane that had actually participated in the Battle of Britain in 1940 in a very special formation. I took off from Coningsby and, as I flew south, Al joined me in Hurricane R4118 having taken off from Cambridge. As we flew past the Queen Elizabeth II bridge at Dartford, I looked out across the ellipsoidal wingtip of my Battle of Britain Spitfire at this actual Battle of Britain Hurricane flying alongside, over the River Thames where so much of the fighting had taken place in 1940, on our way to land at the famous Battle of Britain airfield of Biggin Hill. It was all and more than I could ever have dreamed of. What a marvellous experience. Then it was back to focusing on the task in hand.

Leuchars

The RAF air shows at Leuchars were annual events during my time with the BBMF and were very popular with the Scottish air show enthusiasts. One of the things that the Leuchars air show team did very well was the hosting of veterans and they had a special marquee set up for them. Over the years I met many interesting veterans with amazing stories to tell and they often wanted to sit in our aircraft, which we were always happy to let them do. I remember, for example, Wing Commander Roger Morewood with his handlebar moustache. He had flown Hurricanes with 56 Squadron before the Battle of Britain and then moved on to Bristol Blenheims. With him sitting in the cockpit of the Hurricane which I had taken to the show and me standing on the wing beside him, I asked him if he had ever flown Spitfires. He had. I asked him which he preferred, the Hurricane or Spitfire, and without hesitation he said, 'This. This has an undercarriage. You can't call that an undercarriage,' pointing to the Spitfire alongside.

Another wartime Hurricane pilot I met at Leuchars was Gerry Brady who lived in Aberdeen and became a particular friend. We wrote to each other often and telephoned for chats; we met up every year at the Leuchars air show. I went to find him in the veterans' tent at the show in 2002, wearing my black BBMF flying suit and, whilst I was talking to him and some of his veteran friends, the Chief of the Air Staff, Air Chief Marshal Sir Peter Squire, was doing the rounds of the veterans to shake hands and chat with them along with HRH The Duke of Kent. As a flight lieutenant Sir Peter had been my flight commander when I was a student on Hawker Hunters at RAF Valley in 1973 and he hadn't forgotten me. I had also flown him in a Tornado F.3 earlier in 2002. Much to Gerry Brady's surprise, when the Chief of the Air Staff and the Duke of Kent arrived at our little group, the Air Chief Marshal immediately shook my hand and said, 'Hello, Clive,' before chatting some more. I soon stepped back to let the veterans in the group have the limelight. When the VIPs had moved on, Jerry turned to me and said, 'Is everyone in the RAF on first-name terms now then?'

(When Sir Peter Squire retired from the RAF in 2003 I was delighted and honoured to be able to provide the flypast before his retirement dinner at the RAF College Cranwell, Trenchard Hall Officers' Mess, in Hurricane LF363.)

*****

At one of the Leuchars air shows I attended, the BBMF display was the last of the day, closing the show. The Air Officer Scotland and Northern Ireland, an air commodore based at Leuchars, had decided that he wanted to hold a sunset ceremony in front of the VIP tent with the Leuchars pipe band and an RAF ensign on a flagpole to be lowered whilst he saluted from a dais. We were told that, when we taxied our Spitfire and Hurricane back after landing from the display, we were to park at the far end of the temporary parade ground to form a backdrop to the ceremony. As soon as we had parked, we climbed out and stood to one side with our BBMF ground crew to watch the event unfold as the RAF Leuchars pipe band marched on. The air commodore was yet to mount the dais which was just a large box with a step up to it and no rails, so it was vacant as the band marched towards it and turned to march back through their own ranks. Unfortunately, and much to our amusement, the bass drummer in the centre of the band couldn't see the dais over the large bass drum on his chest, marched into it and fell forward with his momentum rolling him onto the top of his drum on the dais, with neither his hands nor his feet in contact with the ground. As he flapped his arms and legs, the drum gracefully rotated through 90 degrees and then he fell off onto his back with the drum still on his chest, like the proverbial dead ant. Military people will always be amused when ceremony goes wrong, as long as you are not part of it, and the BBMF pilots and ground crew were now in fits of laughter.

Battle of Britain Events

In the late 1990s the RAF began a policy of holding dinners in the officers' messes at RAF stations in September to commemorate the Battle of Britain. The BBMF was increasingly asked, often at fairly short notice, to provide flypasts or displays at these evening events, usually during the pre-drinks before the dinner, with the audience being mainly RAF Officers in mess dress and their guests. These sorties would sometimes take in several venues and would often lead to landings virtually in the dark until we moved the published last landing times forward by thirty minutes to avoid it.

In September 1999 I took off from Coningsby on a sortie in Spitfire PR XIX PM631 to complete flypasts at the officers' messes at RAF Waddington, Staxton Wold, Fylingdales and Leeming, with a flypast at Masham, Yorkshire, thrown in. The landing would be at absolute last light at Leeming for a night stop, returning home the following day.

The final flypast of that evening at Leeming, in front of their officers' mess, was in the gathering dusk and must have looked spectacular. When I broke off to land it was virtually dark. I had sensibly turned on the Spitfire's limited cockpit lighting before take off expecting this and it was just enough to see the air speed indicator and the engine instruments. In the darkness the brightly-coloured flickering flames from the banks of six exhaust stubs down each side of the nose, which are not visible in daylight, were almost mesmerising. With every movement of the throttle they danced and flickered, changing colour and shape; it was really quite distracting.

When I had landed and was taxiing in it was very dark as I made my way around the peri-track to the hangar where the Spitfire would spend the night. As I approached the hangar, I passed a group of Northumberland University Air Squadron (NUAS) students who had been ejected from the mess because of the dinner that evening and so were having a barbeque and some cans of beer beside their squadron building. I waved from the cockpit as I passed in my burbling Spitfire, weaving the nose to see where I was going and spitting flames from the exhausts. I found my two BBMF ground crew, who had driven up from Coningsby, and I parked in front of the hangar under their direction. I ran the engine up for the magneto checks, with the sound reverberating off the hangar doors behind me, and then shut down. The sudden silence was shattering and I could hear the 'tink, tink' noise of the cooling exhausts. It was now pitch dark, and as I sat in the cockpit turning off all the switches, I became aware of another sound – clapping. As I peered into the darkness I spied the NUAS students, who had followed

291

me to my parking spot, applauding what they had seen. It was really very moving and hopefully for them it was inspiring. This was the same airfield where twenty-eight years earlier, as a young student pilot, I had watched Ray Hanna displaying a Spitfire, wondering if one day I might fly one. Now a group of new young student pilots, boys and girls, had just been watching me displaying a Spitfire at the same airfield. I climbed out, walked over to them, demanded a beer and answered their eager questions about what it was like to fly a Spitfire. When the BBMF ground crew were ready to push the Spitfire into the hangar there were plenty of willing helpers.

*****

On more than one occasion I displayed in front of the officers' mess at Coningsby during the pre-drinks for a mess dinner. As the mess was right next to the airfield, guests could walk a few yards across the grass to the edge of the taxiway to watch a full display over the airfield. Being home territory, there was a certain licence to make it a good display although the likely presence of high-ranking guests had to be balanced against that.

In September 2004 I was asked to fly an evening display prior to a Battle of Britain dinner at Coningsby attended by a large number of visiting USAF officers, headed up by USAF four-star General Ronald Keys. As the time to fly approached, 19:30, the wind was still blowing at 25 knots straight down the runway and the display line but on the limit for BBMF operations. Even taxiing to and from the runway could be difficult in such wind strengths. I decided not to fly the Baby Spitfire that I had originally intended to use, but Hurricane PZ865 instead, having asked the BBMF ground crew to prepare it as a back-up. The Hurricane would behave better on the ground in the strong wind.

This particular sortie, which I logged as ten minutes in my logbook, is just about the only time I ever flew what I could call a perfect sortie. Perfection was something that I spent my entire flying career striving towards but constantly failed to achieve. There was always some little error, something I didn't do perfectly or something I could have done better. This sortie probably went perfectly from start up to shut down simply because it was so short. I could not have displayed the Hurricane any better, especially making the necessary adjustments for the strong wind down the display line. I have to admit that for this special show I felt I had some leeway and I flew lower than normal, but exactly as I intended and well within my personal limits. The icing on the cake was a perfect landing at the end.

I subsequently received a personal letter from the RAF Coningsby Station Commander, Group Captain Mark Swan, who also flew the fighters with the BBMF and so knew what was involved. He thanked me for hosting the USAF General and officers at the BBMF and for my display, writing, 'Your Hurricane display was astonishingly skilful in the prevailing weather conditions and many experienced aircrew fully appreciated this.' It is certainly one that I have always remembered.

Hurricane Forced Landing

On 17 September 2000 I flew Hurricane LF363 in company with the Lancaster and a Spitfire, to conduct flypasts at West Runton on the north Norfolk coast, Norwich Cathedral and at Hempnall, Norfolk, on the way to an air display at Biggin Hill. The flypast at Hempnall was particularly poignant as we were to overfly St Margaret's Church in the village over the grave of Battle of Britain Hurricane pilot Sergeant John Lansdall on the sixtieth anniversary of his death. He had been shot down and killed over Kent by a Messerschmitt Bf 109 on 17 September 1940 whilst flying with 607 Squadron from Tangmere in West Sussex. He was 23-years-old when he died. At the churchyard, local people, ex-servicemen and members of the Air Training Corps were gathered to pay tribute to one of 'The Few', who was also one of their own. Our BBMF flypast was timed to follow the sounding of the 'Last Post' by a lone bugler.

As we climbed away from the low flypast over the church in close formation and I increased the power on the Merlin engine of my Hurricane it began to pop, bang and misfire alarmingly. My heart rate shot up. It seemed I had a significant engine problem and, as I didn't have much altitude, my options were distinctly limited. I moved out of formation and reduced the power to a setting that reduced the misfiring, but allowed me to continue climbing, and I transmitted a PAN emergency call on the radio, explaining my problem for the benefit of the other members of the formation and the Norwich air traffic controller whose frequency we were on. He immediately replied with a steer for Norwich Airport but, as that would have meant overflying the Norwich built-up area with an engine that I no longer trusted, I declined that offer. He then came back suggesting a diversion to Seething, a private airfield to the south east of Norwich. Seething hadn't featured in my pre-flight planning as a diversion but it sounded a good idea, as the engine continued to pop, bang and misfire. I set course towards it, gradually climbing to 3,000 feet which allowed a full precautionary forced-landing pattern to be flown, and being shadowed by the Spitfire, which was comforting. Once level at 3,000 feet, and with reduced power, the misfiring was less evident, but a precautionary forced landing still seemed the best option. The Lancaster crew provided me with the Seething radio frequency as my hands were rather full and I contacted them with my PAN emergency status, explaining the problem and requesting a diversion for a precautionary forced landing. Seething acknowledged my emergency and gave me the runway.

When I arrived overhead the runway it looked very short, so I asked how long it was. Back came the reply '800 metres'. The minimum runway length for the BBMF fighters was 2,400 feet so this was very close to that. Nonetheless, I had few other options. I reached the 'high key' position for the forced-landing pattern, set the throttle to just off the idle stop and began to glide down whilst lowering the undercarriage. When I tested the engine again, it once again popped and banged, so this definitely seemed the right thing to be doing and I knew I had to get it right as overshooting was not going to be possible. The seriousness of the situation focused my mind and brought out the best in my flying and I landed very near the beginning of the short runway and stopped about halfway down it, drama over. The Lancaster then appeared, crossing the far end of the runway, with the crew checking that I had got down safely. It and the Spitfire then left to continue to Biggin Hill, leaving me to sort out my own problems on the ground at Seething.

The flying club at Seething was very welcoming and people assisted me to get the Hurricane into a new hangar with an, as yet unfinished, turntable floor. One of the civilian pilots then kindly offered me a flight back to Coningsby in a Mooney four-seater light aircraft. He and a friend climbed in insisting that I took a front seat and subsequently that I flew it back to Coningsby and landed it there as they were concerned about landing over the cable which stretches across the runway. It seemed they thought that if I could fly a Hurricane I could fly anything, although I had to keep asking for speeds and how to operate things like the flaps. On the way I noticed that the horizontal situation indicator did not work. Apparently, it had been that way for some time. After my somewhat firm landing at Coningsby it suddenly sprang into life; they were delighted.

During the subsequent rectification of the Hurricane at Seething, the problem was found to have been caused by a faulty ignition harness. The Major never praised me in any way for my successful forced landing on a short runway and merely complained that he would have to take off from it to prove that the problem had been fixed.

Queen Mother's Funeral

On 9 April 2002 I was one of the two BBMF fighter pilots each flying a Spitfire on the wing of the Lancaster over the Queen Mother's funeral motorcade as it drove along the Mall after her funeral service at Westminster Abbey. When I was told that I would be flying in the BBMF formation for the occasion I felt enormously honoured to be involved in paying this special tribute to a marvellous lady. I flew Spitfire PR XIX PS915 in formation with the Lancaster, on its left wing, and the Major flew Spitfire PR XIX PM631 on the right wing.

We had an enthusiastic send-off (and subsequent greeting on our return) from a larger than normal crowd of all ages, gathered along the perimeter fence by the BBMF hangar at Coningsby, in some cases waving Union flags. On the flypast itself, my fighter pilot's view, flying in close formation, was restricted to the intricate details of the Lancaster's left side and occasional glimpses of the heavily built-up areas beyond it.

We had been told that the cavalcade would take exactly seven and a half minutes to drive from Westminster Abbey to the centre of the Mall and so our formation was released from our hold, near Fairlop Reservoir, as the hearse set off, to arrive seven and a half minutes later. In fact, on the day, it took nine and a quarter minutes for the vehicles to drive the short distance, significantly longer than planned. The result was that the BBMF formation arrived, exactly on time, over the Mall lined with crowds but missing the reason for us being there. The BBMF ground crewman in the Lancaster's rear turret told the crew in the cockpit that the motorcade was just turning into Admiralty Arch.

We two fighter pilots were blind to events below us and the first we knew of the difficulties was when the Lancaster crew, captained by Squadron Leader Stu Reid, transmitted on the radio something to the effect that 'We are going around again. Any objections?' The Major as the fighter leader asked why (a reasonable question and one I was also posing in my mind). The Lancaster crew replied with something like 'There was nothing in the Mall'. The air traffic controller and our operating authority agreed the decision and we turned around over London to make a second pass. On the re-attack the timing was perfect as the many pictures of the event published afterwards prove. I was told that the Queen looked up at us through the glass roof of her car as we passed over the top in tribute to her mother.

Having cleared London, the two Spitfires raced ahead of the Lancaster to land well before it. I thought that the Major sounded even more grumpy than usual when making radio calls during the flight home. When we had shut down after landing and I went to meet him at his aircraft he was fuming and shaking his head. 'That seemed to go well, with the re-attack,' I ventured. He clearly didn't think so and raged, 'but they missed the Mall.' Now I could see that, somewhat amusingly, a certain amount of confusion had set in. 'No, they said that there was nothing in the Mall first time round,' I explained. This revelation produced an instantly calmer and happier Major who had apparently misheard the radio transmission, something that was very easy to do in the ambient noise level of a Spitfire cockpit. It was a good thing that I had been able to correct his airborne perception of events before he met the Lancaster crew on their return.

In fact, the flypast had been a truly significant contribution to a most historic and memorable occasion and the Lancaster crew deserved due credit. It was an honour to be involved.

Almost Wheels-up

On 6 July 2002 I was very fortunate to avoid a wheels-up belly landing in Spitfire PR XIX PS915 at Ronaldsway Airport, on the Isle of Man. As I circled the airfield that day, the chances of inflicting damage on this precious Spitfire were looking disconcertingly high.

I had taken off from RAF Coningsby just over an hour earlier. After completing singleton flypasts at Woodhall Spa and the Yorkshire Air Museum at Elvington, I had joined up with a BBMF Hurricane and the Dakota for the transit across the Irish Sea to the Isle of Man for a display at the old, now disused, RAF Jurby airfield. When the Spitfire and Hurricane part of the display was complete, we left the Dakota behind and I led the Hurricane down the eastern side of the Isle of Man to Ronaldsway Airport where we were due to land for a night-stop on the Island. The weather was deteriorating as we flew south and Snaefell Mountain was in cloud as I followed the coast down and round to the airport.

We arrived at Ronaldsway in close formation and broke into the visual circuit. Rolling out downwind, I moved the undercarriage lever in the Spitfire towards the down position to lower the undercarriage as I had done hundreds of times before. Unlike the hundreds of times before, though, the lever jammed halfway and the undercarriage remained locked up. Suspecting that I may have moved the lever too quickly – a known problem – I re-selected up and then operated the lever towards down again, taking care to use the correct technique and to move it smoothly and slowly, but the lever refused to budge beyond the halfway point. I could actually feel the cable that withdraws the undercarriage up-locks stretching as I tried to force the lever rearwards towards the DOWN gate. It refused to move further. I put it back to the UP position. For now, the undercarriage was stuck up. I broke off the approach and started to circle the airfield to sort out the problem whilst the Hurricane landed.

In the Spitfire, to lower the undercarriage, the selector lever has to be moved forward from the UP gate and held forward for about two seconds so that the undercarriage is raised hydraulically off the mechanical up-locks. Then, when the lever is moved rearwards 'smoothly and smartly', to quote the advice in the *Pilot's Notes*, the up-lock pins are withdrawn by a cable. With the lever all the way back to the DOWN gate, the undercarriage is then lowered hydraulically and locked down.

Unknown to me, my aircraft was suffering a problem with the retractable tail-wheel jack (unique, with the BBMF Spitfires, to the PR XIXs). This, it transpired, had developed a leak across itself, past the seal from the up side to the down side, which was creating a sort of idling circuit in the aircraft's hydraulic system, reducing the hydraulic pressure available to lift the main undercarriage off the up-locks. As the weight of the gear was resting on the up-locks, the pins could not be mechanically withdrawn by the cable and the gear remained firmly locked up. The Spitfire's emergency undercarriage lowering system cannot be used either, unless the undercarriage lever is in the down position.

I was unaware of the exact cause of the problem at this point but carried out the landing-gear malfunctions drill in the Flight Reference Cards with the aim of reducing the effects of gravity on the system to relieve the weight on the up-locks.

As recommended, I dived the aircraft towards the ground, pitched up into a steep climb of about 60 degrees and then bunted using zero G over the top until I had a windscreen full of ground and had to pull out of the dive. Whilst I had zero G applied over the top of this manoeuvre, flying with my left hand, I tried to operate the undercarriage selector lever with my right hand. Several attempts at this produced no change to the situation and I was not being helped by the lowering cloud base which was restricting my room for manoeuvre.

I advised Ronaldsway Air Traffic Control (ATC) that I might have to execute a wheels-up landing on the grass beside the runway, having first jettisoned the cockpit canopy over the airfield. The ATC controller clearly did not want me crashing on his airfield and told me that they did not have a suitable area of grass and that I would have to go somewhere else. I responded that I had identified the ideal strip and would be going nowhere.

I had one last hope, which was that the expert BBMF ground crew, flying as passengers in the Dakota to service all three aircraft on the ground, might be able give me some advice when the Dak arrived at Ronaldsway and on the same radio frequency. Meanwhile, I kept trying the climb, bunt, dive manoeuvres to no effect and with increasing concern. Whilst I knew that a wheels-up landing could be potentially injurious to my precious self, I was surprised to discover that I was not actually worried or fearful for myself. Of far greater concern to me was the damage that I was about to inflict to this treasured and rare example of the nation's aviation heritage.

The Dakota came up on the tower frequency and I asked ATC for permission to speak to the crew. Permission granted, I explained my problem and asked for any expert advice that the technicians on board might be able to offer. After a short pause, back came the response from the BBMF airframe specialist on board, relayed by the Dakota navigator, 'You need to fly straight and level inverted and operate the lever.' 'Easy for you to say,' I replied, speaking my thoughts.

The BBMF does not normally permit the use of negative G on its historic aircraft. To conserve airframe fatigue, all aerobatic manoeuvres in the BBMF Spitfires and Hurricanes are flown with positive G applied. In addition, with Merlin-engine aircraft, the engine could falter under negative G. Fortunately, I was sitting behind a fuel-injected Griffon engine so that shouldn't be an issue, I hoped. However, having never before flown straight and level inverted in a Spitfire, I had no idea what minimum speed was required. The undercarriage limiting speed is 140 knots but if I rolled inverted at that speed would I have sufficient control authority to hold the nose up or would I go into an inverted dive, possibly with insufficient sky to roll the right way up and pull out? As the cloud base was now down to 1,000 feet, this seemed a distinct possibility. I decided that I would deliberately ignore the 140 knots limit on the undercarriage and fly at 180 knots which I thought would guarantee sufficient nose authority to hold level, inverted flight.

I positioned the Spitfire so that, if the engine did stop whilst I was upside down, I would be able to glide to the runway or my chosen piece of grass beside it. Then, flying at 180 knots and at about 800 feet, I rolled upside down and pushed forward hard on the control column spade grip with both hands to hold the nose up in level flight. The engine grumbled but kept running. Hanging in the straps, I reached for the undercarriage lever with my right hand. Relief and gratitude surged through me as the lever slid easily into the

DOWN gate. The negative G had caused the undercarriage inside the wings to fall away from the up-locks under gravity and the Spitfire's undercarriage was now lowering beautifully. Actually, it was going up as we were upside down.

The undercarriage locked down and, with all the correct cockpit indications, I rolled the right way up. It was then simply a case of turning finals and landing. It was now two hours since I had taken off and there was not much fuel left when I finally touched down on Ronaldsway's runway.

The successful outcome was an enormous relief to me, obviously, but also to the many other interested parties and observers on the Island, to those in the BBMF Dakota and especially to the Ronaldsway air traffic controllers who didn't want me making a mess of their airfield. I don't mind admitting that, as I would not be flying the next day, I enjoyed a few beers in Castle Douglas that night.

Five days later I collected the Spitfire from Ronaldsway after it had been fixed by the hard-working BBMF ground crew. I gave them, and the people at the airport who had assisted the BBMF with the Spitfire's rectification, a low, fast fly by, as I departed to return PS915 home to Coningsby unscathed.

I remain eternally grateful to the BBMF technician, Corporal Clive O'Connell, on board the Dakota, who with his expert knowledge of exactly how the Spitfire undercarriage functioned, provided that vital piece of advice to fly straight and level inverted. All I had to do was make it happen.

Officer Commanding BBMF

In 2003, after the Tornado F.3 Operational Conversion Unit had moved to RAF Leuchars, I became a full-time BBMF pilot in preparation for taking over as the Officer Commanding from the Major when he retired. This coincided with the runway at Coningsby being dug up and refurbished before the new Eurofighter Typhoons moved in, so for the 2003 display season the BBMF aircraft were based at RAF Barkston Heath. During 2003 the Major provided a gradual handover and all sorts of useful advice. I began to bring the BBMF into the twenty-first century with office computers, much to the Major's annoyance. I also planned the Flight's 2004 display season. as I would then be in charge.

In January 2004 I took over command of the BBMF. This was '
my final tour with the RAF, another flying tour so I could say th'
never had a ground tour. I couldn't think of a better or a more r
way to complete thirty-five years of regular service and I wa^c
have been selected for the post. I had already been a volun'

with the BBMF for eight display seasons and I felt ready to take on the responsibilities of OC BBMF.

Command of the Flight brought with it the responsibility for the eleven historic and priceless aircraft, overseeing the team of twenty-five aircraft technicians under the Warrant Officer Engineering Officer and all the necessary administration for the unit with only an Operations Officer, an Operations Assistant and an Administrative Assistant to assist. I also became responsible for all the flying supervision on the unit and managing the currency and training of all the volunteer aircrew who flew with the Flight, a task complicated by the fact that all the other aircrew were in other full-time posts elsewhere. In addition, by its very nature, the BBMF was a high-profile unit and I was frequently called upon to host VIP and VVIP visits and to deal with the press and media on a regular basis. Meanwhile, I continued to fly and to conduct the air tests on the BBMF fighter aircraft and to train others to fly them, whilst also being the BBMF Chipmunk QFI. It was, and still is, one hell of a job for a squadron leader.

When Squadron Leader Paul Day, the 'Major', retired after forty-three years of service with the RAF he wanted no fuss and no retirement party, which was typical of him. His wife, Judy, and I managed to secretly arrange the event he didn't want, under the excuse of him attending a low-key dinner with just the BBMF officers and wives at the nearby Petwood Hotel. In fact, we invited many of his old friends and colleagues, all sworn to secrecy, some of whom had subsequently reached very high rank, so it was quite a high-powered occasion. The Major was genuinely surprised and I think impressed. In a letter he wrote to me after the event he said:

> I write as a good loser should to thank you for the uniquely memorable event you organised to mark my retirement last Saturday. It certainly outstripped my 'cheap as chips' option. I am particularly grateful for the chance to give a no-notice audience-initiated rewrite of a speech which I had not rehearsed and which I had little intention of delivering! I am encouraged that I have nothing to teach you about underhanded deceit!

Spitfire Forced Landing

On 30 May 2004 BBMF Spitfire PR XIX PM631 and I were both fortunate to escape unscathed from a potentially dangerous incident. After taking off from RAF Coningsby in company with the BBMF Lancaster and a Hurricane, our three-ship formation completed flypasts at Conington, Mildenhall and Leiston before arriving at Southend for the seafront air display. We had been airborne for one hour and forty-five minutes and we were just completing the display at Southend when, unbeknown to me at the time, an oil pipe detached in PM631's engine bay. As I flew the Spitfire, in company with the Hurricane, down the display line to join up with the Lancaster, PM631 was streaming oil. The air traffic controller on the beachfront noticed what he thought was smoke coming from the Spitfire and transmitted an immediate warning to this effect on the display radio frequency. I checked the engine instruments and, particularly, the oil-pressure and temperature indications inside PM631's cockpit but could see nothing amiss. As I joined up on the Lancaster's port wing, the BBMF ground crew manning the bomber's turrets, alerted by the radio call, saw that PM631's starboard side was black with oil. The groundcrew informed the Lancaster captain, Flight Lieutenant Andy Sell, who rolled out halfway round the turn for the planned final three-ship fly-by, pointing us straight at Southend airfield, whilst the Lancaster navigator transmitted to me on the radio, 'Spitfire you have a serious oil leak.'

I broke out of formation, again checking for any adverse engine indications but seeing none. It subsequently transpired that the oil leak was on the return side of the Griffon engine's oil system which meant that the oil-pressure indications would remain normal in the cockpit until the engine was almost empty of oil, at which point the oil pressure would fall instantly to zero. Without delay, I positioned for a precautionary forced landing at Southend airfield, via a 'low key' point at 1,500 feet, declaring an emergency on the radio. Abeam the threshold of the runway, I throttled the engine to idle, lowered the undercarriage and started to glide down in a curving final turn. The oil-pressure and temperature indications were still normal. I began to wonder whether it was a lot of fuss about nothing and concentrated on judging the glide approach correctly. Rolling wings level at 200 feet on the approach to land, I checked the oil pressure again and this time it was zero. Not wishing to be distracted from making a correctly judged glide approach, I elected to allow the engine to continue running at idle whilst I concentrated on the landing, and brought the aircraft to a halt before shutting the engine down.

The Griffon engine had run at idle for about a minute with zero oil pressure. The subsequent strip of the engine showed that the main bearings had just begun to show signs of failure and they had to be replaced; there was no other damage to the engine. This had been a very serious incident and both good teamwork and luck had played significant parts in the successful outcome. It was most fortunate that the failure had occurred so close to an airfield, as the engine had been entirely drained of oil in about two minutes. In other circumstances this failure would have led, at best, to an off-airfield wheels-up forced landing in less than ideal circumstances with the potential for significant damage to the aircraft, not to mention the possibility of some to me. Unfortunately, the BBMF did not have a spare, serviceable Griffon engine that year, so PM631 had to be recovered to Coningsby by road with the wings removed. It played no further part in the 2004 display season but was repaired in time for the following year.

Lancaster Poppy Drops

I was most fortunate to fly a Spitfire in formation with the BBMF Lancaster on two occasions when one million paper poppies were dropped from the Lancaster's bomb bay as part of high-profile ceremonial events.

The first of these was during the D Day sixtieth anniversary commemorations in June 2004. These D Day anniversary events demanded a massive effort from all on the BBMF, both behind the scenes and in the limelight. Just loading the one million paper poppies into the Lancaster's cavernous bomb bay by hand took the groundcrew a couple of days. The end result was a series of high-profile successes with live TV coverage of the BBMF display at Portsmouth over the commemorative fleet's departure to Normandy, the poppy drop from the Lancaster over a ship carrying D Day veterans to Normandy (the first for nine years and only the third in BBMF history), a para drop from the Dakota, and a flypast for no fewer than seventeen heads-of-state, plus numerous assorted royalty, at Arromanches, on the D Day anniversary itself, 6 June.

Due to the number of high-profile and VVIP guests that would be attending the ceremonies in Normandy, including HM The Queen and the President of the USA amongst others, the French set up strictly-controlled and heavily-defended airspace over Normandy with full radar coverage, fighter combat aircraft patrols with armed jets and surface-to-air missile systems. Entering the airspace required all the correct notifications, flight plans, clearances and permissions. We set off across the English Channel on 5 June with the Lancaster and two actual D Day Spitfires. I was flying Spitfire IX MK356, which had flown over the invasion beaches sixty years previously. We were tasked to fly past the cruise ship the MV *Van Gogh* off the Normandy coast, to drop one million poppies for the veterans aboard her, and we thought we had all the necessary permissions in place. We were therefore somewhat concerned to find that once we were talking to the French controller he didn't seem to know anything about us or what we were tasked to do. In the other Spitfire, D Day veteran Vb AB910, we had Wing Commander Paul Willis, a fluent French speaker, so we put him on the radio to try to sort things out in French. It didn't seem to help. I then spotted a French Mirage 2000 jet fighter, fully armed with missiles that had intercepted our formation over the sea and was turning in on the Lancaster. I told the Lancaster crew on the radio. Things were beginning to look serious. The Mirage sat alongside the Lancaster for a few moments, at a very high angle of attack, and then powered away, only to be replaced by a second Mirage which did the same. The second one only cleared us just in time as we tightened into close formation for the flypast over the MV *Van Gogh*.

When the Lancaster opened its bomb-bay doors and the red poppies streamed out, it was as if it had haemorrhaged. The poppies made a stream of bloodlike red, some 1,500 yards behind the bomber and then fluttered gently down. It was spectacular from my seat in the Spitfire cockpit and must have been very moving for those below on the ship, including some 450 D Day veterans as the sound of our engines receded.

When we had landed at our planned operating base of le Havre, I telephoned our RAF French liaison officer from the British Embassy and asked why we had been intercepted by live-armed French jets. He told us that the pilots just wanted to take a look at the BBMF aircraft. We then discovered that a slight language problem with the French had failed to reveal the lack of a fuel bowser at le Havre; there was only a static fuel pump in a cul-de-sac location. This was fine for the fighters, which could easily be pushed to the fuel pump, but it was going to make refuelling the Lancaster and Dakota virtually impossible. The result was that the Lancaster and the Dakota had to be manhandled into position and out again, twice each, to refuel. Such an aircraft push/pull would normally be a charity fund-raising event, but here it was a necessity.

The following day we flew a three-ship flypast with the Lancaster and the two D Day Spitfires over Juno Beach, where some 5,000 spectators, including 1,000 Canadian veterans of D Day were gathered to be addressed by HM The Queen at the Juno Beach Centre. In a letter I received later, Canadian Major General Rohmer wrote: 'Your D Day flypast at Juno Beach was a "show stopper". It was executed exactly on time with excellent formation precision. Her Majesty was much impressed.'

As we routed back to le Havre from the flypast, the two Spitfires were flying 2,000 feet higher than the Lancaster, like a fighter escort, when the Lancaster was intercepted by an Armée de l'Air Tucano aircraft from a low-speed combat air patrol. The pilot clearly hadn't seen the higher Spitfire escorts but turned in on the Lancaster and sat in formation with it for a few minutes. When it broke away, high and to the Lancaster's left side, it was climbing up towards me and, as the pilot didn't seem to have seen me in Spitfire MK356, there was a potential collision hazard, so I waggled my wings to attract his attention. It was quite obvious when he suddenly spotted me and turned in on me as if positioning for a guns' attack. My fighter pilot instinct took over and I couldn't resist breaking hard into him, forcing him to overshoot and then reversing so that I was in a shooting position behind him. I was thinking, 'You don't want to mess with a Spitfire, Sonny Jim.'

*****

The second Lancaster poppy drop that I was privileged to be involved with took place over the Mall and Buckingham Palace for the sixtieth anniversary commemorations of the end of the Second World War, held on the so-called National Commemoration Day in July 2005. Only three days earlier there had been a terrorist bombing atrocity in London, when four suicide bombers detonated explosives on the London Underground and on a bus, killing fifty-two people and injuring hundreds more. Wonderfully, the British people refused to be cowed by these tragic occurrences and thousands – 250,000 in fact – turned out for the celebrations in London on 10 July, including the Royal Family, led by HM The Queen and the Duke of Edinburgh, who defied the threat of terrorism and rode down the Mall leading the parade of Standards in an open-top Range Rover.

The flypast down the Mall and over Buckingham Palace consisted of nineteen historic aircraft, in five waves, taking off from Duxford during the Flying Legends Air Show. They included the BBMF Dakota and the BBMF Lancaster with me in Spitfire IIa P7350 on its left wing and Squadron Leader Al Pinner in Hurricane LF363 on its right wing. The other aircraft were all civilian-owned historic aircraft and all twin- or multi-engine types as the CAA will not permit overflight of London by civilian-registered single-engine aircraft. The BBMF Hurricanes and Spitfires are military aircraft and the permission for them to overfly London comes from a high level within the RAF. The Lancaster carried a special guest on board, 82-year-old Marshal of the Royal Air Force Sir Michael Beetham GCB CBE DFC AFC, who had flown a full tour of bombing operations in Lancasters during the Second World War and who had flown a Lancaster over London as part of the 1946 Victory Parade.

The Lancaster was flown by Squadron Leader Stu Reid and his crew who positioned perfectly for the poppy drop and released the one million poppies exactly on time. Once again I experienced the amazing sight, from my privileged position in formation on the Lancaster's wing, of the big bomber apparently haemorrhaging as the bright red poppies poured out of the bomb bay. The people on the ground heard the Merlin engine noise recede and then silence fell as the poppies drifted down. It made brilliant TV and good photos, too.

Typhoons

In September 2005 I was tasked to execute a flypast for the RAF Coningsby Annual Formal Inspection in Spitfire IIa P7350 with two Eurofighter Typhoons in close formation on my wingtips. This was the first time that I had Typhoons in close formation with me.

The requirement was to overfly the Air Officer Commanding on time to the second and exactly on track, to cross directly over him as he took the salute from the dais with the guard of honour presenting arms. I flew at 180 knots to give the Typhoon pilots a better chance of being comfortable in close formation with me. I set up a timing hold to the south of the airfield some two minutes out and the Typhoons joined me and slid up into close formation.

The Typhoon is obviously an aircraft that inspires confidence in its pilots and they fly very close formation. It was amazing to look out to my left and right, across those Spitfire wingtips, to see the two Typhoons tucked in alongside at high angles of attack, noses up in the air, looking like cobras about to strike. It was special to be flying the oldest aircraft in RAF service with two of the newest in close formation with me. It also seemed strange that, with all the Typhoon's state-of-the-art navigation systems, it was me with nothing more than a map and a stopwatch who was having to make the navigation work to the second. I managed to achieve it and I have a photo to prove it.

Battle of Britain 65th Anniversary

One of the most remarkable experiences I had during my time flying with the BBMF was at a special event at RAF Northolt, on 15 September 2005, to commemorate the sixty-fifth anniversary of the Battle of Britain. The event was attended by more than eighty surviving members of 'The Few', including some from Australia, Canada, New Zealand and the USA, as well as being honoured by the presence of HRH The Duke of Edinburgh.

The BBMF was tasked to be present on the ground with Battle of Britain Spitfire IIa P7350 which was to provide a static backdrop at a gala dinner to be held in a large hangar at Northolt that evening. Meanwhile, Spitfire Vb AB910 and Hurricane II LF363 were to provide a flypast. We met many of the veterans during the late afternoon as they were drawn to our aircraft, survivors of the types they once flew in anger. Then, prior to the gala dinner, there was a sunset ceremony parade outside the hangar with the pageantry provided by the RAF Regiment's Queen's Colour Squadron. We completed the flypast over the general salute to HRH The Duke of Edinburgh, making two passes, with me in Spitfire AB910, leading Wing Commander Russ Allchorne in Hurricane LF363, followed immediately by a Eurofighter Typhoon from Coningsby.

On landing at Northolt from the flypast, we two BBMF fighter pilots were invited to attend the dinner in our black BBMF flying suits as there was no time to change into dinner jackets and black ties, which was the dress for everyone else. I was seated at a table which included Battle of Britain fighter pilots Tony Pickering and Ken Mackenzie, who had both flown Hurricanes during the Battle, and I sat next to Warrant Officer Luiz 'Bert' Flower, a wireless operator/air gunner on Bristol Blenheims with 248 Squadron during the Battle. Wartime films of Battle of Britain action and people were being projected onto the inside walls of the hangar during the dinner and, at one point, Tony Pickering exclaimed with obvious surprise, 'That's me.' To be part of it all and to dine in the presence of so many of 'The Few' was an amazing experience and I felt very privileged.

Queen's 80th Birthday Flypast

On 17 June 2006 I was back over London in a Hurricane as part of a BBMF formation in the flypast for the official eightieth birthday of HM The Queen.

Just a few days before, I had notched up 500 hours of flying on the BBMF fighters which felt like a milestone.

Following the normal format, after Trooping the Colour, the Queen and the Royal Family appeared on the balcony of Buckingham Palace to watch the RAF flypast in her honour. The flypast consisted of forty-nine aircraft, with the BBMF formation leading and eight further sections behind with the Red Arrows at the rear. The BBMF formation comprised the Lancaster, flanked by two Spitfires and two Hurricanes. I flew in Hurricane LF363. It had been many years since four single-engine piston fighter aircraft had been seen together over London. It was to be the final time that I was to do it.

End of an Era

In early 2006 I reached my normal retirement date from the RAF at the age of 55. I handed over command of the BBMF to Squadron Leader Al Pinner but as he did not yet have the required minimum of four years of BBMF flying, I had been asked to stay on for an extra year beyond my normal retirement date as a full-time reservist squadron leader. I was needed to act as the BBMF Fighter Leader (and also as the RAF Coningsby Station Flight Safety Officer) which, of course, I was very happy to do. As far as the system was concerned, I was retiring from regular service after thirty-five years, which was true, and I received various official and unofficial correspondence about it. It was nice to get the letters. I have known other officers who left the service after very many years and got virtually no thanks or recognition at all. It is sometimes said that it's the only job where, when you leave, you have to hand your watch back rather than being given one as a leaving present.

*****

I spent some time during my extra year as a full-time reservist writing new Aircrew Manuals for the BBMF fighter aircraft types. The wartime *Pilot's Notes* were no longer accurate and Aircrew Manuals in the modern style did not exist for the BBMF aircraft until I wrote them. This was something I could do for the Flight for the future and the manuals were subsequently approved, produced and updated by Boscombe Down Handling Squadron. In addition, I played a full part in the BBMF 2006 display season and made sure to provide the best possible handover of my remaining duties and all that I knew to those who were taking over the reins at the BBMF.

My full-time service and my eleven years with the BBMF were coming to an end at the close of the BBMF 2006 display season. In September, my last month with the BBMF before retirement, I was offered a flight in a two-seat Eurofighter Typhoon with Flight Lieutenant 'Parky' Parkinson who was just about to join the BBMF as a fighter pilot. The Typhoon was great fun, nice to fly and the performance was awesome, like the Lightning but even better. It was a great way to round off a career as a fighter pilot.

On 23 September I had my last flight in a Hurricane, carrying out a couple of solo flypasts and a display for 3 Squadron at Coningsby. My final flight and final display in a Spitfire were planned to be at the annual Lincolnshire's Lancaster Association (LLA) Day at RAF Coningsby, a small air show for members of the Association which traditionally ends each BBMF display season. I flew in clipped-wing Spitfire IX MK356 on a sortie that took in a flypast with the Lancaster and a Hurricane over Flixton in Norfolk, some air-to-air photography, a flypast over the LLA Day event at Coningsby with six fighters in formation behind the Lancaster and my individual Spitfire display.

I am the first to admit that for my final display I broke a few rules that day. Some people who saw it say that I flew between the tall trees or that I rocked the light stanchions with my prop wash; these were obviously visual illusions or simply exaggerations. It was the best fun though, licensed hooliganism (well almost licensed). When I taxied in and shut down outside the BBMF hangar, the crowd of enthusiastic and knowledgeable LLA members were applauding. I stood up in the cockpit and kissed the Spitfire before climbing out. Meeting me outside the cockpit was long-serving BBMF technician Corporal Nigel 'Sticky' Bunn, a harsh critic of pilots' and aircrew performances. 'That was fantastic,' he said. Now that was praise indeed.

*****

Although I was not due to retire officially until February 2007, I had accumulated so much untaken and carried-over annual leave, terminal leave and resettlement course time that I effectively finished work in October 2006.

I had already decided that in retirement I would become a volunteer guide with the BBMF Visitor Centre and I started straightaway, the first ever ex-OC BBMF to become a guide. I was well versed in the history and associated stories of the BBMF historic aircraft and had become very used to showing all sorts of people around the aircraft in the BBMF hangar, so this seemed a natural progression. No training was required. Eventually, I also became the editor for all of the BBMF publications and the Flight's historian, providing the research for new colour schemes for the BBMF aircraft when they were repainted, as well as other historical background information

As soon as I finished flying with the BBMF, I started flying Grob Tutor training aircraft as a volunteer with the Air Experience Flight at RAF Cranwell, becoming a Volunteer Reservist flying officer when my full-time reservist status finally ceased in February 2007.

*****

Being a volunteer reservist, permitted to fly RAF aircraft, led to an unexpected recall to the BBMF in May 2007. The Flight was celebrating its fiftieth anniversary that year and put on a special show and air display at Duxford with all its aircraft flown into Duxford, a remarkable achievement by the BBMF engineers. The OC BBMF, Squadron Leader Al Pinner, wanted to fly all seven of the Flight's fighter aircraft in the display, but with only five fighter pilots on the strength, he needed two more. It was agreed that he could recall Squadron Leader Ian 'Shiney' Simmons, who had ten years' experience with the BBMF as a fighter pilot and had left at the end of the 2005 display season. He was still serving and flying in the RAF as a flying instructor. I was recalled as a volunteer reservist flying officer.

During April Al gave us both a dual check in one of the BBMF Chipmunks, some further Chipmunk refresher flying and then the Flying Ability Test, which all amounted to five hours Chipmunk flying and more than the minimum number of tail-wheel landings required by the rules. Al then went through the pre-season 'fighter quiz' with us, covering all the necessary information on the fighter aircraft and the rules. We were word perfect as we had been doing it for years; indeed I had written the quiz and we were both well prepared. Halfway through, Al realised that he was wasting his time quizzing us and gave up.

Then we each had a Spitfire re-familiarisation sortie; mine was thirty minutes in Spitfire Vb AB910. On the next trip I flew AB910 in a three-ship formation from Coningsby to Duxford, with Al leading, during which we practised close formation. Two days later, on 5 May 2007, I flew Spitfire AB910 in a seven-ship formation of the BBMF fighter aircraft behind the

Lancaster and then with just the fighters, wheeling around over Duxford at the special BBMF fiftieth anniversary air show. It was a remarkable and entirely unexpected thing to be doing and when I landed it was a case of 'They think it's all over. It is now.' That really was it, my last flight in a Spitfire.

My wife, Elaine, had flown to Duxford in the BBMF C-47 Dakota and was there to watch my final display and joined me at the special party held that evening, in a marquee at Duxford, for the fiftieth anniversary of the BBMF.

Shiney and I flew back to Coningsby the following day, not in Spitfires, but in the Flight's two Chipmunks, after I had led him on a low-level close-formation flypast at Duxford.

Chapter 13

Volunteer Reservist

Retirement from full-time service with the RAF did not mean that I wanted to stop flying, nor that my flying career with the service was to come to an end. When I finished flying with the BBMF, I immediately started on the Grob Tutor training aircraft as a volunteer with the Air Experience Flight (AEF) at RAF Cranwell, initially in my existing rank as a squadron leader. When my full-time reservist status finally ended, in February 2007, I became a volunteer reservist flying officer.

It was fortunate that one of the flight commanders at No. 7 AEF was Phil Owen who had served with me on 19 Squadron in Germany in the mid-1970s, flying Lightnings. He had retired from regular service as a group captain and dropped three ranks to become a full-time reservist QFI to continue flying. He was very happy to let me join his AEF at Cranwell. Three days after what I believed was my last flight with the BBMF, in a Spitfire, I flew my first with the AEF in a Grob Tutor, the RAF's elementary training aircraft of the time.

The Grob 115E Tutor T.1 had replaced the RAF's Scottish Aviation Bulldogs in 1999. The Tutor fleet was owned and maintained under contract by a civilian company, Babcock. It was a pooled fleet, providing elementary flying training (EFT) for the Army Air Corps, Royal Navy Fleet Air Arm and the RAF and also equipped fifteen University Air Squadrons and twelve AEFs. The aircraft carried British civilian registrations. The Tutor was an all-composite single-piston-engine training aircraft with a fixed tricycle undercarriage and side-by-side seating with a large cockpit canopy providing an excellent view. It was fully aerobatic with limits of 6G to minus 3G. It made an ideal AEF aircraft to provide air experience for air cadets. It was fun to fly and you could do some quite fancy aerobatics in it.

Within a couple of weeks I was flying air cadets on air experience sorties. These were short flights, usually of about twenty minutes duration and the pilots would normally remain in the cockpit to fly four or five

311

cadets one after the other. It was quite common to fly ten or even twelve cadets in a day. The cadets varied enormously in their appetite for flying and their reaction to the environment but, almost without exception, they left the cockpit with enhanced self-esteem and confidence, and usually with a big grin. I felt I was paying back the start I had been given in aviation as an air cadet myself.

*****

In September 2007 I was given the opportunity to take on the role of flight commander for 7 AEF at Cranwell in a job-share arrangement with Phil Owen, working alternate weeks Wednesday to Sunday. I had to apply formally and be interviewed and selected for the post in competition with other applicants but I was successful.

Having been selected, I needed to ratify my QFI ticket on the Tutor and so I completed a short refresher course with the Central Flying School at Cranwell in September, resulting in a competent-to-instruct QFI qualification on the Tutor. I was also promoted to flight lieutenant (again). I had held three ranks that year, in the order squadron leader, flying officer and flight lieutenant. I then helped to run the Flight, as one of the two flight commanders, for a year, from October 2007 to October 2008. It was very easy working with Phil in the job-share arrangement.

At the end of the twelve-month period I returned to volunteer reservist status, but kept my flight lieutenant rank and also retained my QFI ticket on the Tutor. I often converted new AEF staff pilots to the Tutor and I conducted many dual checks. I also instructed student pilots on the co-located East Midlands University Air Squadron and even student pilots on the EFT course at Cranwell. There were various occasions when circumstances required me to step back into the flight commander role for short periods. As a volunteer, I usually flew with the AEF on two days most weeks and generally achieved around 120 hours flying each year.

*****

On 23 August 2012, when I was 61 years old and had forty-one years of RAF flying behind me, there was a sting in the tail of my long career in aviation. I was nearing the end of a one-hour Convex 2 conversion sortie for a new AEF staff pilot, Squadron Leader Paul 'Mufti' Smith. I had previously had a hand in training Mufti when he went through the Tornado F.3 OCU course and now he was a Typhoon pilot. We had been beating the visual circuit at Cranwell for the previous thirty minutes, had just completed a touch-and-go on the grass runway and were climbing up for our final low-level circuit at 500 feet. Everything had been completely normal up to this point.

As we were levelling off at 500 feet, with Mufti flying the aircraft, without any warning and for no apparent reason, there was an extremely loud bang, followed by very severe, lumpy and loud vibration and a significant loss of power. In the split seconds that followed, my thoughts were 'What the f***?' and 'This can't be happening to me'; but I immediately took control, set the aircraft into a glide and declared a Mayday, stating my intention to force land into a field beyond the A17 road. The noise and the intense vibration were almost creating a sensory overload but I was not surprised to find myself thinking and acting calmly and quickly. It was fortunate that the field straight ahead was ideal, with cut stubble, ruts in the right direction and a fairly firm surface (up until about a week before it still had uncut crops in it) and it was directly into wind.

I was now very much focused and prioritising the flying of the aircraft and the execution of a good landing and I did not let completing drills interfere with that. My hands were occupied with trimming, using the flaps and just flying the aircraft. With my training from my BBMF flying drummed into me, I used the option of bringing the RPM lever fully back, setting the propeller pitch to fully coarse, to optimise the gliding range. The total time from the initial failure to touchdown in the field was probably only about forty seconds. The result was that I didn't get the engine shut down until on the landing roll. During the glide down to land the banging, crashing and vibration were still present, and at about 300 feet the oil-filler cap flew open and the dipstick flew out. If we had any doubt up until now that this was a mechanical failure, it was now confirmed. Both Mufti and I tightened our shoulder straps, as neither of us was expecting a good outcome and we braced for the landing.

I used full flap to minimise the touchdown speed and landing roll. I had always been aware that landing a tricycle undercarriage aircraft on a rough field had the potential to break off the nose wheel. I had pre-determined that if I ever had to do it I would land in a tail-down attitude, as slow as possible, holding the nose wheel off. As it turned out, the landing was lovely, one of my best, on the mainwheels with the nose wheel held off until it had to be lowered onto the ground, after which I kept full back stick to keep it unloaded. The aircraft stopped without the use of brakes and without further incident (in fact some soil had built up against the left wheel and spat and it wasn't going to roll any further). When it became apparent that we had got away with it, Mufti said to me 'Good job mate' and when we were stopped I turned to him; we were both smiling with relief and I said 'Bloody Hell! That was quite exciting for a moment.' I made the cockpit safe, we unstrapped and, when we were standing on the wing walkways, we shook hands across the cockpit, having just shared a moment. Then, wandering round to the front of the aircraft to check the damage whilst awaiting the crash crews, we found that one of the three propeller blades had sheared off near the root and there was a large hole in the propeller spinner, caused, it transpired, by the blade counterweight flying off. Mufti took some pictures of me and the broken propeller with his phone as by now we were both feeling slightly euphoric.

This incident caused a temporary suspension of Tutor flying until early October. I was subsequently awarded a Green Endorsement for my logbook. The citation, signed by the Air Officer Commanding 22 (Training) Group, described the incident in detail and went on to say:

> An engine failure immediately after take off is one of the most demanding emergencies in a light aircraft. Flight Lieutenant Rowley displayed an outstanding degree of professionalism and composure throughout the incident, in the highest traditions of the Royal Air Force. His swift and decisive actions, combined with his excellent aircraft handling skills, enabled a safe and successful landing.

It seemed that, even this far into a long flying career, my mettle was still being tested and it proved that aviation is no respecter of age or experience. I was just glad that once again I had measured up.

In January 2013 an almost identical failure and incident occurred on another Grob Tutor at Cranwell with, fortunately, another successful forced landing in a field off the airfield. This time the inquiry determined the exact cause and the result was the fitting of a new composite propeller to the Tutors before flying resumed in July 2014 after a much more prolonged grounding of the fleet.

*****

I continued to fly the Tutor with No. 7 AEF for a total of just over nine years, until December 2015, when I was approaching my 65th birthday.

The RAF regulations prevented pilots over the age of 65 from flying as the only pilot in command of an aircraft, due to a perceived increase in the risks of suffering health problems in the air, such as a stroke or heart attack. I knew that at the age of 65 my RAF flying days would come to an end and I was resigned to that.

When the end came and I finally hung up my flying gloves, I had flown just short of 1,200 flying hours on the Grob Tutor as a volunteer reservist pilot. I had also flown 1,570 cadets on air experience sorties, more than paying back the start I had been given in my career. I had been flying RAF aircraft for more than forty-four uninterrupted years, I had never had a ground tour and I had accrued over 8,500 hours in the air, all, as I like to tell people, in aircraft that I could turn upside down. I had been extremely privileged to have had the opportunities to fly such iconic aircraft as the Hunter, Lightning, Hurricane and Spitfire and to have experienced all that my long career in military aviation allowed.

Now it was time to stop. I knew that I was lucky to be alive and to be fit and healthy. In truth, especially in the early years when accident rates were so much higher, I hadn't expected to survive to this point and to be able to claim the same number of landings as take offs. I was, indeed I am, proud of that fact. I know that an element of that achievement was due to professionalism, skill, determination and even a little courage; but I also know that a greater part of it was down to sheer luck.

Appendix 1

Record of Service

Squadron Leader Clive Rowley MBE

Dec 1970 - Jun 1971	Officer Cadet Training Unit RAF Henlow	Officer Training
Sep 1971 - Aug 1972	No. 3 FTS RAF Leeming	Basic Flying Training
Oct 1972 - Mar 1973	No. 4 FTS RAF Valley	Advanced Flying Training
Apr 1973 - Aug 1973	229 OCU RAF Chivenor	Tactical Weapons Unit
Sep 1973 - Jan 1974	226 OCU (65 Squadron) RAF Coltishall	Lightning OCU
Jan 1974 - Jan 1977	19(F) Squadron RAF Gutersloh	Squadron pilot (Lightning)
Feb 1977 - Jul 1977	CFS RAF Cranwell & RAF Leeming	QFI course (Bulldog)
Aug 1977 - Nov 1978	MASUAS RAF Woodvale	UAS QFI (Bulldog)
Nov 1978 - Oct 1979	LUAS RAF Woodvale	UAS CFI (Bulldog)
Nov 1979 - Dec 1980	CFS RAF Woodvale	Standards QFI (Bulldog)
Jan 1981- Jun 1981	No 1 TWU (234 Sqn) RAF Brawdy	TWU course (Hawk T.1)
Jul 1981 - Feb 1984	No 2 TWU (63 Sqn) RAF Chivenor	TWU staff (Hawk T.1A)

Feb 1984 - Jun 1984	LTF RAF Binbrook	Lightning refresher course
Jun 1984 - Dec 1984	XI Sqn RAF Binbrook	Squadron pilot (Lightning)
Jan 1985 - Feb 1986	5 Sqn RAF Binbrook	Dep Flt Cdr (Lightning)
Feb 1986 - Apr 1987	LTF RAF Binbrook	OC LTF (Lightning)
Nov 1987 - Mar 1991	5 Sqn RAF Coningsby	Flt Cdr (Tornado F.3)
Apr 1991 - Sep 1995	Tornado F.3 OEU RAF Coningsby	Trials pilot (Tornado F.3)
Sep 1995 - Mar 2003	56(R) Sqn (F.3 OCU) RAF Coningsby	Instructor (Tornado F.3)
Oct 1995 - Jan 2004	BBMF RAF Coningsby	BBMF fighter pilot
Jan 2004 - Jan 2006	BBMF RAF Coningsby	OC BBMF
Feb 2006 - Oct 2006	BBMF RAF Coningsby (FTRS)	BBMF Fighter Leader
Oct 2006-Dec 2015	7 AEF RAF Cranwell	VR AEF pilot (Tutor)

Appendix 2

Flying Hours

Squadron Leader Clive Rowley MBE

Hunting/BAC Jet Provost T.3 and T.5	162
Hawker Hunter T.7, F.6, F.6A and FGA.9	122
BAC Lightning F.1A, F.2A, F.3, T.4, T.5, F.6 and T.55	1,188
Scottish Aviation Bulldog T.1	1,011
Hawker Siddeley Hawk T.1 and T.1A	812
Panavia Tornado F.3	3,074
DHC Chipmunk T.10	426
Hawker Hurricane IIC	162
Supermarine Spitfire IIa, Vb, IX and PR XIX	381
Grob 115E Tutor T.1	1,180
TOTAL	**8,518**

Index

Author's note: The individuals' ranks shown are those mentioned in the text, not necessarily their final ranks.

INDEX

INDEX